Passions, Sympathy and Print Culture

Palgrave Studies in the History of Emotions

Series editors:
David Lemmings, Professor of History, University of Adelaide, Australia
William M. Reddy, William T. Laprade Professor of History, Duke University, USA

Palgrave Studies in the History of Emotions includes work that redefines past definitions of emotions; re-conceptualizes theories of emotional 'development' through history; undertakes research into the genesis and effects of mass emotions; and employs a variety of humanities disciplines and methodologies. In this way, it produces a new interdisciplinary history of the emotions in Europe between 1100 and 2000.

Titles include:

Rob Boddice (*editor*)
PAIN AND EMOTION IN MODERN HISTORY

Kyra Giorgi
EMOTIONS, LANGUAGE AND IDENTITY ON THE MARGINS OF EUROPE

Andrew Lynch, Stephanie Downes, and Katrina O'Loughlin (*editors*)
EMOTIONS AND WAR

Claire McLisky, Daniel Midena, and Karen Vallgårda (*editors*)
EMOTIONS AND CHRISTIAN MISSIONS
Historical Perspectives

Stephanie Olsen (*editor*)
CHILDHOOD, YOUTH AND EMOTIONS IN MODERN HISTORY
National, Colonial and Global Perspectives

Heather Kerr, David Lemmings, and Robert Phiddian (*editors*)
PASSIONS, SYMPATHY AND PRINT CULTURE
Public Opinion and Emotional Authenticity in Eighteenth-Century Britain

Forthcoming titles include:

Erika Kuijpers
TRAUMA, MEMORIES AND EMOTIONS IN EARLY MODERN EUROPE

Jennifer Spinks and Charles Zika (*editors*)
DISASTER, DEATH AND EMOTIONS IN THE SHADOW OF THE
APOCALYPSE, 1400–1700

Palgrave Studies in the History of Emotions
Series Standing Order ISBN 978–1–137–36634–4 (Hardback)
(*outside North America only*)

You can receive future titles in this series as they are published by placing a standing order. Please contact your bookseller or, in case of difficulty, write to us at the address below with your name and address, the title of the series and the ISBN quoted above.

Customer Services Department, Macmillan Distribution Ltd, Houndmills, Basingstoke, Hampshire RG21 6XS, England

Passions, Sympathy and Print Culture

Public Opinion and Emotional Authenticity in Eighteenth-Century Britain

Edited by

Heather Kerr

David Lemmings

and

Robert Phiddian

palgrave
macmillan

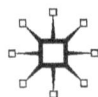

First published 2016 by
PALGRAVE MACMILLAN

Palgrave Macmillan in the UK is an imprint of Macmillan Publishers Limited, registered in England, company number 785998, of Houndmills, Basingstoke, Hampshire RG21 6XS.

Palgrave Macmillan in the US is a division of St Martin's Press LLC, 175 Fifth Avenue, New York, NY 10010.

Palgrave Macmillan is the global academic imprint of the above companies and has companies and representatives throughout the world.

Palgrave® and Macmillan® are registered trademarks in the United States, the United Kingdom, Europe and other countries.

ISBN 978–1–137–45540–6

This book is printed on paper suitable for recycling and made from fully managed and sustained forest sources. Logging, pulping and manufacturing processes are expected to conform to the environmental regulations of the country of origin.

A catalogue record for this book is available from the British Library.

A catalog record for this book is available from the Library of Congress.

Contents

Part IV Afterword

Acknowledgements

We gratefully acknowledge the support of the Australian Research Council (ARC) Centre of Excellence for the History of Emotions, without which it would not have been possible to produce this book. The project began life in September 2012 as an international Collaboratory for the Change Program of the ARC Centre, and we are very grateful to Janet Hart for her kind assistance in convening that meeting. Additionally, we acknowledge the very helpful contributions made by the audience on that occasion. We would also like to thank all the contributors for producing essays of such high quality and for their patience with the production process. Last, but not least, we are very grateful to Jen McCall and her team at Palgrave Macmillan for supporting the project.

Heather Kerr, David Lemmings, and Robert Phiddian
February 2015

Contributors

Emily Cock holds a PhD from the University of Adelaide, Australia, where her thesis explored prostitution and plastic surgery in England in the seventeenth and early eighteenth centuries. She was the 2014 Bill Cowan Fellow in the Barr Smith Library, Adelaide. Her recent publications include: ' "Lead[ing] 'em by the Nose into publick Shame and Derision": Gaspare Tagliacozzi, Alexander Read, and the Lost History of Plastic Surgery, 1600–1800', *Social History of Medicine* (2014); 'Affecting Glory from Vices: Negotiating Shame in Prostitution Texts, 1660–1750', in *Performing Emotions in the Medieval and Early Modern World*, ed. Philippa Maddern and Joanne McEwan (forthcoming); ' "Nonsence is Rebellion": John Taylor's *Nonsence upon Sence, or Sence upon Nonsence* (1651–1654) and the English Civil War', *Ceræ: An Australasian Journal of Medieval and Early Modern Studies* (2015).

Conal Condren is an honorary professor with the Centre for the History of European Discourses, University of Queensland, Australia, and an Emeritus Scientia Professor at the University of New South Wales. He is a member of Churchill College and of Clare Hall, Cambridge, UK, and a fellow of the Australian Academies of the Humanities and of the Social Sciences. His research interests are in the intellectual history of early modern England; politics and Shakespeare; concept formation and linguistic change in politics; and historiographical theory. His recent publications include: *Argument and Authority in Early Modern England* (2006); and *Hobbes, the Scriblerians and the History of Philosophy* (2011).

Kathrine Cuccuru is completing her PhD in philosophy at University College London, UK. She is researching the philosophical history of eighteenth-century British accounts of the sublime.

Amelia Dale holds a PhD from the University of Sydney, Australia. Her thesis, ' "Spots upon the Soul": Reading Quixotic Impressions in Eighteenth-Century Quixotic Narratives', analysed eighteenth-century quixotic narratives' depiction of readers being spotted and stained by the texts that they have consumed. Her work on *Polly Honeycombe* won the University of Sydney's Beauchamp Prize for best literary essay. Her chapter 'Dolly's Inch of Red Sealing Wax: Impressing the Reader in *Tristram Shandy'* is forthcoming in a collection, *Sterne, Tristram, Yorick,* edited by Melvyn New, Peter DeVoogd, and Judith Hawley. She currently coordinates an interdisciplinary Long Eighteenth Century Reading Group at the University of Sydney.

Michael L. Frazer is Associate Professor of Government and of Social Studies and Political Theory at Harvard University, USA. His research focuses on canonical political philosophy and its relevance for contemporary political theory. After receiving his BA from Yale University and his PhD from Princeton University, he spent the 2006–07 academic year as a postdoctoral research associate in the Political Theory Project at Brown University. His book *The Enlightenment of Sympathy* reclaims the sentimentalist theory of reflection as a resource for enriching social science, normative theory, and political practice today. His articles on Maimonides, Nietzsche, John Rawls, and Leo Strauss have appeared in such journals as *Political Theory* and *The Review of Politics.*

Aleksondra Hultquist is an associate investigator for the Australian Research Council (ARC) Centre of Excellence for the History of Emotions. Her work focuses on the literature and culture of the long eighteenth century, especially women writers. Her articles on the role of desire in early British novels have appeared in *Philological Quarterly, The Eighteenth Century: Theory and Interpretation,* and several edited collections. She is a managing editor of *ABO: Interactive Journal for Women and the Arts, 1640–1830,* and is currently finishing her monograph, *The Amatory Mode,* which explores the role of the passions in the development of the eighteenth-century novel. She has worked as an assistant professor in the United States and as a lecturer in Australia.

Heather Kerr is a research fellow in the discipline of English and Creative Writing at the University of Adelaide, Australia, and an associate investigator in the ARC Centre for the History of Emotions. She has published in the areas of early modern drama and poetry, law and literature, ecocriticism, and contemporary cultural studies. Her latest book (edited with Claire Walker) is *'Fama' and Her Sisters: Gossip and Rumour in Early Modern Europe* (2015).

David Lemmings is Professor of History at the University of Adelaide, Australia, and Leader of the 'Change' Program in the ARC Centre for the History of Emotions. He has published extensively on the socio-cultural history of law and the legal professions in eighteenth-century Britain.

His latest books are *Law and Government in England during the Long Eighteenth Century: From Consent to Command* (2011), *Crime, Courtrooms and the Public Sphere in Britain, 1700–1850* (editor, 2012), and *Emotions and Social Change: Historical and Sociological Perspectives* (co-editor, with Ann Brooks, 2014). Together with Katie Barclay and Claire Walker, he is currently working on a monograph that explores the role of emotion in social change through an analysis of representations of the family in the eighteenth-century press.

Jean McBain is a PhD candidate at the University of Melbourne, Australia, where she is working on a thesis provisionally titled 'Liberty, Licence and Libel: Press Freedom and British Periodicals, 1695–1740'. Her chapter for this volume draws upon research from her Master of Arts, undertaken at Flinders University, which explored the participatory dynamics of the early eighteenth-century periodical.

Eric Parisot is Lecturer in English at the School of Humanities and Creative Arts, Flinders University, Australia. He is also an honorary research fellow with the School of Communication and Arts, University of Queensland, and an associate investigator with the ARC Centre of Excellence for the History of Emotions (Europe 1100–1800). His research primarily focuses on eighteenth-century literary responses to death and dying (especially suicide), and his articles have appeared in various journals such as *Eighteenth-Century Studies, Literature Compass,* and *English Studies.* His first monograph, *Graveyard Poetry,* was published in 2013.

W. Gerrod Parrott is Professor of Psychology at Georgetown University, USA. He has served as Editor-in-Chief of the journal *Cognition and Emotion* (1995–99) and as President of the International Society for Research on Emotion, an interdisciplinary organization of emotion researchers around the world (2008–13). His research centres on the nature of human emotion and addresses such topics as cultural differences in emotions, the concept of emotion, and the function of emotions in everyday life. He has published extensively on the nature and function of social emotions such as embarrassment, shame, guilt, envy, and jealousy. In addition to his research articles, chapters, and reviews, he is author or co-author of four books: *The Emotions: Social, Cultural, and Biological Dimensions* (1996); *Emotions in Social Psychology* (2001); *Emotions and Culpability* (2006); and *The Positive Side of Negative Emotions* (2014).

Glen Pettigrove is a senior lecturer in the Department of Philosophy at the University of Auckland, New Zealand, where he teaches both ethics and early modern philosophy. He is the author of numerous articles in academic journals, including 'Hume on Forgiveness and the Unforgivable' (*Utilitas* 2007), 'Meekness and Moral Anger' (*Ethics* 2012), and 'Shame: A Case Study of Collective Emotion' (with Nigel Parsons, *Social Theory and Practice* 2012). His book *Forgiveness and Love* was published in 2012.

Robert Phiddian is Associate Professor of English and Deputy Dean of the School of Humanities at Flinders University, Australia. He is author of *Swift's Parody* (1995) and 30 other publications, principally on eighteenth-century literature and contemporary Australian political cartooning. He is Chair, Adelaide Festival of Ideas (2008–14), Director, Australian Consortium of Humanities Research Centres (2010–), a board member, *Australian Book Review* (2013–16), and an associate investigator, ARC Centre for the History of Emotions (2012–14).

Laura J. Rosenthal is Professor of English at the University of Maryland, College Park, USA, where she specializes in Restoration and eighteenth-century literature. She is the author of *Infamous Commerce: Prostitution in Eighteenth-Century Literature and Culture* (2006) and *Playwrights and Plagiarists in Early Modern Drama: Gender, Authorship, Literary Property* (1996). She has recently edited *Nightwalkers: Prostitute Narratives from the Eighteenth Century* (2008) and is currently completing a manuscript on theatre and cosmopolitanism.

Part I

The Challenge of the Passions to Eighteenth-Century Studies

1
Emotional Light on Eighteenth-Century Print Culture

Heather Kerr, David Lemmings, and Robert Phiddian

1 The public sphere, 'authenticity', and emotional change

An established narrative in eighteenth-century studies of Britain details the early dominance of satire, the increase in sympathetic cultural modes, and the implications for different kinds of sociability generated by the long revolution in print culture.[1] In this book, we do not wish to overturn this scholarship because we agree that it addresses fundamental aspects of change and stability in the society and culture of a nation that was rising to global prominence. Certainly the self-congratulatory Whig reading of history that has everything rising on a tide of progress towards some sort of liberal apotheosis has been very validly exposed to revision. Without the iron teleology, however, the chapters in this volume are unified by a conviction that important changes did occur in culture and society during the 1700s, and that they were linked dialogically with shifts in the ways emotions were experienced and valued.

Eighteenth-century English had a rich and varied language of the passions and the sentiments, and this is the century when the word 'emotion' was first used in a recognisably modern sense.[2] David Hume's *Treatise of Human Nature* (1739) is a central text in the debate about the passions, particularly in its provocative claim that reason serves rather than rules the passions. He is also one of the most sophisticated operators in the period's rich rhetoric of emotion, recently reconsidered by Daniel Gross.[3] Consider the many moving parts in this sentence from the *Treatise*, 2.3.3: 'Now 'tis certain, there are certain calm desires and tendencies, which, tho' they be real passions, produce little emotion in the mind, and are more known by their effects than by the immediate feeling or sensation'.[4] Even without the adjectives

3

and qualifying phrases, we are left with seven intricately distinct nouns for what we might lump together as emotion – desires, tendencies, passions, emotion, effects, feeling, sensation. This is a level of intellectual sophistication that demands to be addressed on its own terms and not mechanically reduced to the categories of modern neuroscience.[5] Movements in the rich lexicon of passions and emotions provide us with our primary resource because we, obviously, do not have direct access to eighteenth-century consciousnesses in the ways open to modern psychology.

Modes of expression and sociability also matter crucially, hence our focus on print cultures, and particularly on the growth of literary sociability often framed as the eighteenth-century public sphere. In its pure form, Habermas' notion of the development of a public sphere in eighteenth-century Britain may be more of a just-so story on which to build a political philosophy than an empirical historical account.[6] It is certainly hard to find the ideally civil and reasonable coffee-house deliberation of the Habermas model in the pamphlet wars that rolled back and forth across late Stuart and early Hanoverian British public life. By contrast, passion and intolerance were very common, especially at moments of high tension like the Exclusion, Sacheverell, and American Revolutionary crises. It is nevertheless worth recognising that the civil wars of eighteenth-century Britain were overwhelmingly *pamphlet* wars, in marked contrast to the seventeenth-century experience. The fundamental cultural and historical change that we seek to explore is that 'something happened' to channel the exercise of both sympathetic and violent passions into various modes of print during a literally unprecedented (if never entirely secure) period of civil peace. Even if the causes of this relative civil peace can be shown to be a string of accidents, the consequences for public sensibilities remain real enough to warrant exploration.

This collection unites literary scholars, historians, psychologists, and philosophers in an exploration of modes of community or expressions of self and feeling that surfaced in print culture during the decades between the 1690s and the mid-1700s. We take many of our bearings from developments in the psychological research into human emotions and seek to put them into a constructive dialogue with cultural analysis properly respectful of historical specificity and difference. Indeed, recognising the insight that emotions can be social, rather than narrowly individual, in origin and expression, the collection deals with the circulation of emotions in 'emotional economies', or 'emotional communities'.[7] Moreover, while some cognitive psychologists write confidently about basic emotions as if they are established trans-historical facts of human experience, we attend also to the older language of the passions.[8] The aim here is to uncover how expressions of feeling in eighteenth-century print came to be accepted as 'authentic' and thus became instrumental in the formation of a variety of eighteenth-century selves and communities. These affinities extended beyond immediate kin and traditional relationships of authority to wider networks of nation, class, or interest. The many new clubs and voluntary organisations of the eighteenth century were institutional expressions of this extension of affinity parallel to and often connected with those permitted by print. The passions shared and expressed in the Kit-Kat Club had their virtual extension through the community of feeling engendered by the *Tatler* and the *Spectator*; the novels of Eliza Hayward extended the experience of metropolitan life to the provinces; the strikingly collegial philosophers of the Scottish Enlightenment developed an ethics and epistemology of sympathy.

Our investigations combine current understandings of the emotions developed in cognitive psychology and other social sciences with a genuinely historical sensitivity to eighteenth-century accounts and explorations of the passions. Heeding Gross's caution, we do not treat 'the passions' as an outmoded account of human motivation to be translated into the new science of emotions research, as that would be scientifically reductive. Similarly, we steer clear of the parallel problem of the cultural constructionism William Reddy has identified in some studies of emotional ethnography.[9] For our purposes, such ethnographies are limited because, for them, 'personal feelings' are only ever 'socially, locally, culturally constructed' and are thus subject to arbitrary changes that permit little meaningful comparability across time and culture. In these circumstances, there is no capacity for understanding historical change.[10] Similarly, our collection does not settle on one side or another of the recent trend to distinguish between emotion and affect.[11] In the turn to affect evident in 'emotional geography' and other studies of space and society, emotion is understood to align with the 'narrative and semiotic', the 'personal and subjective', while affect is aligned with the 'non-narrative and asignifying', the 'impersonal and objective'.[12] Nor does our collection revisit a view of 'affect' as presignifying and abstract that is no longer current in psychology but has a continuing afterlife in literary and cultural studies.[13] Instead, we take eighteenth-century preoccupations with the formation and origins of authentic passions in minds, bodies, and (often via the metaphor of contagion) groups as our principal subject matter.

'Authentic' inevitably proves to be a slippery and sometimes ironic term of analysis for the legitimate expression of public emotions in the following chapters, but it is crucial nevertheless. If chastity comes to be associated more with a state of mind than mere biological intactness (as in Samuel Richardson's *Clarissa*, for example) or if proper British outrage at the severing of Robert Jenkins' ear provokes war with Spain in 1739, then authenticity of emotional motivation matters. According to Hume, in a particularly provocative statement also in the *Treatise* section iii, 'Reason is, and ought only to be the slave of the passions, and can never pretend to any other office than to serve and obey them'.[14] This puts it higher than most others in the period once labelled 'the Age of Reason', and there is a context of paradoxical irony in Hume's prose too complex to be pursued fully here. One aspect of it involves a consciousness in Hume of the chaos wrought in the body politic when inauthentic passions enslaved reason, as often happened in the newly extensive realm of print, where feelings could be simulated and identities hoaxed, from Isaac Bickerstaff (Jonathan Swift, 1708) to Ossian (James Macpherson, 1760) and beyond. Especially in novels, though also in plays, pamphlets, and sometimes newspapers, fiction became a pathway rather than an impediment to authentic passions. Printed simulations of feeling, whether harshly in satires or sympathetically in novels, came to be supplements and even alternatives to 'the real thing'. The word 'authentic' is never used blithely in the chapters that follow, for it can never be self-evident, but it presents a set of issues that cannot be avoided in a history of emotions.

Thus we develop a dialogue between current emotions scholarship and older accounts of the passions because that is essential if we are to pinpoint historical specificity of and change in emotional economies of meaning and social organisation. Just as Habermas's concept of the public sphere has proved useful as a heuristic device for the discussions in this collection, so also ideas about the 'civilising process' that can be traced to the historical sociologist Norbert Elias are constructive, if considered critically.[15] In Steven Pinker's macro-argument about the retreat of violence in the modern world, 'The eighteenth century marked a turning point in the use of institutionalised cruelty in the West'.[16] For Pinker, Britain holds a special place in a neo-Elysian civilising process, remarkable for being the first European nation to mark a steep decline in his main data group of violent deaths. Pinker's talk of a 'humanitarian revolution' in the eighteenth century very probably exaggerates the universal extent of emotional transformation; as Simon Dickie has argued recently through extensive attention to jest-books, comedy remained overwhelmingly a brutally physical phenomenon in the public mind, at least to the end of the century.[17] Indeed, critical consideration of the full range of Norbert Elias's work on emotions and historical change has revealed that his ideas about the civilising process in Europe have been over-simplified by neglecting the survival of alternative emotional regimes.[18] Our collection nevertheless finds evidence to support a more modest version of Pinker's argument and the 'cognitive turn' that underpins it: an evolution of public sympathy, rather than a revolution, evident in a number of vanguard writers and thinkers.

Certainly, it is possible to see cultural developments in the print culture of this period that provide channels for the elaboration of sympathetic and oppositional perspectives previously unavailable in more violent times only a few decades earlier. It is also significant of such a shift that the earliest texts studied in James Chandler's *An Archaeology of Sympathy* are Shaftesbury's *Characteristics* (1711) and Addison and Steele's *Spectator* (1711–12), and that he proceeds towards Dickins via Sterne and Adam Smith.[19] Looking forward, Ildiko Csengei's *Sympathy, Sensibility and the Literature of Feeling in the Eighteenth Century* presents sympathy as the main tributary of the sensibility that permits campaigns such as that for the abolition of slavery in the late eighteenth century.[20] While it is possible to be overly schematic and selective in rehearsing the trajectory of change in the eighteenth century from an age of satire to one of sentiment, the underlying fact of an emotionalisation of public discourse, making space in print for harsh and gentle passions, is hard to dispute.

2 Sympathies, communities, and improving emotions

The essays in the volume respond in a variety of ways to the initial challenge from cognitive psychology posed in the psychologist W. Gerrod Parrott's opening survey. Parrott provides a clear outline of the origins and current scientific understanding of research on emotions, especially relating to their generation in groups, and with an eye to emotional exchange in print culture. While attending carefully to the historical distinction between passions and emotions, he considers the complex conceptualisation of emotion by modern psychologists and explains their ideas about the interpersonal transmission of emotion in terms of sympathy and empathy: a distinction not made in the eighteenth century, but useful for historical analysis all the same. His account also includes a particularly valuable discussion of the extent to which emotions vary with cultural environment. Indeed, Parrott's idea of *ur-emotions* seems especially relevant to the study of emotions and social change, since it allows for the influence of environment in emotional expression, while asserting that there are underlying features common to humans in all emotional displays. The following chapters address a mixture of canonical and non-canonical texts from a variety of disciplinary perspectives. Literary scholars, historians, and philosophers explore ways in which 'authentic' passions came to be conceived and performed in a range of environments, from popular novels, to the new journalism, through the lucubrations of major figures in the Scottish Enlightenment, to last words, aesthetics, and plastic surgery.

Following Parrott's call for humanities scholars to study the social aspects of emotion in different historical contexts, several chapters in this volume consider instances of early eighteenth-century print culture which seem to exemplify a fresh emphasis on appeals to the emotions as a means to lead opinion and constitute moral communities among readers. Robert Phiddian's contribution (Chapter 3) concentrates on the work of Jonathan Swift, and takes as its point of departure Swift's 'savage indignation' at corruption in government as an element of satire: a genre of contemporary print culture that he argues represented anger, contempt, and disgust, rather than mere humour. Political satire of this type is interesting for at least two reasons. Firstly, it is an attempt to conjure an 'emotional public' on the basis of violent dissent, rather than through civil discussion, and therefore offends against the Habermasian view of the emerging public sphere as an environment characterised by politeness and reasoned discussion. Secondly, in the early eighteenth century, such ferocious expressions of opposition in print by authors like Swift and Pope were not openly suppressed by the Whig authorities, and in this official tolerance it is arguable that they conferred a measure of legitimacy on exchanges in print which appeared self-evidently to speak from the heart, as well as the head. Indeed, Phiddian goes on to compare one of Swift's most explicit and public declarations of savage indignation – his self-composed epitaph inscribed on the wall of St Patrick's Cathedral, which bade farewell to a corrupt world – with one of his most intimate – a 'disgusting' poem describing the multiple bodily corruptions of a London prostitute disrobing on retiring for the night. Ultimately he argues that, like contemporary political satire, both convey a powerful criticism of contemporary conditions because they affect moral indignation on behalf of the offended feelings of humanity, rather than mere personal derision. Of course in so far as they emphasised righteous anger, rather than only personal disgust, their passionate sympathy for humanity might also constitute a ringing call for remedial action against corrupt and oppressive authorities, as well as a means of consolation.

In addition to its substantive contribution to understanding the complex roles of emotions in eighteenth-century satire, Phiddian's chapter is valuable because it depends on close engagement between literary texts and the insights of modern psychology. Alternatively, Jean McBain deploys book history in her chapter about Daniel Defoe's creation of a 'textual community' arising out of his correspondence with readers in *The Review* and its 'Scandal Club' (with its subsequent iterations) in 1704–05 (Chapter 4). As she points out, *authorial* authenticity is not an issue here, for some of the earliest letters in question were probably written by Defoe himself, and most of the rest were published semi-anonymously or pseudonymously. McBain insists nevertheless that the success of the Scandal Club in generating a community of readers around correspondence verifies its 'emotional authenticity'. Overall, the Club's expressions of emotions and semi-didactic concern with moral issues (especially of love and marriage) succeeded as legitimate social interactions in the marketplace of print. As she says, whether the letters were fact or fiction, their uncertain status allowed them to operate as parables, and they are therefore fit objects of study for historians of emotions. She goes on to analyse the letters on love and courtship as good evidence for the everyday emotional concerns of the London middle classes, and thereby contributes to scholarly conclusions about ambivalent attitudes to passion as the proper foundation for a successful marriage.

Like Defoe, the early eighteenth-century novelist Eliza Haywood did not just utilise emotional expressions to constitute an audience for her numerous publications. Rather, according to Aleksondra Hultquist (in Chapter 5), the substance of Haywood's oeuvre amounted to a sustained but evolving account of the passions and moral development through human interaction that anticipates the more famous theories of David Hume and Adam Smith. Certainly, as with McBain, Hultquist believes that the work under investigation is an 'authentic' representation of contemporary emotional interactions, in the sense that the novels presented scenarios of love and interpersonal relations which appealed to their readers' interests and thereby created a 'community of feeling'. But authenticity is also applied here at the level of the individual, for Haywood's characters live authentically in so far as they are true to their passions and thereby develop a sense of self-knowledge. Indeed, in her analysis Hultquist is also able to demonstrate the contemporary fluidity of the terms 'passion' and 'emotion'; for Haywood, emotions are psychological 'movements' such as outbreaks of anger, delight, or sorrow, whereas passions are enduring traits of personality, exemplified as an overriding tendency to love, pride, fear, revenge, or slothfulness. Crucially, in Haywood's novels, as for her contemporary Hume, passions drive emotions, and ideally they achieve a state of equilibrium as her characters become aware of themselves and are able to live comfortably in the world. Hultquist also shows that like many of her contemporaries, Haywood strongly believed the passions were gendered; above all, women were more subject to the passion of love than men, although they are not represented by her as any less intelligent. In both her male and female characters the passions are depicted as being age-dependent, however, and growing experience, rather than reason, is the key to satisfaction in life; as their emotional intelligence develops with life, they are able to live more authentically.

It is arguable that for Defoe, as for Haywood, emotional experience was conceived as improving, since the Scandal Club's stories may be regarded as encouraging emotional intelligence among their readers. Jonathan Swift appears to have been less optimistic about the prospects for his appeals to the emotions to effect improvement, at least in the context of the political world, although his 'disgusting' poetry clearly deploys emotive language in the cause of restoring corrupted humanity. As Kathrine Cuccuru demonstrates in Chapter 6, the dramatist and critic John Dennis also believed strongly in the improving power of emotional experience, at least in theory. Certainly, Dennis claimed that the finest poetry inspired moral virtue in readers, since it excited the mind to the sublime, an ideal state of mental harmony associated with divine revelation. Cuccuru establishes that Dennis believed the sublime could only be attained by an elite of particularly sensitive readers, however; and since he insisted that most people would only be moved by vulgar passions, the improving capacity of sublime poetry was quite limited in practice. Moreover, she goes on to show that Dennis's assumed cultural elitism exposed him to the ridicule of Swift's fellow Scriblerians, particularly that of Alexander Pope, whose satirical *Peri Bathos* suggested that the kind of poetry Dennis recommended would be mediocre and passionless because it was based on mere mechanical imitation of greater artists. By contrast, Pope's satire insisted obliquely that truly sublime poetry could only be constructed by a natural progeny (like Pope), because it represents the elements of authentic human nature common to all humankind, but exclusively accessible to genius. If this reading is correct, it is important for the student of eighteenth-century emotions and literature because Dennis, a scholar who rejected the longstanding quarrel between ancient and modern learning, appears ultimately to have had no greater faith in the power of authentically emotional discourse for improvement in the public sphere than Pope, an arch-conservative critic of modernism as well as religious humanist. At the same time as he restricted access to an emotional public with the advantages of a polite education, however, Dennis's ideas about the sublime and poetry betoken a form of knowledge communication associated with moral sentiment and emotional intuition. In other words, he was articulating a theory of aesthetics. Indeed, like Haywood, but in this case via poetry rather than amatory fiction, he recognised the importance of the passions as a positive force for harmonising the individual soul.[21]

As the contretemps between Dennis and Pope reveals, the constitution of proper moral sentiment was becoming a preoccupation of contemporary English philosophical writing. In Chapter 7, Laura Rosenthal discusses Adam Smith's *Theory of Moral Sentiments* (1759), and addresses one of the central issues confronted by the generation of feeling among participants in the public sphere: how to explain and validate the communication of sentiment as the positive expression of human sympathy. She argues that the most direct influence on his thinking about this kind of feeling exchange was a particular form of emotional community: the eighteenth-century theatre. For Smith, according to Rosenthal, the theatre, like the novel, was a place of 'sentimental education', a forum where members of the audience learned to cultivate the appropriate expression of feelings on the basis of a sophisticated moral judgement involving identification with the characters' circumstances. Although she does not use this term, we might argue that for the author of *Moral Sentiments*, theatre-goers, like novel-readers, were learning to recognise 'authentic' emotions: authentic or natural in the sense that they represent the appropriate expression of feelings generated by the apprehension of a shared and virtuous human nature. The Smithian challenge for the emotional labour of playwrights and actors, therefore, and by extension that of anyone contributing positively to the public sphere, was to create subtly moving characters and scenarios which inspired appropriately moral sentiments in the communities manufactured by their art.[22] By implication, cruder forms of dramatic performance, which did not aspire to the improving objective, were like the work of rope-dancers: inferior performers who appealed to much lower and less enduring forms of sympathy for the purpose of mere entertainment only.

Rosenthal also shows that Smith identified the higher moral purpose he associated with the best contemporary European prose as a feature of advanced cultural development. He nevertheless admitted that the theatre was not perfect in its cultivation of progressive moral sentiments. Certainly, 'sympathising up', or the tendency of classical tragedies to emphasise the suffering of kings and great men, rather than those of paupers and women, was a problem for him because it failed to discourage the engrained habit of servility and the concomitant 'inhuman' treatment of the vulnerable and inferiors. Indeed, he believed that English public opinion was highly susceptible to this affective simplicity, as misguided popular sympathy for the travails and corruptions of the Stuart monarchs showed very clearly. As Rosenthal demonstrates in her insightful reading of Lillo's popular *The London Merchant* (1731), however, some contemporary tragedians had already adjusted their art to constitute a more sophisticated and democratic community of sympathetic exchange.

3 Performing emotions: Virtue and corruption in the public sphere

Smith's *Theory of Moral Sentiments* can therefore be read as an account of improving affective communication by studying the arts of story-telling developed in the theatre, arts which ideally encouraged sympathetic feeling around a shared and virtuous recognition of the human condition. At the same time, there was a parallel concern, already recognised by Dennis at the beginning of the eighteenth century: that the arts of dramatic performance could be used to manipulate the passions for the achievement of immoral or amoral ends.[23] Dennis reassured his readers that art in the service of vicious purposes would not engage the passions powerfully, but some other authors were less sanguine about the exclusive utility of affect to constitute authentically humane communities, because they doubted the capacity of consumers to resist the corruption of their affective sensibilities. Chapters 8–12 of this collection consider some of these doubts and reservations about the role of passions and sympathy in the public sphere.

The idea of intuitive sympathy had been around a long time, but part of its history before the eighteenth century lay in the twilight area of supernatural medicine. In her very detailed discussion of representations of rhinoplasty (skin-grafting to cover the facial ravages of syphilis), Emily Cock (Chapter 8) shows that, because of its popular association with supernatural medicine and sexual incontinence, this procedure was exposed to ridicule by some satirical authors and artists, including Butler, Dunton, Hogarth, and Sterne. Indeed, in several humorous skits the absence of the nose seems to have been a marker of moral corruption in the sufferer, and remedial plastic surgery a quack treatment which should engender no moral sympathy whatsoever. Under this critical optic, the procedure was depicted as bound to fail because there was no natural sympathy between the graft and the skin upon which it was fixed. As Cock shows, this particular genre of satirical writing compares emotional sympathy – such as the compassion of a surgeon for a patient who has the pox – with ideas about supernatural sympathy between pieces of separate flesh. She concludes that by doing so ultimately, it may have undermined the authenticity of moral sympathy by associating it with the shameless materialism and quackery of the medical marketplace.

In Chapter 9, Amelia Dale also considers the mockery of sympathetic engagement in humorous literature, via a close reading of Colman's *Polly Honeycombe* (1760), a satire on the popularity of novel-reading among women. In this dramatic farce, the character Polly is represented as reading a romantic novel and 'acting as she reads'; literally mimicking the emotions communicated by the text. She therefore serves to dramatise the dangers of novel consumption for young women, as her body is rendered susceptible to the passion of romance communicated by the text and duly imitated by her unscrupulous social-climbing suitor. The conceit of an eager young girl acting from the pages of an amatory novel therefore enables Colman to show that private novel-reading is just as hazardous and scandalous for impressionable females as public performance in the theatre, in so far as print is equally capable of transferring powerful and unstable emotions, which were potentially corrosive of ideal female honour and the respectable self (characterised in the text as 'a proper Manner of behaving'). Like Smith, he saw many connections between the theatre and print culture, although he seems to have evaluated them less positively. Dale's chapter therefore demonstrates that, by the middle of the eighteenth century, following the rise of sentimental literature, there was considerable ambivalence about the utility of sympathy as a mechanism for the interpersonal transfer of virtuous and improving emotions. As she points out, for Colman, as for some of the other writers analysed in this book, feelings were rendered authentic by their successful performance in 'impressing' themselves on an audience among the public, whether real or virtual; however (and this is exemplified by the catalogue of books from a circulating library mentioned in the prologue to *Polly Honeycombe*), the communities and 'characters' they engendered were not necessarily emotionally consistent, humane, or polite.

Eric Parisot (Chapter 10) examines another manifestation of the anxiety in the mid- to late century about the social consequences of excessive sensibility to the communication of emotions in print. His subject is the representation of suicide in English newspapers, and especially their publication of sentimental suicide notes: a genre of self-representation which critics believed had helped to engender a 'contagion' of sympathetic melancholy leading to more cases of self-destruction. In this case, by contrast with the satirical anti-novel discourse of Colman, opponents mostly deployed explicitly hostile counter-narratives, which were designed to block the experience of sympathy directly. Thus, Parisot shows how anti-suicide campaigners in the press condemned suicide notes as completely inauthentic performances, in the sense that they affected despair and dissent out of a passionately narcissistic imagination. The critics duly attempted to shame suicidal authors with expressions of contempt and disgust, thereby fostering what they believed were emotionally healthy constructions of community. At the same time, published suicide notes themselves began to anticipate these criticisms by insisting on the legitimacy of their feelings and justifying self-destruction as an honourable retreat from a vain and insufficiently sensitive world. As Parisot suggests, conservatives worried that treating them sympathetically threatened to generate a dystopian emotional sub-culture. Certainly this kind of sentimentalism was condemned by the test of utility; for Parisot points out that even Adam Smith's *Theory of Moral Sentiments* dismissed compassion for 'those miseries which we never saw' as 'extreme sympathy', and 'artificial commiseration' which was ultimately 'perfectly useless' because it would only produce more misery.[24] Indeed, from this perspective, printing suicide notes was the publishing equivalent of rope-dancing, and writing sympathetically about it was emphatically rejected as the potential source of a self-destructive community.

This doubt about sentimentalism – how far public expressions of sympathy and individual sensibility for the sufferings of others promoted the common good – was not wholly new. For the moral philosopher Francis Hutcheson, the hallmark of *authentic* emotions (or to use his terminology, 'affections', meaning 'movements of the mind') was whether they conduced to promote virtuous and sociable relations among people, and therefore accurately represented divine creation. But how was the individual to govern his or her behaviour in the world according to this affective standard? As Glen Pettigrove maintains (in Chapter 11), Hutcheson believed human nature included an innate moral sensibility that enabled everyone immediately to distinguish and validate 'kind and generous affections' from vicious ones; and in the 1720s he published four treatises discussing the affective origins of aesthetics and morals. In these writings, besides identifying natural moral sense, he also insisted that humans experienced a 'public sense', a natural sympathy which made them feel pleasure in witnessing another's happiness and pain when they saw people suffer. Ideally, for Hutcheson, this natural benevolence was even manifested towards people who were not obviously deserving, or who were positively vicious.

Insights like these would seem to be a promising foundation for the improving potential of sympathy in the public sphere. Pettigrove demonstrates, however, that while Hutcheson's work warmly recommended virtuous action inspired by natural benevolence, and his writings also directly promoted ethics among the public by engaging the feelings of his readers, his philosophical apparatus did not consistently evaluate 'character' or moral worth in individuals. Rather, in making such judgements about a person's moral 'temper', he ultimately applied a mathematical calculus based on how far an individual's expressions of sympathy for another person were merited by the subject's demeanour or behaviour. According to Pettigrove's reading, Hutcheson's *external* evaluation of appropriately sympathetic behaviour would exclude expressions of patience and mercy, or even generosity or hospitality, because they are not inspired by virtue in the subject of affection: in other words, they were relatively undeserved. Indeed, by resorting to universalising mathematical models of human interaction, Hutcheson tended to neglect the differential influence of custom and environment on people's judgement. Since perception is mediated by these factors, the moral sense of each individual is merely subjective and liable to error; and a judgement based on utilitarian value was therefore the ultimate test of sympathetic affection. As Hutcheson's critics maintained, from this perspective, innate natural sensibility to perceptions of pleasure or pain was no basis for making an authentic judgement about the morality of people and their actions, or for properly moral education of the public.[25]

Hutcheson's moral philosophy was a substantial influence on David Hume and, in Chapter 12, Michael Frazer shows how Hume was a philosopher whose published work vividly exemplifies the contemporary ambivalence about the performance of emotion, in this case in the context of its appropriate role in Enlightenment print culture. According to Frazer, Hume's first philosophical work, *The Treatise of Human Nature* (1739), was originally represented by its author as 'anatomical', in so far as it featured a cold, unemotional, style of writing usually associated with natural science. In writing this book, he claimed to have eschewed the cultivation of moral sentiments via exemplary rhetoric and literary eloquence, thereby indicating some distrust of these arts as superficial colouring, or even affective 'bribery'. Like Hutcheson, Hume believed that moral ideas were derived from feelings of pleasure and pain, but although he argued that practical morality developed through sympathetic communication between people, rather than from a universal instinctive benevolence, his early philosophical priority was to describe and analyse clinically the workings of the mind. Evidently, he was afraid of offending against the dry literary style favoured by the tradition of philosophical writing inspired by Locke. Frazer shows that it was only in his mature works of the 1740s and 1750s, and possibly in response to Hutcheson's criticism, that he began openly to deploy more 'warmth' in recommending virtue as a 'painterly' device for engaging the moral sentiments of his readers in the cause of improving humankind. In fact, when he published the first volume of his *Essays, Moral and Political* (1741), Hume acknowledged that here he had followed the polite and popular model of writing exemplified by Addison and Steele's *Spectator*. As Frazer suggests, despite Hume's initial coyness about adopting a *painterly* style, by imitating the famous literary magazine this leading moral philosopher of the Scottish Enlightenment revealed that he, like the other authors discussed here, consciously strove to constitute a community of sympathetic readers by appealing to their feelings. Thus by 1760, it appears, authentic participation in the British public sphere of print demanded an openly affective performance.

Finally, in his 'Afterword', the historian of political thought Conal Condren critically evaluates the central concerns of this book – emotions, communities, and the development of sympathetic communication in print culture – as they operated between 1675 and 1725, the crucial period when a bourgeois 'public sphere' was first identified in Britain.[26] He considers the thesis that is variously implicit or explicit in all the essays: that by comparison with Britain in the seventeenth century, the conjunction of relative political stability and the growth of commercial print culture over these years resulted in a distinctively different driver of social change, in the form of a marketplace characterised by economies of circulating emotions rather than by coercion and violence. Although doubtful about the heuristic value of the concept 'public sphere', he admits these years saw a shift in the dominant emotional regime, and is relatively persuaded by the essays' concentration on the 'authenticity' of emotions as discussions about collective morality. Indeed, Condren provides an interesting interpretation of functioning *satirical* authenticity as moral censorship and the purging of corruption. Ultimately, therefore, for the satirists Pope and Swift, as for the moralists Haywood, Hutcheson, Hume, and Smith, the expression of passion was legitimate if it was shackled to the cause of virtue. Moreover, Condren's essay makes a substantial contribution to the volume in its comparative analysis of translating and 'modifying' Homer's *Iliad* as evidence of the contemporary reading public's taste for characters who were emotionally intelligent and socially sympathetic, rather than merely simple and passionate. As his treatment of the *Iliad* suggests, the eighteenth century's ambivalence towards the expression of emotion was partly derived from remembrance of political chaos in the seventeenth century, as well as participation in the commercial prosperity of a proto-modern consumer society.

4 Conclusion: Savagery, compassion, and stability of a kind

While this collection connects with existing debates in the field about sentiment, satire, and the public sphere, the explicit development of a dialogue between eighteenth-century passions and twenty-first-century understandings of emotions is a challenge to some settled practices and understandings in the field. It is also unusually even-handed in refusing to side finally with either satire or sentiment, the two poles of scholarship in the field for many decades. Some chapters address the negative passions such as anger and disgust expressed in satire, while others survey warmer feelings of love and sympathy. We take all these passions seriously as part of the economy of authentic emotional expression in print. This is clearly a perspective where the development of the 'Man of Feeling' is important, but the early eighteenth-century 'Rage of Party' is also a crucial part of the ongoing emotionalisation of public discourse, rather than simply a hang-over from the seventeenth century that was exhausted with the death of Pope and Swift. After all, Gillray's savage prints of the 1790s are as much a part of the eighteenth-century public sphere (broadly understood) as Burney's novels or the *Gentleman's Magazine,* and their emotional and aesthetic violence is hard to miss. Our accounts of the passions permit this sort of range, and thus undermine the assumption in some scholarship that the rise of sensibility is straightforwardly a rise of *sympathetic* sentimentality.

In the spirit of vigorous interdisciplinary debate that is one of the abiding virtues of eighteenth-century studies, this book strives always to get beyond the common sense assumption that emotion is a subjective and therefore a specifically personal thing. Hence we focus on print culture as a forum for the performance and reception of passions wherein significant features of new modes of 'authenticity' – of self- and group-consciousness – can be seen to emerge. In doing so, we conceptualise emotions broadly as interactive practices informed by a mixture of embodied cultural norms and individual intentions, arising in particular historical contexts, and contributing with varying success to the constitution of communities of feeling among readers and writers.[27] Nothing so tidy as a public sphere of deliberative debate can be discerned in what we have found, but a more empirically grounded terrain of print cultures as theatres of public emotions does come into view. Passions positive and negative were formed, and sympathy variously exercised across this terrain, thereby constructing communities of feeling which contributed in complex ways to the social and political stability of this century compared to its predecessor. Seventeenth-century Britain had revolutions, restorations, and the first pamphlet wars in history; it would be silly to argue that public opinion mattered less then. Our explorations collected here demonstrate, however, that public opinion in eighteenth-century Britain functioned differently and mattered crucially.

Notes

1. This is presented as a truism in textbooks such as Michael Alexander (2013) *A History of English Literature*, 3rd ed. (Basingstoke: Palgrave Macmillan), pp. 205–6, and is a ground on which fine-grained arguments are made in entire monographs such as Ildiko Csengei (2011) *Sympathy, Sensibility and the Literature of Feeling in the Eighteenth Century* (Basingstoke: Palgrave Macmillan).
2. Thomas Dixon (2003) *From Passions to Emotions: The Creation of a Secular Psychological Category* (Cambridge: Cambridge University Press).
3. Daniel M. Gross (2008) *The Secret History of Emotion: From Aristotle's Rhetoric to Modern Brain Science* (Chicago: University of Chicago Press).
4. David Hume (1998) *A Treatise of Human Nature?: A Critical Edition*, ed. David Fate Norton and Mary J. Norton (Oxford: Clarendon), p. 268.
5. Gross, *Secret History*, pursues this line of argument particularly robustly, notably on pp. 28–39.
6. J. Habermas (1991) *The Structural Transformation of the Bourgeois Sphere: An Enquiry into a Category of Bourgeois Society*, trans. T. Burger and F. Lawrence (Cambridge, MA: MIT Press).
7. See Glen Pettigrove and Nick Parsons (2012) 'Shame: A Case Study of Collective Emotion', *Social Theory and Practice* 38: 504–30; Sarah Ahmed (2004) *The Cultural Politics of Emotion* (Edinburgh: Edinburgh University Press). Barbara H. Rosenwein (2006) *Emotional Communities in the Early Middle Ages* (Ithaca, NY: Cornell University Press) provides a cue for many of our explorations, though it addresses a very different historical context.
8. The debate about basic emotions stems from Paul Ekman's foundational work, beginning with Paul Ekman (1972) *Emotion in the Human Face:*

Guide-Lines for Research and an Integration of Findings (New York: Pergamon Press). And a good overview of the whole area can be seen at Ronald de Sousa (2014) 'Emotion', in *The Stanford Encyclopedia of Philosophy*, ed. Edward N. Zalta, http://plato.stanford.edu/archives/spr2014/entries/emotion/.

9. W. M. Reddy (1997) 'Against Constructionism: The Historical Ethnography of Emotions', *Current Anthropology* 38(3): 327–51.

10. Reddy, 'Against Constructionism', 329. See also J. Plamper, who insists that, to avoid 'a relapse into pure contingency', historical study 'has need of a transtemporal category, which presupposes that much is shared in common' (Plamper (2015) *The History of Emotions: An Introduction* (Oxford: Oxford University Press), p. 38.)

11. Ben Anderson (2009) 'Affective Atmospheres', *Emotion, Space and Society* 2: 77–81.

12. Anderson, 'Affective Atmospheres', 80.

13. Cf. below, Chapter 2; and e.g. Lauren Berlant (2008) 'Intuitionists: History and the Affective Event', *American Literary History* 20(4): 845–60.

14. See above n. 4.

15. Norbert Elias (2000) *The Civilising Process: Sociogenetic and Psychogenetic Investigations*, trans. E. Jephcott, and ed. E. Dunning, J. Goudsblom, and S. Mennell (rev. edn, Oxford: Blackwell).

16. Steven Pinker (2011) *The Better Angels of Our Nature: A History of Violence and Humanity* (London: Allen Lane), p. 176.

17. Simon Dickie (2011) *Cruelty and Laughter: Forgotten Comic Literature and the Unsentimental Eighteenth Century* (Chicago: University of Chicago Press).

18. See D. Lemmings and A. Brooks (Eds., 2014) *Emotions and Social Change: Historical and Sociological Perspectives* (Routledge: New York).

19. Chandler (2013) *An Archaeology of Sympathy: The Sentimental Mode in Literature and Cinema* (Chicago: University of Chicago Press).

20. Csengei (2011) *Sympathy, Sensibility and the Literature of Feeling in the Eighteenth Century* (Basingstoke: Palgrave Macmillan).

21. A. T. Delehanty, (2007) 'Mapping the Aesthetic Mind: John Dennis and Nicholas Boileau', *Journal of the History of Ideas* 68: 233–53.

22. For the concept of 'emotional labour', see A. R. Hochschild (1983) *The Managed Heart* (Berkeley, CA: University of California Press).

23. Delehanty, 'Mapping the Aesthetic Mind', 241.

24. Adam Smith (2002 [orig. 1759]) *The Theory of Moral Sentiments*, ed. K. Haakonsen (Cambridge: Cambridge University Press), p. 161 (sect. III.3.9).

25. See e.g. 'Philaretus' (i.e. the Rev. Gilbert Burnet), in *The London Journal*, no. 298 (10 April 1725); 'Hutcheson, Francis', in *Oxford Dictionary of National Biography* (www.oxforddnb.com).

26. See Habermas, *Structural Transformation of the Bourgeois Sphere*, esp. pp. 42–43, 57–64.

27. Cf. M. Scheer (2012) 'Are Emotions a Kind of Practice (and Is That What Makes Them Have a History)? A Bourdieuian Approach to Understanding Emotion', *History and Theory* 51: 193–220.

2
Psychological Perspectives on Emotion in Groups

W. Gerrod Parrott

1 Introduction

Historians who study emotions in the cultural and intellectual context of eighteenth-century Britain confront many issues that also preoccupy psychologists of emotion. Historical topics that might attract the interest of psychologists include emotional communication in the eighteenth-century British public sphere, emotional reportage in eighteenth-century newspapers, the analysis of sympathy by philosophers of the Scottish Enlightenment, and the development of group identity through consumption of sentimental novels. These topics overlap subjects studied by cultural and social psychologists, such as the contagion of emotions from one person to another, the characterisation of the emotional climate of a culture at a particular point in history, the ways that emotions pervade groups, and the relation between sympathy and empathy. The purpose of this chapter is to share ideas and research from psychology that might pertain to the topics being addressed from the more humanities-based perspectives in this book.

This chapter's focus is thus rather different from that of the burgeoning literature on how to integrate the social constructionist perspectives characterising the disciplines of history and cultural psychology with the more universalist perspectives characterising neuroscience, evolutionary psychology, and the less culturally aware experimental psychology of the twentieth century. Although psychologists have begun to recognise the importance of historians' research on emotions via historians' contributions to psychological handbooks and journals,[1] the most significant contributions to this literature have tended to come from historians and other humanists who have studied the findings of psychology and neuroscience.[2] Genuine interdisciplinarity, however, demands a fuller reckoning with both disciplines in a way that is difficult to achieve by one discipline alone. While a recent collection edited by Tileaga and Byford opens a more even-handed debate between historians and psychologists, there is yet space for an overview of what psychological research on the emotions has to bring to the table.[3] It is just such an overview this chapter seeks to provide: not an historian's critical reading of psychological research through, inevitably, the lens of their own training, but a glimpse into what some problems in the history of emotions might look like from the perspective of contemporary psychology.

This chapter will survey psychological approaches and findings that pertain particularly to the concerns of this volume. These concerns do include some general theoretical questions: What psychological approaches to describing emotions might make historical and cultural analysis more tractable? If emotions have a genetic and evolutionary basis, how can cultural change be understood to affect them? But in general, this chapter will focus less on general questions about the nature of emotion that have already received much attention and more on specific topics from emotion psychology and social psychology that are tailored to the specific interests of historians working on eighteenth-century Britain. Throughout the chapter I shall supply references to accessible reviews and to classic research in the hope that they will prove useful to historians interested in discovering psychological perspectives on these issues.

In addition, this chapter will consider some of the ways in which psychology benefits from historical research. Historians' research is critical to psychologists' understanding of the origins of their own emotion concepts and phenomena. Historians investigate cultural phenomena that are inaccessible to the research methods of cross-cultural psychology; they document social processes in natural settings that complement psychologists' laboratory and field methodologies. This chapter will report several ways in which current psychological concepts have been shaped by historical research, and subsequent chapters in this volume will surely supply psychologists with useful information about the ways that social circumstances and historical change can influence emotions.

It might appear that the subject matter and research methods of psychology and the humanities are so different as to make for very little common ground, as Gergen and Plamper have recently pointed out, focusing (in Gergen's words) on 'the alienated relationship between history and psychology', a condition whose roots are 'traceable at least to the late nineteenth century debates between those favouring a model of the human sciences as *Naturwissenschaft* as opposed to *Geisteswissenschaft*, essentially the difference between claims to an observational versus hermeneutic grounds for knowledge'.[4] Both agree, however, that the disciplines' commonalities should not be underestimated, and Scheer has gone a step further to suggest that 'what needs to be emphasized is the mutual embeddedness of minds, bodies, and social relations in order to historicize the body and its contributions to the learned experience of emotion'.[5]

It is worth noting that psychology spans such a vast range of levels of analysis that psychologists themselves often question the coherence of their discipline. The sorts of questions I ask as a social and cultural psychologist require a set of concepts and research methods that look nothing like those used by psychologists who study emotions by examining the role of the autonomic nervous system, or the activity of various regions and circuits in the brain. *Geisteswissenschaft* is alive and well in cultural psychology. Nevertheless, there remains common ground between the psychological sub-disciplines, and it can be helpful for cultural psychologists to take neuroscientists' research findings into account when, say, examining the metaphors used by different cultures to describe psychological states resembling Western emotions. Incorporating research from such different levels of analysis ultimately can inform thinking about emotions in different cultural contexts.

So too with history and psychology. While there are important differences between a discipline studying the emotions of living people and one focusing on the emotions of those who are long dead, the fields nonetheless share many interests and methodological challenges. For example, historians have made a careful distinction between emotions and emotionologies.[6] Likewise psychologists have needed to distinguish between people's actual emotions and their ideas about emotions (which strongly colour their recollections of past emotions as well as their understandings of others' emotions). This distinction is crucial for understanding the differing perspectives of people who are angry and those who are the targets of others' anger;[7] it explains discrepancies between actual embarrassment and what people believe to be typical embarrassment;[8] it also explains why men and women report remarkably similar emotions when asked about the past hour but dissimilar emotions when asked about emotions that occurred two weeks previously.[9] Thus, both disciplines, for their own reasons, have learned to make careful distinctions between emotions that actually occur and emotional norms, standards, and values. What follows is a somewhat schematic view of eighteenth-century British emotions from the perspective of psychology and what it has to bring.

2 The concept of emotion in contemporary psychology

The term *emotion* has proven impossible to define precisely, probably because the concept of emotion has evolved over centuries, accumulating overlapping but divergent meanings and associations.[10] This ambiguity can present an obstacle to scholarship because researchers may perceive each other as disagreeing about the nature of emotion when they actually are talking about different aspects or senses of emotion.

Psychologists have coped with this imprecision by conceiving of emotion as typically involving a set of components that can each be analysed fruitfully regardless of whether the overall category is itself precisely defined. Unlike some perspectives in the humanities, psychologists generally posit a wide range of emotional possibilities and permutations in the organisation of these components, whether or not a culture or historical moment describes them with a familiar or translatable word. This approach treats emotion as a fuzzy concept that prototypically incorporates a set of components, none of which is essential or sufficient to constitute emotion, but which are frequently present in any given emotional state. This solution, developed over the past 30 years, may be useful to historians as well. Although we lack complete consensus about the list of components, there is in fact considerable agreement among theorists. I shall illustrate this approach by describing a set of components that I have proposed and defended.[11] Other proposals are similar in specifics and in their overarching strategy.[12]

I characterise emotions as entailing five components: feelings, action tendencies, cognition, expression, and self-regulation:

1. Saying that *feeling* is a component of emotion means that emotions typically, although not necessarily, involve a conscious experience of being emotional in some way. Whether the feeling is of anger, satisfaction, envy, or whatever, this feeling is part of what people typically mean when they say they are having an emotion. Feeling sometimes appears to be the central feature of emotion, but at other times is only one aspect of emotion, and at other times is not essential at all – consider an emotion that a person is unaware of (such as unacknowledged shame or repressed anger), or emotions in animals.

2. Similarly, saying that emotions involve *action tendencies* means that emotions typically affect motivation. Emotional action tendencies involve preparation or readiness for action, either physically in the world or mentally with respect to attention, perception, memory, or reasoning.

3. Emotions entail *cognition* in two ways, one being the interpretation that gives rise to an emotion and sustains it (known in psychology as 'appraisal'), the other being the alteration in subsequent thinking that occurs once an emotion is underway (which could be called 'emotional cognition'). Appraisals differ from other perceptions and beliefs because they relate situations and events to a person's cares, concerns, and values. Emotional cognition includes the heightened vigilance that is part of anxiety, the distorted memory that is typical of depression, and the flexible problem-solving that arises as part of playfulness.

4. Many emotions involve an element of *communication or expression* that conveys an individual's emotional state to other people. Expression introduces a means by which emotion can spread from one person to another, as well as a means of inducing complementary or reactive emotions in others. Emotional communication can occur via facial expressions, tone of voice, posture, movement, and gesture.

5. Finally, most emotions involve a component of *self-regulation* by which an emotion's nature, intensity, duration, and expression are modified to suit the circumstances in which it occurs. Although some theorists maintain that regulation should not be considered to be part of the thing being regulated, many psychologists argue that emotions are shaped from beginning to end in ways that cannot be separated from other aspects of emotion, and therefore that regulation and emotion are one.

The componential approach to emotion is a pragmatic approach to a definitional problem that would otherwise impede research. It provides a way to identify emotional phenomena even though emotion itself cannot be defined, and thus promotes clear communication between researchers without committing them to a theory of how the components are bound together.

Each component can be analysed at various levels of analysis. This idea can be illustrated by distinguishing three levels of analysis: the biological, the individual, and the social.[13] In cultural analysis, as in modern everyday life, emotions are often examined on the individual level of analysis, which considers an isolated person's consciousness, thoughts, feelings, and actions when in an emotional state such as anger, embarrassment, or pride. Historians also frequently examine emotions at the social level of analysis, which would situate the anger, embarrassment, or pride within the dynamics of a particular social interaction involving members of a group, a set of groups, culture, and historical period. Although the participants in the social interaction are all individuals having emotions describable at the individual level, their interaction gives rise to social phenomena that are more than the sum of the individual reactions. These social and cultural phenomena require their own terminology and principles of organisation, and often their own research methodologies as well.[14] Less common for historical scholars, but routine for psychologists, is the biological level, which addresses the same set of five components in terms of hormonal, neural, and bodily activity. Yet historians may encounter sources that describe emotions in bodily terms, whether as the result of accurate observation (hearts actually do pound during rage, panic, and agitation) or of folk belief (black bile does not seem related to melancholia), and they may wish to speculate about biological aspects of historical emotions. As with the social level of analysis, the terminology, concepts, and research methods appropriate to biological processes differ markedly from those appropriate to the individual level.

The idea that most characterises the modern psychological approach to emotion is that they are functional, that they affect how a person relates to his or her environment in ways that can (but need not) be beneficial. Emotions' modification of action tendencies and thought processes, their behavioural expressions and conscious awareness, when properly elicited and regulated, can facilitate adaptive functioning in the situations in which they occur.[15] Functionalism posits that emotions exist to be useful; unpleasant emotions typically arise in situations where obstacles need to be confronted, where dangers require vigilance or escape, where relationships are threatened and must be monitored or repaired, where loss or failure requires the abandonment of prior attachments, where social transgression requires submissiveness and making amends; positive emotions typically arise when it is possible to take advantage of opportunities when things are going well.[16] The purpose of emotions is not to make people feel pleasant, but rather to motivate and guide actions that optimise responses to the problems and opportunities at hand. This idea has precedents, but it represented quite a break from the psychology of the mid-twentieth century in which emotions were considered to be disruptions that disorganise behaviour.

3 The historical origins of the contemporary psychology of emotion

Why are these components the ones that psychologists study? Why did psychological research focus on feelings and the biological level of analysis in the nineteenth-century and only gradually recognise the importance of the cognitive, social, and cultural thereafter? The answer to those questions illustrates one way in which psychologists can learn from cultural historians because it entails the history of European conceptions of passion and emotion, with crucial developments occurring in the long eighteenth century.[17]

The historical development of the term *emotion* reveals why conscious feelings were initially the focus of psychological research, and why they are so central to our conception today. Emotion, as a general psychological category, did not exist in English until the late eighteenth and early nineteenth centuries.[18] Prior to that time, the English term most similar to the modern meaning of *emotion* was *passion*. *Emotion* first acquired its psychological meaning as a metaphor for one aspect of passion, namely the manner in which passion stirs up movement. According to the *Oxford English Dictionary* (OED), the earliest uses of the word *emotion* referred to the motion or agitation of physical objects or groups of people.[19] For example, the OED quotes a report from 1579 about 'great stirres and emocions in Lombardye', which referred to social or political agitation. Another example, from 1603, is a reference to 'the divers emotions' of the Turks, which referred not to the Turks' feelings but to their migratory patterns.

The metaphorical extension to psychology occurred about half a century later, in French not English, in the influential philosophical account of René Descartes in *Les Passions de l'âme*.[20] Descartes described passions as being passive, sensory, and highly arousing, and it was to express that latter quality that he described passions as *les émotions*, a term chosen because Descartes asserted that none of the contents of the soul can 'agitate it and shake it so strongly as these passions do'.[21] In English, the physical and social meaning of the word *emotion* also came to be applied to mental states. The first example cited by the OED occurred just 11 years after Descartes' *Les Passions de l'âme* in Jeremy Taylor's work *Ductor Dubitantium, or, The Rule of Conscience*,[22] where the word *emotion* appeared four times and the word *passion* 129 times; the word *emotion* referred to political agitation on one occasion, whereas the other three times it referred to an internal state of an individual.

Based on my own word counts and readings of a few digitised texts from the eighteenth century, the psychological meaning of the word *emotion* continued to gain currency, but it remained subordinate to *passion*. David Hume, in 1739, used the word *emotion* in his *A Treatise of Human Nature*, but it was in a section entitled 'Of the Passions'; *passion* was still his primary concept and *emotion* merely emphasised the agitated aspects of it. In Fielding's *Tom Jones* (1749), the word *emotion* appeared four times, but *passion* appeared well over 100 times. Samuel Johnson's *Dictionary* (1755) included entries for both *emotion* and *passion*, but the one for *passion* was much more extensive and lengthy.[23]

According to Dixon, the word 'emotion' only replaced the word 'passion' when early nineteenth-century natural philosophers wished to create a category that was free of the theological associations attached to 'passion'.[24] The reasons why these natural philosophers tended to focus on emotions as being conscious feelings, and why they turned to physiological measurement to understand their origins, are therefore best found in the intellectual history of the eighteenth century, which indeed was a historical period in which attention increasingly focused on passions' conscious feeling. It was during the eighteenth century that German faculty psychologists such as Moses Mendelssohn and Johan Nicolaus Tetens formulated what is now called the 'tripartite theory of mind', which conceived the mind as divided into three aspects: understanding, volition, and feeling.[25] When tripartite psychology was applied to the passions, they were equated with feeling, not with volition or understanding. This emphasis had enormous implications because, when early psychologists first studied the passions in a scientific manner, they focused on the conscious experience of passions and tended to ignore passions' cognitive, motivational, and social aspects.[26] Meanwhile, in England and Scotland, philosophers also emphasised feeling, although they emphasised passions' role in ethical motivation too. As readers of the chapters by Pettigrove and Frazer in this volume will see, the Earl of Shaftesbury, Bishop Joseph Butler, and Francis Hutcheson discussed emotions and passions as forms of sentiment; their work influenced the thinking of David Hume and Adam Smith, and thereby nineteenth-century psychology.

Faculty psychology and moral sentiment theory helped shape how scientific psychology understood emotion by directing researchers' attention to the conscious feelings that accompany emotional states. The first major approach to psychological research, *introspectionism*, attempted to understand psychological states by careful delineation of their conscious aspects. The phenomenological experience of emotion attracted most attention, and to this day the conscious experience of emotion remains a major focus of psychological research. This emphasis has found its way into the everyday understanding of emotion as well. When I ask my students to define what they mean by the word 'emotion', the most common answer is that emotions are feelings.

A second major characteristic of nineteenth-century psychology was the emulation of the physical sciences. The techniques of physics and chemistry, and later those of biology and medicine, were used to measure the functioning of the brain and body in strong emotional states. Early physiological research on emotion concerned itself with changes in skin temperature and blood pressure during emotional responses, and the earliest psychology texts by Bain and Spencer attempted to relate the conscious feeling of emotion to the accompanying physiological activities of the body.[27] Throughout the nineteenth and twentieth centuries, researchers continued to study emotional reactions at the biological level of analysis, both in the physiology of the body and in the activity and structures of the brain.

From this beginning, it took more than a century for psychologists to develop the multi-componential approach to emotion, to understand emotion at multiple levels of analysis, and to integrate functionalism within that perspective. There are two reasons for this long gestation. The first is that appropriate research methods did not yet exist for most of the components and levels of analysis. The seeds of social psychology, sociology, anthropology, economics, cognitive science, and the other social sciences had barely sprouted in the late nineteenth century, and many would not mature until well into the twentieth. In the long eighteenth century and earlier there had been awareness of all aspects of psychology's contemporary approach: levels of analysis (for example, in Hobbes' *Leviathan*), functionalism and action tendencies (clearly present in Descartes' *Les Passions de l'âme*); emotional expression (consider Charles Le Brun), cognition (Spinoza among others), interpersonal compassion and social bonding (Adam Smith).[28] Despite this awareness, scientific study was not possible for more than a century and the nineteenth-century psychologists therefore focused on feelings and on biology – only those were associated with methods of rigorous empirical study. Thus, one reason why the development of the multi-componential approach took over a century was that the scientists needed to catch up with the philosophers and artists. The second reason was that, once the various social, cognitive, and biological sciences caught up, they tended to view their approaches as competing theories rather than as complementary levels of analysis. It took still more time to find ways to coordinate their various methods, frameworks, and levels of analysis. Add several decades for that, and it was not until the 1980s that contemporary psychology's approach to emotion was formed.

4 The malleability of emotions

Historians and cultural psychologists both investigate how culture can affect emotions. Historians typically examine emotions in the context of diachronic cultural change that may involve emotional change as well. Cultural psychologists, in contrast, study emotions synchronically by comparing multiple contemporary cultures to determine how culture shapes emotion. Historians and cultural psychologists therefore both tend to assume that emotions possess some degree of malleability.

The basis of emotional variability is therefore a fundamental topic for both history and cultural psychology; it is a topic about which the psychology of emotion has much to say. During the last third of the twentieth century, the dominant psychological theories of emotion emphasised their universality across cultures and even across species.[29] These theories postulated the existence of a small number of *basic emotions* that can be identified by universal facial expressions, that are controlled by universal mammalian neurochemical systems, and that can be defined as genetically determined, multi-componential response patterns that are the product of evolution. *Basic emotions theory* allowed for cultural and historical variability with respect to the social norms governing the public display of emotions, but it did not allow for modification of the emotions themselves. Basic emotion theory therefore represented a predominantly nativist approach. In the past two decades, however, basic emotions theory has been subjected to extensive criticism. Evidence suggests that the correlation among the various components of emotion is not tightly bound and that neurochemical systems do not correspond to emotion concepts.[30]

During the period in which basic emotion theory dominated psychology, the principal alternative was social constructionist theory, which construed emotions as social performances that are specific to particular cultures at particular points in their history.[31] Social constructionist theory often minimised the biological bases of emotions, typically by drawing on the two-factor theory of Stanley Schachter to characterise emotions' biology as involving nothing more than arousal of the sympathetic nervous system.[32] Aside from the energising effects of adrenaline, emotions were said to be constituted by verbal labelling and social convention, thus making them nearly unconstrained by genetics or evolution, and highly malleable by language and culture. This form of social constructionism has been extensively criticised, however. The two-factor theory of emotion on which it rests has many shortcomings: it lacks broad applicability; activity of the sympathetic nervous system is not essential to emotional feeling; the theory neglects many fundamental components of emotion, such as action tendencies or expressions; even though emotions lack the fixed universality claimed by basic emotion theory, many emotions possess sufficient similarity across cultures and even across mammalian species to suggest that there is more to emotions than language, culture, and adrenaline.[33]

If we are to account both for emotions' plasticity and for their similarities across cultures and historical periods, an alternative to basic emotions theory and social constructionism must be devised, a task that is the object of considerable research in contemporary psychology. My own proposal is that what we recognise as universal are not emotions themselves but rather more abstract underlying structures that I call *ur-emotions*.[34] When we recognise the similarities between 'anger' in contemporary Australia, 'ikari' in Japan, and 'marah' in Indonesia, we are not noting the identical emotion in three cultures but rather recognising some commonalities despite other differences; we are noting similar appraisals of interference with one's wishes; we are observing action tendencies broadly aimed at stopping that interference; but these general commonalities are expressed in different, culturally specific, even authentic, ways. When we say that taking a bone from a dog might make the dog angry we do not believe that the dog's 'anger' is the same as a human's but only that there are recognisable parallels between the two, such as the preparation to take hostile action to oppose an act. To say that all three cultures and the dog are exhibiting the same basic emotion of anger is unnuanced; to say that the dog's reaction is completely unlike the humans' and that the three human reactions have been independently constructed from their respective unrelated languages and cultures is too arbitrary. A more accurate characterisation would be that all four exhibit an underlying ur-anger that may have developed from common sensory–motor patterns that lead to a mode of action readiness aimed at confronting and modifying an unwanted action.[35]

My distinction between ur-emotions and fully realised emotions provides a basis for understanding emotions' malleability without attempting to describe the determinants of emotions' final form. That task must be addressed by careful analysis of social conditions, child-rearing practices, social norms and values, and cultural practices. These analyses can be performed both by historians and by psychologists, and they are. One path suggested by psychologists postulates that cultures shape emotions by shaping the self-concept, so that certain emotions require assessment of oneself (consider pride, guilt, shame, and embarrassment), and most emotions affect one's relationship with other people (consider anger, jealousy, gratitude, shame, affection, and envy). The cultures produce different conceptions of what it means to be a good person and of how people should treat one another, so these ideals will shape how emotions are expressed, which emotions are considered desirable, and how one ought to feel in a given set of circumstances.[36]

Psychology has proposed numerous other ways in which culture affects the nature of emotions.[37] For example, culture affects the meaning attributed to circumstances; it determines which emotions are appropriate to the social roles that people play; it establishes norms for how emotions are expressed, how emotions are valued, and the ways in which emotions must be regulated. Culture influences the aspects of emotion on which people focus their attention and thereby modify their conscious experience.

Thus, the history and social psychology of emotions converge in understanding that emotions are shaped as profoundly by their social and cultural context as by inflexible biological mechanisms. The ur-emotions that all people share manifest themselves as fully fledged emotions only when attached to culturally variable roles, values, and situations. Just as social psychologists seek to understand how cultures influence emotions, so cultural historians seek to understand how emotions are affected by historical specificity and difference.

5 The social nature of emotions

When emotions are described as consisting of five components, and as having functions and varying levels of analysis, it is easy to focus exclusively on intrapsychic, individualistic aspects of emotion and to neglect the social interactions, groups, and culture that are thoroughly intertwined in this conception of how emotions work. Consequently, social psychologists need to explain how emotions operate in social interaction, how they facilitate group functioning and group interaction, and how they are modified by culture. Equally cultural historians need to understand how emotions adapted to the emergence of print culture during the long eighteenth century and how they led to the formation of authentic selves and communities. To see how thoroughly emotions are affected by their social and cultural contexts, it is worth reconsidering the social aspects of the five components of emotion.

The process of emotional appraisal is easily misinterpreted as referring to a self-centred evaluation of the situation at hand; in fact, appraisal is deeply social. Appraisal is defined as an interpretation of circumstances in light of one's cares, concerns, and values, but nowhere is it stated that the people's cares are only selfish, their concerns merely egocentric, or their values entirely self-serving. People care about other people and become emotional on others' behalf; they can even care for fictional characters. Appraisal is social in other senses as well. The information that leads to emotional appraisal is often provided by other people, and the relevant values and concerns vary strongly across cultures and historical circumstances.[38]

Action tendencies similarly can be misinterpreted as residing entirely within an individual. To the contrary, action tendencies modify the manner in which an individual is in relation to his or her environment, including the social environment of other people, other members of a group, or other groups. Cultural differences and historical change strongly influence the modalities of action that emotions arouse – whether intergroup hostility leads to civil war or to pamphleteering is shaped by the culture of the time.

Feelings, or subjective experience, are often considered to be biologically endowed, so it is a helpful corrective to recognise that attention and meaning have as much influence as do hormones and neuropeptides. The quality of subjective experiences depends on whether people focus on themselves or on their environments, on their identity as individuals or as a member of groups, on whether they are immersed in the moment or detached and observing themselves.[39] People in different cultures are socialised to pay more or less attention to others, to cultivate and savour some emotions in preference to others, and to find some emotions more appropriate or authentic than others.[40]

Although expressions are obviously social in some sense, they are often characterised as being generated by an individual's internal emotional state.[41] It therefore needs to be pointed out that facial, vocal, and other expressions of emotion are strongly modified according to social and cultural context.[42] The magnitude of a person's smile depends on the presence or absence of another person, on emotional closeness with that person, on gender, on relative power, and on social motives. Facial movements can communicate social motives and intentions as well as express an individual's feelings.

Emotional self-regulation is strongly attuned to the particularities of the social situation at hand. Which emotion is most appropriate, at what intensity, and how it is most effectively expressed must all be determined with respect to the social status and personalities of the people present, as well as the social norms that apply to the situation. Social identity and context are intertwined with how an emotional state is regulated.

In short, the statement that emotions can be analysed on multiple levels must be understood as extending emotions' existence beyond the individual. The functions of emotions extend beyond an individual's cognition and biology as well. Emotions modify social interactions, modulate relationships, sustain or challenge social hierarchies, influence group identity, and affect intergroup relations.[43]

6   Emotional contagion

One important social effect of emotion is that the emotions of one person can influence those of another. This influence, of course, can take many forms. One person's emotion, say anger, can arouse a complementary emotion in other, say fear. Alternatively, one person's emotion might lead to an evaluative emotion in another, who reacts to it as surprising, amusing, or disturbing. The social effect that has generated the most interest in psychology occurs when one person's emotion leads other people to experience the same emotion. This influence is known as *emotional contagion* because it results in an emotion 'spreading' from one person to another. Emotional contagion has implications for relationships, work teams, and entire nations. It was the topic of one of the earliest works of social psychology, Gustav Le Bon's *The Crowd: A Study of the Popular Mind*.[44]

Psychologists have proposed a number of ways by which emotions spread from one person to another.[45] These mechanisms of emotional contagion range in complexity from fairly primitive through to highly cognitive. One simple mechanism could occur if the expression of an emotion functioned as an innate (unlearned) elicitor of the same emotion in others. For example, the shrill vocalisations and abrupt movements that express distress or fear may induce distress or fear in others. A second, similar mechanism could work without innate encoding if the association between emotional expression and reaction were learned via classical conditioning. For example, if a person's friend tended to pace back and forth when worried about financial problems, that person could learn to become worried from the sight of the friend pacing.

One of the best studied mechanisms is the mimicry/feedback hypothesis.[46] This account is more complex than the first two in that it involves a sequence of less direct processes, but it is still quite primitive in that it typically proceeds without conscious awareness and bypasses most cognitive interpretation. The first step in the explanation is that people in face-to-face interaction tend to mimic each other's facial expressions, postures, voices, and movements, and to synchronise their non-verbal movements – phenomena that are well-established by researchers of non-verbal behaviour. The explanation's second step connects the mimicry and synchronisation to emotion induction via physiological feedback. If the sensations of making expressive faces, voices, and postures provides part of the feeling of the emotion being expressed, then the sensations of mimicking and synchronising with someone else's expressions should lead to the transmission of one person's emotion to another person. For example, mimicking a happy person will lead to sensory feedback from the cheek muscles that are mimicking the smile and from the arm muscles synchronising with the excited movements of the happy person, and the sensations from those muscles will produce a feeling of excited happiness.

A fourth, more cognitive account of emotional contagion would be based on the inferences that can be made from observing another person's emotion. Because emotions are connected to an appraisal of the situation at hand, we can infer from an emotional display how that person has appraised the situation. For example, someone else's fear informs a nearby person that something in the current situation may be dangerous, and another person's anger implies that that person may be aware of wrongdoing. The exposure to another person's emotion may therefore lead someone to seek out information congruent with the emotion's appraisal. It could also bias the person's interpretation of events so that danger or transgression is perceived when they otherwise would not be.

These four means of emotional contagion have been observed in a variety of studies.[47] In one well-known study, Peter Totterdell equipped players from four professional cricket teams with pocket computers on which they rated their moods and their game performance periodically during a four-day championship match.[48] Totterdell found that happy moods were particularly likely to spread among team members, and that this contagion was not merely due to the outcome of game events. Contagion was only observed during activities in which coordinated action was required, not during activities that depended on individual effort. The effect was strongest in players who were older and who were themselves more susceptible to emotional contagion.

Scholars of eighteenth-century print culture will note that three of these four means of emotional contagion typically involve face-to-face contact, and may well wonder how emotional contagion could be accomplished, say, by the distribution of pamphlets or newspapers. One answer is that the fourth account is quite robust and entirely adequate to bring about contagion. Emotions can be displayed via language – quite vividly so if the writer is skilled. Language can directly supply appraisal information without its needing to be inferred from non-verbal expressions, and can also supply information that affects the intensity of readers' emotional responses; the centuries-long study and practice of rhetoric has codified the theory and methods of doing so. Psychological researchers have a bias toward primitive mechanisms and toward non-verbal aspects of emotion, but other fields (such as rhetoric) fill the gap. A second answer is that skilled writers may employ poetic devices that induce readers to recreate in their imaginations the non-verbal signals that evoke emotions when face-to-face. Tone of voice and rhythmic movement can be conveyed in writing and may contribute to emotional contagion in an audience of readers.

Psychological research has investigated which people are most susceptible to emotional contagion. People who pay close attention to others and those who are good at reading others' emotional expressions will tend to be more susceptible. People who construe themselves as being interrelated with others also have greater susceptibility, which implies that members of cultures that emphasise people's interrelatedness will tend to be more vulnerable to contagion from the emotions of others than will members of more individualistic cultures. Emotional contagion is especially likely with people who are in loving relationships; contagion is especially unlikely if a person dislikes another person, or is engaged in a rivalry, or bears ill will. These findings provide intriguing hints about the sources of emotional contagion. Unfortunately, the original studies provide little information about the underlying processes, so the hints remain speculative. The susceptibility of less powerful people may partly be due to their caring more about and paying more attention to the more powerful person's emotions than vice versa. The less powerful also may engage in unilateral mimicry to communicate allegiance; part of following a leader may be synchronising to that person's emotions. Synchronisation may also communicate intimacy, and reduced emotional contagion in non-intimate relationships may reflect the avoidance of inappropriate intimacy.[49] Certainly historical investigations of such emotions in more frankly hierarchical societies of the past would add valuable complexity to contemporary Western investigations that assume high levels of egalitarianism as 'normal'.

It is noteworthy that disliking a person reduces the contagiousness of that person's emotions. Disliking is also related to sympathy, as was illustrated by a simple psychology experiment on seven- and eight-year-old schoolchildren.[50] The experimenters divided the schoolchildren into two groups and showed each a film that directly manipulated the likability of a boy their own age. In one film, the boy was friendly with his peers, affectionate to his dog, and generous in sharing a sandwich with his little brother; in the other film, the boy acted violently toward his peers, hit his dog, and not only refused to share his sandwich but also deliberately broke his little brother's toy airplane. Each of the two groups of schoolchildren then watched one of two endings to the film. Half of each group saw the boy receive a brand-new bicycle from his parents and happily play with it. The other half of each group watched the boy riding a bicycle, then lose his balance and fall to the ground, grimacing in pain. Schoolchildren who had seen the boy behave benevolently felt happy when they watched the happy ending and shared the boy's pain when they saw the unhappy ending; that is, they experienced some emotional contagion. Those who had seen the boy behaving malevolently reacted the opposite way: they were unhappy when he received the new bicycle and they experienced schadenfreude when they saw him suffer. That is, they not only failed to experience the boy's emotions contagiously, but actually experienced unsympathetic, hostile emotions instead. These findings suggest that emotional contagion shares some features with sympathy, which has also been the topic of psychological research.

7 Sympathy

Central to the philosophy of the eighteenth-century Scottish Enlightenment, sympathy is a complex phenomenon, and because terminology changed between eighteenth-century moral sentiment theory and twenty-first-century psychology, some definitional issues need to be discussed. In the eighteenth century, at least for Adam Smith, the term *sympathy* referred to an appreciation of another person's point of view that was linked to an altruistic motivation to alleviate that person's suffering.[51] The term referred at once to perspective-taking, to understanding another person's emotions, to feeling pity for another's suffering, and to being motivated to see the other relieved of suffering. In modern psychology, the term *sympathy* has mostly been replaced by the term *empathy*, which is of more recent origin but has been used no more precisely. There has been much effort to clarify the issues, but little consensus.

One proposal, put forward by Lauren Wispé, is that *empathy* be used to refer to the comprehension of another person's positive and negative experiences, and that sympathy be used to refer to the heightened awareness of another person's suffering as something to be alleviated.[52] On this view, empathy involves putting oneself in the other's position and knowing what that is like, whereas sympathy combines an understanding of another person's predicament with an urge to take action to relieve it. Of necessity, *sympathy* only applies to unfortunate circumstances and the negative emotions they arouse, whereas empathy can apply to happy circumstances as well. *Sympathy* is thus either an emotion akin to *pity* or an attitude akin to *compassion*. This proposal provides some clarity on a subject long muddled, but it omits some of the components of the eighteenth-century concept (for example, emotional resonance), and it has not been universally adopted. The two best-known psychologists studying empathy both decline to follow suit.[53] I will, nevertheless, follow Wispé's terminology in an effort to impose some clarity in describing psychological research findings.

The topic that has most animated psychologists' interest in sympathy and empathy is altruism, a topic more recently explored in cultural context by historians and anthropologists.[54] Daniel Batson devoted his career to investigating the motivational underpinnings of altruism from a psychological perspective, and particularly wanted to disprove the widely held belief that the ultimate goal of being kind and helpful to others was to benefit oneself. He had to concede, of course, that many cases of helping people are in fact motivated by the desire to gain material rewards, to receive public praise, to raise one's self-esteem, or to escape feelings of guilt or shame: Mandeville and Hobbes made similar points in the seventeenth and eighteenth centuries. Batson attempted to demonstrate, however, that not all cases of helpfulness or generosity were of these types – he attempted to vindicate Adam Smith. Batson did so by carefully distinguishing the types of emotional reactions that arise when one sees a person who needs help and by showing that they lead to different motivational consequences. One emotional reaction is *personal distress*, the tendency to feel upset, disturbed, uncomfortable, and anxious. A contrasting emotional reaction is what Wispé would call sympathy, which for Batson includes tendencies to feel compassion, warmth, pity, and tenderness. Batson predicted that personal distress motivated an egoistic desire to relieve that distress, whereas sympathy motivated an altruistic desire to help the other person. If the sight of a person needing help causes a person to become personally distressed, then that person's primary motivation would be to feel better personally, which could be accomplished by helping the other person but just as effectively by doing something else to feel better. In contrast, if the sight of someone needing help causes a person to experience sympathy, then that person's primary motivation would be to help the other, and no alternative remedy would be available. In a series of ingenious and complex experiments, Batson obtained persuasive evidence that sympathy leads to genuine altruism (in late twentieth-century Americans). In some experiments, he divided people into those who felt personal distress and those who felt sympathy, and showed that the distressed group would avoid helping another person if there were an easier way to feel better, but the sympathetic group would not. In other experiments, he manipulated sympathy by making the victim similar or dissimilar to the experimental participant; greater similarity produced greater sympathy, which led to greater altruism. So, there is now considerable research on the factors that lead to sympathy and on sympathy's role in altruism.[55]

Other aspects of sympathy and empathy have been studied.[56] Sympathy has been shown to play an important role in forgiveness; sympathy toward a person who has wronged one increases motivation to forgive and decreases motivations for revenge and estrangement. Sympathy also inhibits aggression and hostility, possibly due to increased pity for the target's suffering or to increased empathy with the victim's point of view. Either explanation implies that satire and criticism must decrease sympathy to be effective, and that the sort of cruel humour which Simon Dickie described requires an audience willing to suspend sympathy with the butt of the jokes.[57]

8   Group emotions

A group can be said to have emotions, but there are obvious problems with suggesting that the emotions are in the group and not in the group members. There are various ways to make this expression coherent. One is based on individuals' identification with social groups. Self-concepts include elements of both individual characteristics and group membership. When events are appraised for their emotional relevance to the groups with which a person identifies, the resulting emotions can be considered to be group-level emotions. In a series of experiments on undergraduate students at a large state university in the Midwestern United States, researchers demonstrated that the strength of students' identification with their university predicted the occurrence of emotions based on that identity. For example, feeling strong ties with other students at their university and thinking of themselves as students of that university led them to feel group-level emotions (as a university student) that were statistically different from the emotions reported as an individual. These group-level emotions converged with those of other group members, and they motivated actions that were functional for the group as a whole (such as willingness to defend the university's reputation). Group emotions may also affect group cohesiveness, morale, and solidarity. They can function to define social reality, to motivate social change, to influence participation in collective acts, to promote closeness and intimacy, to distinguish in-group and out-group identities, and to define group-related roles and status.[58]

When group emotions are directed toward other groups, they can be said to be *intergroup emotions*. Many of the phenomena of prejudice can be understood as intergroup emotions involving anxiety or hostility. Intergroup emotions can also lead to reconciliation, however. For example, Dutch researchers examined Dutch citizens' collective guilt about their nation's treatment of Indonesians during the colonial era. They asked participants to read a historical account of Dutch treatment of Indonesians and found collective guilt, especially when the Dutch behaviour was presented in the most negative terms. Interestingly, those people who had the strongest Dutch national identity actually reported less collective guilt, presumably because they engaged in defensive denial.[59]

Group identity also can give rise to intergroup fear. For example, after the 11 September 2001 terrorist attacks on New York and Washington, DC, researchers asked Belgian and Dutch citizens to rate their feelings of fear; when the study was described as comparing Westerners and Arabs, they thought of themselves as in the same group as the Americans and felt greater intergroup fear than when the study was described as comparing Europeans and Americans. Other intergroup emotions such as gloating and schadenfreude can be readily observed during sports competitions because sports fans identify with their favourite teams. For example, Dutch football fans express schadenfreude when a rival team such as Germany or Italy is eliminated from World Cup competition.

When group emotions pervade a society, psychologists speak of there being an *emotional climate*. For example, pervasive corruption can give rise to anger and despair that is prevalent in the relationships between group members despite the occurrence of many other emotions; social norms about the Christmas season combine with pervasive cues in the form of twinkling lights, decorations, and carols to give rise to a 'Christmas spirit' of excitement and happiness despite the wide range of actual emotions evoked by the Christmas holiday.[60] Emotional climates are more stable than are reactions to particular events and can characterise a period of time, thus providing a tantalising object of study to cultural historians.

9   Summary

This chapter has surveyed topics in the psychology of emotion that are of particular relevance to understanding the changes in emotional expression and social organisation that occurred in eighteenth-century Britain. Some of these topics have to do with the conception of emotion – understanding emotions' operation and function on multiple levels of analysis, conceiving of them as involving cognition, readiness for mental and physical action, expression, feelings, and self-regulation. This framework promotes interdisciplinary collaboration because the identification of components allows greater specificity and precision, especially when researchers are using different methods and considering different levels of analysis. Understanding this framework requires the tools of literary analysis and history as well as of psychology because the origins of the modern psychological approach lie in the intellectual developments of the early modern period and long eighteenth century.

For the concerns of the present volume, I have surveyed selected topics from social psychology and cultural psychology. The social nature of emotions was emphasised, demonstrating emotions' social effects and functions via all of their components – emotions shape interactions, relationships, hierarchies, and entire groups. The malleability of emotions is underestimated by basic emotion theory and overestimated by social constructionism, so the concept of ur-emotions was presented to allow for cultural variability and the historical development of emotional responses. A number of social phenomena that are of particular significance for understanding public emotional discourse were singled out for more detailed attention. Emotional contagion underlies the spread of emotion. Sympathy and empathy facilitate altruism and long-term relationships. Group emotions operate at the level of collective identity and can characterise historical periods. This research can inform further accounts of emotional communication in eighteenth-century British print culture.

Notes

1. See P. N. Stearns (2008) 'History of Emotions: Issues of Change and Impact', in M. Lewis, J. M. Haviland-Jones, and L. Feldman Barrett (Eds.), *Handbook of Emotions*, 3rd ed. (New York: Guilford Press), pp. 17–31; S. J. Matt (2011) 'Current Emotion Research in History: Or, Doing History from the Inside

Out', *Emotion Review*, 3(1), 117–24; P. N. Stearns (2009) 'Special Issue: History of Emotion', *Emotion Review* 1(4): 291–368.

2. See W. M. Reddy (2001) *The Navigation of Feeling: A Framework for the History of Emotions* (Cambridge: Cambridge University Press); T. Dixon (2003) *From Passions to Emotions: The Creation of a Secular Psychological Category* (Cambridge: Cambridge University Press); B. H. Rosenwein (2006) *Emotional Communities in the Early Middle Ages* (Ithaca, NY: Cornell University Press) and J. Plamper (2015) *The History of Emotions: An Introduction* (Oxford: Oxford University Press).

3. C. Tileagă and J. Byford (Eds.) (2014) *Psychology and History: Interdisciplinary Explorations* (Cambridge: Cambridge University Press).

4. K. J. Gergen, Foreword, in Tileagă and Byford (2014), p. xii; see also Plamper, *The History of Emotions*, 7.

5. M. Scheer (2012) 'Are Emotions a Kind of Practice (and Is That What Makes Them Have a History)? A Bourdieuian Approach to Understanding Emotion', *History and Theory* 51: 193–220, 199.

6. P. N. Stearns and C. Z. Stearns (1985) 'Emotionology: Clarifying the History of Emotions and Emotional Standards', *American Historical Review* 90(4): 813–36.

7. J. R. Averill (1982) *Anger and Aggression: An Essay on Emotion* (New York: Springer-Verlag).

8. W. G. Parrott and S. F. Smith (1991) 'Embarrassment: Actual vs. Typical Cases, Classical vs. Prototypical Representations', *Cognition and Emotion* 5: 467–88.

9. S. A. Shields (2000) 'Thinking about Gender, Thinking about Theory: Gender and Emotional Experience', in A. H. Fischer (Ed.), *Gender and Emotion: Social Psychological Perspectives* (Cambridge: Cambridge University Press), pp. 3–23.

10. A. O. Rorty (1982) 'From Passions to Emotions and Sentiments', *Philosophy* 57: 159–72.

11. W. G. Parrott (2007) 'Components and the Definition of Emotion', *Social Science Information* 46: 419–23.

12. K. R. Scherer (1984) 'On the Nature and Function of Emotion: A Component Process Approach', in K. R. Scherer and P. Ekman (Eds.), *Approaches to Emotion* (Hillsdale, NJ: Erlbaum), pp. 293–317.

13. In fact, the number of levels of analysis is arbitrary; it is always possible to distinguish more or fewer levels depending on one's needs.

14. Averill, *Anger and Aggression*.

15. N. H. Frijda (1986) *The Emotions* (Cambridge: Cambridge University Press).

16. W. G. Parrott (2014) 'Feeling, Function, and the Place of Negative Emotions in a Happy Life', in W. G. Parrott (Ed.), *The Positive Side of Negative Emotions* (New York: Guilford Press), pp. 273–96.

17. W. G. Parrott (2000) 'The Psychologist of Avon: Emotion in Elizabethan Psychology and the Plays of Shakespeare', in B. Landau, J. Sabini, J. Jonides, and E. Newport (Eds.), *Perception, Cognition, and Language: Essays in Honor of Henry and Lila Gleitman* (Cambridge, MA: MIT Press), pp. 231–43.

18. T. Dixon (2003) *From Passions to Emotions: The Creation of a Secular Psychological Category* (Cambridge: Cambridge University Press).

19. *Oxford English Dictionary* (1989) (Oxford: Oxford University Press).

20. R. Descartes (1970 [1649]) *Les Passions de l'âme* [The passions of the soul] (Paris: Librairie Philosophique J. Vrin).

21. R. Descartes (1989) *The Passions of the Soul*, trans. S. R. Voss (Indianapolis, IN: Hackett), p. 34
22. J. Taylor (1660) *Ductor Dubitantium, or the Rule of Conscience* (London: James Flesher).
23. D. Hume (1998 [1739]) *A Treatise of Human Nature*, ed. D. F. Norton and M. J. Norton (Oxford: Oxford University Press); H. Fielding (1749) *The History of Tom Jones, a Foundling* (London: A. Millar); S. Johnson (1996 [1755]) *A Dictionary of the English Language on CD-ROM*, ed. A. McDermott (Cambridge: Cambridge University Press).
24. Dixon, *From Passions to Emotions*.
25. E. R. Hilgard (1980) 'The Trilogy of Mind: Cognition, Affection, and Conation', *Journal of the History of the Behavioral Sciences* 16: 107–17.
26. A good example of early psychological discussion of emotion is A. Bain (1859) *The Emotions and the Will* (London: Parker). For discussion of early psychological approaches to emotion, see H. M. Gardiner, R. C. Metcalf, and J. G. Beebe-Center (1937) *Feeling and Emotion: A History of Theories* (New York: American Book Company), especially Chapter 10; also see Dixon, *From Passion to Emotions*, Chapter 5.
27. Early physiological research methods are described by O. E. Dror (1999) 'The Scientific Image of Emotion: Experience and Technologies of Inscription', *Configurations* 7: 355–401. The first psychology text was arguably that of H. Spencer (1855) *Principles of Psychology* (London: Longman, Brown, Green, and Longmans, 2 vols). Bain's *The Emotions and the Will* relates conscious feelings of emotion to biological activity of the body.
28. S. James (1997) *Passion and Action: The Emotions in Seventeenth-Century Philosophy* (Oxford: Oxford University Press); J. Montagu (1994) *The Expression of the Passions: The Origin and Influence of Charles Le Brun's* Conférence sur l'expression générale et particulière (New Haven, CT: Yale University Press); J. Staines (2004) 'Compassion in the Public Sphere of Milton and King Charles', in G. K. Paster, K. Rowe, and M. Floyd-Wilson (Eds.), *Reading the Early Modern Passions: Essays in the Cultural History of Emotion* (Philadelphia, PA: University of Pennsylvania Press), pp. 89–110; R. Strier (2004) 'Against the Rule of Reason: Praise of Passion from Petrarch to Luther to Shakespeare to Herbert', in Paster et al. (Eds.) *Reading the Early Modern Passions*, pp. 23–42.
29. Two examples are: C. E. Izard (1977) *Human Emotions* (New York: Plenum) and J. Panksepp (1982) 'Toward a General Psychobiological Theory of Emotions', *The Behavioral and Brain Sciences* 5: 407–67.
30. L. F. Barrett (2006) 'Emotions as Natural Kinds?', *Perspectives on Psychological Science* 10: 20–46.
31. J. R. Averill (1980) 'A Constructivist View of Emotion', in R. Plutchik and H. Kellerman (Eds.), *Emotion: Theory, Research, and Experience: Vol. 1. Theories of Emotion* (New York: Academic Press), pp. 305–39; R. Harré (1986) *The Social Construction of Emotions* (Oxford: Basil Blackwell).
32. S. Schachter and J. E. Singer (1962) 'Cognitive, Social, and Physiological Determinants of Emotional State', *Psychological Review* 69: 379–99.
33. R. Reisenzein (1983) 'The Schachter Theory of Emotion: Two Decades Later', *Psychological Bulletin* 94: 239–64. Also see Frijda, *The Emotions*, chapters 3 and 4.

34. W. G. Parrott (2010) 'Ur-emotions and Your Emotions: Reconceptualising Basic Emotion', *Emotion Review* 2: 14–21.
35. N. Frijda and W. G. Parrott (2011) 'Basic Emotions or Ur-emotions?', *Emotion Review* 3: 406–15; W. G. Parrott (2012) 'Ur-emotions: The Common Feature of Animal Emotions and Socially Constructed Emotions', *Emotion Review* 4(3): 247–8.
36. H. R. Markus and S. Kitayama (1994) 'The Cultural Construction of Self and Emotion: Implications for Social Behavior', in S. Kitayama and H. R. Markus (Eds.), *Emotion and Culture: Empirical Studies of Mutual Influence* (Washington, DC: American Psychological Association), pp. 89–130.
37. M. Boiger and B. Mesquita (2012) 'The Construction of Emotion in Interactions, Relationships, and Cultures', *Emotion Review* 4(3): 221–9; Y. E. Chentsova-Dutton, N. Senft, and A. G. Ryder (2014) 'Listening to Negative Emotions: How Culture Constrains What we Hear', in W. G. Parrott (Ed.), *The Positive Side of Negative Emotions* (New York: Guilford), pp. 146–78; B. Parkinson, A. H. Fischer, and A. S. R. Manstead (2005) *Emotion in Social Relations* (New York: Psychology Press).
38. A. S. R. Manstead and A. H. Fischer (2001) 'Social Appraisal: The Social World as Object of and Influence on Appraisal Processes', in K. R. Scherer, A. Schorr, and T. Johnstone (Eds.), *Appraisal Processes in Emotion: Theory, Methods, Research* (Oxford: Oxford University Press), pp. 221–32.
39. N. H. Frijda (2005) 'Emotion Experience', *Cognition and Emotion*, 19(4): 473–97.
40. J. L. Tsai, B. Knutson, and H. H. Fung (2006) 'Cultural Variation in Affect Valuation', *Journal of Personality and Social Psychology* 90: 288–307.
41. For example, P. Ekman (1973) *Darwin and Facial Expression: A Century of Research in Review* (New York: Academic Press).
42. A. J. Fridlund (1994) *Human Facial Expression: An Evolutionary View* (San Diego, CA: Academic Press).
43. A. H. Fischer and A. S. R. Manstead (2008) 'Social Functions of Emotion', in M. Lewis, J. M. Haviland-Jones, and L. F. Barrett (Eds.), *Handbook of Emotions*, 3rd ed. (New York: Guilford), pp. 456–68.
44. C. Anderson and D. Keltner (2004) 'The Emotional Convergence Hypothesis: Implications for Individuals, Relationships, and Cultures', in L. Z. Tiedens and C. W. Leach (Eds.), *The Social Life of Emotions* (Cambridge: Cambridge University Press), pp. 144–63; E. Hatfield, J. T. Cacioppo, and R. L. Rapson (1994) *Emotional Contagion* (Cambridge: Cambridge University Press); J. R. Kelly and S. G. Barsade (2001) 'Mood and Emotion in Small Groups and Work Teams', *Organizational Behavior and Human Decision Processes* 86(1): 99–130; G. Le Bon (1896) *The Crowd: A Study of the Popular Mind* (London: Ernest Benn).
45. Hatfield et al., *Emotional Contagion*.
46. Hatfield et al., *Emotional Contagion*.
47. See Hatfield et al., *Emotional Contagion*; Kelly and Barsade, 'Mood and Emotion'; Parkinson et al., *Emotion in Social Relations* (especially Chapter 7).
48. P. Totterdell (2000) 'Catching Moods and Hitting Runs: Mood Linkage and Subjective Performance in Professional Sport Teams', *Journal of Applied Psychology* 85(6): 848–59.

49. Regarding individual differences, see Hatfield et al., *Emotional Contagion*; regarding cultural differences, see Markus and Kitayama, 'Cultural Construction'. The mechanisms underlying these findings are discussed in Hatfield et al., *Emotional Contagion*, and by Parkinson et al., *Emotion in Social Relations*.

50. D. Zillman and J. R. Cantor (1977) 'Affective Responses to the Emotions of a Protagonist', *Journal of Experimental Social Psychology* 13: 155–65.

51. A. Smith (1976 [1759]) *The Theory of Moral Sentiments* (Indianapolis, IN: Liberty Classics).

52. For advocacy of this proposal along with an informative history of the terms 'sympathy' and 'empathy', see L. Wispé (1986) 'The Distinction between Sympathy and Empathy: To Call Forth a Concept, a Word is Needed', *Journal of Personality and Social Psychology* 50(2): 314–21.

53. Daniel Batson insists on using *empathy* to mean what Wispé calls *sympathy*, while Mark Davis insists that both of Wispé's meanings are facets of a yet more complex process that he refers to as *empathy-related processes and outcomes*. C. D. Batson (1991) *The Altruism Question: Toward a Social-Psychological Answer* (Hillsdale, NJ: Lawrence Erlbaum); M. H. Davis (2004) 'Empathy: Negotiating the Border between Self and Other', in L. Z. Tiedens and C. W. Leach (Eds.), *The Social Life of Emotions* (Cambridge: Cambridge University Press), pp. 19–42.

54. T. Dixon (2008) *The Invention of Altruism: Making Moral Meanings in Victorian Britain* (Oxford: Oxford University Press); D. W. Hollan and C. J. Throop (Eds.) (2011) *The Anthropology of Empathy: Experiencing the Lives of Others in Pacific Societies* (New York: Berghahn Books).

55. See Batson, *Altruism Question*.

56. For a review, see Davis, 'Empathy'.

57. S. Dickie (2011) *Cruelty and Laughter: Forgotten Comic Literature and the Unsentimental Eighteenth Century* (Chicago: University of Chicago Press).

58. E. R. Smith, C. R. Seger, and D. M. Mackie (2007) 'Can Emotions be Truly Group Level? Evidence Regarding Four Conceptual Criteria', *Journal of Personality and Social Psychology* 93(3): 431–46.

59. For a summary of the extensive evidence for intergroup emotions, see Parkinson et al., *Emotion in Social Relations*, Chapter 5.

60. J. De Rivera and D. Páez (2007) 'Emotional Climate, Human Security, and Cultures of Peace', *Journal of Social Issues* 63(2): 233–53.

Part II

Sympathy, Improvement, and the Formation of Virtual Communities

3
The Emotional Contents of Swift's *saeva indignatio*

Robert Phiddian

1 Introduction

According to Joseph Carroll's combative manifesto for a Darwinian approach to literature, 'Together, anger, contempt, and disgust comprise the main emotional components of satire'.[1] Students of satire have done very little to address this statement in the decade since he made it, and not for want of major developments in analysis of these emotions. Anger has long attracted the attention of psychologists, and there is a rapidly developing scholarship on disgust and contempt in their psychological, philosophical, and cultural aspects.[2] Perhaps these emotions' visceral qualities have kept them from attracting much attention among literary scholars of satire. Though satire makes us laugh and is consequently often thought of as a comic activity in the benign realm of humour, it is deeply committed to the mobilisation of essentially negative emotions. They are expressive and affective dimensions of satire rather than the formal aspects that tend to be the focus of literary analysis, but they are essential to an understanding of the cultural and personal function of satires.

Anyone interested in Scriblerian satire and the history of emotions need not follow the full cognitive-behavioural line that Carroll and others map, to find his basic proposition provocative. Swift and Pope may present themselves as beacons of reason in a naughty world, but what keeps bringing me back to them is not that they were particularly correct in their judgements of the world around them. They were not. Instead, the hook is the sheer, exhilarating emotional force of lines that can be imagined as instances of the satirical sublime. Two examples will suffice, first from Pope's *Epilogue to the Satires* (1738):

> Friend You're strangely proud. Pope So proud I am no Slave,
> So impudent, I own myself no Knave:
> So odd, my Country's Ruin makes me grave.
> Yes, I am proud; I must be proud to see
> Men not afraid of God, afraid of me:
> Safe from the Bar, the Pulpit, and the Throne,
> Yet touch'd and sham'd by Ridicule alone.[3]

And from Swift, the King of Brobdingnag's withering summary of European humanity:

> But by what I have gathered from your own Relation, and the Answers I have with much Pains wringed and extorted from you; I cannot but conclude the Bulk of your Natives, to be the most pernicious Race of little odious Vermin that Nature ever suffered to crawl upon the Surface of the Earth.[4]

These passages should, according to their logical content, simply be depressing, but their effect on me is, instead, exhilarating and cathartic. Aristotle's rationale for the cleansing affective power of tragedy, catharsis is also an underappreciated element of satire and its appeal to audiences. While it does not provide a total explanation of the emotional dynamics of satire, it is a substantial part of the story. It is a transhistorical characteristic of the satirical mode – a vicarious sense of glee at judgement rendered in a moment of artistic compression that simultaneously clarifies and purges (often in different measure to different readers). What gives it particular bite in the early eighteenth century is the role played by satire in rapid developments of the conventions and emotional dynamics of print culture.

Pope's visionary anger and Swift's resounding combination of contempt and disgust are strikingly violent and compelling expressions of visceral emotion in the public space provided by publication. And yet, this violence was not treated, at least not formally, as sedition by the Walpole regime they targeted. These passages, and many more specific accusations of corruption and malfeasance, did not have to circulate as underground dissent, or be disguised by anything more than the most transparent claims to fictionality. Such open, spectacular, and sustained dissent to a current regime is a cornerstone of modern notions of freedom of expression, but it was unprecedented before early eighteenth-century Britain. The theory of the development of a public sphere derived from Habermas does not account easily for such satirical dissent and the emotional publics thus called into being, because it focuses on the genesis of modes of civil discourse. As a synthesis of the debate has it:

> In a nutshell, a public sphere adequate to a democratic polity depends upon both quality of discourse and quantity of participation. Habermas develops the first requirement in elaborating how the classical bourgeois public sphere of the seventeenth and eighteenth centuries was constituted around rational critical argument, in which the merits of arguments and not the identities of arguers were critical.[5]

There certainly was a *de facto* expansion of tolerated political utterance in early to mid-eighteenth-century Britain that was different from and more lasting than the previous expansion of press freedom that occurred during the 1640s and 1650s, but the ideal version of an authentically deliberative public sphere laid out in Habermas's classic treatise only tells part of the story.[6] Conal Condren's anti-Habermasian work, with its focus on the acerbically personal aspects of early modern political theory, provides a cue to the robust incivility and personality of Scriblerian satire that is explored here.[7] The central thread of this chapter will be an account of the *saeva indignatio* that is the remarkably harsh driving passion to which Swift lays claim in the inscription above his grave (finalised in his will of 1740), and I will illustrate my case through a reading of one of Swift's most notorious poems, 'A Beautiful Young Nymph Going to Bed' (circulating in manuscript from 1731, and published in 1734).

Beyond the relatively intimate emotional dynamics analysed here, lies a larger argument I can only gesture towards in the scope available, that open satire is a necessary (if not universally sufficient) condition of a relatively free press and liberal institutions. It can be a vector for reform (though the historical instances of this occurring are scarcer than fans of satire care to acknowledge) and a cathartic vent for hostile emotions. In remarkable circumstances satire can trigger revolutions, but that is rare and not the aspect I am exploring here. Nor do I attempt to survey the ecology of satirical writing in the early eighteenth century, recently mapped so impressively by Ashley Marshall.[8] My focus is, rather, the hostile emotions owned by Swift in his epitaph and plausibly mobilised in the readers of one poem which I treat as in some ways representative of his wider satirical work.[9] These emotions cannot easily be reconciled with the civility of the *Spectator*, as idealised by Habermas, but they nevertheless remain necessary and authentic parts of early eighteenth-century public discourse.

2 The Epitaph and the meaning of *saeva indignatio*

How does one find a reasonably direct path to the emotions of so constitutionally ironic a writer as Swift? In a perceptive overview of Swift's poetry, Pat Rogers has upbraided me thus:

> More remarkably still, Robert Phiddian has managed to write a searching book on Swift's parody without devoting anything beyond a few lines to the poems: this, despite the fact that parody is one of the staple elements in the verse, more pervasively so indeed than in the bulk of the prose works.[10]

The burden of the criticism is fair enough. The burden of my excuse depends on a distinction between public and private; more specifically, between personal and mimicked voices. *Swift's Parody* focused on the early prose, particularly *A Tale of a Tub*, and on the many possible personae implied, in the context of the pamphlet wars of the late Stuart era. Swift's prose parody overwhelmingly refunctions discourses that are the object of ironically complex but caustic ridicule, and the voices might be defined as 'anyone but Swift'. This is less obviously true of some of the Irish pamphlets – it is possible to draw a reasonably reliable line between M. B. Drapier (apparent author of the *Drapier's Letters*) and Swift. However, *Gulliver's Travels* and the *Modest Proposal* still vex any gentle reader who wants a narrator who keeps a steady relationship with authoritative meaning in the text. The poems were not the sort of parody I was interested in because they are much more clearly in Swift's voice; as Claude Rawson puts it, 'Swift's poems are his most personal works, if by "personal" you mean something like "confessional" or "autobiographical"'.[11] The voices of the poems are ironic but still personally characteristic, marked by both his reputation as the Dean and by a distinctive way with octosyllabic couplets which sound naïve until you read enough to recognise how perfectly they hit their mark. It is centred in tone and explicit satiric purpose compared to an extensively parodied voice like that of the *Tale of a Tub*'s Hack narrator or the haplessly conflicted arguer for the proposition that 'the Abolishing of

Christianity in *England*, May, as Things now Stand, be attended with some Inconveniencies, and perhaps, not produce those many good Effects proposed thereby'.[12]

A more objective way of arguing this difference is to focus on mode of publication. Just about all Swift's prose was written with print publication in mind, and was published anonymously or pseudonymously. It does not seek to trade on Swift's own authority as a polemicist, but creates authorial fictions that adept readers are supposed to learn to reject. The poems, by contrast, circulated initially and in some senses primarily as manuscripts, within networks of acquaintance and affection where Swift was known. Whatever their parodies and ironies, they were not functionally anonymous, but were known as Swift's, and entered print only belatedly, sometimes even by piracy.[13] Given Swift's temperamental inclination to dominate circles of acquaintance, especially once he became Dean of St Patrick's, poems that circulated in manuscript had a more explicit author-function than and different affective purpose from the formally anonymous prose pamphlets or even *Gulliver's Travels*. As manuscripts, they are markers of membership in a circle of friends defined by opposition to a corrupt world: corrupt in literary taste in *On Poetry: A Rapsody* (1733); corrupt in politics in 'The Legion Club' (1736); physically corrupt in 'The Lady's Dressing Room' (1732) and the other 'disgusting' poems;[14] and civically corrupt in 'A Description of a City Shower' (1710).[15] Arguably, they created and sustained an intimately Swiftian 'emotional community' different from the publics addressed in the formally anonymous printed prose writings.

Before turning to one of the poems, however, I want to look at Swift's most explicit public (if not exactly published) credo. Only two pieces appeared in print signed by Swift and with his acknowledged support in his lifetime – the very early and atypical 'Ode to the Athenian Society' (1692) and the studiously unironic *Proposal for Correcting, Improving and Ascertaining the English Tongue* (1712). But one more piece can be considered as published and openly authorised by Swift, the Latin epitaph that he included in his will of 1740. It has adorned the wall of St Patrick's Cathedral Dublin now for nearly three centuries:

> *Hic* depositum est Corpus
> IONATHAN SWIFT S.T.D.
> Hujus Ecclesiæ Cathedralis
> Decani,
> *Ubi* sæva Indignatio
> Ulterius

Cor lacerare nequit,
Abi Viator
Et imitare, si poteris,
Strenuum pro virili
Libertatis Vindicatorem.
Obiit 19° Die Mensis Octobris
A.D. 1745 Anno Ætatis 78°.[16]

To represent both precision and force in English, consider these translations, respectively literal, fluent, and poetic:

Here is laid the Body of JONATHAN SWIFT, S.T.D., Dean of this Cathedral, Where savage indignation can no longer lacerate his heart. Go, traveller, and imitate, if you can, this strong defender, to the utmost of his powers, of liberty. He died on the 19th day of October, A.D. 1745, at the age of 78.[17]

Here lies the body of Jonathan Swift, Doctor of Divinity and Dean of this Cathedral Church, where savage indignation can no more lacerate his heart. Go, traveller, and imitate if you can one who strove with all his might to champion liberty.[18]

Swift has sailed into his rest;
Savage indignation there
Cannot lacerate his breast.
Imitate him if you dare,
World-besotted traveller; he
Served human liberty.[19]

To understand Swift's purpose in the epitaph, much depends on precisely how one translates *saeva indignatio*, so I will focus on it, as historically as possible, to resist any anachronistic mapping of the term into modern English. Neuropsychological models have their uses (and I will outline some of these below), but they tend to universalise about human response and thus be deaf to cultural and historical difference. A history of emotions or (as it might be more properly named in eighteenth-century context) a history of the passions cannot permit that flattening out of human experience. Swift used a Latin phrase, as was common in epitaphs of the period, especially those of churchmen.[20] Moreover, it does not present immediate difficulties for translation into English. Contemporary dictionaries source indignation directly to the Latin word *indignatio*, while Samuel Johnson gets to savage through

French *sauvage* and Italian *selvaggio*.[21] It is hard to imagine any capable English speaker of the mid-eighteenth century making anything other than a close identification between the Latin words and the English 'savage indignation'.

There is more variety of opinion on the quality of Swift's epitaph. At one end of the range is Lord Orrery's 'An harsher epitaph has seldom been composed. It is scarce intelligible, and if intelligible is a proof how difficult a task it is, even for the greatest genius, to draw his own character, or to represent himself and his actions in a proper manner to posterity'.[22] At the other lies Yeats' enthusiastic evaluation: '...that is why he felt *saeva indignatio*, that is why he sleeps under the greatest epitaph in history. You remember how it goes? It is almost finer in English than in Latin: "He has gone to where fierce indignation can lacerate his heart no more" '.[23] Claude Rawson has recently shown how amenable Yeats was to (mis-)identifying with the energy of the epitaph: 'The grandiloquence of Swift's epitaph...belonged to a lofty style Yeats was readier to see in Swift than Swift was to display'.[24] He certainly was a reader inclined to project his opinions on others, and one can also be pretty confident that he found it 'almost finer in English' because that is how he understood it – he was remarkably bad at any language other than English.[25] Orrery, as a scion of the Boyles, one of the noblest families of the Irish ascendancy, and a good enough Latinist to publish translations of Pliny's *Letters* and two of Horace's *Odes*,[26] was less inclined to be generous, and has a point about the lines 'Strenuum pro virili/Libertatis Vindicatorem'. The Latin syntax of this is pretty tortured, and it seems to me probable that those of us with limited Latin can so easily forgive it because, like Yeats, we instantly grasp the English syntax behind it. For our purposes, the main point is that the phrase, '*saeva indignatio*' is unambiguous. It is clear in Latin, and its translation into current or eighteenth-century English as 'savage (or fierce) indignation' is unproblematic.

As for connotation, Swift's phrase clearly makes a claim based on precedents including Juvenal that he is motivated by emotions which bear comparison with modern psychology's anger, contempt, and disgust. Louis Bredvold links Swift's *indignatio* specifically to Juvenal's '*facit indignatio versum*' (Satire 1, 1.79), though the rest of his article pursues a rather universalised (and dehistoricised) sense of indignation. His purpose is to separate indignation from that lesser thing derision, much as one might seek to distinguish scepticism from cynicism and rank it higher.[27] Rawson follows a similar line when he avers that the addition of *saeva* is 'an incremental intensive, as though bidding to be more

Juvenalian than Juvenal',[28] but it appears that the Renaissance humanist Scaliger had at least got there first with *saeva* and may well be Swift's
more direct source.[29]

Maurice Johnson adds biblical resonances to the mix:

> Indignation in a Dean's epitaph could evoke not only disturbing
> echoes from Juvenal, but echoes from the Bible. The wrathful anger
> of God at Man's weaknesses is expressed in the Old Testament by a
> rhetorical question of 'Who can stand before his indignation? and
> who can abide in the fierceness of his anger?' (Nahum 1:6); or an
> incitement to 'Pour out thine indignation upon them' (Psalms 69:24);
> or a submissive 'I will bear the indignation of the Lord'.
>
> > (Micah 7:9)[30]

Johnson then demonstrates that ascribing indignation to a person on
a grave-epitaph was not normal or even precedented; his one example talks of an indignity done to the interred. It is clearly a remarkable
emotion for a clergyman to claim, especially on his memorial. Pope,
by contrast, emphasised filial piety and his place among the poets, and
Dustin Griffin has recently demonstrated the extent to which Swift and
Pope were in a prickly dialogue of self-definition at this stage of their
careers.[31] Swift's epitaph does not directly present him to posterity as a
writer and, while it presents his credentials as a dean in the Church of
Ireland, it expresses no explicit Christian hope for grace, charity, or an
afterlife. It is a negative peace he expects in the grave, the lack of lacera-
tion, and his take on the *abe viator* convention is a challenge to action,
not a request for sympathy.

All this is very characteristic of Swift's acerbic, restless, and competi-
tive mind. Consequently, I am not persuaded by Griffin's argument that
the effect of *cor lacerare* is to turn the indignation solely into a display of
Swift's pain. The epitaph is more challengingly double-edged than that,
because it activates emotions more militant than sympathy or pity in
readers. It is a final expression of withdrawal from a corrupt world that
cannot help but get up an honest person's (or parson's) nose. Moreover,
the epitaph is also an expression of prophetic anger at corruption and
a call to fight against the forces that constrain freedom. That is what
makes its central term so apt as a credo for Swift's satire. The ambivalence of *saeva indignatio* is the jagged and productive ambivalence of his
work more generally. If we lift a little out of the narrowly historical context, we can see in cognitive terms how it provides him and his readers
both catharsis and impetus, the consolations of disgust and contempt
with the motivating force of anger.

The most recent critic to dwell substantially on the term *saeva indignatio* offers a working definition that has limitations for my purposes:

> Let us begin with a working definition of indignation, ... and a distinction between the righteous and savage varieties. Indignation is qualified anger, born of frustration, rooted in resentment, sophisticated by contempt, seasoned with disgust. Indignation thrives in a place just short of the rage that vents itself in physical violence, but it infrequently crosses that threshold because disdain for the adversary prevents what is constructed as demeaning brutishness. Righteous, that is, virtuous and justified, indignation has the solace of company, the support and confirmation of the community, which can act in concert to redress grievances and eradicate the offensive ..... Wild, fierce, and untamed, savage indignation has no allies, no comfort found in communal norms, no recourse to common judgement or precedent. Frequently, savage indignation finds itself tormented by antithetical competing demands; as a result paralysis, the inability to take positive action, is often its symptom, and that is why it tears the heart.[32]

Maja-Lisa Von Sneidern's formulation includes the emotion terms central to this chapter (anger, contempt, and disgust), plus a few more. Her critique clearly serves a current political purpose in the context of post-September 11 global culture. However, a problem lies in the distinction made between righteous and savage indignation, for it depends on value judgements and runs the risk of valuing older ideological formations according to current standards. For example, to a modern liberal, John Milton's hostility to royal power may count as righteous, while his refusal of freedom of speech for Catholics looks like savage bigotry. At a personal level, I agree with the valuation, but it is hard to see how it can be made to say something useful about the history of emotions, because it depends on contemporary value judgement. Cognitive psychology offers the possibility of something more substantial when it argues that emotions are relatively independent of their particular cultural formulations. In pursuit of this, I will now attempt to map Swift's historical term *saeva indignatio* onto accounts of relevant emotions recognised by cognitive psychology. I do not present this as a scientific solution to Swift's satire, but I do think it can provide a valid interpretative window onto the emotional dynamics of his work. Though satirical works are notoriously bound to a context in time, place, and audience, it is nevertheless clear that satirical cultural work may be apprehended trans-culturally, and with at least some elements of family resemblance in form and purpose.

'Savage indignation' blurs a distinction that is often made these days in cognitive accounts of the emotions. As Von Sneidern's formulation suggests, it is not immediately obvious that indignation as an emotion belongs more to anger or disgust. Yet anger and disgust have very different aspects:

> Although anger may seem like a more natural response to norm violations than disgust, it is worth considering that anger is an approach-related, strongly activating emotion. Hence, it may represent a rather costly response to moral transgressions. By contrast, the withdrawal and avoidance motivation associated with disgust may offer a lower-cost strategy. Indeed, recent modeling work suggests that noncooperation is often a more efficient response to norm violation than is costly punishment.[33]

So, according to Hanah Chapman and Adam Anderson (and their sources), anger is activating while disgust generates avoidance and withdrawal. If we include contempt into the equation, we can arrive at a model of emotional reaction that has three dimensions. William Miller adds that the motion of withdrawal can be parsed between disgust and contempt:

> Both contempt and disgust are emotions that assert a superior ranking against their objects. But the experience of superiority based on the one is quite different from that based on the other. We can enjoy our feelings of contempt, mingled as they often are with pride and self-congratulation. Contrast disgust which makes us pay with unpleasant sensation for the superiority it asserts. Whereas disgust finds its object repulsive, contempt can find its object amusing. Contempt, moreover, often informs benevolent and polite treatment of the inferior. Disgust does not.[34]

Although, as Miller acknowledges, contempt is sometimes viewed as a sub-set of disgust rather than as a separate emotion, a model that has all three emotions in it has considerable explanatory power for the various functions both of Swiftian *saeva indignatio* and satire more generally. To put it schematically, the visceral emotions mobilised by satire are: anger, or aggressive motion towards the object of criticism; disgust, or shocked recoil from the object; and contempt, or cool rising above the object. Of these, disgust seems to me the central negative emotional element of satire; as Miller suggests, it 'is the moral sentiment that does the work of disapprobation for the vices of hypocrisy, cruelty, betrayal, unctuousness in all its forms: officiousness, fawning, and cringing servility'.[35] Neither pure thought nor mere feeling, these 'moral sentiments' engage both passions and reasoning. Thus to talk of satire as expressing disgust is at least a very strong metaphor, and it seems possible from the work in neuropsychology that moral and more strictly behavioural disgust (e.g. revulsion from the look and smell of rotting flesh) are essentially the same thing, using the same neural pathways.[36] All this allows interpretation to make distinctions between satire that generates anger in an audience that might or might not lead to active intervention by them, compared to contempt- and disgust-generating satire that leads to shocked or superior withdrawal. Certainly, satire often seems to operate on its audiences in a broadly cathartic way, as a substitute for action rather than as a trigger for it. This can be seen from Swift's *Modest Proposal* (1729), which deplored the state of Ireland to no effect, to modern stand-up comedians who let us imagine that everyone in public life is a conscious knave or a fool.[37] That satire might shame villains into acting better is a possibility and an enabling fiction, but the fiction disguises a wide range of emotional work, much of which functions more like consolation than incitement.

3 'A Beautiful Young Nymph' and the negative emotions

How does this account help us to understand the emotional economy of particular texts? If the theory boom of the late twentieth century established nothing else, it at least forced us to realise that interpretation has not reached its destination when it arrives at a plausible construction of authorial intention.[38] Can we say anything coherent about the emotions cued in readers of Swiftian satire? In what ways do they reflect the emotional ingredients of *saeva indignatio*, or permit some form of catharsis for the visceral emotions? Without a miraculous finding of a representative group of eighteenth-century readers to hook up to fMRI scanners, we cannot make scientifically certain observations, but literary interpretation can permit some informed opinions. If audiences can be shown to infer satirical purposes and reproduce the dark emotions of satire in experimental conditions today,[39] then we can work on the hunch that something similar occurred in the past, which can be tentatively reconstructed with due attention to historical difference. Swift and his contemporaries thought of passions rather than emotions, and they also valued anger, contempt, and disgust differently from how we value them today: probably, on balance, as more natural and socially valid responses than our sympathetic age prefers to think them.[40] However, the basic assumption that satirical texts are emotion-bearing objects holds, and with it the proposition that they provoke emotions in various but not entirely unpredictable ways in audiences.

One test for this is a reading of 'A Beautiful Young Nymph Going to Bed' (first published 1734, probably written and in manuscript cir-culation from 1731), one of Swift's notorious 'scatalogical poems'. The suite of poems has provoked readers in various ways, and to several acts of naming. Norman O. Brown's venerable Freudian interpretation gave them the name 'excremental poems' among critics for much of the late twentieth century, and Leo Damrosch has recently renamed them (to my mind more accurately, as only some of them address excrement) as 'disgusting poems'.[41] 'Nymph' deals with taboo matters both of the human (particularly the female) body and of social order in couplets that are often but not always ironically detached. There is no explicit narrator (such as Strephon in 'The Lady's Dressing Room'), so there is no formal filter between readers and the routine expectation that the poem's perspective is broadly if ironically the author's. Moreover, it is a witty poem, but not a funny one, which brackets out the comic 'noise' that often attends satirical texts and includes a range of more apparently benign emotional reactions. Among recent critics, 'Nymph' garners arguments about various strange sorts of sympathy with the woman so thoroughly anatomised. Brean Hammond has provided a materialist analysis of this line of argument,[42] but the larger body of work comes from feminists addressing the question of whether this poem can be acquitted of misogyny. After considering the poem in a tradition of definitively misogynist poetry, Felicity Nussbaum decides that 'Swift's point in writing the poems that nauseate their readers is to release men from passion and its attendant madness rather than to reform women's boudoir habits', and that his misogyny is subordinate to the more defensible satiric stance of misanthropy: 'Woman, like man, is not a rational animal, but only *rationis capax*'.[43] Laura Brown sees the account of Corinna as hunting a larger, broadly anti-colonial satirical purpose: 'It is only one quick step from the equation of women and commodities to an attack on the hypocritical female as the embodiment of cultural corruption, the visceral epitome of the alienating effects of commodification and the disorienting social consequences of capitalist accumulation'.[44] In the reading of the poem that follows, I do not seek to contradict these conclusions, but to provide a clear, perhaps even schematic, account of the emotional trajectory of readers' experience of repulsion and sympathy to which many critics of the poem attest. For my purposes, 'Nymph' performs an anatomy of anger, contempt, and disgust in the emotional reactions of readers, a mercurial questioning of the validity of readers' judgements and a paradoxical provocation of sympathy. While there is no single, inescapable, and programmed emotional trajectory through the poem, the full range of indignant response is very plausibly demonstrable.

The opening couplet cues a masculine contempt for a street prostitute: 'CORINNA, Pride of *Drury-Lane*,/For whom no Shepherd sighs in vain'.[45] The cultural superiority is as easy as the gendered contempt, with the mock-pastoral juxtaposition of Covent Garden, in the heart of the metropolis, against the poetic language of shepherds and dactylic maids. Any shepherd in town on a spree can have this Corinna, for money. Indeed, the first ten lines of the poem, that take Corinna from her workplace on the street to her sordid 'bower' in an attic room, can be entirely assimilated with the cruel laughter of ridicule and superiority that Simon Dickie has recently chronicled as persistent through the eighteenth century.[46] In line 11, however, something begins to change: 'Now, picking out a Crystal Eye,/She wipes it clean, and lays it by' (11–12). Putting the eye out breaches any residual pastoral decorum, and brings an actual, fragile body into play. Yet the remarkable thing after the initial shock is the precision with which the object of the opening lines' contempt operates in her nightly care of the self. As readers, we are drawn into a fascinated observation of a disgusting ritual that grotesquely reverses the 'toilet scene' of Pope's *Rape of the Lock*. Her eyebrows come from a flayed mouse. She 'Pulls [them] off with Care, and first displays 'em./Then in a Play-Book smoothly lays 'em' (15–16). She is a virtuoso whose care and skill are remarkable, in the face of physical dysfunction.

Swift's verse is nowhere more deceptively 'simple' than in the emotional range and trajectory of the next lines:

> Now dextrously her Plumpers draws,
> That serve to fill her hollow Jaws.
> Untwists a Wire; and from her Gums
> A Set of Teeth completely comes.
> Pulls out the Rags contriv'd to prop
> Her flabby Dugs and down they drop. (17–22)

He zooms in close, fascinated by the artifice in disguising the disgust-ingly limited and corrupt body, then races to a contemptuous distance of 'flabby dugs' which endure the bathetic rhyme of prop with drop. Such sneering at female sexuality is either an expression of misogyny or a trap for the misogynist reader; it depends on how close to Swift's you imagine the poem's voice to be. Either way, the fascination at 'the Oper-ator's Skill' (25) returns as 'off she slips/The Bolsters that supply her Hips' (27–8) which, if it is ridicule, is ridicule of a peculiarly intimate order. Satire is inevitably an 'othering' process, but 'Nymph' also flirts with sympathetic intimacy towards its object in its most challenging passage:

> With gentlest Touch, she next explores
> Her Shankers, Issues, running Sores;
> Effects of many a sad Disaster;
> And then to each applies a Plaister.
> But must, before she goes to Bed,
> Rub off the Dawbs of White and Red;
> And smooth the Furrows in her Front,
> With greasy Paper stuck upon't.
> She takes a Bolus e'er she sleeps;
> And then between two Blankets creeps. (29–38)

It is possible to hear sarcasm in 'with gentlest touch', and I suppose a misogynist reader will indeed hear that, but this intimate catalogue of wounds carefully tended seems more likely to evoke pity and the beginnings of chivalrous anger in a well-disposed (if still presumptively male) reader. The shankers are weeping scars associated with venereal disease, so there is certainly some patriarchal projection of Corinna's complicity in her fate, but the creature who takes her medicine and creeps between two blankets is as pitiable as she is contemptible. The terms of her existence are clearly an affront to polite and gentlemanly society, but the question of fault – hers or society's – lies ironically open. The 'Pains of Love' – venereal disease – that torment her in the next line are a euphemism that belongs more to the gallant man-about-town than to a woman, be she maid or prostitute. Corinna, an object here of disgust rather than contempt, seems more victim than criminal.

It is possible that, in the starkly moralistic world of the early eigh-teenth century, many readers would, nevertheless, have maintained a judgemental stance to this point. They could be disgusted at her for being the fallen and thus the appropriate recipient of these grotesque carnal punishments. Though I concede that it is well-nigh impossible to detach a determined moralist from judgemental views, such an unsympathetic reader (even from Swift's time) would be increasingly challenged by the note of vicarious anger that appears in the description of Corinna's dreams:

> Or if she chance to close her Eyes,
> Of Bridewell and the Compter dreams,
> And feels the Lash, and faintly screams.
> Or, by a faithless Bully drawn,
> At some Hedge-Tavern lies in pawn. (40–4)

Her dreams are invaded by fears of punishment and oppression – being held in pawn for a bully's debt at a tavern is very hard to distinguish from slavery. And it is now anger towards the bully and the taverner – the militant desire to do something about a bad situation – that is cued here, not the more distancing emotions of disgust and contempt, which encourage us to recoil from or rise above a situation. This militant anger at the hypocritical representatives of authority peaks in the last lines of the paragraph:

> Or, struck with Fear, her Fancy runs
> On Watchmen, Constables, and Duns,
> From whom she meets with frequent Rubs;
> But, never from Religious Clubs;
> Whose Favour she is sure to find,
> Because she pays 'em all in Kind. (51–6)

So the 'Watchmen, Constables, and Duns' either move her on roughly, or shake her down for money, but the religious fanatics are happy to be paid for their attentions 'in kind', which is presumably a combination of sex and disease for their hypocritical 'concern'. This is anger that ends with a snarl, and only the most studious hypocrite could miss the point that Corinna is a victim of men who claim to protect her and society. This is satire at least for a moment angrily telling truth to power.

But 'CORINNA wakes' (57) and the grim decorum of fascinated disgust returns to the poem, as various animals have fastened on her cosmetic shifts. A rat has taken her plaster and her false eye, a cat has pissed on the 'small balls or pads'[47] or cork discs[48] she uses to plump out her cheeks, and her dog has filled her wig with fleas. Most disgusting, perhaps, to the twenty-first century reader, is the 'issue peas'. These early-Modern items of medical apparatus were designed to keep wounds open so that the evil humours could continue to weep out, and Corinna's seem to have been dried peas that a pigeon has decided to eat.[49] As Hammond suggests 'many readers have testified' to sympathy in these lines – it is almost impossible to read competently and avoid pity, but now it is a disgusted rather than an angry pity.[50] We recoil from the scene and from the wreck that is Corinna. It is a pitiful heroism that the narrator describes in the final paragraph, when 'The Nymph, tho' in this mangled Plight,/Must ev'ry Morn her Limbs unite' (65–6). The poet's 'bashful Muse' refuses to give an explanation of how the miracle of reconstruction is achieved, and then leaves off all pity to attempt a stance of absolute contempt: '*Corinna* in the morning dizen'd,/Who sees, will spew, who smells, be poison'd (73–4). This is a profoundly harsh and pitiless note for the poem to end on. Perhaps for some readers it operates as a return to normal moralising conduct, and allows the challenging ambiguities of the rest of the poem to be ignored. Satires can often merely mobilise our negative emotions and, as in Juvenal's *Satires*, permit them to be vented on scapegoats like prostitutes, 'jumped-up slaves', 'inferior classes or races', and the like. However, it is more in tune with Swift's indignant purpose to hear in this couplet a challenge to recognise our part in the disgusting thing exposed and the violent passions with which it engages.

4 Conclusion

A programmatic understanding of anger, disgust, and contempt derived from modern psychology can help explain the emotional dynamics of a compelling, witty, but unfunny piece of satire like 'A Beautiful Young Nymph Going to Bed'. It tells us little directly about poetic form, but there is an elaborate existing scholarship on the forms of satire, and I have argued elsewhere that this focus has become a distraction in satire studies.[51] As this collection accepts the centrality of emotional response, to turn from formal to affective dimensions of the function of satire is not a problem. More pressing, however, is the risk that psychological models tend to universalise from experimental findings that have unrecognised cultural dimensions, and hence to dehistoricise. Satire is a historically and geographically widespread mode that has some basic cross-cultural continuities, but also many distinct cultural functions.

That is why it is important to finish by tracing back the threads of the anger, disgust, and contempt posited above as a response to 'Nymph' to Swift's conscious and historically marked project of *saeva indignatio*.

The emotional ingredients of *saeva indignatio* include 'passions' that map closely onto modern 'emotions' labelled anger, disgust, and contempt; indeed, all those words were current in Swift's time and had historically continuous (though not identical) meanings with their modern usages. Different readers will react to stimuli in the poem in a range of ways that are not 'merely' emotional, but that also involve constructions of meaning and changing climates of sentiment. Visceral and cerebral at once, Swiftian satire provides good Early Modern evidence for cognitive psychology's refusal to make a categorical distinction between reasoning and feeling. Perhaps more strongly than other modes, satire deconstructs the thought/feeling binary by bringing dark emotions to light and, among the Scriblerians, into print and public discourse. The indignation figured in 'Nymph', or in the King of Brobdingnag's condemnation of European humanity is an explosive combination of thought and feeling. It can generate anything from detached contempt to militant sympathy in different readers who put different emotional values on the meanings of the provoking words. It is important not to expect a Pavlovian consistency of response. There are emotionally and historically authentic reactions to satirical texts, but there is no one authentic reaction, because individuals resolve thought and feeling differently. An experience dominated by disgust is likely to be cathartic, one dominated by contempt will generate smug detachment, while one dominated by anger may well be more variable, sponsoring either catharsis or political action. Satirical indignation can contain all the disparate forces contained in what modern psychologists describe as the Contempt–Anger–Disgust triad of emotions.

The larger question for the developing print culture of the eighteenth century is whether and, if so, how the volatile emotions involved in satiric indignation could be contained within public discourse. While this chapter has focused on semi-public utterances by Swift, in his epitaph and a poem designed initially for manuscript circulation, his fully published writing and that of his Scriblerian colleagues have implications for the development of conventions of press freedom in Britain between the absolutist regimes of the seventeenth century and the revolutionary explosions of the late eighteenth century. In an ideal public sphere (such as posited by Habermas for the coffee houses of Queen Anne's and George I's England), rational civility is the universal desideratum of discussion in public and in print. In such a place, the exercise of these passions would obviously be bad. In actual polemical practice, however, a public space needs to exist for them: one of at least limited tolerance, where they are not immediately policed as sedition. If the argument holds that Swift's *saeva indignatio* can work for its author and its readers in something like the way this chapter outlines, then the next stage of investigation should explore whether similar emotional dynamics can be seen to function more widely in the body politic. The growth of modes of sympathy is a well-recognised element of the development of print culture and public opinion in the eighteenth century. Perhaps we need to know more about the necessary persistence of the harsher emotions expressed in satire to attain a fully rounded picture.

Notes

1. Joseph Carroll (2004) *Literary Darwinism: Evolution, Human Nature, and Literature* (New York: Routledge), p. 158.
2. For overviews, see Jonathan Haidt (2003) 'The Moral Emotions', in R. J. Davidson, K. R. Scherer, and H. H. Goldsmith (Eds.), *Handbook of Affective Sciences* (Oxford: Oxford University Press), pp. 852–70; Paul Rozin et al. (1999) 'The CAD Triad Hypothesis: A Mapping Between Three Moral Emotions (Contempt, Anger, Disgust) and Three Moral Codes (Community, Autonomy, Divinity)', *Journal of Personality and Social Psychology* 76: 574–86.
3. Alexander Pope (1963) *The Poems of Alexander Pope: A One-Volume Edition of the Twickenham Text with Selected Annotations* (London: Methuen), Dialogue II, ll. 205–11 (first published 1738).
4. Jonathan Swift (1959) *Gulliver's Travels, 1726* (Oxford: Blackwell), Book II, Chapter 6, p. 132.
5. Craig Calhoun (1992) 'Introduction', in Craig Calhoun (Ed.), *Habermas and the Public Sphere* (Cambridge, MA: MIT Press), p. 2.
6. Jürgen Habermas (1989) *The Structural Transformation of the Public Sphere: An Inquiry into a Category of Bourgeois Society* (Cambridge, MA: MIT Press); first published 1962.
7. Conal Condren (2009) 'Public, Private and the Idea of the "Public Sphere" in Early–modern England', *Intellectual History Review* 19: 15–28; Conal Condren (2011) *Hobbes, the Scriblerians and the History of Philosophy* (London: Pickering and Chatto). See also Nancy Fraser (1990) 'Rethinking the Public Sphere: A Contribution to the Critique of Actually Existing Democracy', *Social Text* 25/26: 56–80.
8. Ashley Marshall (2013) *The Practice of Satire in England, 1658–1770* (Baltimore, MD: Johns Hopkins University Press).
9. Two examples to illustrate the personal nature of the tolerance required: (1) The appearance of Walpole prominently applauding Gay's *Beggar's Opera* when it opened in 1728, perhaps legendary; see David Nokes (1995) *John Gay, a Profession of Friendship* (Oxford: Oxford University Press), p. 435.

(2) The well-attested instance of the Lord Lieutenant of Ireland, Carteret, offering a reward of £300 for discovery of the pseudonymous Drapier in October 1724, while knowing full well that the author of the pamphlets was Swift, a friend he regularly socialized with in Dublin Castle; see David Nokes (1985) *Jonathan Swift, a Hypocrite Reversed: A Critical Biography* (Oxford: Oxford University Press), pp. 288–9.

10. Pat Rogers (2003) 'Swift the Poet', in Christopher Fox (Ed.), *The Cambridge Companion to Jonathan Swift* (Cambridge: Cambridge University Press), p. 182. Rogers is referring to Robert Phiddian (1995) *Swift's Parody* (Cambridge: Cambridge University Press).

11. Claude Rawson (1985) *Order from Confusion Sprung: Studies in Eighteenth-Century Literature from Swift to Cowper* (London: Allen and Unwin), p. 148.

12. The pamphlet commonly known as *The Argument against Abolishing Christianity* (written 1708, published 1711).

13. See Stephen E. Karian (2010) *Jonathan Swift in Print and Manuscript* (Cambridge: Cambridge University Press) for a far more nuanced account than this.

14. See Leopold Damrosch (2013) *Jonathan Swift: His Life and His World* (New Haven, CT: Yale University Press), p. 443.

15. This is an illustrative rather than exhaustive list, and mentions only some of the best-known of Swift's large poetic output. All quotes and dating where not otherwise discussed from Jonathan Swift (1983) *The Complete Poems*, ed. Pat Rogers (Harmondsworth: Penguin).

16. From The Last Will and Testament of Jonathan Swift, D.D. (Dublin, 1746), available in Jonathan Swift (1959) *Directions to Servants and Miscellaneous Pieces, 1733–1742* (Oxford: Blackwell,) p. 149.

17. Claude Rawson (2010) 'Savage Indignation Revisited: Swift, Yeats, and the "Cry" of Liberty', in *Politics and Literature in the Age of Swift: English and Irish Perspectives* (Cambridge: Cambridge University Press), pp. 185–217.

18. Nokes, *Jonathan Swift*, p. 412.

19. Published as a poem in its own right by Yeats in *The Winding Stair and other Poems* (1933). For an account of Yeats' engagement with Swift, see James Lovic Allen (1981) ' "Imitate Him If You Dare": Relationships between the Epitaphs of Swift and Yeats', *Studies: An Irish Quarterly Review* 70: 177–86.

20. See Louis I. Bredvold (1940) 'A Note in Defence of Satire', *ELH* 7(4): 253–64; Maurice Johnson (1953) 'Swift and "The Greatest Epitaph in History" ', *PMLA* 68(4): 814–27; Dustin H. Griffin (2010) *Swift and Pope: Satirists in Dialogue* (New York: Cambridge University Press).

21. Thomas Blount (1656) *Glossographia: Or A Dictionary, Interpreting . . . Hard Words* (London: Tho. Newcomb), p. 336; Samuel Johnson (1756) *A Dictionary of the English Language*, 2nd ed. (London: Printed by W. Strahan).

22. Swift's friend, Lord Orrery writing in 1752, quoted by Griffin, *Swift and Pope: Satirists in Dialogue*, p. 236.

23. W. B. Yeats (1966) *The Variorum Edition of the Plays of W.B. Yeats* (London: Macmillan). The words come from John Corbet, a character in *The Words on the Window-pane* (1934).

24. Rawson, 'Savage Indignation Revisited', p. 189.

25. R. F. Foster (1997) *W.B. Yeats: A Life* (Oxford: Oxford University Press), p. 74.

26. Lawrence B. Smith, 'Boyle, John, Fifth Earl of Cork and Fifth Earl of Orrery (1707–1762)', *Oxford Dictionary of National Biography*, accessed 8 September 2012.
27. Bredvold, 'Note in Defence of Satire'.
28. Rawson, 'Savage Indignation Revisited', p. 211.
29. See William S. Anderson (1962) 'The Programs of Juvenal's Later Books', *Classical Philology* 57(3): 145–60; S. H. Braund and S. M. Braund (1988) *Beyond Anger: A Study of Juvenal's Third Book of Satires* (Cambridge: Cambridge University Press), p. 1; Juvenal (2004) *Juvenal and Persius* (Cambridge, MA: Harvard University Press), p. 20.
30. Johnson, 'Swift and "The Greatest Epitaph" ', 821.
31. Griffin, *Swift and Pope: Satirists in Dialogue*, pp. 232–5.
32. Maja-Lisa Von Sneidern (2005) *Savage Indignation: Colonial Discourse from Milton to Swift* (Newark, DE: University of Delaware Press), p. 14.
33. Hanah A. Chapman and Adam K. Anderson (2012) 'Understanding Disgust', *Annals of the New York Academy of Sciences* 1251: 64–5.
34. William Ian Miller (1997) *The Anatomy of Disgust* (Cambridge, MA: Harvard University Press), p. 32.
35. Miller, *The Anatomy of Disgust*, p. 197.
36. See Paul Rozin, Jonathan Haidt, and Clark R. McCauley (2008) 'Disgust', in Michael Lewis, Jeannette M Haviland-Jones, Lisa Feldman Barrett (Eds), *Handbook of the Emotions*, 3rd ed. (New York: Guildford Press), pp. 757–76; Daniel R. Kelly (2011) *Yuck!: The Nature and Moral Significance of Disgust* (Cambridge, MA: MIT Press); Carolyn Korsmeyer (2011) *Savoring Disgust: The Foul and the Fair in Aesthetics* (New York: Oxford University Press).
37. For a discussion of the silence that greeted the Modest Proposal, see Robert Phiddian (1996) 'Have You Eaten Yet? The Reader in A Modest Proposal', *Studies in English Literature, 1500–1900*, 36: 603–21.
38. See Seán Burke (2008) *The Death and Return of the Author: Criticism and Subjectivity in Barthes, Foucault and Derrida*, 3rd ed. (Edinburgh: Edinburgh University Press).
39. See Kerry L. Pfaff and Raymond W. Gibbs Jr (1997) 'Authorial Intentions in Understanding Satirical Texts', *Poetics* 25: 45–70; also see Paul Simpson (2003) *On the Discourse of Satire: Towards a Stylistic Model of Satirical Humour* (Amsterdam: John Benjamins), pp. 154–8.
40. For the background on this lack of sympathy, see Simon Dickie (2011) *Cruelty and Laughter: Forgotten Comic Literature and the Unsentimental Eighteenth Century* (Chicago: The University of Chicago Press,).
41. Norman O. Brown (1959), *Life against Death: The Psychoanalytical Meaning of History* (London: Routledge); Damrosch, *Jonathan Swift*, pp. 443–53.
42. Brean S. Hammond (1995) 'Corinna's Dream', *The Eighteenth Century* 36: 99–118.
43. Felicity Nussbaum (1984) *The Brink of All We Hate: English Satires on Women, 1660–1750* (Lexington, KY: University Press of Kentucky), pp. 112, 113.
44. Laura Brown (1990) 'Reading Race and Gender: Jonathan Swift', *Eighteenth-Century Studies* 23: 425–43, 430.
45. I have worked with the editorial apparatus, including line numbers, of Rogers' edition of *The Complete Poems*; see especially pp. 453–5 and 830–1. However, to retain original spelling and accidentals, I quote from Jonathan

Swift, *A Beautiful Young Nymph Going to Bed. Written for the Honour of the Fair Sex. Pars Minima Est Ipsa Puella Sui. Ovid Remed. Amoris. To Which Are Added, Strephon and Chloe. And Cassinus and Peter* (London, 1734).

46. Dickie, *Cruelty and Laughter*.
47. 'plumper, n.1' *OED Online* (Oxford: Oxford University Press), accessed 6 April 2014.
48. Hammond, 'Corinna's Dream', 106.
49. 'issue pea n. a pea or other small globular body placed in a surgical issue (4b) to keep up irritation'. 'Issue, N.', *OED Online* (Oxford University Press), accessed 25 July 2014.
50. Hammond, 'Corinna's Dream', 107.
51. Robert Phiddian (2013) 'Satire and the Limits of Literary Theories', *Critical Quarterly* 55(3): 44–58.

4

'Love, Marriages, Mistresses, and the Like': Daniel Defoe's Scandal Club and an Emotional Community in Print

Jean McBain

> we must ask leave of our Grave Querists, to descend to something
> of Mirth and Madness; for we shall always meet with both in the
> Articles of Love, Marriages, Mistresses, and the like.
>
> *Supplementary Journal*, to the Advice from the
> Scandal Club 3, *November 1704*[1]

1 Introduction

Through 1704 and 1705, Daniel Defoe maintained correspondence in print with readers via the Scandal Club: a sub-section of, and then supplement to, the famous *Review*.[2] This feature began as an appendix, the *Mercure Scandale: Or Advice from the Scandalous Club*, and in its first incarnation was a forum for Defoe to critique his peers in the periodical trade. In the course of 1704, a shift occurred, and the retitled *Advice from the Scandal Club* began to present letters and queries from readers on matters personal, political, and whimsical. These were supposedly answered by a learned society, although Defoe's singular responsibility for the answers was only thinly veiled. The influx of reader letters outgrew the *Review* in September of 1704, when the first of five monthly supplements was published as *A Supplementary Journal, to the Advice from the Scandal. Club*.[3] The next year, Defoe experimented with another standalone iteration of the Club with a bi-weekly *Little Review* printed from June to August 1705.

This Scandal Club corpus has enormous, untapped potential for the study of eighteenth-century English emotional preoccupations. In the letters and responses published in the *Review*, the *Supplementary Journal* and the *Little Review*, passions and related moral, social, and ethical issues are constantly discussed. From a debate between Defoe and a reader on the rationality of 'beasts' (referring to animals, and including debate over their capacity to feel and control passions), to discussion of abortion and debate on human nature, passions feature as a common matter of concern and curiosity.[4] Amongst these matters, the most ink is spent discussing love, both in the abstract, and in the context of courtship and choice of spouse. Defined broadly, this issue is discussed in 34 out of 90 letters answered in the *Supplementary Journal*, and 18 of 92 letters in the *Little Review* (37.7 per cent and 19.5 per cent, respectively).[5] In this extended conversation a tension emerged between the necessity of love for happiness in marriage, and the false paths down which love could lead; while the interplay between passion and rationality, in this case in choice of spouse, is a central concern for the community as a whole.

The term 'community' has a historiographical significance here. This follows the influential work of Barbara Rosenwein, who has proposed that the history of emotions should approach past 'systems of feeling' via the identification and analysis of 'emotional communities'.[6] For Rosenwein, 'emotional communities are, almost by definition (since emotions tend to have a social, communicative role), an aspect of every social group in which people have a stake and interest'.[7] This is because 'emotions are above all instruments of sociability' and 'expressions of emotions should thus be read as social interactions'.[8] In the wake of Rosenwein, this essay is focused on emotions in their social, interpersonal aspects. It uses the Scandal Club as a case study of the social role, and the social negotiation, of emotions in early eighteenth-century communities.

Using print materials in such a way raises distinct methodological questions that this essay seeks to uncover and address. The central issue surrounds emotional authenticity. The *Review* was typical of early eighteenth-century periodicals in that almost all of its content was printed pseudonymously. We must therefore consider the possibility of dissimulation in authorship – of correspondents presenting assumed identities and emotional states in writing to the Scandal Club. Further, amongst the submissions from genuine correspondents, it is likely that a number of letters printed in the *Review* were written by Defoe himself. Yet, I propose that these are problems of authorial authenticity, not necessarily of emotional authenticity. Rosenwein has suggested that historians of emotion 'should not worry about whether an emotion is authentic unless the particular emotional community that we are studying is itself concerned about authenticity'.[9] In the case of the *Review*, where pseudonymous and anonymous contributions were the norm, there have never been reference points outside the published form of letters against which to test the congruence of their reported emotions. This emotional community operated via authorial dissimulation, and such disguised authorship was central to its function. Thus, in exploring the idea of emotional authenticity in print culture, a distinction should be made between emotional authenticity and authorial authenticity. In the study of 'systems of feeling', I propose, scholars can seek the former, without requiring the latter.

The following analysis thus begins with an exploration of the origins of the Scandal Club community and of the question of emotional authenticity. It then deploys this analytical apparatus to consider discussions of love and courtship in the Club. These form a useful case study of emotional negotiation and authenticity because, as previously noted, love is a major preoccupation for the Scandal Club. Love and courtship are also significant here because, in the context of marriage and familial relations, love is a particularly social passion. The role of love in choice of spouse, the nature of betrothing love, and the solution for unrequited love all govern interpersonal relations, and are all the subject of complex social codes. Such emotions can be major constituents of the norms of emotional communities, and were of primary interest to that community who aired their issues in the pages of the Scandal Club.

2 An emotional community in print

Daniel Defoe's engagement with readers via the Scandal Club was quite typical for early eighteenth-century periodical editors. The vanguard of this participatory periodical type was John Dunton's *Athenian Mercury* (1691–7).[10] Each issue of the *Athenian* contained between 8 and 15 questions sent by readers.[11] These were answered by the semi-fictitious Athenian Society, who purported to be an association of learned gentlemen.[12] Dunton's periodical targeted a wide cross-section of the English social strata, but Helen Berry has shown that its core readership was almost certainly 'the middling sort'.[13] This readership posed questions on a range of topics, including conduct, courtship, marriage, occupation, medicine and health, religion, relationships, money, philosophy, law, and legend.[14] Thus, the *Athenian* represents a major moment at which a non-elite group could express an idea, opinion, or query in print regarding the issues that pressed upon them.

The *Athenian*'s lead was widely followed in the early decades of the eighteenth century, and Defoe's *Review* is amongst those seen to be inheritors of this question-and-answer tradition. Indeed the received interpretation of Defoe's printing letters from readers in the *Review* is that he sought to ape the *Athenian* in order to broaden his readership and improve the financial returns on his journalistic efforts. The first to make this claim was Dunton himself, who in his 1710 book *Athenianism* listed Tom Brown in his *Lacedemonian Mercury*, Defoe in his *Weekly Review*, Povey in his *General Remark on Trade*, and 'H—' in his *British Apollo* as all being 'Interlopers' in his 'Question-Project'.[15] Scholars from more recent decades, including John J. Richetti and Stephen Parks, have supported similar accounts of the Scandal Club as a popularising feature.[16] Evidence for this explanation has been found in Defoe's own experiences with the *Athenian*; he was informally associated with Dunton's project and contributed the occasional answer to a question. Defoe's family also belonged to the congregation of Dr Samuel Annesley, Dunton's father-in-law.[17] Further, Defoe himself suggests at a number of points that 'the first Design [was] making the Diverting Part, an Inducement, an *Innocent Bait*, to bring some People in love with the more substantial Part'.[18]

I would like to disrupt this narrative of design, however, and consider the extent to which the Scandal Club became a participatory space through the impetus of readers rather than the discretion of Defoe. If we consider the actual content of the Scandal Club from the first issue of the *Review* through the remainder of 1704, a clear distinction emerges between the original nature of Defoe's 'Diverting Part' and the question-and-answer format that came to dominate, and which eventually spilled over into the supplements and the *Little Review*.[19] This distinction is very clear in Defoe's introduction to the first *Supplementary Journal*:

> This Society, having been design'd for examining and censuring Things Scandalous, and openly deserving Reproof; has insensibly been drawn into the difficult, nice, and unsatisfying Work of resolving Doubts, answering Questions, and deciding Controversies, Things absolutely remote and foreign to their first Design.[20]

He goes on to claim that this intention was as remote, 'as making a Map of the World in the Moon'.[21] This same argument is made in the introduction to the first issue of the *Little Review*, and in the preface to the first collected volume of the *Reviews*.[22]

Thus, for Defoe there was a clear shift in the nature of the Scandal Club. Indeed, at the start of the *Review*, Defoe primarily used the *Mercure Scandale: Or Advice from the Scandalous Club* to mount covert attacks on other periodical writers. In the first issue of the *Review*, he gave warning to news-writers to 'be careful, not to Impose Absurdities and Contradictions in their Weekly Papers' to ensure that they 'meet with no Ill Treatment from this Paper'. He continued: 'Our Scandalous Club is a New Corporation Erected on purpose to make Inquisition of such Matters, and will treat them but scurvily as they deserve.'[23] Early examples can be found in the third issue of the *Review*, from 4 March, in which Defoe lampooned the writer of the *Gazette* for being unintelligible in reporting on a battle. He asks: 'If the whole Sentence were put into Latin, Which would be the principle Verb?'[24] He moves on to charge the authors of the *English Post* with being tedious, as well as confused in their geography in reporting on European military engagements. In this case the Society concluded:

> That they were a Triumvirate of Blook-selling [sic], Nonsense-Writing, Ignorant, News-Merchants, and were Entred in the Books upon Record, never to be cross'd out till some Coxcombs are brought before the Society for giving any heed to what they Write.[25]

This attitude towards his peers in the periodical trade left Defoe exposed to all the barbs and complaints other writers could muster, and it is in the midst of a clash with the author of the *Daily Courant* that the first letter is printed in the *Review*.

The *Daily Courant* (1702–35), edited by Samuel Buckley, was London's first daily newspaper. By the end of April 1704, Defoe had so irritated Buckley with his constant nit-picking that Buckley dedicated a full issue of the *Daily Courant* to answering the *Review*.[26] The argument between Defoe and Buckley centred upon debate over whose linguistic skills were the worst, with Buckley striking a stinging blow when he suggested that *Mercure Scandale* will not 'pass either for French or any other Language'.[27] This precipitates a very self-conscious change in the *Review* in the issue of 6 May, as Defoe drops *Mercure Scandale* and leaves the title of the addenda as *Advice from the Scandalous Club*. He attributes this to the criticism from the *Daily Courant*, but also because he was 'wanting Room in this Paper', before going on to defend his use of *Mercure Scandale* in any case.[28]

In this same issue, the first letter is published in the *Review*. The Club's attention is drawn to errors in a recent issue of the *London Gazette* in exactly the kind of sarcastic tone that Defoe had used just a few months earlier. The issues of 13 and 16 May publish letters along a similar vein.[29] The convenience of these letters aroused suspicion among those targeted for rebuke, so that by early June Defoe took to assuring readers that the originals of published letters had been 'left at the Printers, for the Satisfaction of the Curious'.[30] By issue 28, from 10 June, the heat of Defoe's rhetoric was turned up even further. In that issue Defoe addresses the author of a letter printed the week before, who is

> humbly desired to do the Society Justice, in a charge of Forgery, Printed upon them by the said Author [of the London Post]; and to let us know where he may be found, since in Case of an Indictment, his evidence may be needful, with Relation to the P[illo]ry or worse Punishment.[31]

Defoe then claims he is unable to print a letter from a 'J. J.', who has complaints to make about the *London Post*, because of these threats. Whether or not these letters were forgeries or authentic submissions from readers, it is clear that Defoe was employing letters in an attempt to attack his peers from a disguised position. Rather than harking back to the *Athenian* and printing letters from readers as a popularising feature then, Defoe's initial use of letters is a rhetorical strategy. While his targets at the *Daily Courant* and other papers were quick to question the authenticity of the printed letters, Defoe maintained emphatically, and almost certainly falsely, that he was simply printing material sent by readers.

What happened next is the crucial development for this study of an emotional community, for a portion of the *Review's* readership appears to have taken Defoe's assurances at face value, and set to sending letters to the editor with their own concerns. The post-*Athenian* context is significant here – for nearly two decades the middling sorts of London had been able to submit queries to periodical editors with the reasonable expectation that they might appear in print. The letter device Defoe utilised in his spats with other writers thus became a double-edged weapon, as he 'insensibly' gave the impression that the *Review* was open for submissions. By issue 50, from August 1704, this transformation is complete, as the Scandal Club reports that they 'have had so much Business upon their hands this Week, that they are forc'd to intrude upon the more Serious part of the Work' in order to answer all of the letters received.[32] Thus the whole of the paper is taken up with answering questions from readers on topics including astronomy, virtue, love. and religion. There is a letter that notes a conflict between reports in the *London Post* and the *Post Boy*, although the tone is nothing like the condescending letters from May and June. In issue 58, from 23 September, Defoe advertises the forthcoming publication of the first *Supplementary Journal, to the Advice from the Scandal Club*, and puts out the first explicit call for contributions: 'all Gentlemen, who have any thing they think worth Publication, are Desir'd to send it'.[33]

The community that emerged from these rather murky origins appears to have had a similar makeup to that of the *Athenian*. Subscriptions to letters include representatives from both genders, and from a large range of the socio-economic strata. Discussing the readership of the *Review* as a whole, Richetti argues that it was 'aimed at the political nation', and most particularly at 'freeholders and electors, those males who possess the franchise'.[34] He recognises, though, that the Scandal Club courted a broader readership. Many male contributors identified themselves with reference to profession or industry. These range from young gentleman and sons of gentry, to tradesmen, bakers, servants, and apprentices.[35] Females identified themselves in a range of ways, including as 'Lady', 'young Gentlewoman', and 'young Woman', often with some indication of their age.[36] Most letters appear to have sprung from urban sources, but there are missives from the country.[37] Similarly, the nature of questions highlights wide variety in the circumstances of correspondents: from those whose troubles stemmed from poverty,[38] to those who were comfortably off and so could make decisions about marriage without reference to financial means.[39] Almost all letters were signed off with only the initials of the sender, although a few used pseudonyms. These range from one woman's use of 'Urania' in subscription to two letters,[40] to the patently satirical pseudonyms used by a supposed group of pastry cooks and confectioners. The group, including 'George Applepie' and 'William Custard', wrote to thank Defoe for furnishing them with so many unread copies of the *Review* with which to line their pies and wrap their goods.[41]

3   Emotional and authorial authenticities

The pastry cooks, and indeed the more widespread use of pseudonyms and assumed identities amongst the contributors to the Scandal Club, bring the question of authenticity into focus. If we are to use the Scandal

Club corpus as material for the history of emotions, a question must be resolved: How can we hope to approach emotional authenticity, using sources of unknown, or even forged, authorship? The first aspect of this to consider is how sceptical we should generally be about the authorship of the letters. While there has been no specific study of letters printed in the *Review*, scholarship on the *Athenian* and even the *Spectator* provides guidance towards assuming that most printed letters were genuine reader submissions. In her analysis of letters printed in the *Athenian* and other papers of the 1690s, Helen Berry has put forward a convincing argument that 'detailed textual references, to handwriting, and to problems with non-payment of postage, suggest either authenticity [of submissions], or an extraordinarily elaborate fiction, in which the authors of several different periodicals colluded'.[42] Similarly, regarding the *Spectator*, Greg Polly has summarised the current position as follows: 'critics generally agree – with some hesitation – that the larger part of the letters are genuine'.[43] Thus, by issue 50 of the *Review*, and certainly by the time the first *Supplementary Journal* was published, it is likely that the printed letters were genuine reader contributions rather than forgeries by Defoe.

Yet, even if the letters were not written by Defoe, their authorial authenticity is not necessarily certain. There remains a likelihood that some submissions came from readers who assumed an alternate persona and related fictionalised events in their letters. Indeed, it transpires that the Scandal Club is an ideal case study through which to explore this question precisely because the issue of authorial authenticity was toyed with throughout the business of the Club. For a start, the identity of the Society itself was the subject of ongoing discussion and dissimulation in the paper. Defoe maintained an ongoing vacillation about the nature of the Society, and in the introduction to the first *Supplementary Journal* he stated matters quite bluntly:

> And as, perhaps, the Hand that operates in this Work, being allegorically rather than significantly call'd a Society, may be for sundry Reasons uncapable of Performance in so vast a Variety as is like to come before him: So he thinks no Injury to the Undertaking, to let the World know they must be content to be answered in the best manner he can.[44]

He went on to discuss 'the Author' in the singular. But this was not the end of the matter. In both the fourth supplement and in the *Little Review*, letters were printed in which the existence of the Society was questioned. In the latter, the correspondent was particularly concerned with how to address letters to the Society correctly. Defoe answered:

> We are one Person, sometimes Mr. Review, sometimes the Scan-dal Club, sometimes one single Body, sometimes a Body Corporate; So that, Sir, if you Write or Address your self to Us, I shall receive your Letter; or if you send to Me, We shall give you all the Satisfaction I can, for We are your Friend and Servants, Nos Ego.[45]

Defoe clearly found entertainment in such play, and he did not con-fine himself to casting aspersions on the veracity of his own materials. In prefaces to a number of letters, Defoe expressed doubts about the authorship of the contribution. This includes a letter from 'Astrea', which 'seems to be Written rather by the Lady's Lover than by the Lady herself'.[46] At other points, the scepticism is less overt, expressed in variations of the formula: 'The following Story, if matter of Fact'.[47]

Yet, while authorial authenticity in the *Review* is both impossible to gauge and the subject of overt dissimulation and play, this does not necessarily preclude the use of this periodical as a source for emotions history. This comes back to the social dimension of emotions, and the role of the Scandal Club in a system of emotional negotiation and norms. We need to look at the uses to which reader letters were put in the Scandal Club, which were at least in part didactic. In the intro-duction to the first *Little Review* Defoe expounded his aim to attack vice and improve morality: 'the design of this Paper being to make due Inquisition after the Improvement the Devil makes in the Manufacture of Vice, and to discover him as far as possible, in all his Agents, and their Meanders, Windings and Turnings in the Propagation of Crime'.[48] He went on to assure readers that he intended to target vice in the abstract, rather than attacking named individuals: 'In the Purformance [sic] of this Paper, he professes to avoid all pointing at Persons, and hopes no Gentleman will make this Paper be the Handle of Private Resentments'.[49]

In this effort to reform the manners and morals of readers, lack of external referents was part of their use. The pseudonymity of letters uni-versalised the stories told, and made them all the more improving. They become allegories or parables, from which the reader could draw infer-ences about their own life. As a result, even in cases where the Society cast doubt on the authorial authenticity of a submission, this did not prevent them from answering the details of the query. The philosophy behind this is set out in the preface to a letter in the *Little Review*:

Whether the following Case be Real or Allegorick, the Society are not concern'd; but as it includes the Substance of sundry other Letters, and the Reply to it may serve for an Answer to the Gentlemen concern'd in those other Enquiries, the Society resolv'd to bring it in here.[50]

Such parable-type cases were deeply useful to Defoe, who suggested 'The Custom of the Antients in writing Fables, is my very Laudable Pattern for this'.[51] So while Defoe repeatedly drew attention to the issue of authenticity, he had more use for disembodied parables than for cases with little or no allegorical or universal relevance. Thus the letters and responses printed in the Scandal Club can be read as traces of the emotional preoccupations of its community. Those matters discussed in the Club were cases of emotional difficulty and negotiation for individuals within a broader system of feeling. The responses of Defoe, and the opinions provided by other readers, show efforts by members of this community to moderate the behaviour of others. The Scandal Club can thus provide a map of the emotional concerns of the London middling classes in the early eighteenth century: the typical issues individuals faced, and the modes of action the group approved. So while the authenticity of specific cases can never be addressed, the didactic purpose of the Scandal Club made authorial authenticity irrelevant, and the result is a corpus with particular power to speak to the emotional cares of a wider community.

4   Emotional preoccupations of the Scandal Club: Love and courtship

What can the Society say to such a Gentleman as this, but that he [being] a Slave to that he calls Love, stands in direct opposition to his happiness.[52]

Thus, the Society exhorted poor young 'X.X.' who wrote to complain of his broken heart in a letter printed in the fourth *Supplementary Journal*. This young man was suffering from unrequited love in double form. He was both the unhappy lover of an uninterested young woman, and the object of the love of a paragon in female form, whose attentions were tedious to him. This second woman appeared to the Society to be 'sent from Above, to Cure his Moon Blind Passion', but they despaired of his coming to his senses to appreciate this gift.[53] This young man presented precisely the kind of personal case that Defoe found useful in expounding a broader philosophy around the role of love in courtship. Indeed the didactic purpose of the Scandal Club is particularly evident in answers to confused or conflicted lovers. In the remainder of this essay, I turn to such matters of the heart to consider the evidence of middling English attitudes towards love and courtship preserved in the Scandal Club corpus.

These traces of a system of feeling have a particular significance, as they are situated in an historical moment that has become the focus of intense scrutiny over the last 40 years. This followed the discovery of substantial demographic shifts over the eighteenth century in England. In 1983, E. A. Wrigley and R. S. Schofield reported the findings of the Social Science Research Council Cambridge Group for the History of Population and Social Structure. They found that age at first marriage was higher at the start of the eighteenth century than the end for both men and women;[54] the percentage of the population who never married dropped from around 22.9 per cent in 1650–99 down to around 9 per cent in 1750–99;[55] and rates of pregnancy outside, or at the time of marriage rose over the eighteenth century. As Tim Hitchcock summarised it in 1997, the eighteenth century in England began 'with a demographic regime in which many people remained celibate throughout their lives, perhaps only 80 per cent ever marrying, while only a tiny proportion were having penetrative sex outside the confines of courtship or marriage'.[56] These findings inspired a wealth of research on the economic, social, and cultural mores of sex and marriage across the eighteenth century, as scholars worked towards an explanatory framework to describe these changes.[57] Any summary of this historiography is outside the scope of this essay,[58] but it is useful to address one influential thesis that has been proposed: Lawrence Stone's argument that the eighteenth century saw the rise of a companionate model of marriage.[59] In the companionate regime, according to Catherine Crawford, 'marriage organized around emotional attachment and sexual desire came to dominate'.[60] While this argument has been challenged on fronts such as chronology, geography, and class, the core concept of the rise of companionate marriage remains current.[61]

As Katie Barclay has recently highlighted, however, the companionate marriage thesis does not adequately address the role of romantic love in courtship and in choice of spouse, as distinct from love within marriage itself. Barclay's book, examining Scottish elite marriages from 1650 to 1850, reveals some of the broad implications of courtship mores in a social system. As she argues: 'The importance placed upon love in courtship and its role in courtship rituals provides important insights into the relationship between love and power throughout the period.'[62]

Thus, the requisite demonstrations of love for men and women were profoundly gendered and were both influenced, and in turn constitutive of, the power structures of spousal relationships and the broader Scottish patriarchal system.[63] Such an examination of love and courtship in relation to the early modern English middling classes is still wanting, but the Scandal Club corpus would provide significant material for such a programme of research.

In the course of the Scandal Club a multi-faceted philosophy of love and its role in courtship and marriage is developed: from love in allegorical abstraction, to love as a factor in the choice of husband or wife. In this philosophy, love is portrayed as the highest consideration in marriage, but also as a potentially destructive, or at the very least distracting, force. In this way, the *Review*'s emotional community reflects mixed ideas about love, in a manner that Susan James has argued was typical of seventeenth- to early eighteenth-century accounts of the passions. James suggests that the passions were 'conceived as simultaneously functional and dysfunctional'.[64] When the former, 'our emotions incline us to seek out states of affairs that we think conductive to our well-being, and to avoid circumstances that we think detrimental to it'.[65] But passions are simultaneously 'treacherous and wayward, and lead us to misery, frustration, and despair. These dangers stem from the fact that, although not blind, the passions are acutely myopic.... They are consequently described as arbitrary, unpredictable, enslaving, uncontrollable and even pathological'.[66] Discussions of love in the *Review* are often associated with its opposition or interaction with rationality. Again, this is typical of the period. As Stephen Gaukroger has suggested 'it is in terms of the contrast between reason and the passions that fundamental philosophical questions – the nature of wisdom, goodness and beauty – were explored in the seventeenth and eighteenth centuries'.[67]

Thus, in the exposition of the Scandal Club, love can hinder long-term happiness, through influencing impractical courtship decisions, or preventing suitable matches. This dysfunctional aspect of love is discussed in allegorical form in the first *Supplementary Journal*. In response to a letter from 'Astrea' asking which of two suitors she should choose, the Society suggest that she should first look to her affections: 'there is a certain Trifle not much thought of in Modern Marriages, call'd *LOVE*; and they can by no means dispense with it'. Whilst love is placed as the highest consideration, the Society goes on to bemoan the often irrational way in which love is given:

'Tis true, Affection is not always Grounded upon Merit; but still they reckon Love so Essential to the Happiness of a Conjugal State, that however absurdly that Unaccountable Passion may be Grounded, they think a Woman ought to choose a Man She Loves best; let the Qualifications of the other Pretender be what they will.

...And this they take to be what was meant by the Ancients, when they represented Love Hoodwink'd and Blind.[68]

This theme is expanded upon in the next letter, which the 'Author of this *Supplement*, could not but think it very agreeable to place...immediately after this Story', and which the author claims to have had on hand quite some time. This letter describes the correspondent's attempt to trace the history of love's blindness, including a voyage to the temple of Venus in Cyprus, and travails through many archives and countries. Almost at the point of despair, the gentleman 'luckily touch'd at France in my Return, where meeting with the Ingenious De la Fontaine, he gave me the best Hint I met withal'. There follows a translation of Jean de la Fontaine's fable *Love and Folly* (originally *L'Amour & la Folie*, published 1694) here entitled *'The History of LOVE's Blindness'*. In this fable, we learn that Love was one day at play with Folly, when they fell to disagreement, causing Folly to seek revenge:

> Therefore with Fury on his Foe,
> He did discharge a deadly blow;
> Which made his Cyprian Excellence,
> As Poets sing, wink ever since.

Petitioned by Venus to spare her son, the Gods considered the case and:

> Resolv'd, That to atone the blow,
> Which Folly did on Love bestow;
> He should henceforth for ever prove,
> A Guide to the blind God of Love.[69]

With this final couplet, the poem and submission conclude. Paired as it is with the petition of Astrea, this letter argues for the dysfunctional workings of love, and the unfortunate actions it can inspire.

Nevertheless, the Society consistently supports the importance of love in choosing a spouse and they ridicule the idea that courtship can be a matter of rational matching of fortunes alone. For example, in response to a young man, 'B.T.', whose love for a woman of equal fortune and circumstances to himself is unrequited, the Society retort:

Here's a Gentleman tells us his Mistress and He are upon equal Terms, and yet she wont have him! – A strange thing truly, and very unkind! – But then, Sir, must it needs be, that because your Mistresses Age, Fortune and other Circumstances are pretty much alike, that therefore she must have you, and can have no Reasons against it? – Perhaps she don't like you, or perhaps she likes some body else, whose Age, Fortunes and Circumstances agree as well as yours; and if she is not at liberty to choose, then, Sir, she is no more your Mistress, but you are her Master: Therefore, Sir, all your Arguments of that sort, are very odd ones.[70]

Indeed, in a number of cases the Society positively champion the pre-eminence of love in courtship considerations. In one such iteration, the Society rejects a young man's scruples in marrying a woman whose fortune is much less than his. The letter, prefaced with the exclamation 'O How many are the Plagues of Love!', suggests that this man is foolish, for 'Here is *Mutual Love*; the Essence of Matrimony, and makes it a Heavenly Life'.[71]

The question of how to recover from a broken heart is also considered by the Society. Again, this is a topic in which the interplay between passion and reason is a central consideration. In the case of B. T. from *Little Review* 12, the Society turn from their initially mocking tone to far more sympathetic advice: 'There are, Sir, abundance of Remedies for Love; and among the rest, Reason, Patience, Absence, Time, change of Objects, are some of the best'.[72] The proposed cure required concerted effort on behalf of the young man 'Let your Reason dictate that, since she won't have you, you can't have her; and so turn round two or three times and ask your self *what's next* . . . divert your self with learning to despise what you cannot obtain'.[73] Similarly, in response to X. X. from the fourth supplement, the Society advises that he 'Labour to forget, what he cannot obtain'. They complain, though, that 'Talking Reason to a Man in Love, seems to be *Talking Gospel to a Kettle Drum*' and so doubt that their exhortation will have much effect.[74]

5 Conclusion

The Scandal Club corpus provides a rich source for the study of emotional negotiations, particularly with regards to love and courtship, in an early eighteenth-century emotional community. Mining the corpus in such a way requires an approach to emotional authenticity, and in particular an appreciation that authorial inauthenticity can in fact be constitutive of an emotionally authentic set of sources. Such an approach allows us to consider print sources as evidence of the emotional preoccupations of a group. For the Scandal Club itself, the tension between passion and reason in choice of spouse emerges as the major concern. For while love can be wilful, destructive, and misleading, the Society nevertheless finds it essential in making a wholesome marriage. Reason itself is represented as a necessary category of consideration, but not one that can dominate in this matter. As B.T.'s case of unrequited love shows, matching fortunes and circumstances cannot rule the heart.

In developing research on eighteenth-century marriage mores, this material has particular significance. If the thesis that the eighteenth century saw the rise of a companionate model of marriage is to be tested anew, the Scandal Club shows that at the turn of the eighteenth century both passions and reason were seen to be essential in making a good match. There is a hierarchy however, and while love appears to be able to rule reason, the inverse cannot occur. Such a prioritisation foreshadows philosophical developments of the mid-century, particularly Hume's famous invocation that 'reason is, and ought only to be the slave of the passions'.[75] Indeed, the use of pseudonymous, parable-type cases and the didactic purpose of the Scandal Club make this material something of a Grub Street philosophy.

Most significantly, this is a philosophy that develops out of multiple voices and lived experiences. The printed form of the Scandal Club emerges out of a participatory discourse: one where a central editor holds a position of particular power, but where the emotional preoccupations of the group set the agenda. For the middling men and women of London, the culture of readerly participation in periodicals provided an opportunity to make their mark on print culture. Bringing the Scandal Club and similar periodicals into the historiography of emotions provides a unique possibility of accessing the ideas of these middling sorts. We will never know whether young X. X. saw sense and married his paragon, or which match Astrea eventually made, and of course we have no proof that these individuals in fact existed. Yet, their cases were evocative enough to be printed by Defoe, and they are compelling still.

Notes

1. In all quotations from periodicals the 'long s' has been silently transcribed as roman 's'. All other spellings and punctuations are original. Periodical issues are referenced by title, volume (where relevant), issue number and date. Dates are in old style, although the year is taken to have begun on 1 January rather than 25 March.

2. Initially, the *Weekly Review of the Affairs of France* was an eight-page pamphlet. The format changed with the fifth issue to a four-page dual-column layout, using a smaller typeface to fit the same material into a smaller, and therefore cheaper, publication. The frequency of publication was the next change, with a Tuesday issue appearing in addition to the Saturday paper with the seventh issue (at this point 'Weekly' was also axed from the title). A third issue was added to the weekly schedule in March 1705, and in January 1706 the title changed to the *Review of the State of the English Nation*. Following the Act of Union with Scotland in 1707, that was changed to *Review of the State of the British Nation*. Finally in 1712, the title was changed to simply the *Review*. A. W. Secord (1938) 'Introduction' in *Defoe's Review*, D. Defoe and A. W. Secord (Ed.), 22 vols. (New York: Colombia University Press), Vol. 1, pp. xvii–xviii.

3. See M. Nicholson (1970) 'Introduction', in W. Payne (Ed.), *The Best of Defoe's Review* (Freeport, NY: Books for Libraries Press), p. xv.

4. *Supplementary Journal* 5, January 1705, letter 9; *Supplementary Journal* 5, January 1705, letter 8.

5. This count includes any discussion of love, courtship, marriage, or sex.

6. B. Rosenwein (2010) 'Problems and Methods in the History of Emotions', *Passions in Context: Journal of the History and Philosophy of the Emotions* 1: 11.

7. Rosenwein, 'Problems and Methods', 11–12.

8. Rosenwein, 'Problems and Methods', 19–20.

9. Rosenwein, 'Problems and Methods', 21.

10. The first issue was titled the *Athenian Gazette*, but this was changed with the second issue to the *Athenian Mercury*. The collected volumes were titled the *Athenian Gazette; or Casuistical Mercury*.

11. H. M. Berry (2003) *Gender, Society and Print Culture in Late-Stuart England: The Cultural World of the Athenian Mercury* (Burlington, VT: Ashgate), p. 18.

12. The editorial team in fact comprised Dunton, Richard Sault (a mathematician), and Samuel Wesley (Dunton's brother-in-law, a preacher, and father of John and Charles Wesley, founders of the Methodist Church). Dr John Norris, a Cambridge philosopher, also advised the editors on occasion, but 'was unwilling to become a permanent member of Dunton's board of editors'. S. Parks (1976) *John Dunton and the English Book Trade* (New York: Garland), p. 80.

13. Berry, *Gender, Society and Print Culture*, p. 63.

14. Berry, *Gender, Society and Print Culture*, p. 245.

15. J. Dunton (1710) *Athenianism* (London: printed by Tho. Darrack . . .), p. 113.

16. See, for instance, J. J. Richetti (2005) *The Life of Daniel Defoe* (Oxford: Blackwell), pp. 87, 89; Secord, 'Introduction', xviii; Parks, *John Dunton and the English Book Trade*, p. 84.

17. Parks, *John Dunton and the English Book Trade*, p. 83.

18. *Supplementary Journal* 2, October 1704. See also the introduction to the very first serial issue of the *Review*: 'After our Serious Matters are over, we shall at the end of every Paper, Present you with a little Diversion, as any thing occurs to make the World Merry; and whether Friend or Foe, one Party or another, if any thing happens so scandalous, as to require an open Reproof, the World may meet with it there' (*Review* 1.1, 19 February 1704). Also discussed in the introduction to the first *Supplementary Journal* (1 September 1704).

19. Maximillian E. Novak is one of very few analysts to have noted that letter answering was not a feature of the *Review* as initially incarnated. M. E. Novak (2001) *Daniel Defoe: Master of Fictions* (Oxford: Oxford University Press), p. 214.
20. *Supplementary Journal* 1, September 1704.
21. *Supplementary Journal* 1, September 1704.
22. *Little Review* 1, 6 June 1705. First collected volume published 1704.
23. *Review* 1.1, 19 February 1704.
24. *Review* 1.3, 4 March 1704.
25. *Review* 1.3, 4 March 1704.
26. *Daily Courant* 635, 28 April 1704.
27. *Daily Courant* 635, 28 April 1704.
28. *Review* 1.18, 6 May 1704.
29. *Review* 1.20, 13 May 1704; 1.21, 16 May 1704.
30. *Review* 1.26, 3 June 1704.
31. *Review* 1.28, 10 June 1704.
32. *Review* 1.50, 26 August 1704.
33. *Review*, 1.58, 23 September 1704.
34. Richetti, *Life of Daniel Defoe*, pp. 87–8.
35. Baker (*Supplementary Journal* 1, September 1704, letters 2 and 3); Young men of means, often self-identified as Young Gentleman (*Supplementary Journal* 2, October 1704, letter 9; *Supplementary Journal* 4, December 1704, letter 2); Apprentice (*Supplementary Journal* 2, October 1704, letter 11); Sons of gentry (*Supplementary Journal* 2, October 1704, letter 17); Tradesman (*Supplementary Journal* 4, December 1704, letter12); servant (*Little Review* 10, 6 July 1705, letter 5).
36. Lady (*Supplementary Journal* 4, December 1704, letters 19 and 21); young Gentlewoman (*Supplementary Journal* 5, January 1705, letter 5; *Little Review* 9, 4 July 1705, letter 1); 'young Woman, about Eighteen Years of Age' (*Supplementary Journal* 5, January 1705, letter 7).
37. Contributions from the country (*Supplementary Journal* 5, January 1705, letter 10; *Little Review* 2, 8 June 1705, letter 4).
38. See, for example, *Supplementary Journal* 5, January 1705, letter 8; *Little Review* 3, 13 June 1705, letter 3; *Little Review* 12, 13 July 1705, letter 3.
39. See, for example, *Little Review* 9, 4 July 1705, letter 1; and many of the stories discussed above, in which love is a primary criteria in choice of spouse.
40. Urania writes to the Scandal Club with reference to her courtship in *Supplementary Journal* 5, January 1705, and with regards to her subsequent marriage in *Little Review* 4, 15 June 1705.
41. *Little Review* 16, 27 July 1705, letter 3.
42. Berry, *Gender, Society and Print Culture*, pp. 35–8.
43. G. Polly (2005) 'A Leviathan of Letters', in D. J. Newman (Ed.), *The Spectator: Emerging Discourses* (Newark, DE: University of Delaware Press), p. 127.
44. *Supplementary Journal* 1, September 1704.
45. *Little Review* 21, 15 August 1705.
46. *Supplementary Journal* 1, September 1704.
47. *Supplementary Journal* 2, October 1704.
48. *Little Review* 1, 16 June 1705.
49. *Little Review* 1, 16 June 1705.

50. *Little Review* 3, 13 June 1705.
51. *Review* 1, preface, 1704.
52. *Supplementary Journal* 4, December 1704.
53. *Supplementary Journal* 4, December 1704.
54. E. A. Wrigley and R. S. Schofield (1983) 'English Population History from Family Reconstitution: Summary Results 1600–1799', *Population Studies* 37(2): 162.
55. Wrigley and Schofield, 'English Population', 176; Note, the figure of 9 per cent for the end of the century is a revised figure, for which see Schofield cited in A. Macfarlane (1986) *Marriage and Love in England: Modes of Reproduction, 1300–1840* (Oxford and New York: Blackwell), p. 25 (note 17).
56. T. Hitchcock (1997) *English Sexualities, 1700–1800*, (New York and Houndmills: St Martin's Press and Macmillan), p. 26.
57. For discussion of the impact of these findings, see for example Hitchcock, *English Sexualities*, pp. 3–4, 25–7; Macfarlane, *Marriage and Love in England*, pp. 25–8.
58. A useful summary of the historiography on eighteenth-century love, sex and marriage is provided in Hitchcock, *English Sexualities*.
59. L. Stone (1977) *The Family, Sex and Marriage in England 1500–1800* (London: Weidenfeld & Nicolson). See also L. Stone (1992) *Uncertain Unions: Marriage in England, 1660–1753* (Oxford and New York: Oxford University Press).
60. K. Crawford (2007) *European Sexualities, 1400–1800* (Cambridge: Cambridge University Press), p. 19.
61. Hitchcock, *English Sexualities*, p. 27; Crawford, *European Sexualities*, p. 47; K. Barclay (2011) *Love, Intimacy and Power: Marriage and Patriarchy in Scotland, 1650–1850* (Manchester and New York: Manchester University Press), p. 94; Macfarlane, *Marriage and Love in England*, p. 175. Each of these writers suggests that Stone's account must be complicated, but that the basic features are convincing.
62. Barclay, *Love, Intimacy and Power*, p. 87.
63. Barclay, *Love, Intimacy and Power*, p. 119.
64. S. James (1998) 'Explaining the Passions: Passions, Desires, and the Explanation of Action', in S. Gaukroger (Ed.), *The Soft Underbelly of Reason: The Passions in the Seventeenth Century* (London and New York: Routledge), p. 21.
65. James, 'Explaining the Passions', p. 21.
66. James, 'Explaining the Passions', p. 21.
67. S. Gaukroger (1998) 'Introduction', in S. Gaukroger (Ed.), *The Soft Underbelly of Reason: The Passions in the Seventeenth Century* (London and New York: Routledge), p. 2.
68. *Supplementary Journal* 1, September 1704.
69. *Supplementary Journal* 1, September 1704.
70. *Little Review* 12, 13 July 1705.
71. *Supplementary Journal* 2, October 1704.
72. *Little Review* 12, 13 July 1705.
73. *Little Review* 12, 13 July 1705.
74. *Supplementary Journal* 4, December 1704.
75. D. Hume (2007 [1738]) *A Treatise of Human Nature*, eds. D. F. Norton and M. J. Norton (Oxford: Clarendon Press), p. 266.

5
Eliza Haywood's Progress through the Passions

Aleksondra Hultquist

1 Introduction

Eliza Haywood (1693?–1756) was a popular and prolific author of early eighteenth-century Britain. Noted by one of her earliest critics as 'the Great Arbitress of Passion'[1] and some of her most recent as the 'Fair Philosopher',[2] she successfully synthesises both of these authorial personas throughout her oeuvre.[3] This chapter argues that Haywood's sustained and specific discussion of feeling in her fiction theorises emotions in narrative form; her novels effectively demonstrate how the intersection of philosophy and narrative provide authentic representations of private emotion in a public format. As a significant place to explore, plan, and test emotional theories of sentiment, sensibility, and sociability, the emergent novel may be one of the most dynamic modes of eighteenth-century print culture. Fiction can explore emotions from first-person accounts and comment on characters through third-person omniscience, so it is one of the few genres in which philosophy, personal experience, and critical analysis can occur simultaneously. By examining two of her texts, *Reflections on the Various Effects of Love* (1726) and *Life's Progress through the Passions; or the Adventures of Natura* (1748), I show that, over this 22-year span, she explores a discourse for the passions – what I call an ethics of emotion – in a fictional narrative form.

The word 'emotion' is contested and, in discussions about feeling, a relatively new term.[4] Earlier definitions of the word dealt with movement, especially relating to migration and political unrest, and while the term's early connotations also referred to emotions as 'an agitation of mind; an excited mental state', an aspect of movement has always been an intrinsic part of the word's meaning.[5] For Haywood too, passions give movement to feelings. Haywood uses the words 'emotion', 'passions', and 'feeling', but not interchangeably. In *Life's Progress*, she argues that

86

'all the various emotions which agitate the breast...which, tho' they bear the name in common with those other more natural dispositions of the mind, I look upon rather as consequential of the passions, and arising from them, than properly passions themselves'.[6] Emotions are the 'movements' that passions give rise to – sometimes, they are the physical evidence of feeling: blushes, palpitations, tears, and bloody noses. At other times, they refer to feelings raised by the passions: fury, wrath, joy, or grief. The 'passions', in contrast, are inborn character traits, more in line with humoral understandings of emotion. Examples of 'the Passions' include sorrow, anger, and spleen, but also include avarice and pride (concepts that modern thinkers do not refer to as emotions). She does not provide an inclusive list of emotions or passions, and there is slippage between her terms from time to time.[7] Despite this uncertainty in diction, there are clear rules for passionate living in Haywood's texts, and the passions provide structure for an eighteenth-century notion of individuality.

Passionate motifs pervade Eliza Haywood's early novellas – usually the passion of love and the dangerous consequences of hyper-emotionality – and dictate critical interpretation of her corpus. This repetition of emotionality, and the sustained analytical voice which comments on the episodes of her fictional stories, create a code of passionate living. Whereas 'ethics' often refers to a code of principles that govern a person's behaviour, what is *morally* good or bad, right or wrong, Haywood creates a structure of passionate ethics, a scheme based on the principles of what is *emotionally* good or bad, right or wrong, which eventually leads to a sense of individualism for her characters. Rather than a systematic code of examples of the passions or a precise working theory of the passions, Haywood explains how to live authentically and passionately through a fictional paradigm. This ethics of emotions contains specific truths of emotional life, as outlined by Haywood throughout her fiction, which become increasingly specific and encompassing as her work matures. Haywood's novels, then, create a community of feeling that draws upon the public philosophical discussions of emotions, but develops that discussion because her fiction is most interested in private understanding of how to negotiate passions and how those negotiations lead to individual identity.

2 Haywood and the passion conversation

The conversation about the passions was centuries old by the time it reached the eighteenth century, spanning the work of the ancients, such as Aristotle and Plato, through the Medieval period, especially in Augustine and Aquinas.[8] But it had reached a kind of fevered pitch in the eighteenth century, the supposed Age of Reason. Dixon has gone so far as to argue that 'The debate about the proper relationship of reason with the passions, sentiments and affections was one of the characteristics concerns of eighteenth-century thought'.[9] Perhaps more than any other era, the eighteenth century was embroiled in trying to best understand how the passions created public systems, such as governmental structures, and how controlling those passions would lead to a harmonised society. Much work has already been done on what the passions meant to eighteenth-century philosophers such as Francis Hutcheson, John Locke, Adam Smith, and David Hume, especially in an eighteenth-century literary context, and while I will not repeat those arguments here, I will outline a general understanding of the passions by the eighteenth century.[10] Primarily, the passions were thought to be public, rather than private; they were a social phenomenon which was anchored by a shared morality. Emotions were not settled to one particular person, but seemed to wander from individual to individual, belonging to no one. Because of this almost physical movement, they were remarkably hard to pin down, and caused a great deal of anxiety, as inner feeling and outward demonstration of feeling could be at odds with one another. Most importantly, passionate experience should cultivate judgement and moderation; the expression and understanding of the passions should be controlled and used for the public good. By the early eighteenth century, philosophers such as John Locke had transformed the seat of the passions from the body to the mind, a distinction that supposedly provided greater control over the passions.[11] Haywood's explorations of the passions incorporate many of these ideas, but her conclusions are not the same. She mixes humoral and cognisant understanding, but gives precedence to feeling and the body rather than the mind. Her characters learn much about themselves, but rarely put their gained knowledge to social action. Haywood's prescriptions for the passions are not treatises or essays, but rather folded into her specific brand of literary form, amatory fiction.[12] Haywood's work develops an ethics of passionate experience: her prose effectively forms a vocabulary for the passions, demonstrates their significance in the experience of the fictional characters, and analyses the outcomes through authorial commentary. Thus, Haywood's community of feeling differs from those of philosophical treatises by its interest in the private understanding of feeling in the eighteenth century, rather than the more public conversation about harnessing passions for the greater public good.

Haywood's fiction is a space for the detailed expression, exploration, and philosophical engagement of passionate experience for the characters in her novels. The authenticity of feeling in Haywood's fiction comes from its paradoxical ability to involve its readership in the personal vocabulary of shared passions in a public forum of print. The emergent novel allowed the public ideas that circulated about the passions to be accessible to a broad private readership, and represented authentic personal emotional experiences. Because the prose of the novel is multi-layered, it contains several aspects of emotional exploration not available to other forms, thus creating a specific space for a community of feeling. In the first layer, Haywood uses third-person narrative to describe plots of feeling, wherein a character must contend with an overwhelming passion (often that of love). In the second layer, she articulates the personal experiences of her protagonists in the first person, often in the form of letters or monologues that allow for readers to understand the personal experience of the protagonist. In the third layer, she again uses a third-person narrative voice to comment on the story's emotions and outcomes, a voice that clarifies the meaning (and sometime corrects the protagonists' mistaken impressions) of emotional experiences and analyses the situation in terms of her emotional ethical schema. The acts of interpretation are thus guided by Haywood's narrative voice. In this way, Haywood becomes a participant in the public debate about passions in the eighteenth century.

Recent work in literature and the history of emotion notes that literature is particularly able to represent aspects of emotions that are concerned with movement, change, ambiguity, multiplicity, process, complexity, instability, and creativity. Jon Elster has argued, 'we can read plays and novels as the closest thing to a controlled experiment involving high-stakes human emotions'.[13] According to scholars, depictions of emotion in the literature of the eighteenth century provided not only a laboratory of feeling and a platform for social change, but also a way to articulate and understand the early modern individual.[14] The work of Eliza Haywood is a particularly fertile place to examine the passions' place in individual development. Much of her early fiction takes emotion as its starting point, where she defines the major and minor meanings of the passions, creates characters dominated by their emotional life, and then places them in dynamic plots, as if to see how their passions will determine their character and the course their lives will take. The genre has a special capability to represent authentic emotion in the guise of a fictional world, a concept that Haywood always seems to grapple with. The very structure of *Reflections*, which according to Patrick Spedding is a *roman-à-clef*, demonstrates this scuffle between the tensions of fact and fiction.[15] The text fictionally represents real people and events, and the commentary on those events and people would therefore represent a truth of experience. Without the key, we cannot necessarily understand the larger political or public context of these tales, but we can read and understand the 'real' passionate experience of the individuals. The importance of the passion of love is further verified in the frame that Haywood provides: a long discourse of what the passion of love is, how it affects individuals, and how the public understanding of that passion is often misconstrued. *Life's Progress* too tussles with the divide between fact and fiction. Haywood makes it very clear in the first pages that she is 'an enemy to all *romances, novels,* and whatever carries the air of them ... and it is a real, not fictitious character I am about to present'.[16] It is curious that Haywood argues that Natura is 'real' not 'fictitious', partially because she rather too obviously states a falsehood. As a writer of romances and novels, Haywood was someone heavily invested in fictional representations (especially by 1748), so this statement smacks a bit of the lady protesting too much. What the line points out, though, is how 'truthfully' she wishes to represent her protagonist. If his name is too obvious a falsehood, if the plots are heavily contrived, she argues that his nuances of character ring true, she is 'obliged ... to draw him such as he was' (3). Natura is passionate, flawed, and, importantly, he represents authentic emotional experience. Such contexts demonstrate that even if the people or events of the novels are not 'real' *per se*, there is a verisimilitude of feeling in each of the texts, an authenticity of the passions within the fictional setting.

Haywood often pointed out that her earlier works were written not just to raise the passions, but to demonstrate that passions cannot be subdued or cured as effectively as their indulgence and acceptance can teach a person about the self. In Haywood's work, moralistic interludes between semi-erotic stories are in fact philosophic commentaries that explicate a complicated understanding of an eighteenth-century emotional system. The fictional descriptions raise the passions, but the authorial interludes demonstrate the intense relationship between feeling, thinking, and existing in Haywood's prose.[17] Both *Reflections* and *Life's Progress* take emotional experience as their subject matter. These two texts reveal Haywood's ethics of emotion and her specificity, refinement, and expansion of this ethics over a 22-year period. Each text offers examples of how the passions drive learning and ultimately provide self-knowledge through authentic emotional experience. She creates a system of emotions in which passions are not 'good' or 'bad' in and of themselves, in which reason is not 'better' or 'worse' than feeling; rather, what is important is how they create balance in an individual. The earlier of the two texts, *Reflections*, examines the specific passion of love, and how nature, gender, and experience combine to create knowledge of self through the experience of that particular passion. *Life's Progress* offers a sustained philosophic treatise on the passions one encounters through one's life and defines Haywood's sophisticated understanding of the relationship between reason and emotion. The latter text offers a broader range of the passions, a more complex and nuanced understanding of how the passions function, but the basic emotional ethical framework is visible in both texts.

In broad terms, Haywood's ethics of the emotions is structured around specific 'truths' of passionate experience. First, reason and passion are not oppositional forces battling for control over an individual, but stages on a singular continuum. Second, passions are so ingrained into one's nature that they are present from birth onward, growing more defined and powerful with age. Third, experiencing and processing the passions is heavily dependent on gender. She provides an extensive reading of how the passions affect women, one that is in contrast to many of the accepted norms of expected female behaviour in eighteenth-century culture. Fourth, reason does not control the passions, other passions do. Fifth, experience is absolutely necessary to understanding and regulating the passions. As reason increases, so do the passions, and as experience increases, so does the individual's understanding of the passions and the self. And finally, the passions are necessary for mental capability. The absence of passion denotes absence of reason and these two correspond, and will increase and decrease together. This emotional philosophy is defined and put into the laboratory of feeling of fictional episodes, and is bookended by the narrator's analysis. Haywood's earlier text is particularly interested in how the specific passion of love can be defined, experienced, and understood; she outlines what is emotionally good and bad, right and wrong, about love.

3   An ethics of love: *Reflections on the Various Effects of Love*

In *Reflections on the Various Effects of Love* (1726), Haywood offers a distinct philosophy of passionate love, and the text can be read productively as a treatise on the effects that passionate love causes. Her first and most important claim about love is that this passion can reveal the exact core of belief that exists within an individual's nature. Love gets blamed for many of the world's wrongs; people fall in love and perform uncharacteristic deeds that lead to disaster: the love of Paris for Helen and the fall of Troy, the love between Antony and Cleopatra and the fall of Egypt. Haywood argues, however, that this passion amplifies personalities rather than altering them:

> Love, like the Grape's potent Juice, but heightens Nature, and makes the conceal'd Sparks of Good, or Ill, blaze out, and show themselves to the wond'ring World! It gives Energy to our Wishes, a Vigour to our Understanding, and adds to the Violence of our Desires, but alters not the Bent of them.[18]

According to Haywood, love essentialises one's nature, increases the desires that are already present, but it cannot change a person's inclinations. Love sharpens desires and puts into relief what the person always wanted to begin with. In this configuration, love can add to self-knowledge by making it very clear to individuals what or who is at stake, because it adds 'vigour' to 'understanding'. Thus, 'Love itself cannot be considr'd either as a Virtue, or a Vice; it often, indeed excites to both, but never changes the one to the other; there must be some secret Propensity on the Soul, tho' perhaps long (by the Prejudice of Education or some other Motive) conceal'd, on which this Passion must work, and create Consequences, which without that Aid, it would be impossible to bring to pass' (11). If love moves a person to virtues or vices, it is not a virtue or a vice on its own, and cannot change a vice to a virtue or vice versa. Instead, love works on the core desires or personality traits already present, even if those traits are concealed by education or social restraint. For Haywood, those desires that are suppressed by social motivations can be unearthed by the passion of love, but love cannot alter or create desires, instead it makes conscious desires previously unknown to the individual. This idea is the first step in what will become a full vocabulary of the passions and how and why individuals respond to them. By heightening one's nature, love presents authentic self-knowledge to an individual. Once this truth is acknowledged, Haywood moves on to the specific effects of love in relation to gender.

Haywood argues that love is especially destructive to women. For Haywood, men and women are fundamentally different beings, and thus their very constitution affects how love plays out for each:

To prove the Truth of this assertion, one need, methinks, only consider with how much greater Force that Passion influences the Minds of Women, than it can boast on those of a contrary Sex, whose Natures, being more obdurate, are not capable of receiving those deep Impressions which for the most Part are so destructive to those softer Species. (11)

In this passage, Haywood remarks on the ways in which love more easily penetrates women, who are capable of receiving 'deep impressions'. Females were considered more pliable in terms of their emotions and desires, and the experience of love would influence their minds in unexpected ways (a truth universally acknowledged in amatory fiction and in fiction by eighteenth-century women writers more generally). Because of this caveat, women need more than usual judgement when they first fall in love because

> there is something so very pleasant in the first approaches of that Passion, when new Desires play round the Heart ... that there had need be a great Strength of Judgment than is usually found in a female Mind, to defend it from giving Way to the ruinous Delight, which when once enter'd, I need not say how difficult to be repelled. (19)

The very pleasure-ability of love, its all-encompassing effects, make it impossible to resist once begun – therefore, a good wit, a kind of emotional intelligence, must be activated before a woman enters into love. Firm judgement is necessary in love, especially for women. Unfortunately, this also makes love more painful to intelligent women. The more wit she has, the more painful the effects of love, because she has the reason to see all the hazards, but not the ability to stop the emotion:

> A Woman of Wit when thus ensnar'd, is infinitely more unhappy than one of a less distinguishing Capacity, because she sees and knows the Dangers into which she is about to plunge herself, yet withal finds them unavoidable, with open Eyes she gazes on the vast Abyss where her dear Peace of Mind is already lost, and which also threatens the Destruction of her Fame, her Honour, and all that is valuable, yet still blind to every Path that might guide her from the impending Mischiefs. (19)

With her new-found knowledge of self through the experience of love, and the intelligence to understand how love will threaten, 'all that is valuable', the intelligent woman cannot use reason to guide her away from such destruction of her reputation. Rather her reason only makes manifest the dangers and troubles associated with (it seems mostly illicit) passion, and does not show her a path away from the 'mischiefs' associated with love.

This early construction of the passions, love, and gender is restricted to women; she waxes eloquent when exploring how women experience love and can be dismissive of men's experiences.[19] The constancy of passion is a given for women and she philosophises that

So difficult it is to vanquish a real Tenderness! Or chase from the Mind Ideas which have once afforded us so much Delight! Hence it is that Women, when they love with that kind of Passion of which I am speaking, generally love for ever: They have not Strength of Mind to repel the sweet Remora's [remorse-?] which past Pleasures yield, – they re-enjoy them in Imagination. (55)

Not only is gender a crucial factor in women's inability to throw off love, but in this passage, the very strength of intellectual ability makes it more difficult as well. By re-enjoying past pleasures in imagination, the intelligent, reasonable, witty woman will feed passion rather than extinguish it. Though they have not strength of mind to repel such pleasures, they have intelligence enough to relive them, recreate them, re-imagine them and thus create a memory and experience of love that is impossible to shed. In addition to the very constitution of the female mind to re-play love, the social ideologies and practices are against them: 'they have more Leisure, as well as more Desire to indulge their thoughts, and soothe deluded Fancy' (55). Haywood's ethics of love underscores the impossibility of reason to overcome passion in such situations. Social habits, as it were, are against women, their natures are softer, and their wit cannot help, only push them deeper into love. Haywood argues, 'Love is therefore, for many Reasons, dangerous to the softer Sex; they cannot arm themselves too much against it, and for whatever Delights it affords to the Successful few, it pays a double Portion of Wretchedness to the numerous Unfortunate' (56). Because women are so impressionable to the destructive results of love, the only way to avoid mishaps in love is to guard against it; wit and reason can only help so much. Haywood carefully outlines the dangers of love to women, but she believes that a lack of experience in love is also a factor in its damaging effects as well as in its ability to teach the lover about herself.

The necessity of experience in love to the creation of character is made manifest when Haywood begins to put her ethics into the practicum of fiction. When she turns to the explanatory fictional tales of those who have found love destructive, she is, in effect, putting her ethics to the test, explaining their veracity through exempla. To support her ethics, she frames the story of Sophiana in third-person narrative detail, as an example that 'till Experience has made us wise, we know as little of ourselves as of the World' (30). For Haywood, maturity and experience are necessary to true reason *and* true passion, and Sophiana's wavering feelings from one lover, Aranthus, to another, Martinus, demonstrate her lack of experience in understanding her passions and thus herself. Additionally, Sophiana's determined personality and her 'Birth and Quality', which accustoms her 'to receive only Admiration' (41), are significant factors in her difficulties with love, as these traits are heightened by her experience of love. Her first affair with Aranthus goes horribly wrong; infatuated with him, she 'at last grew guilty of such Irregularities, and indeed, indecent Fondness, even in Publick, that she fell into the utmost Contempt' (31). The difficulty of love is further heightened by her gender and her intelligence: she has 'an infinite deal of Wit and Penetration' and 'these Faculties render'd her all the more wretched, by an immediate and poynant Intelligence of the Misfortune her Inadvertency had brought upon her' (32). As Haywood has pointed out above, the intelligent woman cannot protect herself against love, and is made more miserable by her understanding of the situation. Haywood shows Sophiana's emotional despair by quoting her impassioned letters of accusation where she speaks of her wretchedness and misery in the loss of Aranthus's love, with Sophiana eventually claiming that 'I own I cannot, will not live without you' (36).

Haywood continues to outline her emotional philosophy in the narrative vein. Sophiana's guardian tries to impress upon her that 'Time...wears every Thing away; in a few Years the Memory of the whole Affair will be lost, Absence will also contribute to the Cure of your unhappy Passion, and we may have you again, both with more Ease to your self, and less Disadvantage to [your] Reputation' (50). According to her guardian, the pain of unhappy love will lessen with time, thus allowing Sophiana to gain her understanding of herself. Loss of memory coincides with the gain of self-knowledge, and a return to a self that was lost while in the throes of passion. But her youth prevents her from gaining knowledge from the experience, and she quickly 'a second Time [became] the slave of Love, and no less devoted to this, than to her former Passion' (51). Her second intimate affair with Martius (in which she ends up disgraced as his paid mistress) is evidence 'sufficient to convince any one of the Instability of a very young Person's Affection' (54), because she cannot make use of the information that the first disastrous love affair has given her. Haywood pulls out of the narrative voice to a didactic voice in which she reviews the story and explicates on the information to be learned from the affair. In youth, or 'the Dawn of Inclination', Haywood argues that 'there is always a kind of wandering and uncertain Fire which plays about the Heart' (54); people are more likely to be consistent in feeling and mind as they age. 'The Mind', Haywood philosophises, 'must therefore first be settled before the Passion can be so' (54). Because Sophiana is too young to understand her mind, she cannot understand her passions and cannot control them; thus Haywood argues that reason and emotion are linked and abetted through personality, gender, age, and maturity. Sophiana's gender and youth, in addition to the ways in which her extreme passions waver and stick, highlight the need for knowledge and understanding of self that one is supposed to gain when experiencing passions.

In the next 20 years of Haywood's career, she clarified her ethics and narrative strategies. She returns time and again to the specific plot of Sophiana and Arathus (in which the female lover is seduced, abandoned, writes embittered letters, and attempts suicide) in order to demonstrate how the passion of love simultaneously destroys young women and makes them more self-actualised; it recurs in *The City Jilt* (1726), and *The British Recluse* (1722) among other texts. The later heroines fare better than Sophiana, who cannot make use of her passionate experience; for Glicera (*The City Jilt*) and Belinda (*The British Recluse*), the experience of love gone wrong matures them and brings them to an understanding of self within the larger public world. They regain reputations and gain self-knowledge through their experiences. As Haywood's narrative techniques developed, a maturity of her ethics also advanced. In *Life's Progress*, Haywood departs from the singular passion of love, to all of the passions by following the life story of Natura. Haywood's ethics of love matures into an ethics of the passions, and she creates a character that lives and dies by her understanding of emotion.

4   An ethics of the passions: *Life's Progress through the Passions*

In *Life's Progress through the Passions* (1748), Haywood continues her discourse on the passions and reason through the tale of Natura, a young gentleman, who grows and experiences life through his emotionally authentic experiences of love, anger, grief, and more.[20] Haywood explains his growth by documenting his progression from a young, feeling, thoughtless man, to a mature married man whose feelings and reason decline in proportion. She bookends each fictional episode with an analytical reading of the text, connecting the tale to her explanations of how to read the passions in each incident, thus creating an emotional ethical code playing out in a fictional laboratory of feeling. In this text, Haywood solidifies her main concepts of the passions, and she argues for certain truths of experiencing the passions. In some ways, her philosophies are established enough for her to expound upon them; she no longer needs to convince her readership that the passions are natural, for instance; she simply creates the name Natura, a charactonym that reiterates how passions are 'natural' character traits, the deep sense of self that Natura must come to know and understand throughout his life. Secondly, she develops her argument that the passions are meant to be experienced; they cannot be suppressed through engagement with reason, and – though they might be tempered by maturity, experience, and self-knowledge – they bring a person to maturity, experience, and self-knowledge. In this later work, Haywood offers that reason, knowledge, experience, and emotion are interrelated; each depends on the intensity of the other; and all can 'enflame' the passions, even reason. She articulates that passion and reason are intertwined, not oppositional, as a way in which to balance and contain each other.

Haywood develops the discussion of 'nature' and the passions, by explaining how the passions are in fact deeply rooted personality traits in addition to states of emotional movement. By beginning with Natura as a child, she establishes his core characteristics, especially his tendencies to 'amorous inclination' which 'begin to peep out long before the difference of sex is thought on; as *Natura* proved by the preference he gave the girls over the boys who came to play with him, and his readiness to part with any thing to them' (5–6). Natura's love of girl children and disinterest in boys, sets the stage for a guiding passion of Natura's life – love will always be an issue for him. As this passion grows stronger, so will his reason and experience grow correspondingly strong and help him to understand his passions and make good decisions. Many of the narrative episodes, especially in his youth, centre on experience gained through love, and the last grand incident of his life, his final marriage, focuses on love and his understanding of it and himself. As in *Reflections*, experience is significant to both knowing the passions and understanding the self, thus passion and reason are inextricably linked. One of Haywood's chapter headings exemplifies this importance: 'Chap. II. *Contains some proofs by what swift degrees the passions gain an ascendant* [sic] *over the mind, and grow up in proportion with our reason* (no page number)'. Age, the growth of the mind, and the strength and understanding of the passions are all proportionate to each other. They will increase as he grows and decrease as old age commences.

But the main tenet of Haywood's ethics in *Life's Adventures* is the absence of using reason to control the passions. One gets to understand one's passions, but it is not in order to deploy reason to subdue them. Reason is not a counterbalance to the passions in Haywood's ethics; other passions are:

> As [Natura's] understanding increased, the passions became stronger in proportion; and here is to be observed the wonderful wisdom of nature, or rather the Great Author of nature, in the formation of the human system, that the passions given to us, especially those of the worst sort, are, for the most part, such opposites, that the one is a sufficient check upon the other. (7)

Rather than passions being controlled through careful reason, stoicism, or prayer, as they had been in past configurations, Haywood remarks upon the ways in which the passions themselves counterbalance and create a self.[21] She even names some of the counterbalanced pairs: pride will be checked by fear, sordid covetousness controlled by ostentation; sloth is roused by ambition, 'and so of the rest' (7–8). There are a few interesting things to point out in these passages. First her choice of passions is informative as to how the eighteenth-century mind understood emotion. 'Pride' and 'fear' are both passions in Haywood's configurations; only the latter would be deemed an emotion by modern definitions. Similarly, 'sloth' would today be considered a personality trait, as would ambition. By naming them 'passions' the eighteenth-century mind acknowledges an inextricability to the ways in which personalities and emotions are intertwined, the way that the personal and the public are never truly separate in the eighteenth-century construction. Additionally, a system of balance is at work here. Rather than a positive/negative continuum that privileges reason over emotion, the eighteenth-century arrangement of emotion sees passionate traits as balancing and controlling each other. Other passions will compensate for passion before reason will. One of the best demonstrations of the passion and reason working together occurs after the death of Natura's son.

Through the example of this sad event, Haywood shows how emotions and the mind operate in connection to each other, reading melancholy as the absence of passion and therefore reason. Natura's emotional and intellectual qualities decline together because of his grief; emotion and reason are necessarily corresponsive. Significantly, it is not reason that prompts Natura's recovery, but rather an extreme increase in passion to 'refill' that which is siphoned off by melancholy, the most dangerous effect of which is 'the gloomy pleasure it gives to every thing that serves to indulge it: – darkness and solitude are its delight and nourishment, and the person possessed of it, naturally shuns and hates whatever might alleviate it' (181–2). Natura's family tries to arouse other passions in him. His second wife has had a very public affair with his step-brother. Thinking that thrusting the news upon him in a surprising manner will re-engage his mind, they inform him of the unhappy news, but 'there appeared not the least emotion in his countenance' (184). This lack of passionate response is subsequently read as evidence of declining reason: 'This strange insensibility afforded cause to fear his faculties were all too deeply absorbed in melancholy for him ever to become a man of the world again' (184). The relationship of passion and reason in this passage demonstrate the inextricability of one faculty over the other in Haywood's emotional ethics. Natura's inability to feel emotion is evidence of declining reason and a threat to his mental capacity. The situation gives his family 'an infinite concern' (184). However, as is true to Haywood's ethics, it is not reason that can pull Natura from his emotional melancholy, but rather another passion: revenge.

Haywood's ethics of revenge bears examination. It is the greatest of passions, and 'once entertained, is scarce ever extinguished' (185). Though revenge can oust other passions, nothing can oust it, neither reason nor another passion: '*Revenge* alone is implacable and eternal, not to be banished by any other passion whatsoever'; (185) and though properties of reason, such as morality or religion, might 'hinder a man from putting into action what this cruel passion suggests, but neither of them can restrain him who has revenge in his heart, from wishing it were lawful for him to indulge it' (185–6). Where reason has little to no power to extract Natura from his melancholy, the passion of revenge can, though it then pushes out all other feelings until it is sated. Once he processes the feelings of injustice 'he was for ever lost to the sense of any other passion, than that [revenge] which so powerfully engrossed him' (186). His successful revenge plot (he obtains a divorce, thus financially destroying his wife and her lover) both allows him to uphold his reputation and rouses him from the melancholic episode, the existence of which has been so destructive to both his emotional and mental capabilities.

More significant in controlling the passions are age and experience. As a child, Natura has an inordinate amount of the passion 'curiosity' and has difficulty controlling it because 'reason was not ripe enough in him to enable him to distinguish between what were proper subjects for the exercise of this passion [curiosity] and what were not so' (17). As his age increases, so does his inclination for curiosity, and so does his reason, which will guide the passion, though not control or diminish it. In fact, in Haywood's ethics, age and experience trump reason and morality: '*Pride* seldom, I believe it may be said, *never*, wholly dies in us, tho' it may be concealed; whereas *wrath* diminishes as our *reason* increases, and seems intirely evaporated after the heat of youth is over' (18). While morality teaches that pride should be concealed, it cannot be diminished by reason, but by other passions, such as wrath; age and experience can be just as, if not more, effective than reason in regulating passions. Age and experience are pre-eminent in Natura's journey to self-awareness because they match the passions in strength as they go.

In *Life's Progress*, as in *Reflections*, Haywood posits that the excess or dearth of experience determines the strength of passions and which ones get indulged when a new incident arises. The culmination of Haywood's ethics is demonstrated most clearly in Natura's third marriage, which occurs late in the text and is indeed a laboratory in which to observe the effects of maturity on Natura's feelings. Haywood's description of Natura's marriage to Charlotte begins by the narrator's asserting that 'We are apt to ascribe to the strength of our reason, what is in reality the effect of one or other of the passions' (206). Haywood demonstrates how reason and passion often get conflated and confused with one another. In his third marriage, reason almost thwarts the generous affection of the soul that he has for Charlotte, his third wife.

Natura's love for Charlotte, which Haywood calls 'the tender passion', first demonstrates the way in which experience of his passions has brought him to a place of emotional maturity, a place that allows love and friendship to be '*truly worthy of the names they bear*' (206). His earlier disappointment in love allows him to admire Charlotte's wit, manner of conversation, and their matching 'sympathy of humour' (208) rather than be dazzled by her beauty or bowled over by sexual need as in past relationships. Indeed, it is not sexual difference which most attracts them to each other, but matching souls, 'the flame which warmed their breasts, was meerly spiritual, and platonic; – the difference of sex was never considered' and even 'she thought she discovered more charms in his soul, than in that of any other man or woman' (209). Natura and Charlotte's past marriages, their similar ages, their past experiences, allow them a knowledge of themselves that gives them great pleasure in the company of each other. This connection is at first superficially felt, but creates a solid base of their growing affection, and 'The acquaintance between them soon grew into an intimacy, and that intimacy, by degrees, ripened into friendship, which is the height and very essence of love' (209). The most tender of the passions, deep, soulful love (we might say 'true love') is possible only after experience allows friendship to recognise the value of each other's souls.

Reason in this case does more to hinder the passion than help it, preventing their union, because both, so disappointed in their previous marriages, convince themselves they have an aversion to the married state. By thinking hard about their previous relationships and coming to the logical conclusion that marriage is not beneficial, they actually prevent their ability to deeply love one another in a culturally acceptable manner. Emotional fear over losing her to another suitor whose 'passion was not of that delicate nature, which fills the mind with a thousand timid apprehension' (215) and who quickly looks 'into her family and fortune, and finding there was nothing of disparity between them, he declared his passion to her' (216). The passion of fear, rather than the logic of reason, induces Natura to throw off his reasonable objections to marriage, and get Charlotte to throw off hers. Whereas earlier love scenes offer reason as a way to positively prevent bad effects from love, here it almost prevents the good effects and 'thus does passion triumph over the most seemingly fixed and determined resolution', and Natura and Charlotte are united by 'a parity of principles, humours, and inclinations' (223). This is not a case of passions overriding the reason; instead, the two work together to align a person's passions. The mind and the senses combine to create emotional connection, a desired end in this case. Haywood philosophises,

A platonic and spiritual love, therefore, between persons of different sexes, can never continue for any length of time. Whatever ideas the *mind* may conceive, they will at last conform to the craving of the *senses*; and the *soul*, though never so elevated, find itself incapable of enjoying a perfect satisfaction, without the participation of the *body*. (223)

When the mind is attracted, the bodies of two people will eventually attract as well. In this case reason brings this couple to recognise their 'tender passion' for each other; reason leads to passion, a realisation of feelings, and an understanding of the self.

5 Conclusion

Kathryn R. King notes that, by the publication of *Love in Excess* (1719), Haywood's first successful novel, she had begun to establish herself as 'an edgy, excitingly modern kind of writer' who was remarkable for her creation of an 'affective consensus'.[22] Part of this excitement, I contend, had to do with her ability to place the theory of the passions into a personal and stimulating discourse of authentic passionate living through fiction. By the publication of David Hume's *Essays Moral and Political* in 1741, early modern thinkers generally understood the passions to be significant motivators in the creation of public and social structures. Controlling the passions was paramount to this discussion, as ordering the passions lead to society's organisation. Haywood's contribution to the passion dialogue of the eighteenth century placed emphasis on private experience of the passions; for Haywood, understanding the passions could lead to an understanding of the self. She experimented with the effects of the passion by creating fictional characters living out fictional experiences in laboratories of feeling, but she was very insistent that the passions that she explored were authentic. Because of fiction's ability to create verisimilitude of emotional life through its author's capacity to control the character, circumstance, and outcomes, the community of feeling constituted in Haywood's novels was a significant site for understanding the passions and the individual.

Notes

1. J. Sterling (1732) 'To Mrs. Eliza Haywood on her Writings', *Secret Histories, Novels, and Romances Written by Eliza Haywood* (London). No page number.
2. L. M. Wright and D. J. Newman (Eds.) (2006) *Fair Philosopher: Eliza Haywood and* The Female Spectator (Lewisburg, PA: Bucknell University Press).
3. The myth of 'two Haywoods', the first as an enthusiastic writer of trash fiction, the second a post-1740 reformed advice novelist, has been debunked at least since Kirsten T. Saxton and Rebecca P. Bocchicchio's collection *The Passionate Fictions of Eliza Haywood* in 2000. Nevertheless, the myth remains both among eighteenth-century non-specialists and in the greater, generalist discourse of Haywood. For work that emphasises the continuity of her late and early work, see especially S. Carlile (Ed.) (2011) *Masters of the Marketplace: Women Novelists of the 1750s* (Lanham, MD: Lehigh University Press).
4. T. Dixon (2012) ' "Emotion": The History of a Keyword in Crisis', *Emotion Review* 4: 338–44. Dixon argues that modern usage begins in the early nineteenth century.

5. *Oxford English Dictionary* (2014) 'Emotion' http://www.oed.com.ezp.lib. unimelb.edu.au, accessed 18 June 2014.

6. E. Haywood (1748) *Life's Progress through the Passions; or The Adventures of Natura* (London), p. 6.

7. My own use of the terms passions, emotions, and feelings is somewhat interchangeable in order to vary my prose. If using Haywoodian terms, I clarify those meanings according to her examples.

8. See Dixon, 'Emotion' (2012): 338–44.

9. Thomas Dixon (2003) *From Passions to Emotions* (Cambridge: Cambridge University Press), p. 72.

10. See S. James (1997) *Passion and Action* (Oxford: Clarendon Press); Dixon (2003); J. Elster (1999) *Alchemies of the Mind* (Cambridge: Cambridge University Press); D. M. Gross (2006) *The Secret History of Emotion* (Chicago: University of Chicago Press); A. Pinch (1996) *Strange Fits of Passion* (Stanford: Stanford University Press).

11. N. Armstrong and L. Tennenhouse (2006) 'A Mind for Passion: Locke and Hutcheson on Desire', in V. Kahn, N. Saccamano, and D. Coli (Eds.), *Politics and the Passions 1500–1850* (Princeton: Princeton University Press), pp. 131–50.

12. Amatory fiction is a sub-genre of the early novel written by women between the 1680s and 1740s. The tales generally have female protagonists and tend to follow the story of her seduction and downfall. See R. Ballaster (1992) *Seductive Forms* (Oxford: Clarendon Press); and T. Bowers (2011) *Force or Fraud* (Oxford: Oxford University Press).

13. Elster, *Alchemies*, p. 108.

14. Examples include A. T. McKenzie (1990) *Certain Lively Episodes*; N. Eustace (2008) *Passion is the Gale* (Williamsburg, VA: Omohundro); J. A. Stern (1997) *The Plight of Feeling* (Chicago and London: University of Chicago Press); and R. Tierney-Hynes (2012) *Novel Minds* (Basingstoke: Palgrave Macmillan).

15. Despite its being advertised as being 'In Two Parts', the second part (along with the character key) has yet to be discovered. It is, frustratingly, the only text that we know Haywood wrote for which we cannot account. P. Spedding (2004) *A Bibliography of Eliza Haywood* (London: Pickering and Chatto), p. 244.

16. E. Haywood (1748) *Life's Progress through the Passions; or the Adventures of Natura* (London), Eighteenth Century Collections Online http://find. galegroup.com.ezp.lib.unimelb.edu.au/ecco, 3. All subsequent references are from this edition.

17. The rigour of Haywood's ideas about the passions is probably far greater than her earliest critics believed. Kathryn R. King and Earla Willputte, for instance, both argue for the sophisticated conversations about the passions within her literary circle and her texts. K. R. King (2007) 'Eliza Haywood, Savage Love, and Biographical Uncertainty', in *Review of English Studies*, pp. 722–39. E. Wilputte (2011) 'Eliza Haywood's *Poems on Several Occasions*: Aaron Hill, Writing and the Sublime', in L. V. Troost (Ed.), *Eighteenth-Century Women: Studies in Their Lives Work and Culture*, Vol. 6 (New York: AMS), pp. 79–102.

18. E. Haywood (1726) *Reflections on the Various Effects of Love* (London) Eighteenth Century Collections Online http://find.galegroup.com.ezp.lib. unimelb.edu.au/ecco, 10. All subsequent references are to this edition.

19. In Haywood's texts, men are easily sated and inconstant in their affections; these supposed 'truths' of character demonstrate men's slowness to emotional intelligence.
20. The gender of Natura is intriguing, especially given the feminine ending of his name and the fact that most of Haywood's explanatory nature of the passions takes place through the example of women. I suspect the choice in gender has more to do with male mobility; many of his most important emotional experiences happen while he is encountering specifically masculine developmental markers, such as while he is away from home at university, while on the Grand Tour, or dealing with issues of inheritance.
21. The theory of countervailing passions had grounding in moral philosophies of the era, though it was not necessarily a significant idea in controlling the passions. See A. O. Hirschman (1977) *The Passions and the Interests* (Princeton, NJ: Princeton University Press).
22. K. R. King (2012) *A Political Biography of Eliza Haywood* (London: Pickering and Chatto), p. 24. The phrase 'affective consensus' is from G. G. Starr (2004) *Lyric Generations* (Baltimore and London: Johns Hopkins University Press).

6
That 'Tremendous' Mr Dennis: The Sublime, Common Sense, and Criticism

Kathrine Cuccuru

> Mrs. Phoebe Clinket: I perfectly agree with Sir Tremendous: your modern tragedies are such egregious stuff, they neither move terror nor pity.
>
> Plotwell: Yes, madam, the pity of the audience on the first night, and the terror of the author for the third. Sir Tremendous's plays indeed have rais'd a sublimer passion, astonishment.
>
> John Gay, Alexander Pope, John Arbuthnot,
Three Hours After Marriage (1717)

1 Introduction and background

Lampooned here as *Sir Tremendous*, the literary critic and aspiring dramatist John Dennis (1657–1734) tends to be remembered as a prominent, frequent butt of the Scriblerus Club's many satirical jokes.[1] Quick to find offence, and slow to offer forgiveness, short of temper, and even shorter of finances, gruff, yet eloquent, and tending to self-importance and retaliation, Dennis proved an easy target for the Scriblerians. The Scriblerus Club, who mainly met in 1714, were an informal literary group of educated gentlemen and political–cultural satirists. Central members Alexander Pope, Jonathan Swift, John Gay, John Arbuthnot, and Thomas Parnell were behind the satirical creation *Martinus Scriblerus*.[2] Pope most actively perpetuated the Scriblerian project, and most actively targeted Dennis, with their fierce bouts played out in print. Pope lampooned Dennis's plays and his fondness for the word tremendous, while lambasting his literary criticism.[3] Dennis responded by colourfully criticising Pope's poetry and writing as, for instance, 'whenever he Scribbles, he is emphatically a *Monkey*, in his awkard servile Imitations'.[4] Looking beyond their public name-calling, the printed exchanges between Dennis and the Scriblerians, especially Pope, broach important issues that permeated serious public debate throughout eighteenth-century Britain. My focus will be Dennis's account of the greatest, sublime poetry, and Pope's serious response to it.

Dennis is thought to be the first to offer a theory of the sublime in England.[5] He is particularly known for adopting and critically expanding upon the ideas in the treatise *Peri Hypsous* (usually translated as *On the Sublime*) attributed to 'Longinus', where the sublime is the rhetorical effect of excellent poetry and oratory to irresistibly transport the hearer.[6] My discussion will show that Dennis's account of the sublime implies a special *sublime sense* that he associates with the 'best and wisest natures' (CW: 340). Although Dennis does not describe it in this way (instead he refers to 'regular' or 'reasonable' nature (for example, CW: 202)), these morally virtuous characters may be understood to correspond with the height of *authentic* human nature. Problematically, this introduces a tension between what the sublime is, that is, the highest, authentic, state of moral virtue, and what the sublime is meant to do, that is, instruct our moral development towards this authentic moral height. Dennis distinguishes the extraordinary sensing of 'Enthusiasm' from the common sensing of the ordinary 'vulgar' passions. Since Dennis connects the sublime with those certain natures that can rightly sense Enthusiasm,[7] I shall demonstrate that he introduces a special *sublime sense*. However, if the sublime cannot be commonly sensed, especially by the morally imbalanced (that is, those with seemingly inauthentic natures), then, how is the greatest, sublime poetry supposed to perform its instructive role of reforming the moral character?

Dennis appears generally motivated to make a distinction between a special *sublime sense* and *common sense* for two interrelated political reasons. The first is that he wishes to realign the term Enthusiasm with authentic divine inspiration of the poetic genius, while distancing it from the contemporary malign and politically dangerous religious sense associated with rabble-rousing zealotry, mass hysteria, and political radicalism. Dennis's second motivation is his hope to preserve the separation between the minority aristocratic elite and the common masses, and the assumed social order this separation is meant to maintain. Such a social division may be reflected in his distinction between those natures with the rare *sublime sense* and majority with *common sense*. The social elite are identified with the rare genius of the sublime poet and critic, the men of letters, while the common masses correspond with general readers and audiences.[8] Despite hints of social equality and religious tolerance, Dennis's critical theory appears to support an exclusive intellectual community that directly maintains the established institutions of a relatively elite public sphere. Significantly, being a Whig, he views the proper elite public sphere in terms of Whiggism. I shall argue that, by maintaining such a distinction, Dennis unavoidably makes the greatest sublime poetry's instructive value either redundant or largely ineffectual.

I suggest that this tension is critically played upon in the Scriblerian satire *Peri Bathous*.[9] Its mock praise of Dennis, and others, who consider that the sublime requires some sort of special sense, is meant to draw attention to (primarily) Pope's criticism that this undermines the proper understanding of the sublime in poetry.[10] On Pope's view, the sublime most powerfully expresses our authentic, *common* nature, that is, those passions common to all natures, and thus, commonly sensed (to some degree) by every nature. Therefore, contra Dennis, Pope considers that this *common sense* of the passions is central to the efficacy of the sublime. Moreover, aspirants to an intellectual elite based on *sublime sense* are wildly lampooned by the Scriblerian project; their aim being to ridicule 'false tastes in learning'.[11] As *Martinus Scriblerus*, Pope went on to antagonise and subvert the political establishment, consciously pushing forward the politicisation of the literary public sphere, especially in the various versions of the *Dunciad* and in his *Imitations of Horace*.[12] Significantly, Pope's (and his fellow Scriblerians') political view is Toryism. However, I shall show that these cheap shots belie the Scriblerians' own desire to set themselves apart from their satirised opponent, and similarly maintain an intellectually elite community of their own.

2 Dennis's account of poetry and the sublime

Dennis mentions the sublime throughout his critical works but his main discussion appears in *The Advancement and Reformation of Poetry* (1701) (CW: 197–278) and *The Grounds of Criticism* (1704) (CW: 325–74). The principal aim of these works is to offer an account of genuine and great poetry. His underlying motivation is to address two important debates of the day. *The Advancement* primarily engages with the Ancients and Moderns debate, known in Britain as 'The Battle of the Books',[13] where the basic argument is over whether or not ancient poetry and knowledge are superior to modern forms.[14] Although agreeing with the excellence of the Ancients and the degeneracy of the Moderns, Dennis argues that the Ancients' advantage is not insurmountable. He demonstrates that their only advantage is the greatness of the Ancients' subjects:

those being, the sacred and divine (CW: 214). Therefore, modern poetry may be reformed and advanced by the proper poetic subject of 'True Religion', that is, the biblical God of revelation (CW: 251–66). In *The Grounds* (and more forcefully elsewhere)[15] Dennis defends the value of poetry in Christian religious teaching and argues against any Church role in regulating the stage by recapitulating and expanding upon his claim that genuine and great poetry has True Religion as its subject. Within this context is to be found his account of the passions and the sublime. My discussion will be primarily concerned with two claims that arise from it. The first claim is that the final end of *all* poetry is to instruct morally by the proper excitement of the passions, with the correlate that the greatest poetry is the most passionate, and hence the most instructive. The second claim is that the greatest poetry is the sublime.

Dennis's first claim comes from his general account of poetry. He defines poetry as 'an Imitation of Nature, by a pathetick and numerous Speech' (CW: 215). In the context of his account of True Religion as set out in *The Advancement* and appealed to in *The Grounds*, he understands authentic human nature to be 'Rule and Order, and Harmony' as universally prescribed by eternal divine law (CW: 202). He locates both moral perfection and beauty in this regularity of nature (CW: 202, 335). Further, he believes that what pleases us aesthetically is the morally virtuous because the design of True Religion is happiness, and the most aesthetically pleasing or happiest nature is the highest moral power, that is, the divine creator, God (CW: 252–3). He argues that poetry has the same design as True Religion (CW: 251). Thus, the most aesthetically pleasing poetry imitates the most morally virtuous character.

Like True Religion, Dennis argues, poetry attains the height of virtuous pleasure by (at least momentarily) restoring the harmony of reason, passion, and the senses (CW: 234, 263). Dennis considers that this perfect harmony of the faculties is analogous to the 'Primitive State' in which humans were 'created Holy, Innocent, Perfect', prior to the Biblical fall (CW: 255). For him, this is our authentic human nature and the one that poetry must imitate. The parallel that Dennis draws between poetry and True Religion is explicit:

> as that alone is the True Religion, which makes the best Provision for the Happiness of those who profess it; so [like True Religion] that must be the best and the noblest Art, which brings the greatest Felicity with it. But as the Misery of Man proceeds from the Discord, [...] it follows, that nothing can make him Happy, but what can remove that Discord, and restore the Harmony of the Human

Faculties. So that that must be the best and the noblest Art, which makes the best Provision at the same Time for the Satisfaction of all the Faculties, the Reason, the Passions, the Senses. But none of them provides in such a sovereign Manner as Poetry, for the Satisfaction of the whole Man together.

(CW: 263)

He holds that poetry, as the greatest human art,[16] requires an 'end' (or purpose), and a 'means' (or rules/principles), for acquiring that end (CW: 215, 335).

Following the analogy with True Religion, Dennis takes the two complementary ends of poetry to be 'subordinately' pleasure and 'finally' moral instruction (CW: 335). Assuming its obviousness, Dennis only implies the connection between poetry's definition as the imitation of nature and its purpose to reform manners and develop the morally virtuous character. I take his line of thinking to be as follows: the highest morally virtuous character is one who attains Dennis's described state of harmony, that being our authentic human nature, and it is the one that poetry must imitate. However, as fallen beings our faculties are in varying states of imbalance, or as Dennis terms it irregularity, all humans require moral instruction in order to experience our authentic nature. Thus, poetry not only imitates (the virtuously pleasurable) authentic human nature, but makes it possible for the imbalanced, irregular nature to be *moved* toward this imitated state.[17] Dennis describes instruction as this movement toward harmony: 'to instruct..., that is, to bring Mankind from Irregularity, Extravagance, and Confusion, to Rule and Order'(CW: 335). Furthermore, Dennis insists that poetry must be instructive in this way; otherwise it would not be an 'art' (CW: 336).

Dennis considers that effective instruction of the human character is achieved by the appropriate excitement of the passions. He holds the passions to be the most influential force over human nature. Again, this is derived from his account of True Religion where he believes that the Biblical Fall resulted from our greatness of passion, specifically, that we 'diverted Affection' from God to inferior objects of passion (CW: 257). In general, he argues, all human thought is attended by some passion, and we will be moved by that passion. So, he claims 'that all Instruction whatever depends upon Passion' (CW: 337). For Dennis, it follows that 'Poetry, at the same time that it instructs us powerfully, must reform us easily; because it makes the very Violence of Passions contribute to our Reformation' (CW: 337). Thus, to achieve its instructive aim as an art, Dennis takes the principle of authentic poetry to be that 'poetry must everywhere excite the passions' (CW: 216, 337, 338). And conversely he states this rule as: 'That where there is nothing which directly attends the moving of it [that is, Passion], there can be no Poetry' (CW: 338). Significantly for my discussion, Dennis correlates the efficacy of instruction with how much poetry moves the passions. He states: 'The more Poetry moves, the more it pleases and instructs' (CW: 338). Therefore, the most passionate poetry is the most instructive. Further, he asserts: 'Now if the chief Thing in Poetry be Passion, why then the chief thing in great Poetry, must be great Passion' (CW: 215). So it is clear that Dennis holds that *all* authentic poetry must instruct morally by the proper excitement of the passions, and that the greatest poetry is the most passionate, and hence, the most instructive.

The second claim that I am interested in from Dennis's account is that the greatest poetry is the sublime. He critically adopts and expands Longinus's account of the sublime as the irresistible transport of the hearer of excellent or lofty poetry and oratory. Following Longinus, Dennis describes the sublime effect provocatively when he writes that it:

> Ravishes and Transports us, and produces in us a certain Admiration mingled with astonishment and with surprise [...it is an] invincible force which commits a pleasing Rape upon the very Soul of the Reader; that whenever it breaks out where it ought to do, like an Artillery of Jove, it Thunders blazes and strikes at once.
>
> (CW: 359)

Dennis criticises Longinus for only describing this sublime effect and failing to explain its cause (CW: 223, 359). Dennis considers that his own understanding of poetry and True Religion is consistent with and completes Longinus's study of the sublime by determining its cause. Dennis argues that, ultimately, the sublime is the coming together of its cause and effect (CW: 223). His simplest definition of the sublime is 'a great thought exprest with the Enthusiasm that belongs to it' (CW: 222, 359). Significantly, for Dennis, the authentic sublime can only be attended by Enthusiastic passions.

Dennis's most focused discussion of Enthusiasm occurs in *The Grounds* where he defines 'Greater Poetry' (CW: 331, 338–40). This branch of poetry, he writes, 'is an Art by which a Poet justly and reasonably excites great Passion, in order to please and instruct, and make Mankind better and happier' (CW: 338).[18] By definition, then, Dennis holds that 'Greater Poetry' must fulfil his principle by everywhere exciting *great* passion. He further claims that 'it is impossible for a Poet every where to excite in a very great degree, that which we vulgarly call Passion' (CW:

338, see also 216). This leads him to distinguish 'two sorts of Passion': the vulgar passions, and Enthusiasm (CW: 338).

The key difference between the vulgar passions and Enthusiasm is the object that excites the passion. Vulgar passions are excited by the direct, or related, ideas of objects of everyday experience. He says, for example, that the passion 'pity' is excited by 'the Sight of a mournful Object' (CW: 338). Enthusiasm is the strong passion excited during the contemplation of, or meditation on, ideas of objects 'that belong not to common life' (CW: 338), or, 'when their Cause is not clearly comprehended' (CW: 216). Initially, the objects of Enthusiasm appear to be simply God and other divine creatures, but he also suggests Enthusiasm is excited by a certain experience of everyday objects (CW: 339). This is the case when Dennis adapts the classical example of the sun. He says that the vulgar idea of the sun is 'of a round flat shining Body, of about two foot diameter'; while, he continues, in meditation the idea of the sun is 'of a vast and glorious Body, and the top of all visible Creation, and the brightest material Image of all Divinity' (CW: 339). Recall that he believes that the Biblical Fall resulted from diverting our passion from the objects of God's divinity to profane, earthly objects (CW: 257). As such, we may take the objects of Enthusiasm to correspond with the divine and the vulgar to correspond with the earthly. Moreover, he claims, because originally all creatures, even the dreadful and dangerous, were created perfectly harmonious by God, when poetry restores harmony we can be virtuously pleased by objects that we would ordinarily dread or fear (CW: 264). So, in the state that Dennis calls meditation, it is possible to glimpse the virtuously pleasurable harmonious state of an everyday object, that is, as it was created by God's divine nature; and in such a state, Enthusiasm may be excited by that object.

Although he lacks clarity and consistency with his terminology, Dennis generally takes the 'soul' to encompass all our internal faculties of reason, passions, and sense (CW: 253); whereas the 'mind' is our faculty of reason, where we have, reflect upon, and imagine thoughts and ideas (CW: 217). Meditation, then, is a particular activity of the mind, specifically, the imaginative reflection of the mind on the ideas that occur in it (CW: 217). Unlike mere reflection, where the mind recalls ideas of everyday sensed, or even mental, objects, meditation generates the idea of God's divine nature, in heavenly or everyday objects of God's creation. Consider again his example of the sun: in meditation, the idea of the ordinary image of the sun requires the mind to work on it in certain ways in order to generate the divine image of it. The most effective mental image is one that has the same liveliness and movement 'as if [the divine object] were, before our very Eyes' (CW: 218, see also 339); however, he does not offer any details of how the imagination generates it. Instead, he considers the mind's workings to be a wondrous mystery of God's creation beyond human comprehension. This incomprehensibility contributes to the excitement of Enthusiasm because, by generating the imagined object, the mind has a 'conscious View of its own Excellence' (CW: 217). Thus, there is a two-fold sense in which the causal objects of Enthusiasm are beyond common life and full comprehension. Firstly, the imagined object is beyond common life, specifically, the objects that manifest God's nature, be they either heavenly objects or the created divine nature of everyday objects. Secondly, the process of generation by the human mind is beyond its own full comprehension. In meditation we appear to be aware of both the wonder of the object and the wonder of our mind's (God given) capacity to generate it; together these excite Enthusiasm (CW: 217–18, 360).

Since the sublime's attendant passion is Enthusiasm, the object of meditation in the sublime state is God's divine nature. Also like Enthusiasm, the sublime state combines the wonder of these divine objects and the conscious awareness of the wonderful incomprehensibility of our human mind to generate it. Thus, Dennis says in *The Grounds*:

> That which is truly sublime has this particular to it, that it exalts the Soul, and makes it conceive a greater Idea of it self; filling it with Joy and with a certain noble Pride, as if it self had produc'd what it but barely reads.
>
> (CW: 360)

This captures, for Dennis, the coming together of the sublime cause and effect; that is, the irresistible transport of the soul (the effect) with the idea of God's divine nature as generated by the human mind (the cause).

According to Dennis, this sublime state is achieved in the perfect meditative state where, analogous to the Primitive State, reason, passion and the senses are in complete harmony. He describes the Primitive State of harmony where the internal faculties of the soul are perfectly balanced and solely focused on God's divine nature as sublime. He states: 'So that Man, in his Primitive State, was always in lofty ravishing transports' (CW: 256). Analogously, he says that 'in a *sublime* and accomplish'd poem, the Reason, and Passions and Senses are pleased at the same time superlatively' (my emphasis, CW: 263). In both cases, the passions are at their greatest level of excitement (CW: 256, 263). Consistent with Dennis's claimed instructive end, the sublime in poetry is the affective transport or movement of the mind from an imbalanced state to the height of harmony, that is, the state of highest morally virtuous character, our authentic nature. Because it attains such heights, and is the most passionate, the greatest poetry is the sublime.

3   A tension in Dennis's account

Taking his two claims together – that is, the greatest, most passionate poetry is the most instructive, and the greatest poetry is the sublime – we might suppose sublime poetry to be the most instructive. However, because of a further distinction Dennis makes between sensing the vulgar passions and Enthusiasm, the instructive value of sublime poetry appears to be largely ineffectual or redundant. This raises a tension between what the sublime is, that is, the greatest poetry, and what the sublime is meant to do, that is, morally instruct. To demonstrate that this is the case, I shall set out the relevant notion of *common sense*, and then show how Dennis's account problematically implies a *sublime sense*.

As now, eighteenth-century usage of the term *common sense* has some association with practical wisdom or acting sensibly. However, unlike the present, eighteenth-century usage of the term *common sense*, or even just *sense*, is most usually grounded in or refers to the idea that, in virtue of our given human nature, all humans have the internal faculty to perceive the world, through the senses, in a common way. In eighteenth-century critical discourse and aesthetic theory *common sense* usually refers to a common internal disposition or sensible faculty to perceive or have feeling for the aesthetic (broadly construed as emotional response) in objects of experience.[19] On this usage, all humans, in order to count as human, have *common sense*. However, like all human faculties, the level of sensitivity and development of *common sense* varies, so not everyone has equally *good sense*. Nevertheless, it seems, through instruction and the right kinds of exposure to certain objects of experience, those with insensitive or underdeveloped *common sense* may improve it. Similarly, in terms of the aesthetic, all humans may develop their capacity to experience and appreciate beauty. Also in the closely related terms of eighteenth-century moral theory, especially where the proper emotional response to beauty is morally virtuous, the development of aesthetic appreciation may correspond with the development of the morally virtuous character.

Considering Dennis's account of poetry then, it seems correct to summarise him as follows. In virtue of our (God-)given human nature, all passions, both the vulgar and Enthusiastic, are felt by or excited in *common sense*; but since all humans are, to some extent, in a state of moral imbalance, our appropriate sensitivity to or excitement of the passions requires development; and thus, poetry, the design of which is to instruct by the appropriate excitement of the passions, best develops the authentic morally virtuous character. Significantly, the most instructive poetry is that which best moves the fallen nature from irregularity or inauthenticity to harmony, that is, what he calls sublime poetry, which is attended by Enthusiasm.

However, in drawing out his distinction between the vulgar passions and Enthusiasm, Dennis asserts a difference between the common human capacity to feel vulgar passions and a special capacity to feel Enthusiasm. This difference is made apparent in the following passage from *The Grounds*:

> Thus there are two sorts of Passions to be rais'd in Poetry, the Vulgar and the Enthusiastick; to which last, the Vulgar is preferable, because all Men are capable of being moved by the Vulgar, and a Poet writes to all: But the Enthusiastick are more subtle, and thousands have no feeling and no notion of them. But where the Vulgar cannot be moved in great degree, there Enthusiastick are to be rais'd. Therefore in those parts of Epick Poetry, where the Poet speaks himself, or the Eldest of Muses for him, the Enthusiastick passions are to prevail, as likewise in the Great Ode. And the Vulgar Passions are to prevail in those parts of the Epick and Dramatick Poem, where the poet introduced Persons hold Conversation together. And perhaps this might be one Reason, for which Aristotle might prefer Tragedy to Epick Poetry, because the Vulgar Passions prevail more in it, and are more violently mov'd in it; and therefore Tragedy must necessarily both please, and instruct more generally than Epick Poetry. We shall then treat of the Vulgar Passions when we come to speak of Tragedy, in which Poem they ought most to prevail: we shall then more particularly shew the surest and most powerful ways of raising Compassion and Terror, which are the true Tragical Passions.
>
> (CW: 339)

In this passage, Dennis describes sensing the vulgar passions as a common capacity across all human natures. So these passions may be described as being felt by the sensible faculty of *common sense*.

In contrast, Dennis writes that Enthusiasm is 'more subtle, and thousands have no feeling and no notion of it', implying a different or special capacity to feel it. The nature of this difference in capacity is further described when Dennis writes:

For Men are mov'd for two Reasons, either because they have weak Minds and Souls, that are capable of being mov'd by little Objects, and consequently by little and ordinary Ideas; or because they have Greatness of Soul and Capacity, to discern and feel the great ones: for the Enthusiastick Passions being caus'd by the Ideas, it follows, that the more the Soul is capable of receiving Ideas whose Objects are truly great and wonderful, the greater will the Enthusiasm be that is caus'd by those Ideas. From whence it follows, the greater the Soul is, and the larger the Capacity, the more will it be mov'd by religious Ideas; which are not only great and wonderful, but which almost alone are great and wonderful to a great and wise Man; and never fail to move very strongly, unless it is for want of due Reflection, or want of Capacity in the Subject.

(CW: 340)

Clearly, Dennis considers that the human capacity to feel Enthusiasm depends on a certain 'greatness of soul'. He holds that such a soul has both a great mind capable of thinking great, religious ideas, and a special sense capable of being enthusiastically moved by these thoughts. This implies that a great soul has a (God-)given or established special capacity – a *sublime sense* – for Enthusiasm, and its correlate, that the weak soul can only feel the vulgar passions in *common sense*.

However, if *sublime sense* is limited to great souls, then Dennis renders sublime poetry's instructive value either redundant or completely ineffectual. It becomes redundant because those rare few who naturally possess *sublime sense* already have a developed morally virtuous character, which requires no instruction. Conversely, for the common majority having no *sublime sense*, or way of acquiring it, sublime poetry is completely ineffectual as they can never feel Enthusiasm and be moved by it in sublime poetry. For them, only poetry that excites the vulgar passions in *common sense* can be morally instructive. So Dennis is going against his central claim that, as the greatest, most passionate poetry, the sublime best reforms the irregular or inauthentic nature.

A tempting alternative reading of these two passages is that there are rare sublime geniuses with a given *sublime sense* who produce the greatest, sublime poetry; while the common majority are generally, perhaps irresistibly, affected and instructed by their sublime poetry. This fits well with the associated Longinian tradition. However, Dennis's account does not explicitly assert the mass effect of sublime poetry; whereas he explicitly limits the feeling for Enthusiasm while asserting the mass feeling for the vulgar passions. A better fit for Dennis seems to be that the greatest poetry need not generally instruct (that is, the greatest number of souls), rather it may simply have the greatest instructive effect on certain souls. He may accept that in the course of moral development some souls' *common sense* may potentially be refined into *sublime sense*.[20] If so, then poetry which excites the vulgar passions remains the most effective initial instruction for the undeveloped character. Nevertheless, he may claim that greatest developmental step is between merely attaining a feeling for Enthusiasm – a *sublime sense* – and attaining authentic harmony of the faculties – the sublime state; and hence, the most significant point of instruction. But Dennis clearly correlates the greatness of capacity of sense with the extent of passionate movement, that is, the greatest souls are the most moved by Enthusiasm precisely because of their attained greatness. The sublime, then, marks the height or completion of moral development, leaving its instructive value largely ineffectual or redundant. As such the greatest sublime poetry may, in the authentic morally virtuous character, excite the greatest passion; however, it fails to excite, or instruct, the irregular, undeveloped character. This is in tension with Dennis's claim that all poetry is to morally instruct, and that the sublime is the most instructive.

4 *Peri Bathous*: Or Martinus Scriblerus his treatise of the art of sinking in poetry

Now that I have demonstrated the tension in Dennis, I shall turn to how this tension is played upon in the mock praise of the Scriblerians' *Peri Bathous* (The Profound). *Peri Bathous* is foremost a political and cultural satire. Nevertheless, modelled on Longinus's *On the Sublime* and aimed at prevailing inept Modern poets, Martinus Scriblerus's *ars poetica* may, with caution, be read as an inversion of (primarily) Pope's view on poetry. According to Pope, poetry must imitate nature and sublime poetry is the highest expression of authentic human nature. It is produced by the natural genius who has an imagination capable of intuiting this nature. Such expressions of nature are regulated by *common sense*. Pope understands *common sense* in a way that is consistent with how I have described it here, that is, in virtue of our given human nature, all humans have a disposition or sensible faculty to perceive and feel the sensible world in a common way. For Pope, then, the imitated nature in poetry is limited to the shared commonalities experienced in *common sense*, and may not appeal to the uncommon peculiarity or idiosyncrasy of any individual nature. This makes *common sense* the measure of authenticity. So the sublime poet not only imaginatively intuits nature but can rightly judge which intuited aspects are common to all human natures. The greatest, sublime poetry most vividly and effectively expresses common nature as it really is, that is, authentic human nature. In turn, the reader is immediately struck by this expression of authenticity, and rightly moved by the poetic realisation of the authentic passions of the soul. Thus, Pope holds the sublime to be the height of *common sense*, and the sublime poet to be the one who can most clearly express it.[21]

If we consider that *Peri Bathous* is the inversion of Pope's view, the implied significance of *common sense* is seen in Scriblerus's encouragement of the Profound poet to avoid or deny it. Scriblerus's 'first principle of the Profound' poet is to:

> studiously detest, and turn his head from all ideas, ways, and workings of the pestilent foe to wit and destroyer of fine figures, which is known by the name common sense. His business must be to contract the *gout de travers*; and to acquire a most *happy, uncommon, unaccountable way of thinking.*
>
> (Original emphasis, PB: 200–1)

Moreover, according to Scriblerus, the Profound end of poetry is 'tranquillity of mind', that is, the complete dulling of the passions, and where passions are raised they must be from 'low-life' (PB: 213). Scriblerus considers that the mastery of this Profound mediocrity or poetic descent is best achieved by unnatural, or we may put it nonironically as inauthentic, imitation. Scriblerus gives two sorts of imitation: 'the first is when we force to our own purposes the thoughts of others; the second consists in copying the imperfections or blemishes of celebrated authors' (PB: 213). But unnatural imitation is also generally achieved by the surprising (mis-)matching of the marvellous and the improbably low, or simply base vulgarity (PB: 201, 207). One such unnatural pairing Scriblerus gives is 'a footman speaking like a philosopher'; however, the most unnatural is low metaphors for God's divine nature (PB: 201, 203–5).

Despite their apparent differences, Pope's view here (as the inversion of Scriblerus) is similar to Dennis's account of poetry in a number of ways.[22] Like Dennis, Pope considers poetry to be the proper imitation of uniform or regular (God-)given nature, in that it rightly excites the passions, and reflects moral refinement. However, unlike Dennis, Pope denies any special or *sublime sense*. Instead, as I have suggested, he considers the sublime to be the highest expression of authentic *common sense*.

Pope is most critical of theories of the sublime that aim beyond or away from what is naturally central to *common sense*. If the sublime appeals to something outside *common sense*, then the sublime collapses into its antithesis, the Profound. This is implied by Scriblerus when he writes:

> The Sublime of nature is the sky, the sun, moon, stars, etc. the Profound of nature is gold, pearls, precious stones, and the treasures of the deep, which are inestimable as unknown. But all that lies between these, as corn, flowers, fruits, animals, and things for the mere use of man, are of mean price, and so common as not to be esteemed by the curious: it being certain, that any thing, of which we know the true use, cannot be invaluable: which affords a solution, why common sense hath either been totally despised, or held in small repute, by the greatest modern critics and authors.
>
> (PB: 200)

On Pope's view, since Dennis distinguishes Enthusiasm from the commonly sensed Vulgar passions, this attendant passion of Dennis's sublime mirrors Scriblerus's Profound. This is because it does not properly excite what is common to *all* human natures. As such it is not regulated by *common sense*, placing it outside authentic nature and importantly beyond the sound judgement of taste. On Pope's harshest charge, Dennis's sublime only manages to excite the peculiarities or idiosyncrasies of certain natures, not the *common sense* of the best and wisest characters.

Pope's critical account generalises the tension in Dennis from instruction to poetic appreciation. It is now between what the sublime is, that is, the greatest expression of authentic nature, and who may rightly *appreciate* it as such. In this case, Pope charges Dennis with turning the sublime into the inauthentic expression of peculiar and idiosyncratic natures, unregulated by *common sense,* and outside good taste. Beneath the lampooning and cheap shots, I consider this a serious point made in the Scriblerian response. Problematically, though, Pope's own account of sublime poetry may also suffer a similar charge and collapse into Scriblerus's bathos. Despite placing *common sense* at the centre of his account, Pope appears to hold that sound judgement of the authenticity of nature in poetry requires a specially developed *common sense*, one that can rightly sense authentic nature (PB: 198). Further, he implies that the majority lack such a capacity or sense, especially those he mocks as having pretentions to the sublime. But, if the mark of poetry is the expression of what is common across all natures, that is, our authentic human nature, then why cannot all natures sense and judge it as common and authentic? Pope does not appear to explain why only certain natures have this (reintroduced) *sublime sense* and how those without it can come to appreciate the sublime. Without such an explanation, Pope's account is reduced to a switching of intellectual elites. He seems to be simply replacing his satirised opponent with his own intellectual community, namely, the Scriblerians, as the proper judges of authenticity and the authority on good taste. However, Pope does not reveal what makes the Scriblerians's particular natures the measure of authenticity, and not just as peculiar and idiosyncratic.

5 Concluding remarks: Eighteenth-century criticism

Dennis's personality may have ensured his satirical targeting by Pope and the Scriblerians; but by insisting that the greatest, sublime poetry may only be properly sensed by a special *sublime sense*, his critical theory reinforced it. The tension identified in Dennis, and criticised by Pope, is that the greatest poetry – the sublime – is supposed to rightly express, and irresistibly, excite the authentic common passions of human nature. This implies that these passions should be properly felt (to some extent) by all human natures in *common sense*. Although initially making such a claim, Dennis points out, that the majority of natures do not, or perhaps not appropriately, sense the sublime. So, he concludes that only a few special natures that he distinguishes as having *sublime sense* are able to authentically appreciate sublime poetry, which denies the initial claim of the general effect of the sublime on the common human nature.

Despite rightly identifying the problem of distinguishing *sublime sense* from *common sense* in Dennis, Pope's critical response ultimately endorses a similar distinction between *common sense* of the majority and a special *common sense* of poets. Indeed, Dennis's and Pope's focus on promoting and defending their opposing intellectual, political, and religious, views appears to have blinded them to the similarities of their literary critical accounts. Since both describe a special sense for the sublime, their actual point of difference is not that Dennis endorses *sublime sense* and Pope endorses *common sense*; rather, they differ as to advocating who may authentically possess this sense. Both Dennis and Pope believe that their own respective intellectually elite literary communities are the authentic possessors of it, and in turn, the one that can properly lay claim to have the corresponding authentic moral and political opinion in the early eighteenth-century public sphere. However, if neither side can (or does) appeal to general *common sense*, on what grounds can we judge one to be the actual authentic *sublime sense*? What forms the standard of authenticity of human nature? Or is there only idiosyncratic preference?

This tension dogged the emerging fields of literary criticism and more broadly aesthetic theory throughout the eighteenth century. Even as aesthetic value, the standard of taste, was gradually decoupled from moral value and its political consequences, theorists continued to struggle to reconcile the apparent common sensing of the aesthetic with the proper appreciation of it. Importantly, these theorists maintained that *good taste* or *good sense* ought to be recognisable and generalisable throughout time, the unfathomable alternative being that there may be *no* standard of appreciation. Any theory that amounted to there being only idiosyncratic preference was fervently denied. So, being charged with peddling idiosyncrasies and the false sublime proved clear provocation for the ferocious printed exchanges of 'that *Tremendous* Mr Dennis' and 'that *Monkey* Mr Pope'.[23]

Notes

1. For biographical information on Dennis, see, for example, J. Prichard (2004) 'Dennis, John (1658–1734)'. *Oxford Dictionary of National Biography Online* (Oxford: Oxford University Press), accessed 1 July 2014.
2. For general information on the Scriblerians, see, for example: V. Rumbold (2004–12) 'Scriblerus Club (act. 1714)'. *Dictionary of National Biography Online* (Oxford: Oxford University Press), accessed 1 July 2014.
3. A. Pope (1993 [1710]) 'An Essay on Criticism', in P. Rogers (Ed.), *Alexander Pope* (Oxford: Oxford University Press), pp. 17–39, especially, pp. 26, 34–5.
4. J. Dennis (1939) *The Critical Works of John Dennis*, E. N. Hooker (Ed.) (Baltimore: The John Hopkins Press), Vol. 2, p. 104. (Henceforth, in-line as CW: pp; all subsequent page references are to Volume 1.).
5. S. H. Monk (1960) *The Sublime: A Study of Critical Theories in XVII-Century England* (Ann Arbor, MI: University of Michigan Press), p. 45. For a further exposition of Dennis's account of the sublime, see D. B. Morris (1972) *The Religious Sublime: Christian Poetry and Critical Tradition in 18th-Century England* (Lexington, KY: The University Press of Kentucky).
6. For a recent discussion on Longinus, see M. Heath (2012) 'Longinus and the Ancient Sublime', in T. M. Costelloe (Ed.), *The Sublime: From Antiquity to the Present* (Cambridge: Cambridge University Press), pp. 11–23.
7. The term Enthusiasm will be capitalised throughout to indicate that it is being used as defined by Dennis.
8. For further discussion of Dennis's political motivations, see J. Morillo (2000) 'John Dennis: Enthusiastic Passions, Cultural Memory, and Literary Theory', *Eighteenth-Century Studies* 34(1): 21–41.
9. A. Pope (1993) 'Peri Bathous: Or, Martinus Scriblerus his Treatise of the Art of Sinking in Poetry', in P. Rogers (Ed.), *Alexander Pope* (Oxford: Oxford University Press), pp. 193–239. (Henceforth in-line as PB: pp.)

10. Although a Scriblerian collaboration, it is reasonable to treat it as representative of Pope's view; see E. L. Steeves (1952) 'Introduction', in A. Pope, *The Art of Sinking in Poetry*, E. L. Steeves (Ed.) (New York: King's Crown Press), pp. xi–lxix.
11. Pope, quoted in Rumbold, 'Scriblerus Club'.
12. See: J. Habermas (1989) *The Structural Transformation of the Public Sphere*, T. Burger (Trans.) (Cambridge: Polity Press).
13. This description is attributed to Jonathan Swift in his satire *The Tale of Tub* (1704); see J. Swift (2010) *The Tale of Tub and Other Works*, M. Walsh (Ed.) (Cambridge: Cambridge University Press).
14. For one discussion on this debate, see J. M. Levine (1991) *The Battle of the Books: History and Literature in the Augustan Age* (Ithaca, NY: Cornell University Press).
15. See, for example, *The Usefulness of the Stage* (1698), CW: 146–93.
16. Where 'art' is the method for best fulfilling poetry's design to simultaneously satisfy the faculties. CW: 246, 263.
17. Conversely, poetic imitation of irregular or debauched human states is not genuine poetry and can only give false pleasure to the weak minded or those lacking taste. CW: 328.
18. Great poetry includes epic, tragic, and greater lyric. The other branch is 'Lesser' poetry, 'which excites less Passion for the formention'd ends;' it includes comedy, satire, the little ode, elegy, and pastoral poems. CW: 331, 338.
19. This notion of *common sense* is seen in the writings of the Earl of Shaftesbury, Francis Hutcheson, and David Hume; see, for example, L. E. Klein (1994) *Shaftesbury and the Culture of Politeness: Moral Discourse and Cultural Politics in Early Eighteenth-Century England* (Cambridge: Cambridge University Press).
20. Dennis implies a version of Aristotelian habituation for moral development. A parallel analysis of moral development in Aristotle is given in M. F. Burnyeat (1980) 'Aristotle on Learning to be Good', in A. Rorty (Ed.), *Essays on Aristotle's Ethics* (Berkeley, CA: University of California Press), pp. 69–92; and a difficulty for Dennis's adoption of *habitus* in A. T. Delehanty (2007) 'Mapping the Aesthetic Mind: John Dennis and Nicolas Boileau', *Journal of the History of Ideas* 68(2): 243.
21. These summarised features of Pope's sublime appear explicitly and implicitly throughout his critical works; see especially 'An Essay on Criticism', pp. 19–24. For an in-depth discussion on Pope's understanding of and relation to 'nature', see G. Tillotson (1958) *Pope and Human Nature* (Oxford: Clarendon Press).
22. A discussion on the political motivation for pushing these differences is given in C. Gerrard (2005) 'Pope, Peri Bathous, and the Whig Sublime', in D. Womersley (Ed.), *'Cultures of Whiggism' New Essays on English Literature and Culture in the Long Eighteenth Century* (Newark, DE: University of Delaware Press), pp. 200–15.
23. Acknowledgements: Thanks to the collection editors; my supervisor Professor Sebastian Gardner; and my UCL Ph.D. colleagues who commented on this as work in progress, especially Margaret Hampson, who also read earlier drafts.

7
Adam Smith and the Theatre in *Moral Sentiments*

Laura J. Rosenthal

1 Introduction

In the opening of *The Wealth of Nations*, Adam Smith pauses briefly to consider exchange itself. We cannot credit any wisdom for this capacity, he observes; instead, it is part of human nature to 'truck, barter, and exchange one thing for another'.[1] Animals can cooperate, but 'nobody ever saw a dog make a fair and deliberate exchange of one bone for another with another dog'.[2] Smith doesn't see the need for further evidence or speculate as to why people exchange: 'it belongs not to our present subject to inquire'.[3] By contrast, in his earlier *Theory of Moral Sentiments* (1759), Smith not only explores the equally fundamental operation of sympathy, but devotes considerable attention to demonstrating its existence and character. For Smith, that people sympathise is less obvious than that they exchange; the process thus demands considerable explanation. Smith opens with a similar statement about human nature: 'How selfish soever man may be supposed, there are evidently some principles in his nature, which interest him in the fortune of others, and render their happiness necessary to him, though he derives nothing from it except the pleasure of seeing it'.[4] Unlike exchange, however, the evidence for this process demands continual attention throughout the text.

Literary critics have described the fledging eighteenth-century novel as similarly concerned with an inquiry into the prevalence of sympathy, and have thus often turned to Smith's *Theory of Moral Sentiments* (*TMS*) to illuminate the novelistic project of the cultivation of private sentiment.[5] Inevitably, these discussions have been informed by Smith's economic writing: that one of the first political economists began his career analysing feelings rather than profits has persistently raised interesting questions about the relationship between sympathy and exchange in the novel. Some critics have seen the projects of *The Wealth of Nations* (*WN*) and *TMS* as separate and even contradictory: while one treatise argues for compassion, the other justifies exploitation. Steward Justman has proposed that *TMS* provides a counterbalance to *WN*;[6] alternatively, Jonas Barish has suspected that *TMS* presents the emotional structures that will keep the exploitation of capitalism in place.[7] Sceptical of the recent attraction to Smith for the study of the novel, James Chandler argues that Smith's *TMS* stabilises and reinforces the hierarchies of a commodity culture through its central observation of the tendency to sympathise up. In this essay, however, I shall suggest that the relationship between these two works comes into better focus when we look closely at the evidence on which Smith's theory of sympathy rests. In exploring Smith's considerable influence on the novel, critics have shown how fiction developed fresh ways of recording and validating private feelings. Yet, if we look not just at how Smith shaped the literary scene but how the literary scene shaped *Smith*, we shall see that the emotions he describes commonly take place in public rather than private. To best understand Smith's own analysis of sympathy, we will need to turn from the novel to another literary genre, for most of what Smith comes to know about human feelings he learned from the theatre.[8]

2 The theatre of feeling

In the opening of *TMS*, Smith explains the mechanics of sympathy by appealing to a dramatic public scene: viewing 'our brother on the rack'. We do not experience our brother's pain, but we imagine what it would be like to be in his position; 'we enter as it were into his body' (12) and endure emotional distress, the intensity of which depending on 'the vivacity or dullness of the conception'. We know people sympathise, Smith suggests, by 'many obvious observations'. These observations come from visceral experience: when we see a stroke about to fall on the arm or leg of another person, we shrink back or draw in our own limbs; we twist our bodies to balance them when watching a rope-dancer. Particularly delicate people feel itchy and uneasy when looking at the sores and ulcers of others. Even strong men can experience this unease in vulnerable body parts, such as their eyes. In seeking persuasive support for his opening claim about the human propensity to sympathise, Smith looks to immediate and observable bodily responses. The involuntary examples open the explanation because they suggest an unreflective response to the perceived feelings of others that can be observed, in public, by a third party.

When Smith moves away from 'pain or sorrow' to the more conscious feelings of 'pity and compassion', however, he turns from casual observation of unselfconscious bodies in public to the more organised form of public gazing in the theatre:

> Whatever is the passion which arises from any object in the person principally concerned, an analogous emotion springs up, at the thought of his situation in the breast of every attentive spectator. Our joy for the deliverance of those heroes of tragedy or romance who interest us, is as sincere as our grief for their distress, and our fellow feeling with their misery is not more real than that with their happiness. (13)[9]

Smith has moved through three categories of example in his opening explanation: (1) first, the brother on the rack, which is vivid but unlikely to be experienced by his readers; (2) visceral unpleasant examples from quotidian experiences observable in public that would persuade readers of their own involuntary tendency to sympathise; and (3) perhaps the payoff of sympathy that involves more complex experiences. For the third category, Smith turns to the theatre, a move crucial to Smith's presentation of sympathy inspired by public experience.

Smith does not distinguish between sympathy generated by the axe approaching the limb, the brother on the rack, the balancing rope-dancer, and the hero of the tragedy, except in terms of emotional range, which is richer in the last example. He moves seamlessly from life experience to theatrical representations, a move worth pausing to consider given that most discussions of literary sympathy focus on the private experience of the novel. In a particularly resonant study, Catherine Gallagher has argued that reading novels functioned as a sanctioned form of emotional practice for women: that is, they learned to grant and withhold sympathy through fictional characters, a skill that would serve them well in a marriage market in which they could only respond to the desires of others.[10] Smith, like the advocates of novel-reading, also believes that literature cultivates sympathy, but for him this sentimental education takes place at the theatre. Further, sympathy felt in the theatre is not practice, but sympathy's full realisation. Smith envisions audience members sympathising with characters that are not the disembodied figures from fiction, but also not the same as the body of a brother on the rack (or the body on stage). In sympathising at the theatre, we place ourselves in circumstances that demand imagination, but the imagined circumstance emerges from collaboration between writers, actors, scene painters, costumers, and various artisans. This is not a substitute or lesser version of sympathy, but for Smith, it seems, a richer version than those experienced by the observation of unselfconscious people watching an axe approach a limb. Sympathy, we recall, for Smith does not require that its object feel what the sympathiser is feeling. We can be embarrassed for someone who does not feel any shame (15). We can also sympathise with the dead, who feel nothing, and with the mad, who lack the rationality to lament their state (16). The sympathy generated by the performance of a tragedy, then, is not an imitation of sympathy or practice for sympathy, but its full fruition and, for Smith, the best evidence of its importance.

Smith's vision of commercial society is itself, as David Marshall has shown, fundamentally theatrical.[11] Smith depicts a world in which all actions and expressions take place in front of an audience: the 'impartial spectator'. Smith, he argues, 'is concerned with the inherent theatricality of both presenting a character before the eyes of the world and acting as a beholder to people who perform acts of solitude'. Jonas Barish argues that this theatricality reveals a weakness in the argument, oscillating between positing an actual spectating crowd that needs to be pleased and a theoretical 'impartial spectator' with more perfect judgement.[12] Marshall, however, finds in this oscillation an expression of vulnerability on the part of the author. The impartial spectator with impeccable judgement offers the best hope for comfort against the persistent threat of being beheld by an unsympathetic gaze, a predicament in which actors continually find themselves. Thus we cling to the impartial spectator, in Marshall's reading, because sympathy in Smith, unlike in Hume or Hutcheson, only comes to us under certain circumstances. As Marshall observes, the motives for accumulating wealth in Smith can be explained by the terrifying spectre of public exposure without sympathy suffered by the poor: 'nothing', Smith writes, 'is so mortifying as to be obliged to expose our distress to the view of the public, and to feel, that though our situation is open to the eyes of all mankind, no mortal conceives for us the half of what we suffer'.[13] This fear explains the otherwise mysterious motive behind seeking riches so far beyond what a person can actually manage to consume or enjoy.

But as we have seen, it is not clear that for Smith sympathy can be withheld. In the opening example demonstrating the human propensity to sympathise, Smith cites a combination of voluntary and involuntary acts. Pulling in one's arms when observing a stroke about to descend on the arm of another involves no reflection, nor does physical discomfort prompted by looking at sores on another's body. Yet at the same time, as Marshall notes, Smith explains that we fear poverty for the risk of falling outside of the circle of sympathy. Smith also explains that excessive complaint can diminish sympathy, although in this case it might just be that no one else's sympathy can match that of the sufferer. Smith thus distinguishes between kinds of sympathy on a spectrum that ranges from simple, visceral forms to more sophisticated kinds that can in fact be granted or withheld. These different degrees of sophistication in the practice of sympathy, as we shall see, find a parallel in different kinds of theatrical performance.

Yet while both Barish and Marshall observe the profound *theatricality* of Smith's vision of human experience, they both, oddly, overlook the importance of the *theatre*. In Smith's presentation of the three examples that demonstrate the tendency to sympathise, the spectator's feelings for the hero in the tragedy offer the most conscious and complex. Those are the kind that Smith most wants to cultivate. When watching the hero, we do not simply cringe or draw back, but feel grief for his distress and joy for his deliverance. But that's not all: we also feel gratitude toward his loyal friends and resentment against those who injured him. This is a more complicated experience than cringing as a stroke approaches another's limb, not just for the multiplicity of feelings associated with the sympathy for the hero, but for the intellectual effort demanded by the production in sorting out of the nuances regarding which characters deserve which feelings, and in what proportions, in the kinds of complicated plays to which *TMS* regularly refers. Before you sympathise with the hero, you have to figure out who he is and what various claims to heroism the production offers. Further, a collaboration of artists with a sophisticated sense of how sympathy operates has already figured this out and has manipulated it for your entertainment and edification. Thus sympathy can, but does not necessarily, become a form of cultural or literary criticism.

Theatre potentially offers the richest forms of sympathy in Smith; some of the simpler experiences of sympathy, however, have thespian origins as well. Before turning to tragedy, Smith, as noted, points out that spectators watching a dancer on a slack rope twist in sympathy with his peril. This example resembles the stroke that threatens another's arm in the way it generates a visceral reaction; spectators move their bodies in an unconscious way without recognising that their contortions will, of course, not be able to help the dancer. This example, however, nevertheless differs from the threatened limb in that it describes a consciously contrived piece of theatre rather than a spontaneous event. Rope-dancing was a popular commercial form of entertainment in which the possibility of the dancer's loss of balance and subsequent inquiry created part of the entertainment. Surely the best rope-dancers became adept at frightening their audiences by appearing to be about to fall and then recovering their balance. But while the example of the rope-dancer implies that entertainers had long understood the emotional dynamics that Smith codifies, Smith here also distinguishes between *kinds* of sympathy in terms of levels of refinement that would have been apparent to eighteenth-century readers. Rope-dancing became the go-to example in eighteenth-century periodicals for the corruption of the stage. Most notably, Joseph Addison and Richard Steele, who influenced Smith considerably,[14] compare rope-dancing as a senseless form of entertainment to tragedy as the more sophisticated one.[15] In Swift's Lilliput, courtiers who want to gain favour must dance on a rope before the king. The lowest point for rope-dancing might have been in 1766 when the Haymarket Theatre created a stir with a rope-dancing monkey, whose act provided the opportunity to satirise the London theatre world in *A Letter from the Rope-Dancing Monkey in the Hay-market, to the Acting Monkey of Drury Lane.*[16] Satirists distinguish here between rational propriety and sensational exploitation, and Smith draws on this cultural hierarchy when choosing his examples. Finally, even the opening example of the brother on the rack probably owes a debt to the theatre. While eighteenth-century Britons certainly engaged in inhumane punishments, probably the only place that most people would have seen a rack of the kind used for torture would have been on stage in a tragedy. Our brother on the rack, then, is probably not really our brother and not really on the rack, but rather an actor on a prop.

Having established the human propensity to sympathise through three different examples from the stage, Smith considers which performances attract the strongest feelings of sympathy. Theatre provides the answer here as well. Sympathy itself in Smith, as Alexander Broadie argues and as the example of the vulnerable limb suggests, is initially a mechanical process,[17] involuntary and brief: 'Mankind, though naturally sympathetic, never conceive, for what has befallen another, that degree of passion which naturally animates the person principally concerned. That imaginary change of situation, upon which their sympathy is founded, is but momentary' (27). Anyone seeking consolation must figure out how to sustain this attention. Smith proposes that the best way to attract the desired 'concord of affection' would be to flatten the actual feeling so as not to alienate the sensitive spectator with a short attention span and no natural desire to feel your pain beyond the involuntary initial spasm (27); we are 'disgusted with that clamorous grief, which, without any delicacy, calls upon our compassion with sighs and tears and importunate lamentation' (29). Sympathy for pain is real, but brief and limited. Here is the evidence: 'The loss of a leg may generally be regarded as a more real calamity than the loss of a mistress. It would be a ridiculous tragedy, however, if which the catastrophe was to turn upon a loss of that kind' (35–6). Greek tragedy offers a possible counter-example: in *Philoctetes*, the title character cries out in constant pain; Hercules and Hippolytus also suffer in Greek tragedy. Smith explains, however, that the impact of these tragedies emerges not from the actual presumed physical suffering of the heroes, but for the solitude of Philoctetes, and the impending doom of Hercules and Hippolytus.

Similarly, we cannot sympathise with a friend in love because, not being in love with the same object, we will always feel the beloved to be overvalued (38). Yet in some tragedies and romances, 'this passion appears so wonderfully interesting'. But as Smith explains, the story of two people in love with no impediments to their happiness would make a terrible play. In tragedy, love needs to be improper not to advocate impropriety, but because the audience will foresee the 'dangers and difficulties' of that love. Thus, women make particularly interesting heroines in these kinds of tragedies because the laws of society demand greater reserve from them. This explains how we can be 'charmed' with the love of Phaedra in Racine's play – not from her guilty passion, but the 'secondary passions' of her 'fear, her shame, her remorse, her horror, her despair' (40). While Otway's *The Orphan* confirms the impossibility of sympathising with the emotion of love but the propensity nevertheless to sympathise with distress over obstacles in its way, *Othello* demonstrates that

> Mankind, at the same time, have a very strong sense of the injuries that are done to another. The villain, in a tragedy or romance, is as much the object of our indignation, as the hero is that of our sympathy and affection. We detest Iago as much as we esteem Othello; and delight as much in the punishment of the one, as we are grieved at the distress of the other. (42)

Smith's crucial argument for the need to restrain emotion finds its best evidence at the theatre, both through heroic suffering on stage and the demand to control one's own emotions as part of the audience:

> It is agreeable to sympathise with joy; and wherever envy does not oppose it, our heart abandons itself with satisfaction to the highest

transports of delightful sentiment. But it is painful to go along with grief, and we always enter into it with reluctance. When we attend to the representation of a tragedy, we struggle against that sympathetic sorrow which the entertainment inspires as long as we can, and we give way to it at last only when we can no longer avoid it: we even then endeavor to cover our concern from the company. If we shed any tears, we carefully conceal them, and are afraid, lest the spectators, not entering into this excessive tenderness, should regard it as effeminacy and weakness. (56)

A reader would have no need to hide her tears when indulging in a novel in private; it is only public experiences of sympathy that cultivate this crucial restraint while demanding complex moral judgements. *The Orphan*, as well as *Oedipus* and Thomas Southerne's *The Fatal Marriage*, demonstrate that 'the distress which an innocent person feels, who, by some accident, has been led to do something which if it had been done without knowledge and design, would have justly exposed him to the deepest reproach' (126). Racine and Voltaire, among others, 'best paint the refinements of delicacies of love and friendship, and of all other private and domestic affections'. Voltaire's *Tragedy of Mahomet* supports Smith's claim that 'it may sometimes happen, that with the most serious and earnest desire of acting so as to deserve approbation, we may mistake the proper rules of conduct, and thus be misled by that very principle which ought to direct us' (205). Voltaire's plays show us 'what ought to be our sentiments for crimes which proceed from such motives' (206). Wisdom and virtue attract our favour, which is also something we know from the structure of tragedy in general but also, according to Smith, from Voltaire's *Orphan of China* in particular.

Smith seems aware that he draws his evidence for human behaviour mostly from the stage, for at one point he concedes that tragedy and romance do not always align precisely with life. In some we 'meet with many beautiful and interesting scenes, founded upon, what is called, the force of blood' (261), the natural affection that related people supposedly have for each other. This force of blood, however, only exists in these fictions, 'nowhere but in tragedies and romances' (261). Yet, even though Smith acknowledges here a distinction between tragedy and life, he nevertheless qualifies this observation in a way that retains the authority of theatre:

Even in tragedies and romances, it is never supposed to take place between any relations, but those who are naturally bred up in the same house; between parents and children, between brothers and sisters. To imagine any such mysterious affection between cousins, or even between aunts or uncles, and nephews or nieces, would be too ridiculous. (261)

Eighteenth-century drama reveals some consistency with Smith's sense of the 'force of blood'. In Richard Steele's *The Conscious Lovers* (1722), which the author promoted as a new sentimental kind of comedy, a father and daughter reunite in the final scene through the accidental recognition of a bracelet. Before that moment, there is no 'force of blood'.

Theatre then becomes for Smith a stable source of authority and evidence for emotions, tendencies, and behaviour, both for the moral complexities it presents and the public visibility of one's own emotions to others. He only mentions the novel briefly. We cannot account for this through any limits on Smith's scope of reading. His *Lectures on Rhetoric and Belles Lettres* show his broad familiarity with literary genres and suggest the particularity of theatre in relation to other arts.[18] We learn from these lecture notes that for Smith literary genres belong to distinct stages of cultural development. All cultures, Smith argues, produce beautiful poetry; poetry is cultivated in 'the most Rude and Barbarous nations, often to a considerable perfection' (137). Every culture has the need for leisure and diversion, and all indulge in singing, dancing, and verse. Prose, however, has only developed in commercial societies: 'No one ever made a Bargain in verse' (137). The development of prose also demands greater time and leisure than 'Savage' nations have available. Thus, while the *Lectures* say little about drama, they reveal Smith's understanding of particular literary genres as products of particular economic systems or historical stages. But if poetry emerges in all cultures as a form of entertainment and prose emerges as the necessary product of commerce, then what remains for drama? The answer, I want to suggest, is that theatre spans both forms of economic production (traditional and commercial); these two phases of history, however, have produced different kinds of theatrical productions and thus different kinds of emotional circulation.

3 Tragedy and commerce

Smith, James Chandler argues, aestheticises the inequalities of a commercial society, beginning with the key observation that in *TMS* 'we sympathise more readily with those better off than ourselves' (561).

This tendency to sympathise 'up' has attracted much attention in readings of Smith; less attention, however, has been paid to its foundational evidence in tragedy, which is where Smith turns to explain this key argument:

> It is the misfortunes of Kings only which afford the proper subject for tragedy. They resemble, in this respect, the misfortunes of lovers. Those two situations are the chief which interest us upon the theatre; because, in spite of all that reason and experience can tell us to the contrary, the prejudices of the imagination attach to these two states a happiness superior to any other. To disturb, or to put an end to such perfect enjoyment, seems to be the most atrocious of all injuries. The traitor who conspires against the life of his monarch, is thought a greater monster than any other murderer. All the innocent blood that was shed in the civil wars, provoked less indignation that the death of Charles I. A stranger to human nature, who saw the indifference of men about the misery of their inferiors, and the regret and indignation which they feel for the misfortunes and sufferings of those above them, would be apt to imagine, that pain must be more agonizing, and the conclusions of death more terrible to persons of higher rank, than to those of meaner stations. (63)

Chandler's astute observation of Smith's aesthetic point of reference comes through in this passage as well: the death of a king and lovers facing obstacles make compelling tragedies. What complicates this issue, however, is Smith's perspective on this harmony. Presumably, Smith believes death comes to every one of every rank with equal terror; thus, he criticises the tendency to believe that those of higher rank suffer more. Smith is clearly also critical of the way so much 'innocent blood' has been overlooked because of the fascination with the death of the king in the civil wars. Thus, we can see in this passage some tension between what tragedy teaches us and moral sentiments.

Smith briefly takes up the practice of featuring kings in tragedy in the *Lectures* as well, but in a way that is even more clearly critical:

> Kings and Nobles are what make the best characters in a Tragedy. The misfortunes of the great as they happen less frequently affect us more. There is in human Nature a Servility which inclines us to adore our Superiors and an inhumanity which disposes us to contempt and trample under foot our inferiors. We are too much accustomed to the

misfortunes of people below or equall with ourselves to be greatly affected by them.

(Lecture 21, p. 124)

Rather than advocating hierarchy as a natural order and thus aesthetically pleasing as presented on stage, Smith explains that kings work best in tragedy because of the flaw of 'servility' and the 'inhuman' disposition to trample inferiors under foot. Thus, on the one hand, Smith assumes throughout that theatre reveals the truth about human sentiments, and some of those observations are more flattering than others. On the other hand, Smith consistently admires the stage, and even proposes in *WN* that the state should encourage theatre to mitigate the alienation of those in 'low condition' and lessen the temptations of religious fanaticism.[19]

This apparent discrepancy can only be solved by thinking about Smith's understanding of theatre as, like society itself, historically evolving. This is revealed by the mismatch between Smith's discussions of drama in general, which tend to define the genres in highly traditional ways, and the plays that he discusses with admiration. While it is true that the misfortunes of a king provide the traditional structure of tragedy, most of the plays that Smith cites as evidence for his theory of moral sentiments do not follow this pattern. Certainly, *Oedipus* follows the misfortunes of a king, but *Othello* does not. When we 'esteem' Othello, we cannot be simply identifying 'up', given Othello's complicated position. Audiences admire him not for his rank, but for his eloquence and his accomplishments. He is neither royal nor noble. Not all of the other characters in the play look up to Othello: some clearly look down on him and others certainly look at him askance, especially when he aspires to the hand of Desdemona. David Marshall puzzles over the 'almost total absence of women from the world of *The Theory of Moral Sentiments*' in spite of having been written 'in an age that closely associated both sympathy and sentiment with "feminine" sensibilities'.[20] And yet if we look at *theatre* as well as theatricality, we can observe that the more recent plays that Smith uses to explain sympathy place vulnerable women rather than monarchs at the centre of tragic action. Smith turns to Thomas Southerne's *The Fatal Marriage; or, The Innocent Adultery,* in which Isabella marries Villeroy, believing that her husband has been killed in battle, for evidence of the way humans sympathise. In the play Isabella's original husband Biron, to the surprise of the other characters, returns alive – an event that precipitates the tragedy. The play was immensely popular. Elizabeth Barry played the original Isabella; in the mid-eighteenth century, David Garrick adapted the play in a way that drew even more attention to the heroine, retitling it *Isabella; or, The Fatal Marriage*. Isabella became a signature role for the great Sarah Siddons, who heightened the pathos of the play by casting her own young son in the role of Isabella's son, the care and protection of whom becomes the motive for this second, unknowingly adulterous marriage. Thomas Otway's *The Orphan* features a similar 'innocent adultery': here Monimia, secretly married to one brother, gets tricked into sex with the other. Both of these plays encourage sympathy for a woman regarding her unwitting sexual missteps rather than any kind of loss of political power. While Monimia in Otway's play bears some responsibility, since she enters into a secret marriage, Isabella remains a paragon of innocent virtue torn between her loyalty to her (believed to be dead) husband and the need to protect her son.

So how does Smith reconcile this difference between his own definition of the 'proper subject of tragedy' and the tragedies that he describes as particularly compelling but that do not fit the formulation? While it would be possible to write this off as a simple inconsistency, I think there might be a more interesting answer: Smith offers his theory of upward identification not, as Chandler assumes, as a complacent view of human nature that demonstrates the effectiveness and appeal of a commercial market society through our constant tendency to want what others have when they have more, but as historically formulated critique. Smith did not see cultures as static, but rather defined by different stages shaped by different economic practices. The impulse to sympathise 'up' belongs for Smith to an earlier, less enlightened moment defined by classical rather than modern tragedy. Sympathy for the great in Smith follows from 'those delusive colours in which the imagination is apt to paint' their condition. They are never what we think they are. The passage discussing this point becomes increasingly ironic, and is worth quoting at length. We admire the great and feel

a particular sympathy with the satisfaction of those who are in it. We favour all their inclinations, and forward all their wishes. What pity, we think that any thing should spoil and corrupt so agreeable a situation! We could even wish them immortal; and it seems hard to us, that death should at last put an end to such perfect enjoyment. It is cruel, we think in Nature to compel them from their exalted stations to that humble, but hospitable home...Great King, live for ever! is the compliment, which, after the manner of eastern adulation, we should readily make them, if experience did not teach us its absurdity. (63)

Attachment to monarchs and the related default tendency to sympathise up emerge here as a superstitious weakness. While this is an admittedly subtle argument in Smith – or perhaps more of an implication than an argument – he nevertheless presents the apparent fact that 'all the innocent blood' shed in the civil wars provoking less indignation than the death of the king as a kind of vulnerability related to the 'eastern' irrational adulation of a monarch rather than, by implication, a presumably more 'western' democratic spread of sympathy. It is worth noting that, in addition to admiring she-tragedies, which demand our sympathy for vulnerable and abused women,[21] Smith also holds up Samuel Richardson, in one of his very few references to a novel, as an expert in moral sentiments. Richardson, I believe, makes the grade for similar reason to the authors of the she-tragedies: his most prominent novel tells the story of a virtuous woman who is raped by an aristocratic man who keeps her prisoner in a brothel. Clarissa refuses his later offer of marriage, stops eating, and eventually dies. One of Lovelace's arrogant mistakes, we might say, was his assumption that everyone, including ultimately Clarissa, would sympathise 'up', and that his status would earn him forgiveness. The politics of this novel have generated a rich discussion and the narrative itself offers many different points of entry; nevertheless, at the more immediate level the narrative clearly demands sympathy with the vulnerable, non-aristocratic woman before the titled male, a plot indebted to she-tragedies.

Smith associates the Stuarts with this misguided and outdated mode of sympathy that has been surpassed by modern tragedies like *The Orphan* and *The Fatal Marriage*. Because the people 'cannot stand the mortification of their monarch', compassion takes the place of resentment; past provocations are forgotten and 'they run to re-establish the ruined authority of their old masters, with the same violence with which they had opposed it. The death of Charles I brought the restoration of the royal family. Compassion for James II almost prevented the Glorious Revolution' (*TMS:* 65). The unreflective compassion for the Stuarts corrupted a whole generation under Charles II, when 'licentiousness' became connected with 'generosity, sincerity, magnanimity, loyalty', and regularity of conduct became 'altogether unfashionable'. To 'superficial minds', Smith warns, 'the vices of the great seem at all times agreeable' and the 'virtues of the inferior ranks of people' seem 'mean and disagreeable' (*TMS:* 235). In the case of Charles II, then, upward identification ruined the virtue of a generation. Some of the tragedies written soon after, however, point to ways that sympathy needs to operate in many different directions.

4 Conclusion: *The London Merchant* – Sympathy and its failures

Throughout, I have discussed how Adam Smith turned to the theatre for evidence of how human feeling operated, and how some neglected passages about theatre can help us better understand *TMS*. In conclusion, I want to turn this question around, and very briefly suggest how *TMS*, in turn, can then help us understand eighteenth-century drama by showing the importance of Smith's implied distinction between tragedies that belong to an earlier generation and more recent ones that demonstrate the significance of sympathising in multiple directions. Extensive critical discussions about how theories of sympathy shaped the eighteenth-century novel have overshadowed its earlier significance to the stage. While Richard Steele characterised his own *Conscious Lovers* (1722) as a breakthrough in drama as a reformed, sentimental comedy, tragedy had long since moved away from or complicated the classical model lamenting the death of a king.[22] As we can no longer think about *TMS* without thinking about Smith's theory of political economy, it seems appropriate to turn to a play known for its vigorous defence of commerce: George Lillo's *The London Merchant* (1731). I make no claim here that Smith was familiar with this play and am not aware of any writing in which he mentions this play. Nevertheless, it was one of the most popular tragedies in the eighteenth century and shares Smith's dual interest in moral sentiments and political economy. *The London Merchant* is also significant for its author's claim to initiate a new kind of theatre – in this case, in the play's turn from 'Kings and nobles' to the tribulations of a humble apprentice.

The London Merchant tells the story of an apprentice, George Barnwell, who is seduced by a prostitute named Millwood. He resolves to break away from her after the seduction, but is continually drawn back through her deceptions. First, she persuades him to steal money from his master for her, but eventually she convinces him that he must kill his uncle, who has long served as his patron, and bring her the money. The titular London merchant is Thorowgood, the master who is ready to forgive George for his initial transgressions but can no longer defend him when he murders his uncle. Thus the standard reading has been to treat the play as a fairly straightforward morality tale, although with complicated social implications.[23] Earlier critics disdained the play as overly simplistic; more recent ones, however, have discussed the negotiations of theatricality, class, labour, sexuality, and genre. Most readers, however, have reasonably assumed that Thorowgood represents an idea of the upstanding merchant – the name seems to be a dead giveaway! – and that as a prostitute Millwood represents the darker side of capitalist exchange, and that George serves as a lesson to the audience of the dangers of falling into temptation. It has also been widely observed with interest and curiosity that Lillo allows the prostitute Millwood to tell her side of the story. Some have read this as a destabilising force in the play, although others have suggested that this confession is part of the temptation that she represents. One critic has even fruitfully compared her language to that of Milton's Satan, suggesting that Lillo has her draw in audiences to experience the temptations of George for themselves.[24]

I would like to suggest, however, an alternative way of reading this play that may better account for its popularity and that Smith can help us see. *The London Merchant* demonstrates that Smith was right to see theatre as already grappling with the ways that commercial society renegotiates affective relationships. Like the rope-dancer, theatre managers learn from immediate feedback. As Jean Marsden and Lisa Freeman have in different ways shown, tragedy in particular reveals national political obsessions in the eighteenth century.[25] While these critics have shown the way tragedy in this period expresses new relations of class and gender, I would like to turn here to its negotiations of commerce and sympathy, in Smith's sense of the term. The play's significance as a tragedy is not just that it replaces the king with an apprentice, as the author himself announces in the prologue, but its representation of a series of events that happen beyond the control of the characters. It is ultimately less a morality tale than a tragedy about a failure of sympathy in commercial modernity.

It will be difficult to claim that the titular merchant Thorowgood is anything but thoroughly good, and yet that is what I am going to try to do. He is, of course, good in the sense that he uses his position to defend his country, he is willing to forgive George for his initial transgression, and he wants his daughter to follow her heart in her marriage choice. At the same time, like those who weep over Charles I but can't see the rest of the devastation from the wars, Thorowgood can only sympathise up.[26] His daughter rejects the titled gentlemen courting her because she loves her father's apprentice, which escapes his notice in spite of living with both of them. Obliviousness is not an act of will, of course, but later

George gives him an explicit opportunity to sympathise that he refuses. When George first falls for Millwood's charms, he attempts to confess to Thorowgood the reason for his overnight absence. Thorowgood immediately forgives him, which has been taken as more evidence of the master's generous virtue, rendering the apprentice's misdeeds all the more poignant. But George begs him again to hear his 'confession'. This is a crucial moment in the play, for here the tragic outcome could have been avoided. Sex with Millwood need not lead to murder. Thorowgood assumes the sexual nature of George's transgression and forgives him because sex, while a form of disobedience in George's situation, is nevertheless not a fatal indulgence for a young man. George, however, is not looking for forgiveness but for *sympathy*: he wants his master to momentarily see the world as he does. Because Thorowgood lacks this crucial capacity, he misses what George wants, even when George declares it unambiguously: 'Hear me, then, on my knees confess' (II. vi. 34), he begs. Had the master allowed the apprentice to tell his story, he would have been able to see how Millwood was manipulating George and prevent further mischief. Had he been able to sympathise down, Thorowgood would have listened to George and figured out Millwood's plot, which George lacks the experience to understand.

The reason that sympathising would have prevented the tragedy is because Millwood knows that she cannot tempt George to return through the promise of more sex. After the initial seduction, George vows to avoid Millwood forever. She returns, however, with a story that her cruel guardian discovered their tryst. Previously, the cruel guardian has been demanding marriage, but she had managed to keep him at bay. Now, however, this (fictional) guardian demands illicit sex because of his discovery of her night with George; he will otherwise leave her impoverished. Thus she sets up for George a genuine ethical dilemma. He can rescue Millwood by stealing money from his master, which violates his duty to Thorowgood. But to turn off Millwood at this point also seems wrong to George, given the (false) information that his night with her has ruined her prospects. George instinctively sympathises with Millwood, as Smith would predict; he is impressed with her beauty, her clothes, and her expensive lifestyle. Millwood need not actually experience the feelings which George attributes to her (distress, fear) in order for *George* to experience them in this act of sympathy. George knows that stealing from Thorowgood would be wrong, but he cannot sympathise with his master because the master has shut down the avenues for an exchange of feelings. Millwood, however, has the greater success here. She sympathises in turn enough with George to recognise that sex will not tempt him to steal on her behalf. In both directions, we see a Smithian kind of sympathy that does not require compassion; it only requires the sympathiser to imagine herself in the position of the other. It remains essentially theatrical on one side, since George sympathises with Millwood's performance, and on the other side strategic, since Millwood, unlike Thorowgood, takes the trouble to figure out what makes George tick. Both count as sympathy for Smith, for in his view we can sympathise with the dead, where there is no chance of the return of feelings.

Millwood has a significant advantage over the other characters because she is not blinded by the tendency only to sympathise up. She succeeds in spite of her precarious position by sympathising with George and even with Thorowgood. Her capacity to free herself from the limiting upward tendency of sympathy is displayed in a remarkable speech in which she suggests that all social rank is simply conventional (IV. xviii. 25–35). Thorowgood, by contrast, cannot understand George's predicament and cannot even see the heartbreak of his own daughter. His daughter and his other apprentice know, however, that he would only be able to detect a problem if the books do not balance, and so they scramble to prevent this from happening. George, unfortunately, only sympathises upward as well, following Thorowgood's directive to keep his problems to himself. Even looking upward, he does not sympathise particularly well. Had he been aware of Maria's affection, he would never have been tempted by Millwood, but he lacks the capacity to see the world through her eyes and detect what she feels. The discovery of her affection shocks him; he dared not even consider that one so much 'above' him would find him worthy. When he kills his uncle, his sympathy and awe for the uncle's greatness so overpower him that he becomes unable to rob the estate. Thus, it is no coincidence in the play that Millwood is only caught when betrayed by those immediately beneath her: the servants, whose wavering loyalty she fatally misses.

For both Smith and Lillo, these hierarchies stand in the way of productive exchange, both financial and emotional. Thorowgood loses control of his apprentice, placing his business and the life of George's uncle in danger through his inability to sympathise down. He understands what he needs to do for his monarch, but not for those in his own household. Millwood does better through the advantage of her own degraded position, but she fatally overlooks the feelings of her servants. Apparently Lucy had been growing disgusted with the plots of her mistress for quite some time. In private, she and her fellow servant Blunt discuss Millwood's plotting in disapproving terms early in the play (I. vi), a dynamic missed by the lady of the house. For both Smith and Lillo, a cosmopolitan economy of exchange depends on emotional as well as financial circulation and sophistication unimpeded by these blind spots produced by outdated hierarchies. Neither Smith nor Lillo make this point out of revolutionary idealism, but instead at least partly out of the observation that exchange can open up new forms of vulnerability that neither are able to resolve. Whatever Lillo's intentions, it is impossible to see that the playwright does not allow us, however briefly, to glimpse the predicament of those (like Millwood) exploited by the commercial system. The play also, however, shows that a clever victim of exploitation can exploit in return. Thus, we do not watch *The London Merchant* as a warning against the temptation of bad women, but instead for the less comfortable insight that the maintenance of power depends on more than the hollow statements of morality that we get from Thorowgood. Instead, it demands the capacity to sympathise down, for that is the direction from which future trouble will come.

Notes

1. Adam Smith (1997) *The Wealth of Nations*, ed. Andrew S. Skinner. 2 volumes (New York: Penguin Books), Vol. 1, p. 117. Future references are to this edition.
2. Smith, *The Wealth of Nations*, Vol. 1, p. 118.
3. Smith, *The Wealth of Nations*, Vol. 1, p. 118.
4. Adam Smith (2002) *Theory of Moral Sentiments*, ed. Knud Haakonssen (Cambridge: Cambridge University Press). Future references from this edition are cited in the text.
5. See, for example, Anne Jessie Van Sant (1993) *Eighteenth-Century Sensibility and the Novel: The Senses in Social Context* (Cambridge: Cambridge University Press); Gilliam Skinner (1999) *Sensibility and Economics in the Novel, 1740–1800: The Price of a Tear* (New York: St Martin's Press); Markman Ellis (1996) *The Politics of Sensibility: Race, Gender, and Commerce in the Sentimental Novel* (Cambridge: Cambridge University Press); Claudia L. Johnson (1995) *Equivocal Beings: Politics, Gender, and Sentimentality in the 1790s: Wollstonecraft, Radcliffe, Burney, Austen* (Chicago: University of Chicago Press).
6. Stewart Justman (1996) 'Regarding Others', *New Literary History* 27(1): 83–93.
7. Jonas A. Barish (1982) *Anti-Theatrical Prejudice* (Berkeley, CA: University of California Press); James Chandler (2010) 'The Politics of Sentiment: Notes Toward a New Account', *Studies in Romanticism* 49: 553–75.
8. Smith, of course, spent much of his life in Glasgow, which did not have a theatre until after the first edition of *Theory of Moral Sentiments* appeared. He did, however, see plays during his stay in France, and possibly also in London and in Edinburgh. Theatre was an important part of this early education, as acting out plays was part of the curriculum (Nicholas Phillipson (2010) *Adam Smith: An Enlightened Life* (New Haven, CT: Yale University

Press), pp. 18–19). Much of Smith's knowledge about drama, however, probably came from reading. There is some evidence that Smith opposed the building of a theatre in Glasgow. His eighteenth-century biographer Dugald Stewart, however, believed that he was writing a book about theatre at the time of his death.

9. Romance, of course, can also refer to the prose form as well as drama, but the emphasis here is theatrical.

10. Catherine Gallagher (1994) *Nobody's Story: The Vanishing Acts of Women Writers in the Marketplace, 1670–1820* (Berkeley, CA: University of California Press), especially Chapter 4.

11. David Marshall (1984) 'Adam Smith and the Theatricality of Moral Sentiments', *Critical Inquiry* 10(4): 592–613; see also David Marshall (1986) *The Figure of Theater: Shaftesbury, Defoe, Adam Smith, and George Eliot* (New York: Columbia University Press). On the theatricality of sympathy beyond Smith, see Elizabeth D. Samet (2003) 'Spectacular History and the Politics of Theater: Sympathetic Arts in the Shadow of the Bastille', *PMLA* 118(5): 1305–19. While Smith, as we shall see, takes the sympathy generated in the theatre very seriously, Samet notes how Mandeville, who Smith attempts to refute, in contrast saw this kind of sympathy as similar to 'an imitation spawned by imagination and enthusiasm' (1305). See also Jean-Christophe Agnew (1986) *Worlds Apart: The Market and the Theater in Anglo-American Thought, 1550–1750* (Cambridge: Cambridge University Press).

12. Barish (1981) *The Anti-Theatrical Prejudice.*

13. Quoted by Marshall, 'Adam Smith and the Theatricality of Moral Sentiments', 605.

14. Phillipson, *Adam Smith*, pp. 21–3.

15. See *The Tatler*, 12, 99, and 108.

16. London, 1767. On the monkey's performance, see George Winchester Stone, Jr (Ed.) (1960) *The London Stage, 1660–1800: A Calendar of Plays, Entertainments & Afterpieces, Together With Casts, Box-receipts and Contemporary Comments: Part 4, 1747–1776*, 1st ed. (Carbondale, IL: Southern Illinois University Press).

17. Alexander Broadie (2006) 'Sympathy and the Impartial Spectator', in Knud Haakonssen (Ed.), *The Cambridge Companion to Adam Smith* (Cambridge: Cambridge University Press), pp. 158–88.

18. In a few places, Smith comments on Shakespeare's metaphors; in lecture 21, he discusses which modern playwrights have followed the three unities, although he ultimately, like Samuel Johnson, diminishes their significance since the audience knows from start to finish that they are observing a performance rather than real life (122). With two notable exceptions (lectures 21 and 23), Smith mostly leaves out theatre in favour of prose and poetry. Adam Smith (1985) *Lectures on Rhetoric and Belles Lettres*, ed. J. C. Bryce (Indianapolis: Liberty Fund).

19. The first remedy is an education in science and philosophy, and 'The second of those remedies is the frequency and gaiety of public diversions. The state, by encouraging, that is by giving entire liberty to all those who for their own interest would attempt without scandal or indecency, to amuse and divert the people by painting, poetry, music, dancing; by all sorts of dramatic representations and exhibitions, would easily dissipate, in the greater

part of them, that melancholy and gloomy humour which is almost always the nurse of popular superstition and enthusiasm. Public diversions have always been the objects of dread and hatred to all the fanatical promoters of those popular frenzies. The gaiety and good humour which those diversions inspire were altogether inconsistent with that temper of mind which was fittest for their purpose, or which they could best work upon. Dramatic representations, besides, frequently exposing their artifices to public ridicule, and sometimes even to public execration, were upon that account, more than all other diversions, the objects of their peculiar abhorrence'. *WN*, Vol. 2, p. 384.

20. Marshall, 'Adam Smith and the Theatricality of Moral Sentiments', 604. For Smith's presumed masculine orientation, see also Stewart Justman (1993) *The Autonomous Male of Adam Smith* (Norman, OK: University of Oklahoma Press).

21. The appeal of the she-tragedies cannot be explained simply by Smith's other traditional category of a couple in love facing some kind of block. These plays instead focus specifically on the suffering of a vulnerable woman rather than a couple in love. On this point, see Jean Marsden (1996) *Fatal Desire: Women, Sexuality, and the English stage, 1660–1720* (Ithaca, NY: Cornell University Press), chapters 3 and 5.

22. See Marsden, *Fatal Desire*, Chapter 3.

23. Lucinda Cole (1995) 'The London Merchant and the Institution of Apprenticeship', *Criticism: A Quarterly for Literature and the Arts* 37(1): 57–84; Lisa A. Freeman (1999) 'Tragic Flaws: Genre and Ideology in Lillo's *London Merchant*', *South Atlantic Quarterly* 98(3): 539–61; Lee Morrissey (1998) 'Sexuality and Consumer Culture in Eighteenth Century England: "Mutual Love from Pole to Pole" in *The London Merchant*', *Restoration and 18th Century Theatre Research* 13(1): 25–39. See also Laura Mandell (1999) *Misogynous Economies: the Business of Literature in Eighteenth-Century Britain* (Lexington, KY: University of Kentucky Press).

24. Clay Daniel (1987) 'The Fall of George Barnwell', *Restoration and Eighteenth-Century Theatre Research* 2(2): 26–37.

25. Freeman, 'Tragic Flaws'; Marsden, *Fatal Desire*.

26. At the end of the first part of *WN*, Smith actually warns against merchants, arguing that, while they have a broader understanding of society than common workers, their judgements cannot be trusted because they will not be able to see beyond their own interests.

l

Part III

Performing the Self: Communicating Feelings and Identifying Authentic Humanity

8
'Off Dropped the Sympathetic Snout': Shame, Sympathy, and Plastic Surgery at the Beginning of the Long Eighteenth Century

Emily Cock

1 Introduction

This paper explores the intersection of two facets of sympathy in the late seventeenth and early eighteenth centuries. The first is the concept of medical sympathy that posited a system of physical communication between like matter, which rose to prominence in the seventeenth century. As this idea of medical sympathy waned, the discourse of sympathy as an authentic moral sentiment was on the rise. I examine the interplay of these two discourses within medical and literary treatments of rhinoplasty, a treatment popularly associated with repairing damage to the nose caused by syphilis and its customary mercury treatment. This brought the procedure under fire for enabling the syphilitic patient to pass as healthy, thus avoiding the shame that onlookers considered rightly due to the sexual transgressor. The satirising of rhinoplasty through the story of the 'sympathetic snout' formed a means of shaming the procedure, the doctors, and the patients, and uniting the reading public into a community separate from those under attack. The association of the procedure with medical sympathy arose through the misapprehension that skin or flesh for the reconstructed nose would be taken from a different person; it was believed that unable to supersede the more authentic attachment to its original body, the graft would fail to adhere to the new one. This was the effect of medical sympathy which, as I shall discuss in relation to the poetic account given by Lady Hester Pulter, could be directly antithetical to any sympathetic feelings and desires of the doctor or the graft's donor.

145

In *De curtorum chirurgia per insitionem* (Venice, 1597), Bolognese surgeon Gaspare Tagliacozzi (1545–97) explained in detail how a skin flap from the arm could be used to reconstruct a patient's nose, lip, or ear. Despite this variety, Tagliacozzi became synonymous with the reconstruction of the nose. By far the single most frequently cited example of the popular myth around Tagliacozzi and the sympathetic snout – from which I take the phrase itself – is Samuel Butler's great comic-epic poem *Hudibras* (1662–63). Butler describes the 'learned Taliacotius', who

> ...from
> The brawny part of porter's bum,
> Cut supplemental noses which
> Would last as long as parent breech,
> But when the date of nock was out,
> Off dropped the sympathetic snout.[1]

Throughout the eighteenth century, these lines glossed almost all English references to Tagliacozzi, and served to bring rhinoplasty and the communicative effects of medical sympathy into general knowledge and ridicule.

At its base, the story of the sympathetic snout relates a failed nasal reconstruction. It thus occupies an important place in the history of plastic surgery. Yet it also represents an as yet unexplored satirical representation of sympathy's troubling intersubjective potential. In the first part of this paper, I shall outline the importance of the nose in the late seventeenth century, and the state of medical discussion around Taliacotian rhinoplasty. I shall then examine the role of sympathy in this narrative, considering the manner in which the medical and emotional discourses of sympathy are entwined in these sources. As in later surgeons's glossing of references to Tagliacozzi with *Hudibras*, medical and 'literary' treatments of rhinoplasty and sympathy were in dialogue throughout this period, and each offers interesting mediations of the discourse.

2 The significance of the nose

By the early eighteenth century, any missing nose was suspected to be the effect of venereal disease – specifically 'the pox' (syphilis), although this was often conflated with 'the clap' (gonorrhoea).[2] The pox had appeared suddenly in Europe at the end of the fifteenth century, and rapidly became endemic. While there is some debate as to the level of shame attached to the pox in its early years, by 1662 John Graunt was able to note that 'only HATED persons...have died of this too frequent malady', since as the earlier Barnabe Rich had explained, 'in poore men we use plaine dealing, and call it the Poxe, but in great personages, and a little to gilde over the loathsomeness, we must call it the Gowt, or the Sciatica'.[3] Advertisements for alternative venereal cures stressed their discretion, in addition to efficiency, in distinguishing themselves from the time-consuming and body-marking mercurial treatments; in one 1700 example, 'Dr. Rivers' promises to provide patients with 'an Effectual Cure, by a *Safe, Easy,* and *Pleasant Method,* without any Confinement from *Business,* or knowledge of their nearest *Relations,* even their very *Bedfellows'.*[4] The pox was not only a disease to avoid – it was one to hide.

Syphilis can destroy a patient's nose in several ways. Firstly, babies born with congenital syphilis can lack the nasal cartilage, resulting in a sunken bridge, or simply a hole; this is the Phantom of the Opera's problem in Gaston Leroux's 1911 novel, and the reason that his parents cast him out.[5] Both the disease itself, and the mercury treatment that was standard in the seventeenth and eighteenth centuries, caused bone and cartilage damage, while mercury's stimulation of the saliva glands could also lead to gangrene around the mouth and sinuses.[6] Many of the facial injuries reported in period sources are probably attributable to gummatous syphilis (a manifestation of tertiary syphilis), which has been recorded as taking between 1 and 46 years to develop, and is characterised by gummatous lesions of the skin or bone.[7]

Because of its association with the pox, an absent nose became a shorthand for lewdness. It was employed by William Hogarth, for example, in his depiction of Moll Hackabout's syphilitic bunter in *A Harlot's Progress* (1732), while John Dunton in *Bumography* (1707) joked that 'few that Whore have any NOSE to show'.[8] In 1760, Laurence Sterne hyperbolically decried how 'oft with dire disgrace the nose falls off, sapped by the unrelenting rage of Syphilis'.[9] So great was the mid-century demand for new noses, Sterne added, that 'could Taliacotius rise once more, he'd have as many customers as ever'.[10] Satirical texts position the syphilitic as beyond emotional sympathy, and deserving of the shame and visibility to which their injured nose exposes them; the patient's attempt to deceive onlookers, and any surgeon's assistance in this attempt, is thus even more shameful.

Despite the stigma surrounding venereal disease, its prevalence across disparate communities ensured that treatments and treatises abounded, and there was a long-running search for the best means of treating venereal patients. Tagliacozzi and physicians such as John Cotta (1575–1650) and Timothie Bright (1551–1650) advocated the development of alternatives to the highly injurious mercury treatments, and particularly recommended the use of the South American plant, guaiacum.[11] Easing the suffering of venereal patients was therefore never beyond the pale.

The *reconstruction* of the nose, however, enabled the patient to pass as healthy, with all of the moral and social advantage that provided. In a slight variation on the myth, in William Congreve's *Love for Love* (1704), Valentine avows to Mr Foresight that he should have 'Taliacotius trim the Calves of Twenty Chairmen, and make [him] Pedestals to stand erect upon, and look Matrimony in the Face'.[12] While alluding directly to the effects of syphilis on the legs, Congreve also highlights the capacity of Tagliacozzi's skills to conceal Foresight's extramarital misdemeanours so that he may pass with the respectable face of 'Matrimony'. Irony forms the joke here, since both the audience and Valentine (who is feigning madness) know that the naïve Foresight is the victim of an adulterous wife – any venereal taint he possesses would therefore be the similarly shameful result of cuckoldry.

In several texts, the failure of these noses to enable their new owners to pass in polite society pre-dates their sympathetic detachment. In these texts, such as 'A Dissertation upon Noses' (1733), contrasting skin tones render 'visible, that the Features of [the patient's] Face [are] *not Fellows*'.[13] This premise extends the humour and shame integral to the suggestion that the syphilitic's new nose would be sourced from a lower-class ass, since the pamphlet's 'Serious, Grave, Upright Spanish Don' of 'Tawny' complexion has the misfortune to receive his skin from a porter 'that had not only a very white Skin, but [which was] Cut out of those Parts that are not exposed to the Sun'.[14] The pamphlet is illustrated, and shows a very large, very white nose on a dark-skinned gentleman's face. It goes on to say that,

> to Remedy this Inconvenience for the Future, the Dr. got together a great Collection of Porters, Men of all Complexions, Black, Brown, Ruddy, Fair, Dark, Tawny, Swarthy and Pale: So that it was impossible for a Patient of the most *Out of the way Colour*, not to find a Nose to Match it.[15]

The particular attack on men of colour in this pamphlet highlights the sympathetic snout's affiliation with much broader racialised and nationalist discourses around syphilis that served to unite communities in condemnation of pocky outsiders; it was, after all, the 'Disease, with whose Name one Nation now upbraids another'.[16] This is not, however, the reason such noses fail. Despite having secured a wide assortment of noses, the doctor here is thwarted by the power of sympathy.

3 Reconstructing the nose: The medical view

Throughout this period, restoring the damaged nose was not impossible. In the fifteenth century, the Sicilian Branca family had introduced a technique for twisting a skin flap from the forehead or cheek over to the nose, and shaping it to cover the missing area. They had undoubtedly borrowed this method from India, where the operation had been performed since at least the sixth century BCE.[17] But it was Tagliacozzi who became synonymous with rhinoplasty after the publication of *De curtorum chirurgia per insitionem*. He detailed how the patient's nose, lip, or ear could be reconstructed with a skin flap taken from the patient's arm, which reduced facial scarring. Though he himself had argued that rhinoplasty would be of most use for 'martial injuries to military men', the popular and medical association of his procedure with syphilis tarred it with the shame of that condition.[18]

Medical hesitation to engage with Tagliacozzi's technology may well have been born from this problematic association, which would only increase in the 'medical marketplace' of the eighteenth century wherein, as Roy Porter notes, 'healing was practiced more as a trade than as a profession'.[19] It was thus even further subject to popular prejudices and moral concerns; rhinoplasty became a type of medical knowledge that was itself shameful. Tagliacozzi and his supporters had defended his work by stating that his detractors were jealous, rather than sympathetic to the patients' or wider community's welfare. He attacked the 'wrongheaded ... men ... who not only disapprove of *any* operation (including mine) because of the potential for pain or harm, but who also revile surgery to the point of slander'.[20] Tagliacozzi sought to cast shame upon rhinoplasty's detractors, criticising those who 'circulated fictitious rumours that bear a strong resemblance to old wives' tales and that cannot be substantiated either through reason or the senses'.[21] In contrast, he placed himself and his procedure within a community of rational, modern medical men driven by compassion for their patients.

Histories of plastic surgery currently hold that Tagliacozzi's detractors won, in that after his death, Taliacotian rhinoplasty was neglected and then quickly lost.[22] In 1710, Joseph Addison and Richard Steele warned the 'new fresh-coloured Faces' of the 'young Men of this Town' that '*the Art of making Noses is entirely lost*' and therefore 'beg[ged] them not to follow the Example of our ordinary Town Rakes, who live as if there was a Taliocotius to be met with at the Corner of every Street... [but] to regard every Town-Woman as a particular Kind of Siren, that has a Design upon their Noses'.[23] The first new cases of rhinoplasty from India were reported in England at the very end of the eighteenth century, prompting new European attempts in the early 1800s as medical men such as Dieffenbach and Joseph Carpue (1764–1846) worked to counter the shaming and ignorance around rhinoplasty that had caused its neglect.[24]

In fact, Tagliacozzi's procedure was not entirely lost. Approving remarks dot the seventeenth-century record, and in 1687 and 1696, a full English translation of Tagliacozzi's treatise on noses was printed in London, attached to the complete works of the respected Scottish surgeon, Dr Alexander Read (c. 1580–1641): *Chirurgorum Comes: or, the Whole Practice of Chirurgery. Begun by the Learned Dr Read; Continued and Completed By a Member of the College of Physicians in London.*[25] Ongoing research into surviving copies, and the book's publication and advertising, suggest that this publication was reasonably successful. Christopher Wilkinson, who is listed as the bookseller on the 1687 title page, advertised the book in *The London Gazette* twice, a venue he only used for his more substantial titles.[26] Further archival work will shed light on the extent of professional knowledge of this procedure, and why it was not practised. Here, it is sufficient to note that, while the medical knowledge persisted, the *practice* of rhinoplasty probably did disappear from seventeenth- and eighteenth-century England; all popular and most medical understandings of the procedure were restricted to the story of the sympathetic snout.

4   The sympathetic snout in medicine

Medical sympathy was used to explain everything from the travelling of a yawn, to the coordination of organs in the body, the synchronised ripening of plants, and the curing of patients at a distance from their physician. It was always a controversial doctrine, but was increasingly condemned by medical figures keen to distinguish themselves as members of a professional medical community distinct from quacks and mountebanks. Within eighteenth- and nineteenth-century physiology, Evelyn L. Forget notes, more technical language was adopted to separate scientific phenomena from these associations.[27] The principle of medical sympathy could be applied in a variety of different ways. Flemish physician Johannes Baptista van Helmont (1579–1644) wrote that a doctor might, for example, treat a patient in isolation by working on a sample of his or her blood, or cease milk production in a mother weaning her child by pouring some of it onto a fire.[28] Others, he warned, might utilise the phenomenon to less amiable effect; for example, he advised that if anyone

> Hath...with his excrements defiled the threshold of thy doore, and thou intendest to prohibit that nastinesse for the future, doe but lay a red-hot iron upon the excrement, and the immodest sloven shall, in a very short space, grow scabby on his buttocks: the fire torrifying the excrement, and by *dorsall Magnetisme* driving the acrimony of the burning, into his impudent anus.[29]

In the seventeenth century, sympathetic cures were most prominently at work in treatments for targeting a weapon that had wounded the patient. Robert Fludd's (1574–1637) *Answer to M. Foster* (1631) was an extensive defence of the doctrine in reply to William Foster's *Hoplocrisma Spongus, or A Sponge to Wipe Away the Weapon Salve* (1631). Fludd provided numerous examples of such 'weapon salve' cures, and used sympathy to explain further popular phenomena such as the belief that a corpse would bleed in the presence of his or her murderer.[30] In this pamphlet, Fludd was required to defend sympathetic medicine from allegations of unholy association. Thus, in addition to including a version of the sympathetic snout story, Fludd credited the well-respected Sir Walter Raleigh with sympathetic powers. According to Fludd, Raleigh was able to 'suddenly stop the bleeding of any person (albeit hee were farre and remote from the party) if he had a handkirchers, or some other piece of linnen dipped in some of the blood of the party sent unto him'.[31] That he did so without shame or qualm, Fludd reasoned, should be evidence enough for any rational mind that his powers owed nothing to improper forces.

Taliacotian rhinoplasty became intimately entwined with medical sympathy from a very early date. The sixteenth-century poet Elisio Calenzio provides the earliest recorded account that a graft for the new nose would be taken from another person when describing the actions of Antonie Branca, though like Tagliacozzi, Branca was actually employing an autograft.[32] Though Tagliacozzi considered that 'the skin flap can, in fact, be procured from another person's body', he wrote that in practice it would not suit, since 'the skin flap must be firmly sutured to the mutilated nose or lips until the parts coalesce' and the body immobilised.[33] 'Would two people ever consent to being bound together so intimately and for so long?' he asks; 'I certainly cannot imagine it'.[34] His work was countered, however, by more widely available medical and literary texts that stated that he had purchased his grafts from servants or slaves, therefore rendering them subject to sympathetic influence.

In England, the most influential medical account of Tagliacozzi's supposed use of others' flesh for his new noses was provided by van Helmont in *De magnetica vulnerum curatione* ('On the magnetic cure of wounds', 1621).[35] In 1649, an English translation was published with some of van Helmont's other works as *A Ternary of Paradoxes*. The translator was Walter Charleton, physician to the late Charles I, who added further examples from England's most prominent supporter of sympathetic cures, Sir Kenelm Digby (1603–65). Van Helmont provides a series of examples designed to illustrate the capacity of detached body parts to communicate with the source body through sympathy. As his *pièce de résistance*, he includes Tagliacozzi's alleged nose transplant as the 'one experiment [that], of all others, cannot but be free from all suspect of imposture, and illusion of the *Devill*':

> A certaine inhabitant of *Bruxels*, in a combat had his nose mowed off, addressed himself to *Tagliacozzus*...a famous *Chirurgeon*, living at *Bononia* [Bologna], that he might procure a new one: and when he feared the incision of his owne arme, he hired a *Porter* to admit it, out of whose arme, having first given the reward agreed upon, at length he dig'd a new nose. About 13. moneths after his returne to his owne countrey, on a suddaine the ingrafted nose grew cold, putrified, and within a few dayes, dropt off. To those of his friends, that were curious in the exploration of the cause of this unexpected misfortune, it was discovered, that the Porter expired, neer about the same punctilio of time, wherein the nose grew frigid and cadaverous. There are at *Bruxels* yet surviving, some of good repute, that were eye-witnesses of these occurrences.[36]

Certain that he has provided irrefutable evidence of the power of sympathy, he asks, 'I pray, what is there in this of Superstition? what of attent and exalted *Imagination*?'.[37] Though this was to prove a highly influential account, not all of van Helmont's readers were convinced, and even Charleton rescinded his belief in sympathetic cures four years after issuing his translation.[38]

Van Helmont's account clearly states that Tagliacozzi removed the flesh for the replacement nose from the porter's arm, rather than, as the developing popular account would have it, his backside. A 1664 edition of van Helmont's works retained this translation.[39] Similarly, Fludd provided an account of the sympathetic snout in his 1631 defence of sympathetic medicine. His rendition of the 'famous and remarkable' story stipulated that,

> There was a certaine Lord, or Nobleman of Italy, that by chance lost his nose in a fight or combate, this party was counselled by his Physicians to take one of his slaves, and make a wound in his arme, and immediately to joyne his wounded nose to the wounded arme of the slave, and to binde it fast, for a season, untill the flesh of the one was united and assimulated unto the other. The Noble Gentleman got one his slaves to consent, for a large promise of liberty and reward; the double flesh was made all one, and a collop or gobbet of flesh was cut out of the slaves arme, and fashioned like a nose unto the Lord, and so handled by the Chirurgion, that it served for a natural nose.[40]

Unfortunately for this nobleman, Fludd continues, the manumitted slave travelled to Naples, and 'fell sicke and dyed, at which instant, the Lords nose did gangrenate and rot'. Subsequently, Fludd says, the surgeon cut off the gangrened part of the nose, and constructed a new and ultimately successful nose from the patient's own arm.[41] Athanasius Kircher (1602–80) also recorded that the patient's face would be tied to the slave's wounded arm, and sufficient flesh cut out and shaped into a nose. Kircher thought this account absurd, a story 'which I should say happened in Utopia rather than . . . in Italy'.[42] Kircher was a supporter of medical sympathy, and already thought that the dominance of the sympathetic snout story threatened whatever scientific standing it might achieve.

Fludd's account of the sympathetic snout contrasted the success of an autograft with a failed allograft. Following the death of the slave, he reasons, 'neither the tall Hills of Hetruria; nor yet the high Appenine mountaines could stop the concourse and motion of these two spirits, or rather one spirit continuated in two bodies, as a line being stretched out from two extremes, of so farre a distance'.[43] After the initial nose rotted and was cut away, the Lord,

> followed the advice of the same Physician, which was to wound in like manner his owne arme, and to apply it to his wounded and mutilated nose, and to endure with patience, till all was compleate as before. He with animosity [i.e. spirit] & patience, did undergoe the brunt, and so his nose continued with him untill his death.[44]

Here, he argued, was irrefutable evidence of the agency of sympathetic communication: the authentic sympathetic bond of the body for its components would not only overcome all distances and attempts at alienation, but would also sustain such autografting over the space of the individual's own body.

5   The sympathetic snout in satire

The elaborate and disreputable associations that were attached to rhinoplasty served to discredit the procedure, and helped to dissuade sympathetic medical practitioners from seriously engaging with the grafting techniques detailed in *De curtorum chirurgia per insitionem*. In addition to unflatteringly tying sympathy to Tagliacozzi, Butler mocked it elsewhere in *Hudibras* as the trade of 'mountebanks' and 'quack[s]', and revealed his knowledge of van Helmont's work in a lurid recounting of the latter's laying of a 'red-hot spit' on an enemy's 'dung'.[45] He appears to have been the first author to specify that the graft would be taken from another person's 'bum', but may have been influenced by a Taliacotian reference in James Smith's *The Loves of Hero and Leander: A Mock Poem*, which was attached to a new edition of *Gondibert* in 1653. After swimming across the Hellespont, the prone Leander is approached by a curious watchman named Warton. While '[running] at *Leander* with his bill', Warton trips;

> He lifts up bill to cleave a rock,
> Bill fled from hands, Nose stuck in nock.
> *Leander* with a start did rise,
> And breaks his [Warton's] nose fast by his eyes.[46]

Warton's nose is then stuck in Leander's natal cleft until after Leander has sex with Hero. Then, in a moment of post-coital relaxation, 'Out flew the nose with such a thump,/That *Heroes* Father in next room,/Did leave his bed and in did come'.[47] When Warton and the other watchmen arrive to demand the nose, Hero's father has it pinned in his hat as a token of victory. Failing to wrestle it from him, the noseless man is transformed through the 'pity of the Gods' into an owl, so that his shameful flat face will never be exposed to daylight.[48] Following this transformation, Warton is said to have 'clapt his wings and flue to *Tod*', where 'Tod' is glossed as 'A famous Surgeon in his time'.[49] The most likely contender for this position is Tagliacozzi, although the abbreviation is unusual. The poem's suggestion that Warton is able to sense the location of his detached nose indicates Smith's adherence to the notion of sympathetic communication between the nose and its source body.

Later texts that included references to Tagliacozzi or rhinoplasty adopted Butler's interpretation, and even used *Hudibras* to reinterpret information provided about the procedure in earlier medical works. The satirical 'Dissertation upon Noses' (1733), written to accompany an advertisement for a sympathy cure, included the story of the Taliacotian nose as evidence of sympathy's power. The 'Dissertation' was published with two other short works in which a small dose of science is extended through droll satire: an 'it narrative' following a travelling shilling, and an exploration of the migratory patterns of birds between Earth and the moon, both of which test the attribution of agency to non-human objects by endowing them with the power of sympathy. The pamphlet is an advertisement for 'Dr. *Chamberlen*'s Famous Anodyne Necklace For Children's Teeth, FITS, *Fevers*, *Convulsions*, &c', which relied on the same principle of '*Sympathetic Influence*' as was purported to be demonstrated in the stories of donors' distant effects upon their noses.[50] The author provides van Helmont's account of the nose transplant, accompanied by Charleton's translation, in which the Latin specifies only that the nose was carved from the man's '*Carne*', which is translated as 'flesh'.[51] For the identity of this flesh, he then turns to the familiar quotation from *Hudibras*, which, he says, 'hints, that it was out of his Posteriors'.[52] The 'Dissertation's' account of Tagliacozzi is based on a *Tatler* article of 1710 concerning 'the Rise of that fatal Distemper which has always taken a particular Pleasure in venting its Spight upon the Nose'.[53] This article also took *Hudibras* as its starting point for a discussion of Tagliacozzi's method; subsequently, Addison and Steele also state that the graft was 'cut out of those Parts that are not exposed to the Sun'.[54] Ellis Veryard records seeing Tagliacozzi's statue at the University of Bologna, and credits him with

> the Secret of supplying noses, Lips, Ears, and other mutilated Members; to which purpose he has publish'd his *Chirurgia Curtorum*, where he tells us a Story of a certain Gentleman that lost his Nose in a Rancounter [sic], and had it supply'd by him with a piece of Flesh cut from another Man's Back-side, and so artificially chap'd and join'd that any one would have taken it for natural; but that the Fellow, from whom it was taken, happening to die some time after, the Gentleman's Nose rotted off by sympathy.[55]

Though aware of Tagliacozzi's original text, Veryard relies instead on Butler for his account, and follows this text with the relevant lines from *Hudibras*, as did William Bromley in 1691.[56] Thomas Salmon lifted Veryard's account almost verbatim, including the quotation from Butler, in 1731, and Charles Thompson used Butler to gloss his account of a visit to Bologna in 1752.[57] *Hudibras* continued to be a standard inclusion in *Lancet* authors' discussions of rhinoplasty throughout the nineteenth century.[58] Thus, although cited with amused scepticism, it is evident that the story of the sympathetic snout remained the key association of rhinoplasty.

Satirical representations of the sympathetic snout narrative became increasingly elaborate, balancing anxieties around the exposure of the patient's shame, the inalienability of the body, ridiculing medical sympathy, indebtedness to social inferiors, and more. The *Tatler* included a story of 'Three *Spaniards*, whose Noses were all made out of the same Piece of Brawn' – that is, the same porter's backside.[59] One day the three gentlemen felt their noses painfully 'shoot and swell extremely'; upon investigation, they found that the porter had been beaten up, and that the injuries sustained by his rump had been sympathetically transmitted to their noses.[60] The three men therefore track down the perpetrator of the attack, and deal with 'him in the same Manner as if the Indignity had been done to their own Noses'.[61] Addison and Steele conclude this episode by joking that 'it might be said, That the Porters led the Gentlemen by the Nose'.[62] Carolus Musitanus recorded another story of a man too afraid to blow his new nose, lest it fall off; his physician reassured (and surprised) him by grasping him by the nose and marching him around the room.[63] In a 1752 satire on artificial beautifiers, the purported author, Madame Roxana Termagant, hyperbolically proclaims that she has procured the services of

> a great grand-daughter of Professor TALIACOTIUS, who pares, scrapes, grinds, and new models overgrown noses, cuts off crooked or flat ones to the stumps, and ingrafts new ones on the roots of them from an Italian's snow-white posteriors, who has been fed with nothing but white bread and milk, purely for this purpose.[64]

When Voltaire translated the Tagliacozzi episode from *Hudibras*, he added his own twist to the ending. He concluded that after the man from whom the graft had been taken died, and the nose had subsequently fallen off, it would be reattached to the man's backside, and buried with him.[65] Since Voltaire does not mention any reshaping of the flesh to its original state, we can assume that he intends the grotesque image of a nose sticking out from the man's buttocks. His account might have been influenced by the *Tatler*'s discussion of *Hudibras* and Tagliacozzi, which also stated that 'it was always usual to return the Nose, in order to have it interred with its first Owner'.[66] This version of events reiterated that the flesh was still unequivocally bonded to the source body, as sympathy marked out insurmountable boundaries between human bodies. Sympathy also maintains the shaming connection with the flesh's origins because, like the Spanish noblemen, the patients are forever 'led by' their noses' 'Original Proprietor' – a man base enough to sell his own flesh.[67]

6 Competing sympathies

The sympathetic snout narrative thus stages two competing sympathies: the moral sympathy of compassionate medical and other communities, and the medical sympathy that foreclosed surgical attempts to allow the patient to escape his 'authentic' self through a rhinoplastic disguise. The two strands are brought together by the Hertfordshire noblewoman, Lady Hester Pulter (1607–78) in the poem entitled 'To Sr. W. D. Upon the unspeakable Loss of the most conspicuous and chief Ornament of his Frontispiece'. Here, Pulter offers the poet laureate Sir William Davenant (1606–68) not only emotional support, but most radically her own flesh for the reconstruction of his nose. Pulter's poem is particularly important within the sympathetic snout canon for pre-dating the overbearing influence of *Hudibras* and its mercenary servant, providing instead a unique twist on the narrative by focusing on the sympathetic sentiments of the flesh's donor.[68] This importance is qualified, however, by the fact that Pulter never published her poems. While they may have circulated in manuscript among her closer acquaintances, there is no evidence that Butler or other writers had access to or were influenced by her interpretation of rhinoplasty. In contrast to the wildly popular and influential *Hudibras*, 'To Sr. W. D.' constituted a private early reflection on the relationship of moral and medical sympathies.

Davenant had contracted the pox in the late 1620s or early 1630s (in 1633 he refers to himself as a 'long-sick Poet').[69] He was treated with the customary mercury salivation by the Queen's physician, Dr Thomas Cademan, and addressed public poems of thanks to him that conceded his receipt of 'Devill *Mercurie*', thus acknowledging the venereal nature of his distemper.[70] By the 1630s he was famously noseless.

In 'To Sir W.D.', the staunchly Royalist Pulter was primarily admonishing Davenant for what she perceived was an increasing likelihood that he would defect to serve the Parliamentarians. Here, sexual honour is tied to political honour, with the corruption in Davenant's nose at risk of spreading to his 'Fame [and] Brains', as he may 'Trample...that Honour in the Dust/In beeing a Slave to those are Slaves to Lust'.[71] After losing his nose to seduction, his next episode might take his mind: as Marcus Nevitt explains, Pulter references the episode in Ludovico Ariosto's *Orlando Furioso* where the eponymous hero is jilted by his beloved, Angelica, in favour of an African soldier, Medore.[72] Orlando loses his wits, and can only recover them after his friend Astolpho collects them from the moon, where they sit in a jar, and forces Orlando to snort them. Pulter reminds Davenant that he will have no such recourse: 'You could not then snuf up your Brain/Though all your strenght [sic] you should expose/You want the Organe cal'd a Nose'.[73]

Pulter suggests that she is 'unknown' to Davenant, but that the reports she has heard have moved her to 'extreamly...deplore [his] loss'.[74] She stresses that it is sympathy for Davenant's predicament that has moved her to act, which places her in contrast to the more usual slave or servant donors of the sympathetic snout canon, whose flesh is sold for freedom or profit. 'In pitty', she says to Davenant,

> I think noe man
> But would his Leg or Arm expose
> To cut you out another Nose
> Nor of the Female Sex thers none
> But'ld bee one flesh though not one Bone
> I though unknown would sleight the pain
> That you might have soe great a gain
> Nay Any Fool did he know itt
> Would give his Nose to have yor Wit.[75]

Pulter's hesitation to be of the same 'Bone' as Davenant may be a reference to the skeletal damage caused by syphilis, which as 'rotting shins' was almost as proverbial as the missing nose.[76]

Pulter refers to a strain of sympathetic snout mythology, appearing as early as in Calenzio's account, that stipulated that the donor would actually 'give his [own] nose' to the unfortunate patient.[77] For Pulter, this remedy presented additional problems since the donation of her own nose would leave her open to the charge that she herself had lost that member to the pox – only God, 'that Bright eye above/Would know twere Charity not Love'.[78] 'Love' is here a euphemism for sexual intercourse and venereal disease, rather than genuine affection. Pulter's compromise is that Davenant 'Excuse my Nose [and] accept my Leg' as a source for the skin graft.[79] While this may have carried some sexual connotations in itself, it is highly unlikely that there would have been a suggestion of the buttocks pre-*Hudibras*; the leg, in Pulter's logic, would have been a part of the body easily covered.

Any chance that Pulter's discussion of a skin transplant is purely fantastical, or rhetorical, can be dismissed by her immediate reference to the detrimental effects of sympathy, exactly as they had been promulgated in England by writers like Fludd. After Davenant has received her donation, she writes, he will need to pray for her continued good health, since the nose will expire when she does:

> But yet besure both night and Day
> For mee as for your Self you pray
> For if I First should chance to goe
> To visit those sad shades below
> As my Frail Flesh there putrifies
> Your Nose noe doubt will Sympathize[.][80]

Pulter emphasises the obligation established by her gift: Davenant must now pray 'For [her] as for [him] Self', as her physical safety is now in his interest. Like the Spanish noblemen who found themselves 'led by the nose' by their grafts' source, Davenant's nose will remain sympathetically attached to his benefactor's body. Pulter's object in this poem is not to address the effectiveness, morality, or success of the Taliacotian reconstruction; she is first and foremost concerned with warning Davenant that she can only provide him with a new nose once, and that if he ruins that one through similar bad behaviour (coded in Pulter's poem as both moral *and* political foolishness), he will lack 'Nose, or Fame [good reputation], or Brains'.[81] He therefore must not take her sympathetic gesture for granted.

7 Conclusion

The shaming of rhinoplasty through its association with syphilis and the sympathetic snout narrative essentially wiped skin graft technology from early modern medicine, despite its preservation in specialist texts like *Chirurgorum Comes*. Sympathy's effect on the new nose was always to thwart any gesture of good will toward the patient and to remove their disguise. By defeating the syphilitic's attempt to escape the shame of their disease, the body's sympathetic reaction appeared to authenticate their shame.

The sympathetic snout narratives of the seventeenth and eighteenth centuries literalised the competing logics of medical and affective sympathies as existing within *and/or* between individual bodies. Medical sympathy problematised the extent to which one could control one's own body, and physiologised the extent of its alienability. The apparent success of autografts and failure of allografts literalised the limits of communication between individuals; the sympathy of an individual for his or her own state trumps any gestures of sympathy toward others. Pulter did not treat rhinoplasty with the cynicism of Butler and other later writers; instead, 'To Sr. W. D.' situates her gift of flesh in a space of authentic moral sympathy for someone she considers a member of her own Royalist emotional community. In *Hudibras* and its echo texts, however, the motivation of moral sympathy has been overtaken by mercantile reward for the servant or slave who sells their flesh, with all feelings of compassion derived from the willingness of surgeons to perform the procedure – a rare commodity, as I have shown. In either case, medical sympathy is the framework by which the grafts fail, because the privileging of physical sympathy between like substances, represented as the more authentic and powerful form of sympathy, exposes the limits of interpersonal emotional sympathy.

Notes

1. Samuel Butler (1973) *Hudibras, Parts I and II and Selected Other Writings*, ed. John Wilders and Hugh de Quehen (Oxford: Clarendon Press), pp. I. i. 279–84.
2. There is significant confusion during the period as to the exact pathology of the pox, and many writers represented the pox as an advanced stage of the clap; for example, *An Herculeon Antidote against the POX* (London: 1698) frames the pox and clap within the same pathology: 'I do believe thousands of people in this City of *London*, have been brought from a Gonorrhæa to a General Pox': sig. A1^r.
3. Margaret Healy (2001) *Fictions of Disease in Early Modern England: Bodies, Plagues and Politics* (New York: Palgrave), p. 162.
4. Dr Rivers (c. 1700) [...] *for all Venereal Maladies. By Dr. Rivers, who, by this Assiduous Care and Daily Practice, hath for several Years render'd himself Famous in this City, for the cure of the Alamode-Distemper* (London), sig. A1^r; original emphasis.
5. Gaston Leroux (1911) *The Phantom of the Opera* (New York: Bobbs-Merrill), pp. 271, 344.
6. John Emsley (2005) *The Elements of Murder: A History of Poison* (Oxford: Oxford University Press), pp. 35, 39.
7. Carolyn Sutton (2006) 'Syphilis', in Anita L. Nelson and JoAnn Woodward (Eds.), *Sexually Transmitted Diseases: A Practical Guide for Primary Care* (Totowa, NJ: Humana Press), p. 216.
8. John Dunton (1707) *Bumography: or, a Touch at the Ladys Tails* (London), sig. G3^r.

9. Laurence Sterne (1760) *Yorick's Meditations Upon Various Interesting and Important Subjects* (London), p. 18.
10. Sterne, *Yorick's Meditations*, p. 18. The stigmatisation of syphilis continued to haunt plastic surgery through the nineteenth century; see further Gilman (1998) *Creating Beauty to Cure the Soul: Race and Psychology in the Shaping of Aesthetic Surgery* (Durham, NC: Duke University Press), p. 34.
11. John Cotta (1612) *A short discoverie of the unobserued dangers of severall sorts of ignorant and unconsiderate practisers of physicke in England* (London), sig. B4^v; Timothie Bright (1580) *A Treatise Wherein is Declared the Sufficiency of English Medicines* (London), sig. D4^r.
12. William Congreve (1969) *Love for Love*, ed. M. M. Kelsall (London: Benn), IV. i. 453–5.
13. 'A Dissertation upon Noses' (1733) in *A Solution of the Question, Where the Swallow, Nightingale, Woodcock, Fieldfare, Stork, Cuckow, and other Birds of Passage Go, and Reaside, when absent from us. With the Travels of a Shilling, and a Dissertation upon Noses* (London), sig. A7^v; original emphasis.
14. 'Dissertation', sig. A7^v.
15. 'Dissertation', sig. A7^v; original emphasis.
16. Member of the College of Physicians, in Alexander Read (1687) *Chirurgorum Comes: or the Whole Practice of Chirurgery* (London), sig. Yy4^r. While most of Europe referred to syphilis as *de morbo gallico* (the French disease), the French termed it the Neapolitan disease, the Dutch called it the Spanish pox, and others attributed it to the New World, or to Jews and Arabs expelled from Spain in the fifteenth century: Jon Arrizabalaga, John Henderson, and Roger French (1997) *The Great Pox: The French Disease in Renaissance Europe* (New Haven, CT: Yale University Press), pp. 6, 11–12.
17. Martha Teach Gnudi and Jerome Pierce Webster (1950) *The Life and Times of Gaspare Tagliacozzi Surgeon of Bologna 1545–1599* (New York: Herbert Reichner), p. 110; David Hamilton (2012) *A History of Organ Transplantation: Ancient Legends to Modern Practice* (Pittsburgh, PA: University of Pittsburgh Press), p. 10.
18. Gaspare Tagliacozzi (1996) *De curtorum chirurgia per insitionem*, trans. Joan H. Thomas (New York: Classics of Surgery Library), p. viii.
19. Roy Porter (1996) ' "Laying Aside Any Private Advantage": John Marten and VD', in Linda E. Merians (Ed.), *The Secret Malady: Venereal Disease in Eighteenth-Century Britain and France* (Lexington, KY: University Press of Kentucky), p. 51.
20. Tagliacozzi, *De curtorum chirurgia*, p. 102.
21. Tagliacozzi, *De curtorum chirurgia*, pp. 80–1.
22. For the standard historical view that this procedure disappeared between Tagliacozzi and the end of the eighteenth century, see, for example, Edward Zeis (1977) *The Zeis Index and History of Plastic Surgery 900BC to 1863AD* (1863–1864), trans. T. J. S. Patterson (Baltimore, MD: Williams and Wilkins), pp. 13–14; Fielding H. Garrison (1929) *An Introduction to the History of Medicine*, 4th ed. (Philadelphia, PA and London: WB Saunders), pp. 226–7; I. Eisenberg (1982) 'History of Medicine: A History of Rhinoplasty', *South African Medical Journal* 62: 289; John Symons (2001) 'A Most Hideous Object: John Davies (1796–1872) and Plastic Surgery', *Medical History* 45: 395; Stephanie Pain (2006) 'A Nose by any Other Name', *New Scientist* 191(2566):

50–1; Paulo Santoni-Rugiu and Philip J. Sykes (2007) *A History of Plastic Surgery* (Berlin: Springer), p. 195; Hamilton, *A History of Organ Transplantation*, pp. 19–20; Bryan Mendelson (2013) *In Your Face: The Hidden History of Plastic Surgery and Why Looks Matter* (Melbourne: Hardie Grant), pp. 92–107.

23. Joseph Addison and Richard Steele (1710) *Tatler*, no. 260; my emphasis.
24. Santoni-Rugiu and Sykes, *A History of Plastic Surgery*, p. 198.
25. For a thorough survey of references to Tagliacozzi and rhinoplasty in European medical texts, see Gnudi and Webster, *Life*; Zeis, *Zeis Index*.
26. *The London Gazette* issue 2012 (26 February 1684), p. 4; issue 2252 (16 June 1687) p. 4.
27. Evelyn L. Forget (2005) 'Evocations of Sympathy: Sympathetic Imagery in Eighteenth-Century Social Theory and Physiology', *History of Political Economy* 35: 283–84.
28. Johannes Baptista van Helmont (1649) *A Ternary of Paradoxes* (London), sig. C4^v.
29. van Helmont, *Ternary*, sigs. C4^v–D1^r; original emphasis.
30. van Helmont, *Ternary*, sigs. P2^{r-v}.
31. van Helmont, *Ternary*, sig. S2^r.
32. Gnudi and Webster, *Life*, pp. 282–3.
33. Tagliacozzi, *De curtorum chirurgia*, p. 75.
34. Tagliacozzi, *De curtorum chirurgia*, p. 77.
35. This was first published in Paris in 1621, then in Cologne in 1624, and within his collected works in Amsterdam in 1648 and later editions: Gnudi and Webster, *Life*, p. 288.
36. van Helmont, *Ternary*, sig. D1^r; original emphasis.
37. van Helmont, *Ternary*, sig. D1^r; original emphasis.
38. Mark A. Waddell (2003) 'The Perversion of Nature: Johannes Baptista Van Helmont, the Society of Jesus, and the Magnetic Cure of Wounds', *Canadian Journal of History* 38: 179–97; Elizabeth Hedrick (2008) 'Romancing the Salve: Sir Kenelm Digby and the powder of sympathy', *The British Journal for the History of Science* 41(2): 181.
39. *Van Helmont's Works Containing His Most Excellent Philosophy, Physick, Chirurgery, Anatomy* (1664), trans. J. C. (London), sig. Eeeee2^r.
40. Robert Fludd (1631) *An Answer to M. Foster; or, the Squeesing of Parson Foster's Sponge, Ordained by him for the Wiping away of the Weapon Salve* (London), sig. S2^v.
41. Fludd, *Answer*, sig. S2^v.
42. Gnudi and Webster, *Life*, p. 293.
43. Fludd, *Answer*, sig. S3^r.
44. Fludd, *Answer*, sigs. S2^v–S3^r.
45. Butler, *Hudibras*, I. ii. 230–40.
46. James Smith (1653) *Hero and Leander: A Mock Poem* in *Certain Verses Written By Severall of the Authours Friends; To Be Re-printed with the Second Edition of Gondibert. With* Hero *and* Leander *the mock Poem* (London), sig. C2^v; original emphasis.
47. Smith, *Hero and Leander*, sig. C7^v.
48. Smith, *Hero and Leander*, sig. D1^r.
49. Smith, *Hero and Leander*, sig. D1^v; original emphasis.
50. 'Dissertation', sig. A1^r; original emphasis.

51. van Helmont, *Ternary*, sig. A7^r.

52. 'Dissertation', sig. A7^v.

53. Addison and Steele, *Tatler*, no. 260.

54. Addison and Steele, *Tatler*, no. 260.

55. Ellis Veryard (1701) *An Account of Divers Choice Remarks, As Well Geographical, As Historical, Political, Mathematical, Physical, And Moral; Taken in a Journey Through the Low-Countries, France, Italy, and part of Spain; With the Isles of Sicily and Malta* (London), pp. 144–5; original emphasis.

56. William Bromley (1705) *Remarks on the Grand Tour of France and Italy. Perform'd by a Person of Quality, in the Year 1691* (London), pp. 88–9.

57. Thomas Salmon (1731) *Modern History: or, The Present State of all Nations* (Dublin), III. 927; Thompson, Charles (1752) *The Travels of the Late Charles Thompson, Esq; Containing His Observations on France, Italy, Turkey in Europe, the Holy Land, Arabia, Egypt, and Many Other Parts of the World* (London), I. 96.

58. See, for example, 'St Thomas's Hospital', in *The Lancet* 1(6) (1823): 204–5; Robert Liston (1835) 'Reunion of Divided Parts – Reconstruction of the Nose', in *The Lancet* 24(606): 40–3; John Houston (1844) 'A Lecture on the Modern Improvements in Surgery', *The Lancet* 44(1113): 393–400; 'Report of the Clinical Society of London', *The Lancet* 109(2806) (1877): 841–4; 'Plastic Surgery', *The Lancet* 165(4256) (1905): 806–7.

59. Addison and Steele, *Tatler*, no. 260; original emphasis.

60. Addison and Steele, *Tatler*, no. 260.

61. Addison and Steele, *Tatler*, no. 260.

62. Addison and Steele, *Tatler*, no. 260.

63. Gnudi and Webster, *Life*, p. 284.

64. 'Roxana Termagant' (1752) *Have At You All: Or, the Drury-Lane Journal* (London), sig. S2^v.

65. Voltaire (1770) *The Works of M. de Voltaire* (London), XII. 168.

66. Addison and Steele, *Tatler*, no. 260.

67. Addison and Steele, *Tatler*, no. 260.

68. The poem appears in the manuscript collection *Poems Breathed Forth by the Noble Hadassas*, apparently compiled between 1645 and 1665. Mark Robson suggests that many of the poems appear to have been written during Pulter's periods of confinement, approximately 1625 to 1648: Mark Robson, 'Pulter, Lady Hester (1595/6–1678)', ed. H. C. G. Matthew and Brian Harrison in *Oxford Dictionary of National Biography* (Oxford: Oxford University Press). Online edition ed. Lawrence Goldman. http://www.oxforddnb.com/view/article/68094, accessed 13 August 2011. 'To Sr. W. D.' can be reliably dated to after 1643, since the second line references Parliament's removal of Cheapside Cross in that year, and Marcus Nevitt dates it to after Davenant's 1652 release from the Tower of London, where he had been held for his Royalism: Marcus Nevitt (2009) 'The Insults of Defeat: Royalist Responses to Sir William Davenant's *Gondibert* (1651)', *The Seventeenth Century* 24(2): 287, 304.

69. Nevitt, 'Insults', p. 287.

70. Mary Edmond (1987) *Rare Sir William Davenant* (Manchester: Manchester University Press), pp. 45–6; original emphasis.

71. Pulter, Hester (2005) 'To Sr. W. D. Upon the Unspeakable Loss of the most Conspicuous and Chief Ornament of his Frontispiece', in Jill Seal

Millman and Gillian Wright (Eds.), *Early Modern Women's Manuscript Poetry* (Manchester: Manchester University Press), lines 44, 51–2.

72. Nevitt, 'Insults', p. 289.
73. Pulter, 'To Sr. W. D.', lines 40–2.
74. Pulter, 'To Sr. W. D.', lines 1, 9.
75. Pulter, 'To Sr. W. D.', lines 4–12.
76. See, for example, Gordon Williams (1994) *A Dictionary of Sexual Language and Imagery in Shakespearean and Stuart Literature* (Atlantic Highlands, NJ: Athlone), pp. 127–30, 857–8.
77. Calenzio refers to Branca building a new nose from the slave's arm, or taking his own nose as a replacement: '*Brauca Siculus, ingenio vir egregio, didicit nares inserere, quas vel de brachio resicit, vel de seruis mutuatas impingit*': quoted in Etienne Gourmelen (1580) *Chirurgicae artis* (Paris), p. 173.
78. Pulter, 'To Sr. W. D.', lines 17–18.
79. Pulter, 'To Sr. W. D.', line 20.
80. Pulter, 'To Sr. W. D.', lines 21–6.
81. Pulter, 'To Sr. W. D.', line 44.

9
'Acting It as She Reads': Affective Impressions in Polly Honeycombe[1]

Amelia Dale

> 'Tis Novel most beguiles the Female Heart.
> Miss reads – she melts – she sighs – Love steals upon her –
> And then – Alas, poor Girl! – good night, poor Honour!
>
> George Colman, *Polly Honeycombe* (1760)

1 Introduction: Polly Honeycombe, print and theatre

George Colman's *Polly Honeycombe* (1760) is a playful farce that satirises novel-reading in the eighteenth century by placing it on stage. Polly Honeycombe, convinced that 'A Novel is the only thing to teach a girl life', imitates novel heroines and uses their example to further her own plans and desires.[2] Her parents are determined to marry her to money, in the person of Mr Ledger, who speaks in the jargon of finance, and in Polly's words is 'more tiresome than the multiplication-table' (86). Clarissa-like, Polly exuberantly defies her parents' choice of Mr Ledger as her husband. She chooses instead the social climber Scribble, who ventriloquises the language of romance. Polly's characterisation both reflects and contradicts the stereotype of the sexually susceptible, overtly sympathetic female reader described in the play's prologue, quoted above. The prologue describes an 'affective economy', to use Sara Ahmed's words, with 'Love' circulating between the body of 'Miss' and the book she reads.[3] The female, reading body becomes malleably impressed with the passions represented in the novel, to the point that she softens in emphatically physical terms (melting and sighing) and becomes vulnerable to sexual penetration ('good night, poor Honour!') (69). This representation of a novel-driven affective economy occurs within a dramatic text, and the circulation of a novelistic 'Love' is thereby implicitly compared to the way passion might circulate in

165

the theatre. Modern scholars have commented on these interactions between the stage and the novel. For example, Ros Ballaster argues that eighteenth-century novels describe the theatre as a place where female audience members are liable to imitate the 'affective force of the tragic actress'.[4] Indeed, emotional transference is central to the way the theatre is described by eighteenth-century acting theorists. Daniel Larlham contends that, for many such theorists, 'the felt truth of theatrical performance depended not upon the interpretative comparison between onstage and offstage worlds, but upon the *mimetic experience of passion*, modelled by the actor and undergone by the spectator'.[5] The prologue, then, points to how *Polly Honeycombe* gleefully participates in these two textual forms – the novel and the theatre – which were both seen to have the affective capacity to impress the bodies of their (female) audience members and thereby induce mimetic emotional responses.

This essay will argue that *Polly Honeycombe* both illuminates and complicates current debate about eighteenth-century audiences' emotional investment with the theatre and novels. Michael McKeon insists that mixed dramatic forms could 'investigate the relationship between – through the self-conscious "mixing" of – the several overlapping realms of publicity and privacy'.[6] Relatedly, *Polly Honeycombe*, with its self-conscious dialogue between the theatre and the novel, demonstrates how public, embodied 'acting' of particular passions overlaps and intersects with 'private', sympathetic identification with characters in novels.

The farce not only destabilises the distinctions between the printed page and stage, but also suggests how the technology and the publicity of print shaped the understanding of emotions in the mid-eighteenth century. It describes the consumption of sentimental literature as entailing a mode of public 'acting' where passions are manifest as legible inscriptions on the body and on the 'self'.

2 Printed selves and the public sphere

Polly Honeycombe was one of the most popular farces of the eighteenth century.[7] An afterpiece, it was written to be only part of a night's performance and performed after a more substantial piece of work. On the night of its premiere (5 December 1760, in Drury Lane), for example, it was performed after Aaron Hill's translation and alteration of Voltaire's *Merope*.[8] The farce was a success and was performed 15 times the first season it appeared.[9] *Polly Honeycombe* also had a successful publication history. It ran into seven printed editions in its first three seasons, and later appeared in collections of Colman's *Dramatick Works* (1777, 1778).[10] Admittedly, this was not unusual for the eighteenth century; Julie Stone Peters states that even 'ordinary' plays normally ran into several editions while popular playwrights 'could generally expect to see some dozen editions of any play'.[11] Even when taking the extensive eighteenth-century consumption of printed plays into account, *Polly Honeycombe* was a notable success. Although interest in *Polly Honeycombe* has recently grown, especially after the welcome publication of the Broadview edition edited by David Brewer (2012), it remains understudied.[12]

The relationship between eighteenth-century novels and the theatre is the subject of growing critical interest. Emily Hodgson Anderson, writing about eighteenth-century female authors' connection with the theatre, notes how 'eighteenth-century writers and audiences saw more connections than divergences between the theatre and the novel'.[13] Both Brewer and Ballaster recently argue that *Polly Honeycombe* exemplifies the complex interrelationship between eighteenth-century print culture and the stage.[14] The farce's full title, designating the text as a hybrid form, a 'Dramatick Novel of One Act', suggests both oppositions and continuities between the novel and drama. During the eighteenth century, an intermingling of what we currently think of as discrete literary forms was not unusual.[15] Ballaster argues that the close ties between novel and theatre in the eighteenth century have been underestimated and that the two mediums set themselves up as rivals, 'at all levels of authorship, plot, character, and reception.'[16] *Polly Honeycombe* indeed positions the mid-eighteenth-century novel and the theatre as rivals. These competing mediums both describe the 'self' as being structured by surfaces and public performance.

This essay will suggest that insofar as the heroine of *Polly Honeycombe* has an 'authentic self', it is a 'self' produced by a layering of legible, external surfaces. Lisa Freeman argues that the conditions of eighteenth-century theatre precluded the sympathetic experience that novels can offer.[17] She claims that the theatre offered an eighteenth-century concept of character 'not as an emanation of a stable interiority, but as the unstable product of staged contests between interpretable surfaces'.[18] The eighteenth-century theatre, according to Freeman, is a 'medium obsessed not with the tensions between interiority and exteriority but with the conflicting meaning of surfaces in themselves. On the stage there was no public/private split; there was only public space and public displays.'[19] I agree with Freeman's claim for the defining exteriority of eighteenth-century theatre. However, when Freeman aligns the novel with interiority and privacy in opposition to the theatre's exteriority and publicity, she also possibly exaggerates the difference between characterisation in the theatre and the novel. By contrast, Deidre Lynch and Dror Wahrman have stressed the way character was constituted as shifting surfaces in the mid-eighteenth century.[20] Moreover, April Alliston suggests that novels which represent quixotic, mimetic readers – novels with characters like Polly – offer an '*anxiety of interiority*' not necessarily involving an 'essential core of selfhood'.[21] However, even such anxiety is absent from *Polly Honeycombe*. Instead, the farce gleefully delights in exteriority and performance. Through Polly's playful performance of sympathy, the farce suggests how, in the mid-eighteenth century, expressions of feeling are 'authentic' because they are externalised and performed in public, rather than reflective of some inner self. Here, truly feeling an emotion involves having it marked upon one's body like words upon the page.

The 'self' in *Polly Honeycombe* is therefore constructed from competing, public, impressed surfaces. During the eighteenth century, definitions and descriptions of the passions and emotions involved figurations of impressions, to describe the way a particular experience could mark a person's character and/or their body. Passions are described as impressions by both David Hume and Aaron Hill, the publisher, poet and theorist on acting. For Hume, the word 'emotions' is sometimes used to describe impressions from sensation, but they are also included with passions as 'secondary impressions': a combination of both the primary impressions from the senses (internal and external bodily sensation) and ideas.[22] Hume famously concludes that the 'self' is governed by the passions, a philosophy which means that impressions themselves become fundamental constituents of the 'self'.[23] His descriptions of affective impressions draw on the association between the word 'impression' and ink on paper.[24] Print, in short, was crucial to formulating ideas of the 'self' and conceiving affective experience in the period. As discussed in the next section, this is apparent in *Polly Honeycombe* when Polly reads aloud from a (parody of a) sentimental novel. The farce's representation of her reading aligns the body of the emoting reader with the actor's body, and both the actor and the reader are 'impressed' by the words on the page. By way of conclusion, this chapter will examine an 'Extract' from a circulating library catalogue enclosed in the preface to the play's printed edition, which describes the novel reader as a surface inscribed by novel titles.

3 Acting as she reads

The farce begins with Polly reading from a (fictive) sentimental novel she later identifies as *The History of Sir George Truman and Emilia*. She is simultaneously a reader and a performer. Her pose mirrors that of an actor at a rehearsal holding a script and the scene playfully queries whether a distinction can be drawn between a reader and an actor. The placement of this scene at the opening of the farce parallels Polly's performed reading with her quixotic imitation of novel heroines throughout the rest of the play. Her reading seamlessly becomes mimetic behaviour, her gleeful 'acting' of what she reads. More immediately, the stage direction '*Acting it as she reads*' signals how Polly's eager sympathy with characters from the novel she reads results in her theatrically mimicking their movements (70).[25] 'Well said, Sir George!' are the first words Polly exclaims, and the first words of the play proper (70). We catch Polly responding to her reading by momentarily addressing a fictional character as though he is a person of flesh and blood, capable of hearing her appreciative words. The farce suggests that absorbed, sympathetic reading in the eighteenth century, which Catherine Gallagher influentially described as a relationship of private ownership and investment, can also be understood as a public performance.[26] Notably, throughout the farce, Polly never reads silently. Even a letter from her lover, Scribble, is joyfully voiced aloud to the audience. Polly's reading is both voiced and imprinted on her body. Though she reads alone, her reading is self-consciously 'staged' to a public audience through print and performance.

Indeed, the public nature of Polly's reading is congruent with a century alive to the theatricality of sympathetic reading. The female novel-reader was fraught with political and symbolic weight and was used in debates unrelated to female consumption of fiction. Jacqueline Pearson writes:

> [t]he reading woman became not only historical reality but also a sign, with a bewildering range of significations. The period's most important debates, about authority, gender and sexuality, the economics and morality of consumption, national identity and stability, class and revolution, use the sign of the reading woman.[27]

The female silent reader, reading alone in her closet (with onanistic implications), at once exemplifies ideas of privacy. However, she was repeatedly mediated to the public through representations on stage, in painting, and of course in print, with contested meanings. Joe Bray's study of the intradiagetic reader in late eighteenth-century novels argues that these texts educate readers in ways to avoid too closely sympathising with the characters and situations of their reading.[28] The numerous eighteenth-century plays that put readers on the stage, and paintings which put the reading subject on display, suggest that there is something intrinsically dramatic about the scene of sympathetic reading.[29] At the same time, the texts' intense interest in scenes of reading articulate a desire to make public the scene of the feminine domestic reader.

In *Polly Honeycombe*, the inherent theatricality of sympathising while reading privately is manifest. The theatre was used as a model for the functioning of sympathy during the eighteenth century, most famously by Adam Smith, as Laura Rosenthal discusses in this volume (Chapter 7). The stage directions have Polly mimicking the gestures of the characters in the novel, *'acting it as she reads'*, placing her own hand to her chest when Sir George presses Emilia's hand 'to his bosom' (70). *The History of Sir George Truman* is figured as an elaborate set of stage directions, with Polly (and thus the actress) mimetically responding to its detailed descriptions of emoting bodies. When Polly reads, 'where the pulses of his heart beat quick, throbbing with tumultuous passion' (70) and touches her own chest, the implication is that Polly's own heart is similarly beating. She seems to mirror the bodily processes undergone by Sir George. The placement of her hand on her heart is not an exact reproduction of either Sir George or Emilia's movement. Instead, Polly's body becomes the location of the love scene; Polly inscribes on her own body both Emilia's bashfulness and George's 'tumultuous passion'. The affective economy described within the book is transposed onto Polly's body, which becomes impressed with both characters' feelings. Her hand is pressed, like Emilia's, but she is feeling the throbs of her own heart. There is the brief, cheeky suggestion of onanism, with Polly's hand taking the place of Emilia's, while her heart stands in for Sir George's. Polly externalises and playfully performs the stereotypical, sexualised infatuation of the enthralled, silent female reader.

When Polly reads from a sentimental novel on stage, before the audience in a theatre, the relationship between novel reader and literary character is brought into the public sphere through staged performance and print. The scene from the novel Polly reads describes Emilia's reaction to Sir George's declaration of love. Emilia says little but there are elaborate descriptions of how her body expresses her emotion: 'She, half raising [...] her downcast eyes, and half inclining her averted head, said in faltering accents' (70). Like the sentimental literature it parodies, the novel Polly reads seeks to transcend speech, describing 'a concern with feeling as articulated by the body'.[30] John Mullan argues that sensibility in such novels, where speech is transcended in an attempt to communicate authentic feelings, results in a sensibility 'both private and public'.[31] The emotions legible on Emilia's body are self-consciously performed by Polly, whose own sentimental transport is, of course, being performed by the actress. Here, 'authentic feelings' or emotional transports are not signs of privileged, individual sensibility or even a private feeling expressed and performed. Rather, there is a sense that the description of Emilia's impressed body is a script for further impassioned performances. Emotions are corporeal impressions which are deftly refracted and parodied in layers of performance.

Performance, rather than an interiorised characterisation that might invite sympathy, would have been paramount in an eighteenth-century production of *Polly Honeycombe*. Catherine Gallagher argues that Hume's model of sympathy suggests that it is easier to sympathise with a character who has never existed, and who does not have a body, than with a 'real', embodied person.[32] The body of the person who is the intended subject of sympathy becomes, to use Gallagher's term, a 'proprietary barrier', impeding the empathetic relationship that she identifies as crucial to the experience of a 'realist' novel.[33] Freeman, building on Gallagher's theory, argues that the bodies of actors in the theatre also present a 'proprietary barrier' to the audience.[34] At Drury Lane, Jane Pope began playing Polly as a teenager, but she kept the role well into her 30s. Indeed, the structure of eighteenth-century theatre encouraged actors to monopolise a part until they retired from a company, which led to close associations between actors and particular roles.[35] According to Freeman's argument, then, Pope's body would have presented an obstacle to the theatre audience's sympathetic identification with Polly. At the same time, however, Pope would have embodied Polly's staging and sympathising with characters from a novel. Thus, novelistic emotional economies might not be replicated on the eighteenth-century stage but *Polly Honeycombe* shows us how they could be *performed* there. The process of sympathetic identification is played and parodied, emphasising how emotional identification was envisaged as performative during the eighteenth century.

Even when consumed solely in print, *Polly Honeycombe*, unlike a novel, significantly offers to its readers the presence, or at very least the *possibility* of the body of the actress playing Polly, and the reader must work out from the concise stage directions such as *'reading and acting'* (70) how the actress playing Polly should act. The stage directions, ostensibly written to guide the actress, serve to direct the performance occurring in the reader's imagination. Peters describes a shift in printed stage directions in this period: directions which aim to 'bring the performance to the reader – that attempt to make it vividly present in the instant'.[36] *Polly Honeycombe*'s extreme self-consciousness means the readers of the printed text never forget that what they are reading is something which has been performed, and has the potential to be performed again. When consumed alone it is sutured to the public space of theatrical performance; like any printed play, the text serves as both a record of previous performances and an impetus for new ones.[37] The title page of *Polly Honeycombe* states, 'As it is now Acted at the Theatre-Royal in Drury-Lane' (57). The phrases 'As it is now Acted' or 'As it is Acted' appear commonly in printed plays of the period, promoting a general likeness between the printed text and its staged equivalent and suggesting that the printed text is produced to replicate as closely as possible the staged version.[38] Both the title and magazine advertisements for the printed edition used the success of the performances as a selling point; for example, one advertisement reads: 'As it is performed at the Theatre Royal in Drury Lane, with great Applause'.[39] 'As it is' also suggests that the silent reading of the farce and its performance in Drury Lane occur simultaneously. Thus the act of reading produces an imagined performance of the farce which is fundamentally connected to the farce's similar, simultaneous performance on stage. Indeed, as Brewer notes, the Drury Lane theatre was situated in close physical proximity to London's circulating libraries in London.[40] The geographical closeness between performance and print is mirrored by a temporal proximity. It was typical for publishers to print plays close to their premiere, and *Polly Honeycombe* was no exception, the printed edition of the play coming out within a week of the play's premiere.[41] The affective economies of print and performance thereby intersect.

Polly Honeycombe is a play which never forgets it is a play and, as is typical for so much eighteenth-century theatre, is alive to its own mediation through performance and print. Brewer stresses how Polly herself is an eager, self-aware performer; she laughs in the middle of the play and in the epilogue in delight at her own performance (102, 109).[42] Rather than being the stereotypical deluded, quixotic reader, she playfully, self-consciously performs the role of the mimetic female reader, with the same avidity that animates her imitation of novel heroines throughout the play. This, on top of the way the play does not end with Polly 'old-maidish' or regretful of her novel-reading ways, points to how

Polly Honeycombe subverts as well as shores up the anti-novel discourse with which it engages.

Polly uses her novel-reading to perform sentiment. The externalisation of her sympathy, of course, stems from *Polly Honeycombe* being written for the stage, but it also underscores the public, performed nature of sentimental reading. Following the conventions of eighteenth-century theatrical performers, Polly, like an eighteenth-century actress, does not remain 'in character' when she reads the part of 'Sir George' and 'Emilia'.[43] Her very act of sympathising with them involves moving in and out of character. She speaks her reactions to the novel out loud, interrupting her absorbed reading to voice her emotional reactions. ' "[T]he lovely face of Emilia was overspread with blushes." – This is a most beautiful passage, I protest!' (70). Her commentary, merely by interrupting her reading, undermines the very declarations of transport it describes. On the pages of the printed play, quotation marks and dashes separate the words of the novel from Polly's commentary; they mark the abrupt shift from the novel's hyperbolic sentimentalism to her exuberant appreciation. Stage directions such as *'affectedly'* suggest an artificiality to Polly's reaction to the novel. She states, 'Lord, lord, my stupid Papa has no taste. He has no notion of humour, and character, and the sensibility of delicate feeling' (70). She seeks to prove, to herself at least, her refined taste and sensibility, her superiority to her 'stupid' parents (70). As a result, Polly's quixotic behaviour appears as a playful acting out of novelistic form, with an awareness that novels do not adequately fit her situation.[44] She is the stereotypical female novel-reader, seduced by her reading and unduly influenced by it, but she is also a masterful performer, using her reading to demonstrate her own sensibility and to forward her own desires. The sense of performance is heightened because the novel that elicits Polly's demonstrative sympathy is an outrageous parody of a sentimental novel. Both the theatre audience and the readers of *Polly Honeycombe* are not compelled to share Polly's passionate sympathy, but are invited to delight in her deft, self-conscious performance of emotion.

Polly's hyperbolic, dramatic reading of a sentimental novel exemplifies the close interconnections between sentimental literature and the theatre in the eighteenth century. On a more general level, it elucidates how texts can make available to their audience specific expressions and emotional practices. Print and drama encourage an impressionable audience to perform, practice, or *try* emotions. For instance, Pascal Eitler, Stephanie Olsen, and Uffa Jensen note how nineteenth-century children's books and advice manuals encourage a mimetic production of emotion that was 'also continually producing differences.'[45] Similarly, Paul Goring writes that during the eighteenth century, '[r]eaders of sentimental fiction were invited to inhabit roles' and 'rehearse a language of gesture'.[46] Goring observes how the bodies of the heroes in sentimental fiction use the 'same tools of suasion' as those in mid-century stagecraft.[47] Both the emoting reader and the emoting actor perform the feeling and gesticulating bodies of the characters on the page they read. Eighteenth-century theories of theatre were indebted to classical theories of passions, in particular, Larlham argues, to the understanding of emotion as a 'motion of the soul', producing changes in the organs and muscles of the bodies.[48] Hill's influential works on acting describe the actor's idea of the passion exerting a physical pressure which moves the spirits and muscles.[49] According to this theory, an expression of emotion becomes a mechanical result of the actor calling it to mind.[50] Hill's *Essay on the Art of Acting* (1753) compares affective impressions with paper being impressed by a printing press; the idea of the passion is 'muscularly stamp'd' on the body.[51] Hill's theory explicitly relates impressions on the body of the actor to those on the printed page. His *Essay* contains quotations from plays as exemplary descriptions of particular passions (such as joy or grief). The budding actor is instructed to use the printed words as the basis for their performance of each passion. In the case of 'anger', for example, Hill quotes Shakespeare's Henry V's rallying of his troops (Act 3, Scene 1), which rouses them to a fierce, battle-ready state of the bodily signs of anger.[52] Both Hill and Shakespeare suggest interchangeability between the description of the physical signs of a passion and the feeling itself. Goring has emphasised the ways eighteenth-century descriptions of moved bodies produced 'real emotional transport' in their readers.[53] In a similar way, in Colman's farce, Polly, the sentimental reader of Sir George and Emilia's raptures, is moved by descriptions of the physical processes of emoting bodies, enough to physically imitate them. Descriptions of affected bodies produce affective impressions on other bodies. Both Polly's imitative reading, and the acting Hill describes, are part of an affective economy, where emotions become heightened through their circulation, where passion is externalised and affected, and where imprinted bodies rehearse representations of passion in print.

4 The circulating extract

Polly Honeycombe's engagement with 'impressed' bodies and affective economies extends to its self-conscious treatment of print. This is exemplified by the 'Extract' contained in its printed edition. It is enclosed in the prologue, which purports to be an extract from a letter critiquing the play from George Colman's mother. Colman's 'mother' writes of how she finds, in the possession of some young female novel-readers, a catalogue of a circulating library, 'a bulky pamphlet'. She encloses an extract from this circulating catalogue, which appears in the pages of *Polly Honeycombe* before the play properly begins. It is a long list in two columns of titles of eighteenth-century fiction, in alphabetical order.[54] The Extract contains a dizzying number of titles, from respectable works, such as Samuel Richardson's *Pamela* (1740) and *Clarissa* (1748–49) and Voltaire's philosophical fiction *Zadig* (1747), to the scandalous, such as *Fanny Hill* (1748). The list demands to be looked at, for the arrangements of the titles of the page and the patterning in the columns to be noted, for our eyes to pick out the longer titles and the italics as we scan the page. Its meaning comes from print devices, the patterning of the listed titles, the repetition, the columns, and the few, well-chosen italics. The bulk of the works in the Extract belong to the 1750s, as William Scott has noted.[55] The Extract lends the play topicality. Its contextualisation suggests that *Polly Honeycombe* is most concerned with modern novels, published and distributed while the play is being performed and sold in print.

Part of the Extract's ostentatious dependence on print for meaning comes from the subtly chosen italics, which work to reinforce the relation between the Extract and a quixotic subjectivity. Italics are used in the full title of *Clidanor and Cecilia*, describing the text as being '*adapted to form the Mind to a just Way of thinking, and a proper Manner of behaving in Life*' (64).[56] The emphasised words represent a work which has been specifically written with the purpose of changing the reader's way of thinking and behaving; the reader's mind is impressed by a novel's description of '*a just Way of thinking, and a proper Manner of behaving*'. In the first printed edition of *Polly Honeycombe*, the only other italicised words on this particular page of the Extract, and indeed the page opposite, are part of the full title of the *Bubbled Knights*: '*Folly and Unreasonableness of Parents laying a restraint upon their Children's Inclinations in the Affairs of Love and Marriage*' and '*sentimental*'. Throughout the (five) pages of the Extract, numerous other long titles refer to the importance of love. The clear implication is that novels are crucial in the circulation of transgressive love. Novels are presented in the Extract as teaching their malleable young readers to both disobey their parents '*in the Affairs of Love and Marriage*' and to associate such disobedience with fashionable sentimentality. Fiction's alteration of the reader in the

Extract is proclaimed in the novel titles, and through print itself, with the titles imprinted on the page symbolising the novels' imprint on the reader. The alterations of the reader's character are part of the advertised experience of reading novels; the books' ability to '*form the mind*' of their reader is part of what makes them desirable objects to be consumed. I am describing the circulating library Extract in this detail because of the way it captures the circulation of texts and emotions and, like Polly's own performed reading, the way it points to the publicity of 'private' reading, in particular the publicity of the affective impressions generated by reading. Moreover, it also implies that the female reader's 'character' may be marked, or even *stained* by 'improper' reading. This danger of corrupting impressions is apparent in the way numerous titles in the Extract refer to works of erotica, such as *The New Atalantis for the Year One thousand seven hundred and fifty-eight* (66), evidencing the overlay between erotic affective economies and the circulation of novels. This particular compendium of erotica was referenced in the 1761 title of *Harris's List of Covent-Garden Ladies; or, New Atalantis*, a catalogue of prostitutes detailing their price and location.[57] The 1761 title of *Harris's List* therefore conflates circulating library books and prostitutes. The Extract lists a large number of prostitute narratives, for example, *History of Some of the Penitents in the Magdalen-House* (1760), *The Juvenile Adventures of Miss Kitty Fisher* (1759), and *Memoirs of the celebrated Miss Fanny M[urrray]* (1759). The listing of these titles in the Extract suggestively sutures the circulation of novels with both illicit commerce and the circulation of female bodies.

The circulating library occupied a privileged place in anti-novel discourse. Emma Clery observes there was a frequent rhetorical conflation between the books which were borrowed and the bodies of the female readers, with library books passing through the hands of temporary owners, getting grubbier and steadily more defaced, suggesting a parallel fate for the female readers who consume and internalise the stories.[58] I have suggested above how this anti-novel discourse, suggesting an illicit economy involving the circulation of a transgressive 'love' between novels and their readers, is also playfully alluded to in *Polly Honeycombe*'s prologue and the first scene. In the Extract, *Polly Honeycombe* articulates the eighteenth-century association between the commercial circulation of printed objects and the commercial circulation of prostitutes' bodies. This is echoed by Polly's behaviour in the play; she sends her nurse to visit Scribble and collect his love letters and instructs her to visit the circulating library on the way (76). The dual purpose conflates Polly and Scribble's love affair with promiscuous reading, tying the circulation of novels to the circulation of the transgressive 'love' between Polly and Scribble.

In other ways, the Extract is suggestively connected to Polly's own character. In *Polly Honeycombe*, the list that is the Extract not only mocks the eighteenth-century novel, but can be read as an allegory of the reading subject. The Extract is as much a portrait of its bookish, quixotic heroine, as the 'Polly' in the play proper. This page, overlain with print of advertised novel titles, describes an insatiable novel-reader, and it appears to refer to contemporary ideas about the acquisition of knowledge. Certainly, John Locke's *An Essay Concerning Human Understanding* (1690) repeatedly and famously uses the figure of white paper being printed to describe human experience: ideas are 'printed' or 'imprinted' on the mind by experience (and occasionally nature and God).[59] As Scott Paul Gordon writes, the quixote's mind is not a blank sheet of paper, but a paper which has been marked by the quixote's favourite texts, 'Don Quixote's mind has been inscribed by the romances he has consumed', and similarly, Polly's mind is imprinted with contemporary sentimental novels.[60] The Extract represents the Lockean *tabula rasa* overlain with contemporary novel titles. The Lockean individual, Lynch notes, is a collector, 'the cumulative product of his private stockpile of sensations and reflections'.[61] This cumulative nature of Lockean individual consciousness is portrayed in the Extract's list form, for each book title signifies both an object to be consumed and an educational experience to be impressed on the reader's mind. This circulating library list, however, is notably not one of acquirable objects, but rather of the transient affective experience which circulating libraries offer, typically represented as the single, fast reading of a novel. The circulating library reader owns nothing after the reading of a borrowed novel, but retains the impressions the experience leaves in the mind, much like someone in the audience of a theatre performance. The novel titles describe the affective experiences of reading the books, as well as the material objects of the books themselves.

5 Conclusion

The circulating library Extract is a series of printed pages or impressed surfaces overlain by novel titles which draws the readers' attention to the technology of print itself. I have suggested above how the Extract can be read as an epitome of a ravenous, impressionable novel-reader's 'self'. Each title, imprinted on the page, represents the affective experience of its consumption. The 'self' of the stereotypical novel-reader (which Polly both is and is not) is the quixotic result of the impressions from her reading. The circulating library Extract is also represented as an object emphatically in the public sphere. It is ostensibly an advertisement for a circulating library, listing other objects that are circulating. Colman's 'mother' can take the catalogue from her acquaintances and reproduce it in a letter to her 'son', which itself is enclosed in a printed play, which is itself reprinted, circulated, and advertised. The Extract compares the eighteenth-century 'self' to a commercial library's catalogue, and by extension, suggests a 'self' subject to commerce and public surfaces: legible, externalised, and part of an affective economy.

Both the circulating library Extract and the scene where Polly reads describe sympathetic reading as an activity which, while having pretensions to the private, is ever in the process of becoming public, through self-conscious mediation by print and theatre. *Polly Honeycombe* playfully describes a close, complicated relationship between feeling and acting. Polly's mimetic *'acting'* of her reading, her embodiment of novels, inevitably exists in dialogue with the actress' embodiment of the script. Polly's *'acting'* and the circulating library Extract describe the reader's sympathetic investment in novels as being publicly articulated through a legible embodiment. Indeed, sympathy is inextricable from performance, from its public, corporeal articulation via imprinted surfaces. Hill's description of an actor's body imprinted by a passion is akin to the representation in the circulating library Extract of the vulnerable reader being imprinted by the experience of reading novels. The farce describes how the technology of print is sutured to eighteenth-century conceptions of 'self'. Print structures the way the 'self' is conceived as a public show of externalised surfaces, layered, competing, and impressed with legible emotions. *Polly Honeycombe* ultimately describes being moved by a novel as a public, dramatic act, involving an emoting and affect-laden 'self' of imprinted, legible surfaces.

Notes

1. A much earlier version of this work won the University of Sydney Beauchamp Literary Prize (2012) and was published online as 'Dramatick Extraction and Polly Honeycombe's &c.', Sydney eScholarship Repository, The University of Sydney, 2012. http://ses.library.usyd.edu.au/.
2. D. A. Brewer (2012) *The Rivals and Polly Honeycombe* (Peterborough: Broadview), p. 72. All further citations to this edition are incorporated in the text.
3. S. Ahmed (2004) *The Cultural Politics of Emotion* (Edinburgh: Edinburgh University Press), pp. 44–6.

4. R. Ballaster (2012) 'Rivals for the Repertory: Theatre and Novel in Georgian London', *Restoration and 18th Century Theatre Research,* XXVII(1): 16.
5. D. Larlham (2012) 'The Felt Truth of Mimetic Experience: Motions of the Soul and the Kinetics of Passion in the Eighteenth-Century Theatre', *The Eighteenth Century* LIII(4): 435 (Larlham's emphasis).
6. M. McKeon (2005) *The Secret History of Domesticity: Public, Private, and the Division of Knowledge* (Baltimore, MD: The Johns Hopkins University Press), p. 394.
7. D. A. Brewer (2012) 'Print, Performance, Personhood, Polly Honeycombe', *Studies in Eighteenth Century Culture* XLI: 186.
8. *The London Stage, 1660–1800; A Calendar of Plays, Entertainments & Afterpieces, Together with Casts, Box-receipts and Contemporary Comment. Compiled from the Playbills, Newspapers and Theatrical Diaries of the Period* (1960–68) (Carbondale, IL: Southern Illinois University Press), Part 4, Vol. 2, pp. 828–34.
9. Cross, the prompter, notes in his diary after the first performance that the farce was 'indifferently received, partly oweing [sic] to the Fright and Confusion of the Performers, who omitted some speeches on which the plot depended'. By the third night, however, the prompter writes, 'Polly Honeycomb [sic] goes off very well'. Quoted in *The London Stage,* Part 4, Vol. 2, p. 828.
10. The English Short Title Catalogue lists a first London 1760 edition, a 1761 Corke edition, an Edinburgh 1761 edition, two different Dublin 1761 editions, a London 1762 'third' edition and a 'fourth' London edition 1778. English Short Title Catalogue, British Library, http://estc.bl.uk (home page), accessed 15 June 2012. Thomas Price argues that an unauthorised edition of *Polly Honeycombe* in Dublin prompted Becket to style his 1762 altered version of the farce 'The THIRD EDITION' in order to avoid confusion with the Dublin edition. G. Colman (1997) *Critical edition of The jealous wife and Polly Honeycombe. Volume 30 of Studies in British Literature,* ed. T. Price (New York: Edwin Mellen Press), pp. 183–6.
11. Joseph Addison's *Cato* (1713) and John Gay's *Beggar's Opera* (1728) were published over a hundred times during the eighteenth century. J. S. Peters (2000) *Theatre of the Book 1480–1880: Print, Text, and Performance in Europe* (Oxford: Oxford University Press), pp. 50, 345, n. 62.
12. *Polly Honeycombe* is hardly unknown, and its historical importance is acknowledged. However, when it is mentioned, it is typically only in passing, as part of a larger discussion of eighteenth-century female novel readers and as an influence on more commonly studied quixotic texts, such as Richard Sheridan's *The Rivals* (1775). There has been little work done on its own literary complexities. Recent exceptions include Brewer, 'Print, Performance, Personhood, Polly Honeycombe', 185–94; Brewer, Introduction to *The Rivals and Polly Honeycombe*; Ballaster, 'Rivals for the Repertory', 5–24. See also the Georgian Theatre and the Novel Project. Ballaster, G. Egan and K. Lawton-Trask, The Georgian Theatre and the Novel: 1714–1830, http://georgiantheatrenovel.wordpress.com, accessed 9 June 2014.
13. E. H. Anderson (2009) *Eighteenth-Century Authorship and the Play of Fiction: Novels and the Theater, Haywood to Austen* (New York: Routledge), p. 3. Nora Nachumi lists 382 female novelists and demonstrates that at least one third

of these novelists were performers, playwrights, or otherwise associated with the eighteenth-century stage. N. Nachumi (2008) *Acting Like a Lady: British Women Novelists and the Eighteenth-Century Theater* (New York: AMS Press), pp. 66–70, 181.

14. Brewer, 'Print, Performance, Personhood, Polly Honeycombe', 185–94; Ballaster, 'Rivals for the Repertory', 5–24.
15. John Richetti writes, 'hybridization seems to come naturally to prose fiction, and many of the novels we identify with the beginnings of modern narrative are intertwinings of different and sometimes conflicting literary modes'. J. J. Richetti (1984) 'Richardson's Dramatic Art in *Clarissa*', in S. S. Kenny (Ed.), *British Theatre and the Other Arts, 1660–1800* (Washington, DC: Folger Books), p. 289.
16. Ballaster, 'Rivals for the Repertory', 22.
17. L. Freeman (2002) *Character's Theater: Genre and Identity on the Eighteenth-Century English Stage* (Philadelphia, PA: University of Pennsylvania Press), pp. 4–5.
18. Freeman, *Character's Theater*, p. 27.
19. Freeman, *Character's Theater*, p. 27.
20. D. Lynch (1998) *The Economy of Character: Novels, Market Culture, and the Business of Inner Meaning* (Chicago: Chicago University Press); D. Lynch (2000) 'Personal Effects and Sentimental Fictions', *Eighteenth-Century Fiction*, XII(2–3): 345–68; D. Wahrman (2006) *The Making of the Modern Self: Identity and Culture in Eighteenth-Century England* (New Haven, CT: Yale University Press), p. 179.
21. A. Alliston (2011) 'Female Quixotism and the Novel: Character and Plausibility, Honesty and Fidelity', *The Eighteenth Century* LII(3–4): 265 (Alliston's emphasis).
22. T. Dixon (2003) *From Passions to Emotions: The Creation of a Secular Psychological Category* (Cambridge: Cambridge University Press), p. 104.
23. Dixon, *From Passions to Emotions,* pp. 106–7.
24. D. Hume (1739–40) *A Treatise of Human Nature: Being an Attempt to Introduce the Experimental Method of Reasoning into Moral Subjects* (London: Printed for John Noon), Vol. 1, pp. 55–6; C. Lupton (2012) *Knowing Books: The Consciousness of Mediation in Eighteenth-Century Britain* (Philadelphia, PA: University of Pennsylvania Press), p. 74.
25. Italics as in the original stage directions.
26. C. Gallagher (1999) *Nobody's Story: Gender, Property, and the Rise of the Novel* (Durham, NC: Duke University Press), p. 194.
27. J. Pearson (1999) *Women's Reading in Britain 1750–1835: A Dangerous Recreation* (Cambridge: Cambridge University Press), p. 1. See also Pearson (1996) ' "Books, my Greatest Joy": Constructing the Female Reader in *The Lady's Magazine*', *Women's Writing* III(1): 3–15; W. B. Warner (2000) 'Staging Readers Reading', *Eighteenth-Century Fiction* XII(2–3): 391–416.
28. J. Bray (2009) *The Female Reader in the English Novel: From Burney to Austen* (New York: Routledge), p. 21.
29. For a description of paintings of absorbed, reading women, see Warner, 'Staging Readers Reading', 391–416.
30. J. Mullan (1990) *Sentiment and Sociability: The Language of Feeling in the Eighteenth Century* (Oxford: Clarendon Press), p. 16.

31. Mullan, *Sentiment and Sociability*, p. 16.

32. Gallagher, *Nobody's Story*, pp. 169–71.

33. Gallagher, *Nobody's Story*, p. 171.

34. Freeman, *Character's Theater*, pp. 18–19.

35. Brewer, Introduction to *The Rivals and Polly Honeycombe*, p. 26; Appendix A to *The Rivals and Polly Honeycombe*, p. 259.

36. Peters, *Theatre of the Book*, p. 62.

37. Brewer, 'Print, Performance, Personhood, Polly Honeycombe', 190.

38. The English Short Title Catalogue has 86 entries of titles with the phrase 'As it is now acted' and 669 of 'As it is acted' published in 1740–70. English Short Title Catalogue, British Library, http://estc.bl.uk (home page), accessed 15 June 2012. 'As it is acted' editions contrast with other forms of printed plays in the mid-eighteenth century that had less immediate connections to performance, such as editions of plays that had never been performed and scholarly editions of Shakespeare.

39. 'On Thursday will be published', *London Chronicle*, 6–9 December, 1760.

40. Brewer, 'Print, Performance, Personhood, Polly Honeycombe', 192.

41. Peters, *Theatre of the Book*, p. 50.

42. Brewer, 'Print, Performance, Personhood, Polly Honeycombe', 188.

43. Freeman, *Character's Theater*, pp. 36–7.

44. Brewer, 'Print, Performance, Personhood, Polly Honeycombe', 188.

45. P. Eitler, S. Olsen, and U. Jensen (2014) 'Introduction', in U. Frevert, P. Eitler, S. Olsen, U. Jensen, M. Pernau et al. *Learning How to Feel: Children's Literature and Emotional Socialization, 1870–1970* (Oxford: Oxford University Press), p. 8.

46. P. Goring (2005) *The Rhetoric of Sensibility in Eighteenth-Century Culture* (Cambridge: Cambridge University Press), p. 14.

47. Goring, *The Rhetoric of Sensibility*, p. 144.

48. Larlham, 'The Felt Truth of Mimetic Experience', 433.

49. A. Hill (1753) 'The Art of Acting', *Works of the Late Aaron Hill Esq. in Four Volumes consisting of Letters on Various Subjects, and of Original Poems, Moral and Facetious. With an Essay on the Art of Acting* (London: Printed for the Benefit of the Family), Vol. 3, pp. 387–408.

50. J. Roach (1985) *The Player's Passion: Studies in the Science of Acting* (Newark, DE: University of Delaware Press).

51. A. Hill (1753) 'An Essay on the Art of Acting', *Works of the Late Aaron Hill* (London: Printed for the Benefit of the Family), Vol. 4, p. 356.

52. Hill, 'An Essay on the Art of Acting', p. 370.

53. Goring, *The Rhetoric of Sensibility*, pp. 1–7.

54. William Scott writes: '[a]ll the titles can in fact be traced, though sometimes the only evidence is to be found in contemporary reviews, advertisements or lists of new publications [...] The only work I have not succeeded in tracking down is *Spy on Mother Midnight, or F – 's Adventures*.' W. Scott (1968) 'George Colman's *Polly Honeycombe* and Circulating Library Fiction in 1760', *Notes and Queries* XV(12): 465. The English Short Title Catalogue lists three records of *Spy on Mother Midnight* (1748). English Short Title Catalogue, British Library, http://estc.bl.uk (home page), accessed 15 June 2012.

55. Scott, 'George Colman's *Polly Honeycombe*', 465.

56. The italics are most likely Colman's. Colman chose the italics for 'Prostitutes of Quality, or Adultery a la Mode; being *authentic* and *genuine* Memoirs of several Persons of the *highest Quality*' (1757); the two extant editions' title pages emphasise 'being' and 'Memoirs' rather than 'authentic,' 'genuine', and 'highest Quality.' According to the English Short Title Catalogue there are no copies of *Clidanor and Cecilia* in existence (or at least in libraries), though it certainly existed; *Thelamont* (1744) advertises itself as 'by the author of *Clidanor and Cecilia*'. English Short Title Catalogue, British Library, http://estc.bl.uk (home page), accessed 15 June 2012.
57. J. I. Freeman (2012) 'Jack Harris and "Honest Ranger": The Publication and Prosecution of Harris's List of Covent-Garden Ladies, 1760–95', *The Library: The Transactions of the Bibliographical Society*, XIII(4), 434.
58. E. Clery (1995) *The Rise of Supernatural Fiction, 1762–1800* (Cambridge: Cambridge University Press), p. 97.
59. J. Locke (1690) *An Essay Concerning Human Understanding* (London: Printed for Tho. Basset, and sold by Edw. Mory). See, for example, Book 1, Chapter 2, p. 4.
60. S. P. Gordon (2006) *The Practice of Quixotism: Postmodern Theory and Eighteenth-Century Women's Writing* (New York: Palgrave Macmillan), p. 20.
61. Lynch, *The Economy of Character*, p. 85.

10
Framing Suicidal Emotions in the English Popular Press, 1750–80

Eric Parisot

1 Introduction

By modern standards, suicide was remarkably ubiquitous in the English eighteenth-century press. By mid- to late century, the frequency of suicide featuring in the popular press – in news reports, correspondence, essays, satirical pieces, and fictional vignettes – helped to establish two significant prevailing perceptions: that suicide formed a distinctive feature of the English national character, and that the scourge had reached unprecedented levels. As one observer remarked in 1772, suicide was perceived 'to be more frequent in England than in any other country', and it was seen to be 'a melancholy truth, that it has of late been more frequent here than at any former period'.[1] The nation, it appeared, was facing an unparalleled social crisis.

When examining the body of writing on suicide in the English press from the mid- to late eighteenth century, it also becomes apparent this problem was recognised as one inextricably tied to the discussion and representation of suicide circulating *in print*. Some observers viewed the popular press as culpable, for a variety of reasons. The frequency of reported suicides in newspapers, as 'melancholy intelligence ... circulated with the other occurrences of the present day',[2] had been cited as a significant inuring factor, especially when compared to France, where the few authorised gazettes tended to avoid the controversial subject. As a Parisian correspondent to the *Morning Post and Daily Advertiser* remarks in 1778, the English are 'better informed of those accidents' by virtue of a liberal press, the very 'means which are

My sincere thanks to Meegan Hasted, for her assistance with newspaper research for this essay.

wanting in a despotic government, where a man can publish nothing without an *imprimatur*'.[3] Such reports, occasionally specifying the method of execution and speculating on possible motives, were also said to imprudently provide detrimental examples to weak minds. Not surprisingly, then, the practice of printing suicide notes, increasingly prevalent from 1750 to 1780, drew particular criticism: concerned by the publication of 'stimulatives to suicide', one correspondent admonishes the printer of the *Morning Chronicle*, attesting that 'The insane productions of such authors, carry with them such an evil tendency, that it is to me a matter of wonder, what end you mean to answer by the publication of them'.[4] Meanwhile, some commentators used the same channels and risked 'publicizing the problem they deplored' (as Jeffrey Merrick observes[5]), by polemically denouncing the act, its actors and its defenders, based on moral, social, legal, philosophical, and/or religious grounds. Suicide was commonly condemned as anti-social for its disregard for family and community; unnatural, for its denial of the principle of self-preservation; and ungodly, for its denial of providence and God's right to property over life. In some rare cases, polemicists would even take up the pen to respond to suicide notes, unwilling to let the suicide have the final say. As the main receptacle for suicidal discourse during the period, the popular press was the key forum in which the minds and souls of the nation's readers were to be fought and won over.

This battle for the reader's sympathies is the focus of this essay. But rather than focus on polemics, it will attempt to expose the emotional strategies (and associated rhetorical and aesthetic devices) employed by conservative commentators attempting to contain the threat of moral contagion and discredit the emotional experience of suicide, and in turn, demonstrate how suicidal authors often adapted like strategies to reassert their sense of self-legitimacy. These emotional, rhetorical, and aesthetic manoeuvres, exemplifying Michael Milner's assessment of 'strategic' emotions as 'having deliberate, tactical importance' recognisably deployed 'in a hegemonic war of position', were primarily adopted to (re)define the relation between the suicidal and the community.[6]

Mindful of both the deleterious and preventive influence of depicting suicide in print,[7] and the capacity of the press to initiate and shape circuits of emotion or 'affective economies'[8] that could ossify into popular opinion, conservative commentators focused their attention on appropriate forms of representation (largely to emphasise abhorrence on moral and religious grounds), and confining the spread of suicidal emotions by way of contagion (largely by discrediting the authenticity of suicidal despair as a genuine experience). These two strategies – representation and containment – lend themselves to the conceit of 'framing'. Anti-suicide commentators framed suicide in order to invoke sentiments such as contempt, disgust, and horror in response to the deed and its exponents. They also presented suicidal emotions as artificial or imaginary, bordered and confined to a space removed from reality: demarcating the boundary between artifice and reality, and enclosing this imaginary activity and its subsequent expression as pride and overwhelming despair, was seen as an important way to limit artifice and affectation permeating into the real world and spreading by contagion via the popular press. The passions of pride, contempt, and disgust, were central to such limiting and socially distancing tactics, but such sentiments often worked both ways.

2 Emotional aversion: Contempt and disgust

In 'Some Observations on the Causes of Suicide', published in the *Gentleman's Magazine* in 1756, an anonymous author comments on appropriate responses to the suicidal: 'To reason with people under the influence of this ridiculous and extravagant pride would be utterly hopeless; for it is a species of madness, and if it can be cured at all, it must be either by contempt or ridicule'.[9] There are several important considerations here. Pride – of the 'ridiculous and extravagant' sort – is cited as the primary cause of suicidal despair; what these descriptors might imply will be considered shortly. That this type of pride-induced despair is pejoratively considered a form of lunacy also points to the increasing medicalisation of suicide; by the mid-century, some writers were compassionately excluding the *non compos mentis* from their moral and legal evaluations of suicide: as articulated in *Two Dissertations* on Samson and Jephtha (1754), 'The Actions of one who is not *Compos Mentis* are neither morally Good, nor Evil. And therefore can neither merit Reward, nor Punishment'.[10] Also worth noting is the author's scepticism towards reason as a method of persuasion. The suicidal cannot be coaxed by reason, or the type of logic found in many polemical essays of the period, but must be induced by emotions, particularly those derived from scorn and derision. Ridicule, that Shaftesburian 'test of truth', evidently retains its currency into the latter half of the century, likely designed to pique the dignity or vanity of the despairing through shame and embarrassment.[11] While Kames asserts that ridicule is a mixed emotion 'qualified with that of contempt',[12] it is the negative emotion of contempt, and its social function in combating suicide, which remains the focus here.

Contempt, alongside anger and disgust, is often considered a socially distancing emotion that asserts or reinforces social position relative to others, often resulting in social exclusion. Ostensibly less social in nature, such negative emotions, as Agneta H. Fischer and Antony S. R. Manstead argue, can still serve a socially strategic function, especially in their capacity to inhibit antisocial or dysfunctional behaviours, and to reinforce community norms and values.[13] Contempt, expressed as derogation and/or rejection, appears to have been recognised by eighteenth-century critics as an important part of the emotional arsenal against suicide.

The passion of pride, as a cause of suicidal despair, serves as a focal point for efforts to discredit the suicidal experience and deny its legitimacy. In his serial 'Essay on Suicide' (1771–72) 'W.W.' proposes that despite variations in experience, 'the Commission of so horrid an Act' will be 'found to proceed from the same cursed Root *Pride*, for Pride is the Parent of all Discontent'.[14] 'Philo', writing to the *Gazetteer and New Daily Advertiser* in 1772, concurs, arguing that the desire for self-annihilation 'proceeds from a proud, froward and wicked heart... [and] owing to a man's suffering discontent be attendant on all his actions, to be ever dissatisfied with the world, or, himself'.[15] These appear to echo earlier sentiments previously noted in 'Some Observations on the Causes of Suicide', which finds the cause of suicide 'to be generally disappointed pride'.[16] While pride is constructed as a dualistic passion in a contemporary anonymous poem, providing 'The spur of honour, or the sting of shame', each author appears to emphasise pride as a catalyst for negative emotions.[17] Where David Hume's definition of pride favours a positive prospect of fulfilment and achievement, of an 'agreeable impression, which arises in the mind, when the view either of our virtue, beauty, riches or power makes us satisfy'd with ourselves',[18] these authors isolate the opposite side of the coin – thwarted pride – as a potentially suicidal emotion; for these authors, pride lends itself towards an acute sense of judgement and 'the sting of shame' associated with a lack of fulfilment, and it is this particular emotional state that is cited as a precursor to suicidal despair. Nevertheless, this descent from pride, to shame, and to mortification – a term invoked here to denote both a state of extreme humiliation and the onset of death or dying – is viewed by conservative commentators of the period as a fall aggravated by an unfettered imagination. '[T]he Devil tempts the Suicide,/With fancy'd woes – imaginary pride', warns an anonymous poetaster in *Lloyd's Evening Post and British Chronicle* (1760); that is, the emotional wounds that stem from pride which precede physical self-harm are represented as often illusory.

Suicidal pride – identified as 'ridiculous and extravagant' in the example cited – is reconstructed by its critics in this period as not only worthy of derision, but conducive of misery absurdly disproportional to given circumstances. Pride, or more specifically, wounded pride, is seemingly discredited as an exaggerated imaginary affect.

With pride decried as an illusory passion, it follows that the legitimacy of suicidal despair is also questioned. In *Two Dissertations*, the author charitably declares in the first dissertation that the imaginary embellishment of misery is 'natural to all in calamity', but nevertheless argues that the despairing tend 'to magnify the *Idea* of the Miseries they suffer, in their own Imagination... [and] are apt to think and cry out, *the Misery is unsupportable*, which to one more hardy, would be but a Triffle [sic]'. This '*Idea*', italicised by the printer to underline its fictitious status, often produces a 'pretended *insupportable Calamity*'.[19] An essayist in the *Morning Chronicle and London Advertiser* (1772) is even less forgiving:

> The extravagant creations of vicious reason and imagination are almost incredible... They can reverse the order of the world in argumentations; they can aggravate tolerable into intolerable misery; they can produce grief out of nothing; they can form substantial woes out of shadows; can convert heaven into hell. It is indeed foolish to be stupid under pains; but it is much greater folly to dream of such as we do not feel, till the greatest calamities overtake us, and refute our false imaginations...[20]

Once again, the intemperance and implausibility of suicidal despair, fuelled by an over-active imagination, is underscored. Doubts over the validity of such states of depression are also articulated by more obvious expressions of incredulity: in 1753, a correspondent to *Gray's Inn Journal* admits 'I cannot look upon any Contingence in this World of Consequence sufficient to urge a Man to this Extreme of Madness';[21] similarly, in *A Dissertation upon the Unnatural Crime of Self-Murder* (1773), Caleb Fleming asserts that 'there truly is not one supportable circumstance, which can possibly enter into the compass of human trial, where man could be justified in taking away his own life'.[22] Such critics are, of course, subject to the accusation of bearing an inflexibly limited sympathetic imagination, but at this stage it is sufficient to note that some commentators refused to admit the possibility of suicidal despair as a legitimate human experience. These 'unhappy mortals', who dispose of themselves 'without any such apparent necessity', are simply 'self-deluded'.[23]

These allegations culminate in a disdainful portrait of a suicide as a conceited, self-deceiving fantasist, unwilling (rather than incapable) to regulate governable passions and wayward thoughts. As 'W.W.' outlines in his 'Essay on Suicide', whether he 'entertains contemptible Thoughts of him who gives the Blow', or suffers from 'the Effect of his own Folly in an unguarded Hour', the suicide 'thro' Pride and Arrogance...continues to cherish Discontent in his Bosom, when he is disparaged and sunk in the Esteem of others'. No longer willing to support 'the Reflexion (of his debased State) in his own Breast', he 'resolves to rid himself (as he vainly thinks) of the Burden he must labour under, to free himself from the galling Chain, which is greatly increased by the Stubbornness of his own proud Will'.[24] Agency, rather than victimisation, is emphasised throughout this portrayal, underlining the choices that remain available to a suicide throughout his crisis. Indeed, according to 'W.W.', this account of purportedly typical suicidal conduct reveals the degree to which despair is the result of bad choices: to harbour rather than seek to alleviate anxiety; to cling to the image of the degraded self, and to allow it to fester into disease; to choose to die, rather than to relinquish pride and vanity.

The sustained denigration of suicidal despair and its root cause, pride, as wilfully cultivated or even contrived emotional experiences, was one form of contempt expressed by conservative commentators of the period. Others preferred more blatant hostility towards suicide, expressing outright disgust, and hoping to cultivate comparable sentiments in their readers. The abhorrence for suicide most commonly rested on natural and moral/religious grounds. Neither were they mutually exclusive; Fleming likens the unnatural depravity of 'self-murder' to an 'equally detestable' perversion of nature, 'of which, an estimate is best made by the sulphurous fiery shower which fell on Sodom!'[25] Before him, in *Two dissertations*, the unnamed author argues that 'licentious Writings...in defence of this unnatural, odious Practice...threaten the contagious Encrease [sic] of it', subsequently calling on 'every Man in his Station, to contribute his Endeavour to give Check to this growing Evil: And more especially a Christian Duty, to represent and inculcate, the hainous [sic] and atrocious Guiltiness of it'. Such diction and rhetoric exemplify how, according to William Ian Miller, 'the Christian language of sin latched on to disgust' as a mode of disapprobation, and also serves to highlight the sermonic vigour used to underline appeals to the readers' sense of (Christian) moral outrage.[26]

The author of *Two dissertations*, however, makes an interesting appeal 'to represent' suicide in all its atrocity. As 'W.W.' observes, 'SHOCKING and dismal as the Catastrophe of such a Conduct must appear to the Imagination of a Considering Person (and there is not anything in Nature can be more so)', some have been 'so injudicious as to dignify it with the Appellation of Heroism'.[27] The problem of appropriate representation, and the call for a greater emphasis on the horrendous, is one that appears to be answered by commentators of the period. Investing in the emotional impact of imaginative representation, a number of discussions considering suicide employed the aesthetics of horror and disgust over the rhetoric of sin and damnation. For one observer in particular, suicide 'requires no Profusion of Imagery, no bold daring Metaphor, no studied Hyperbole to represent this Piece of Impiety in its proper Colours; it strikes the Eye at once in its most flagrant atrocious Dye' – presumably blood red – 'from which any thinking Mind must now start back appalled'.[28] Exposing the physically violent reality of suicide, it would appear, required little artifice. More importantly, as a shock tactic, it was viewed as an effective visceral deterrent.

The horrific representations of suicide seen in print during this period are arguably an extension of the debate surrounding the forms of physical humiliation *post mortem* for suicide, and their capacity to deter the living from following suit. Customs of profane burial or physical desecration – which included interment in the often unconsecrated north side of the churchyard or burial in highways or in crossroads, corpses dragged through the streets, stakes driven through bodies, and anatomical dissection – still operated infrequently in the mid- to late eighteenth century: *The Whitehall Evening Post or London Intelligencer* reports on the fate of William Gumby of Gosport, Hampshire, who in 1761 had his corpse 'drawn on a Hurdle to the Cross-Road...and a Stake drove through his Body: Between his Legs was drove a large Post, which is several Feet above the Ground, and on which his name and the Crime he committed are to be fixed, in order to intimidate others from being guilty of so horrid a Sin';[29] *Lloyd's Evening Post* reports a suicide buried in the crossroad at Elme, Somersetshire, in 1764;[30] *The Public Advertiser* mentions a self-poisoner by the name of Lowe, who was 'buried near the Sea Coast, [with] a stake driven through his body';[31] and, a German gentleman by the name of Jacob Miers, who was adjudged *felo de se* after cutting his throat in 1772, was buried facing north to the poorhouse in Portugal Street in London, despite his request for clemency and a proper burial.[32] In an age of humanitarian concerns, such seemingly barbarous practices were far from universally applied, sparking concern from alarmed observers who often prescribed forms of desecration to combat the perceived growing tide of suicides.[33] A correspondent to the

London Daily Advertiser and Literary Gazette in 1751 – spurred by reports of legal prescriptions against gaming, and possibly by the Murder Act (1751) that handed judges the power to order hanging in chains or dissection – calls for 'some new Law', whereby 'the Person so destroying himself should be exposed for one whole Day upon the Gibbet erected for that Purpose, and afterwards the Body delivered to the Surgeons'.[34] In the same year, writing in the *Gentleman's Magazine*, correspondent 'M.S.' proposes that self-murderers 'should be hanged in chains in some conspicuous place at the four corners of the city'.[35] Likely in response, a further correspondent 'M.A.' adds weight to this campaign in the following month's issue of the *Gentleman's Magazine*, arguing for the suicide's body to be delivered to the surgeon in the next market town for public dissection in the marketplace, and for remaining skeletons to be used and publicly displayed for succeeding surgeons.[36] For each of these correspondents, punishing the dead is no longer the primary motivation for reform; it is, instead, superseded by the greater need to foster abhorrence and disgust. What matters most to these correspondents is that the gruesome displays they recommend are open to public view. This is a variation on R. A. Houston's argument that 'the corpse of the suicide, whose death had created a breach in the social fabric', was used as a location 'to re-make community', for 'punishing the dead had more to do with a language of community than it did with the mechanics of pain'.[37] Indeed, the type of punishments endorsed by such critics function to reinforce a sense of community, but rather than aiming to heal the social body, they are designed to ceremonially exorcise malignant elements of the community to secure the moral welfare of the living.

Disgust, the central emotion provoked by rituals of defilement, operates similarly to contempt in the way it reaffirms social values by way of rejection and exclusion. Although biological in its origin, working as an aversive emotion designed to protect against potential pollutants and toxins, disgust is also, according to Miller, 'a moral and social sentiment', playing 'a motivating and confirming role in moral judgment' and in defining the boundaries of the moral and social community; in short, 'Disgust evaluates (negatively)'.[38] Moreover, as Keith Oatley identifies and, as demonstrated here, it is a form of evaluation that can be extended to symbolic objects and people.[39] When directed against individuals and their actions, the physical experience of disgust can easily slide into socially motivated emotions such as contempt and moral indignation. One might propose, then, that eighteenth-century commentators calling for a greater emphasis on public shaming rituals are arguing for the reversal of the civilising trajectory from visceral disgust to socio-moral contempt; that is, dissatisfied with the efficacy of existing socio-moral structures in preventing suicide, they seek to reinstate barbaric rituals that enable the conversion of socio-moral contempt back into physical revulsion. Part of this necessarily involves the ceremonial transformation of suicides as people into odious symbolic objects, or even biological contaminants. (This might explain the insistence on public dissection in the marketplace, reducing the cadaver to a contaminating agent amongst local produce.) For such critics, contempt might serve as an appropriate form of emotional disapprobation that demarcates the limits of propriety and the moral community; but visceral disgust achieved via ceremonial display, appealing to base human senses, might function more effectively to deter even the basest of social and moral beings.[40]

It is arguably a small step from public displays of corporal punishment to gruesome representations of suicide in the press. The same emotional strategy of promoting disgust is in play, but with two key differences. First, actual witnessing is replaced by virtual, or imagined, spectatorship. Second, scenes of physical humiliation *post mortem* are replaced with the gruesome visions of the immediate aftermath of suicide. For example, George Colman the Elder and Bonnell Thornton propose in their *Connoisseur* (January 1755) that the 'Suicide of Quality' (as opposed to 'every lower wretch' who ought to be 'dragged at the cart's tail' and 'hung in chains at his own door'):

> should be indulged in having his wounded corpse and shattered brains lay (as it were) in state for some days, of which dreadful spectacle we may conceive the horror from the following picture drawn by *Dryden*.

> The SLAYER OF HIMSELF *too saw I there:*
> *The gore congealed was clotted in his hair:*
> *With eyes half-closed, and mouth wide ope he lay,*
> *And grin as when he breathed his sullen soul away.*[41]

In the same month, the *Gentleman's Magazine* published a satirical advertisement for discreet methods of suicide designed for the gentleman of '*wit, humour*, and *pleasure*', which outlined the pitfalls of using a pistol, 'sometimes causing a great effusion of blood, sometimes blowing the brains about the room, spoiling the paintings and other furniture, and leaving the body bloody and mangled, the countenance distorted, and the features defaced . . . so that all attempts to conceal it by pretending apoplexy or sudden death are ineffectual'.[42] These two commentaries evidently attempt to merge strategies of ridicule and disgust, but the rather defusing effect of comedy is removed in later examples. In a letter to the *Town and Country Magazine* in 1772, correspondent 'Anti Suicide' claims that 'If a suicide could for a moment recover life, and view himself mangled, as he lay with his brains scattered on the walls, and his blood streaming on the floor, with his remaining features distorted to agony – how he would shudder at himself and tremble at his own appearance!'[43] The *Gentleman's Magazine* also reports, in 1774, of 'a man of genteel appearance [found] lying dead on the ground, with his brains blown out, and a pistol sticking in his mouth'.[44] Examples such as these paint the act of suicide in all its physical gore, and for some, befitting the odious nature of the crime. They also reveal the serious violence essential to self-destruction that is often left implied: reminders that physical mutilation was in many cases inextricable from the deed itself and not solely the domain of surgeons and local vigilantes. These depicted scenes are also intensely private moments usually concealed from public view, a further reminder of the popular press's capacity to expose readers to deeds and sights they might have never witnessed in reality. Exposing such scenes to public and imaginary view can be read as another strategic effort to foster moral and physical abhorrence for suicide.

Contempt and disgust, then, were mobilised by critics of suicide through the popular press in a variety of ways: the authenticity of suicidal despair was questioned on the basis of its disproportional excess; so too was its perceived root cause, wounded pride, on the basis of its apparently illusory origins; the suicidal were constructed as self-deluded beings, subject to an over-active imagination; campaigning for further rituals of corporal desecration *post mortem* aimed to cultivate both moral indignation and visceral repulsion, as did descriptions of the suicide's body at death. Each in their way attempted to reassert normative values and reinforce the borders of the social body by expunging suicide – the act and its exponents – from the collective moral sphere.

3   Reciprocal aversion: Pride and the antiworldview

Critics of suicide were not the only authors using the popular press for aversive means. Indeed, the practice of printing suicide notes in newspapers and magazines during this period arguably resulted in a unique set of circumstances which allowed the suicidal to answer their critics. This practice was brought to critical attention by MacDonald and

Murphy's landmark study, *Sleepless Souls* (1990), in which the authors claim that by the 1770s the published suicide note was 'well established as a literary subgenre'.[45] Twenty-two suicide notes, both purportedly real and ostensibly fictional, appear to have been printed in London newspapers and magazines from 1750 to 1780, which – as I suggest elsewhere – is 'more than one would expect, but hardly as frequent as MacDonald and Murphy might seem to imply', but syndication also meant that notes were often reprinted in dailies, weeklies, and monthlies, contributing to their perceived ubiquity.[46] Also, 15 of these notes were printed in the 1770s, confirming MacDonald and Murphy's claim that this publishing practice was most prevalent during this decade. This is a significant cultural development in the 'history of opinion' on suicide – it offered suicidal authors a platform to shape public attitudes towards the act of suicide, the authenticity of the suicidal experience, and most importantly, their own selves.

Just as their detractors attempted to undermine pride as a legitimate emotion, suicidal authors would invoke pride as a way to assert and/or refashion their own sense of self.[47] If writing a suicide note is the penultimate act of empowerment for a suicidal author, a moment of active self-fashioning and re-contextualising the relation between the self and the wider community, then pride becomes an expedient sentiment, in that it reaffirms individuality by re-organising the hierarchical relation of self to other.

The suicide note of Mungo Campbell is a case in point.[48] Imprisoned in Edinburgh's Tolbooth in 1770 and sentenced to death for the murder of Alexander Montgomerie, 10th Earl of Eglinton, Campbell hanged himself in his cell, circumventing an inglorious public execution and the indignity of anatomisation. The public stir created by the murder trial and suicide reverberated in the London newspapers. *Lloyd's Evening Post* (5–7 March 1770) reported the existence of 'a very affecting letter' written by Campbell found at the death scene, devoted solely to his wife; the letter was printed in London's *Independent Chronicle* one week later (12–14 March):

> You will find, my long and faithful companion, I have kept my word with you – Since I must die because I would not surrender my arms to a tyrannic Lord, I am resolved to avoid being a public spectacle – 'Ere you receive this I am no more. May every happiness attend you on earth, and may we meet in eternity, is the earnest wish of your's [sic] even in death,
>
> *Tolbooth, Feb. 24.*   Mungo Campbell[49]

This note, along with others of the period, is discernibly aligned with the vogue for sentimentalism, functioning as elaborate performance, framed and understood within a codified set of sentimental literary postures.[50] This suicide note ends a long campaign by Campbell to defend his character, or more accurately, to construct himself as a sentimental hero – a sympathetic and benevolent defender of liberty and justice. Campbell's sensibility is proudly on show here: his note expertly conceals his final act by deflecting all attention to his loving wife, declaring not only his undying devotion to her but also his own tender heart. Campbell's sentimentalism also offers a platform upon which he is able to elevate himself above (and escape from) the vulgar workings of the law. Prideful honour, as a marker of dignity and identity, obliquely functions here to help Campbell achieve or aspire to positive remembrance, as a man of feeling rather than a murderer and suicide.

Prideful shame, on the other hand, is evident in the suicide note of Thomas Davers (printed in the *Gentleman's Magazine* in 1767). The note, mockingly introduced by the editor, reads:

> Descended from an ancient and honourable family, I have, for fifteen years past, suffered more indigence than ever gentleman before submitted to: neglected by my acquaintance, traduced by my enemies, and insulted by the vulgar, I am so reduced, worn down, and tired, that I have nothing left but that lasting repose, the joint and *dernier* inheritance of all.
>
> > Of laudanum an ample dose,
> > Must all my present ills compose:
> > But the best laudanum of all
> > I want (not resolution) but a ball.
> > N. B. Advertise this.
>
> T. D.[51]

Tracing his decline from social distinction to his indecorous exit by poison rather than pistol, Davers' note reads as one final attempt to reclaim his rightful rank in society. Claiming an authority in death that he could not achieve in life, with the final flourish of his pen he contemptuously demands the world's attention – 'Advertise this' – as a way to reassert his honour. Here, we begin to see the transformation of pride as a self-regarding emotion to an outward disdain for the world. It is what G. J. Barker-Benfield labels the 'antiworldview', used to describe the mutation of sensibility into pathological hypersensitivity, the 'devaluation of "the world"' and a retreat into the grave.[52] John Upson, who hanged himself in 1774, adopts this same posture in the following lines reportedly left in a prayer book:

> Farewel [sic], vain World, I've had enough of thee,
> And now am careless what thou say'st of me;
> Thy Smiles I court not, nor thy Frowns I fear,
> My Cares are past, my Heart lies easy here;
> What faults they find in me take Care to shun,
> And look at home, enough is to be done.

Poor John the Glover, June 26, 1774[53]

Despite his appellation, 'Poor John' does not play the victim, instead defiantly reasserting his agency at the very end by rejecting the world, by pen and – his instrument of death – his garter. Evidently anticipating severe rebuke, he caustically turns the tables on his critics, confidently advising that corrective measures are best directed towards the self. A further example is found in the *Morning Post and Daily Advertiser* (1778), where the suicidal author outlines the natural principles justifying his act before insolently dismissing the world: 'Farewell, ye detested tribe of my fellow-creatures; I leave you for ever; I owe nothing; nor do I care how my carcase may be used after my death'.[54] This author's scorn, not for society but for his entire species, takes suicidal pride and contempt to new heights.

The discursive exchange prompted by Philip James O'Neil's suicide, a young Irishman who reportedly shot himself in the head after penning nearly 40 letters to friends and acquaintances in 1771, highlights the inherent dangers posed by printing suicide notes. In the first of two of these to be published, O'Neil proleptically responds to the objections of his readers, attempting to rationalise his decision within the context of Christian providence and predestination in an audacious display of intellectual hubris.[55] O'Neil reveals his disdain for the world in the second letter: 'I am going to depart this wretched world; I have seen nothing in it but vanity and deceit; wherefore should I then stay in it?' In a sense, O'Neil returns the accusations levelled at the suicidal – of being contemptible, self-conceited, and disingenuous – back at society at large, choosing to rid himself of the world. 'If there be another world', he reasons, 'it must certainly be better'.[56] The response to this profane *contemptus mundi* was predictably swift, and while concerned correspondents attempt to correct O'Neil's erroneous justifications, they also expose the prevailing concern over the influence of print. Although O'Neil's first letter cites a motivation to 'insert this unhappy circumstance in the Newspapers' to 'perhaps hinder some young men from coming to the same end', critics are deeply concerned by the opposite effect. Writing to *Hoey's Dublin Mercury*, 'Benevolus' proposes 'the publication of such a letter will be, by way of precedent, dangerous to weak minds', gesturing towards the responsibility of the newspaper editor or printer as a public censor.[57] Writing to the *London Evening Post*, 'Tranquillus' – who is less tranquil than his pen-name might suggest – concludes his letter with a firm caution: 'But consider, O ye youth of England, that the way to ruin is extravagance... That every one may take warning by this gloomy and melancholy self-murderer, is the hearty wish of a friend to society'.[58] This exchange brings the contest for the reader's sympathies firmly into focus. O'Neil and his critics appear to engage in a process of mutual rejection; just as O'Neil chooses to withdraw from the world, his critics attempt to purge the community of his potentially contaminating influence.

The affect most feared by such critics is sympathy. 'To minds replete with philanthropic principles', one correspondent begins his 'Thoughts on Suicide' in *The Sentimental Magazine* (1775), 'who feel a pungent sensation for the multifarious miseries to which their species in humanity are incident... and mourn with a noble sympathetic grief... what subjects of unspeakable anguish are the frequent acts of suicide'.[59] While this degree of sympathetic identification is commended here as an act of *'Christian benevolence'*, the problem with this – especially from the perspective of conservative commentators – is that any admission to such heightened sensitivity is also an admission to the very same state of emotional sensitivity that renders one susceptible to self-destruction. '[T]his extreme sympathy with misfortunes which we know nothing about', as Adam Smith suggests in his *Theory of Moral Sentiments* (1759), 'though it could be attained, would be perfectly useless, and could serve no other purpose than to render miserable the person who possessed it'.[60] Herein lies the danger of 'emotional extravagance' when considered in the context of suicide and the press; extreme emotions such as despair and contempt for the world, circulating in print and trespassing personal boundaries by sympathy, carry the risk of suicidal contagion.

The rejection of sympathy, however, might be interpreted as the height of suicidal pride, as exemplified by a long translated note signed by S. Warin – a young Frenchman who shot himself in Spa (then Germany) – and printed in the *Morning Chronicle and London Advertiser* in 1779. Warin anticipates his detractors, but also addresses his potentially sympathetic reader: 'It is unnecessary to enquire what were the motives that have induced me to shorten my life; I do not think there

exists in the world a man of my age who has experienced so many misfortunes, and even if there did, that would afford no ground for blaming
my conduct'.[61] Warin is pointed in his claims for utter subjectivity here,
attempting to reclaim his individuality in the only way available, by
claiming his experience as utterly unique and inconceivable to all others. But in doing so, unusually, his disregard is extended to include
the only remaining connection to the world, his reader, described as
'not competent judges of my situation'. For Warin, subjectivity poses an
obstacle to the sympathetic imagination, and it is deployed to shield
himself against any form of moral judgement. What Warin attempts
to construct here is an emotional or sympathetic impasse, where a lack
of shared experience becomes an insurmountable barrier to sociability.[62]
This provides an apt description of the relation between suicidal authors
and their detractors. In the previous section, we encountered a series of
commentators who refused to admit the possibility of suicidal despair as
a genuine, rather than an imaginary, emotion; by limiting the circumference of their own sympathetic imagination, they fostered social fracture,
strategically intended to reassert the moral boundary separating their
community from destructive influences. Many suicidal authors of the
period attempted to counter this exclusionary tactic by adopting prevailing codes of sentimentalism, designed to win over the sympathetic
reader and to enable posthumous social rehabilitation. The suicide notes
highlighted here, however, laid out to show the emotional progression
from suicidal pride to utter contempt, culminate in Warin's extreme
example of social aversion, one that reverses the direction of abjection
imposed by morally conservative commentators. By forcibly imposing
limits on his reader's imagination, Warin actively locates himself outside
the circumference of the social, moral, and sympathetic sphere.

4   Conclusion: The authenticity of suicidal emotions

The hundreds of reported suicides found in the English popular press
during the mid- to late eighteenth century constitute a grim catalogue
of the failings of community. Each report marks an occasion at which an
individual has irrevocably rejected society and chosen to seek an alternative state, whether as annihilation or an afterlife. Collectively, they are
a disturbing record of a civilised society's inability to curtail the suicidal
impulse, exerting a profoundly unsettling influence over the living.

   It is this disquieting effect that conservative commentators of the day
attempted to limit, by discrediting the authenticity of suicidal emotions.
Wounded pride, and attendant feelings of shame, was at once invoked

as a root cause of suicidal despair and contemptuously dismissed as a fanciful emotion caused by obstinate and excessive self-regard. The legitimacy of suicidal states of mind that resulted from such illusory origins, then, was also questioned; critics openly doubted whether any circumstance, in the entire compass of human experience, could justify suicidal desires, and instead constructed such despair as the passionate ebullition of an over-indulgent imagination. Suicides, consequently, were scornfully dismissed as self-deluded beings. Underwriting such rhetoric was the emotion of contempt, strategically enlisted to inhibit dysfunctional social behaviours, to reinforce normative community values, and to curb the impact of suicidal thoughts and behaviours left lingering in the print record. Similarly, disgust was also employed as an emotional form of disapprobation by critics who campaigned for rites of physical desecration as a visceral deterrent, and by those who exposed the horrific gore of self-violence that was often obscured by polite representations of suicide.

What is left implied in such efforts to frame suicidal emotions – that is, to represent and enclose them as artificial – is the withholding of sympathy, and the desire to limit sympathetic engagement via the press. The failure to offer sympathy to the suicidal should not be viewed as an emotional *tabula rasa*, but rather, as yet another negative evaluation, another performance of moral censure.[63] From this perspective, sympathy is not an expression of Christian benevolence, but a moral concession; it is imperative, then, for concerned commentators of the period to discredit representations of suicides as appropriate subjects for compassion as a way to reinforce the moral fibre of the community. Conversely, for suicides, sympathy can mean validation. Suicidal authors of the period often adopted sentimental postures as a way to foster sympathetic response as a surrogate for absolution and social rehabilitation. When such notes are placed alongside a body of contemporary writing that seeks to undermine the legitimacy of suicidal emotions, it becomes clear that sympathy also functions as a form of authentication. While many published suicide notes make ostensible claims for forgiveness or justification, or to air grievances or to apportion blame, they are also intrinsically attempting to write extreme states of mind into sympathetic legitimacy.

Other suicidal authors, however, chose to authenticate their experience differently by reasserting their individuality. In doing so, they often reciprocated the emotionally aversive strategies deployed by their critics, by expressing disdain for the world they were set to depart, by dismissing the desire for sympathy and placing themselves outside the sphere of the sympathetic community, and by further investing in pride as a self-affirming emotion. Pride, characterised as illusory by some, is recast as a means to self-legitimacy by suicidal others. Rather than make claims for sympathetic and social rehabilitation, these authors instead engage with their critics in mutual processes of abjection, culminating in the construction of a living moral community and its suicidal others.

Perhaps this, above all, was the greatest fear for concerned critics of suicide: the construction of suicide not only as an alternative to community, but as an alternative community. For instance, suicide is satirically depicted as a clubbable quality in George Colman's *Connoisseur*, with the invention of 'the Last Guinea Club', where 'a few broken gamesters and desperate young rakes' define their membership by self-destruction;[64] elsewhere, in a letter to *The World*, John Anthony Tristman outrageously proposes a 'RECEPTACLE FOR SUICIDES', a country club of sorts designed to fulfil the needs of 'the numerous fraternity of DISTRESSED GENTLEMEN'.[65] Although suicide is clearly the subject of ridicule here, these comic pieces also expose the serious dystopian fears held by conservative commentators of the day. Suicide, perceived to be occurring on an unprecedented scale, was not only a matter of individual morality, or the moral integrity of the community; if left unabated, suicide threatened to form the basis of a paradoxically asocial counter-community, bonded by common experience and sustained by circulating print. It called for no less than a campaign to strike the problem at its root, and to discredit the authenticity of suicidal emotions altogether.

Notes

1. *Gazetteer and New Daily Advertiser* (1772) 6 January, [4]. Cf. *Gazetteer and New Daily Advertiser* (1765) 26 December, in Mark Robson, Paul Seaver, Kelly McGuire, Jeffrey Merrick and Daryl Lee (Eds.) (2013) *The History of Suicide in England, 1650–1850*, 8 vols. (London: Pickering & Chatto), Vol. 6, p. 227.
2. *Lloyd's Evening Post and British Chronicle* (1762) 19–22 February, 177–8.
3. *Morning Post and Daily Advertiser* (1778) 24 September, [2]; see also Jeremy L. Caradonna (2010) 'Grub Street and Suicide: A View from the Literary Press in Late Eighteenth-Century France', *Journal for Eighteenth-Century Studies* 33(1): 23–36.
4. *Morning Chronicle and London Advertiser* (1772) 12 September; also in Robson et al., *History of Suicide in England*, Vol. 6, p. 260.
5. Robson et al., *History of Suicide in England*, Vol. 6, p. 185.
6. Michael Milner (2012) *Fever Reading: Affect and Reading Badly in the Early American Public Sphere* (Durham, NH: University of New Hampshire Press), p. 15.

7. See Donna T. Andrew (2013) *Aristocratic Vice: The Attack on Duelling, Suicide, Adultery, and Gambling in Eighteenth-Century England* (New Haven, CT and London: Yale University Press), pp. 83–125; Michael MacDonald and Terence R. Murphy (1990) *Sleepless Souls: Suicide in Early Modern England* (Oxford: Clarendon Press), pp. 301–37.

8. Sara Ahmed (2004) *The Cultural Politics of Emotion* (Edinburgh: Edinburgh University Press), p. 45.

9. 'Some Observations on the Causes of Suicide', *Gentleman's Magazine* (1756), January, 28; also in Robson et al., *History of Suicide in England*, Vol. 6, pp. 204–5.

10. *Two Dissertations: The First on the Supposed Suicide of Samson* . . . (1754) (London: Innys and Richardson), p. 5.

11. Despite popular belief, Shaftesbury never actually used this phrase; see Alfred Owen Aldridge (1945) 'Shaftesbury and the Test of Truth', *PMLA* 60(1): 129–56.

12. Henry Home and Lord Kames (1762) *Elements of Criticism*, 3 vols. (Edinburgh: Millar; Kincaid, and Bell), Vol. 1, p. 341.

13. Agneta H. Fischer and Antony S. R. Manstead (2008) 'Social Functions of Emotion', in Michael Lewis, Jeannette M. Haviland-Jones, and Lisa Feldman Barrett (Eds.), *Handbook of Emotions*, 3rd ed. (New York and London: Guilford Press), pp. 460–1.

14. 'An Essay on Suicide', *Westminster Journal and London Political Miscellany* (1771), 28 December, in Robson et al., *History of Suicide in England*, Vol. 6, p. 239.

15. *Gazetteer and New Daily Advertiser* (1772) 10 November, in Robson et al., *History of Suicide in England*, Vol. 6:, pp. 264–6.

16. 'Some Observations on the Causes of Suicide' (1756), 28; also in Robson et al., *History of Suicide in England*, Vol. 6, pp. 204–5.

17. *Pride: A Poem* (1766) (London: Almon), 2; cf. Kristján Kristjánsson's (2002) term 'pridefulness', in *Justifying Emotions: Pride and Jealousy* (London and New York: Routledge), pp. 104–10.

18. David Hume (1978) *A Treatise of Human Nature*, ed. L. A. Selby-Bigge, rev. P. H. Nidditch, 2nd ed. (Oxford: Clarendon Press), p. 297.

19. *Two Dissertations* (1754), pp. 24–5.

20. 'Considerations on Self-Murder; Continued', *Morning Chronicle and London Advertiser* (1772), 28 July, [1–2].

21. *Gray's Inn Journal* (1753) 24 March; also in Robson et al., *History of Suicide in England*, Vol. 6, pp. 192–4.

22. Caleb Fleming (1773) *A Dissertation upon the Unnatural Crime of Self-Murder* (London: Dilly), p. 4.

23. Charles Collignon (1765) *Medicina Politica, or Reflections on the Art of Physic as Inseparably Connected with the Prosperity of the State* (London: Thurlbourn and Woodyer, et al.), p. 25.

24. 'Essay on Suicide', *Westminster Journal and London Political Miscellany* (1772) 4 January, in Robson et al., *History of Suicide in England*, Vol. 6, p. 246.

25. Fleming, *A Dissertation*, p. 15

26. William Ian Miller (1997) *The Anatomy of Disgust* (Cambridge, MA and London: Harvard University Press), p. 193. Sermons were seen to be an

important component of reform: see *Gentleman's Magazine* (1751) October, 464–5; *Public Advertiser*, Friday 30 August 1771, [2]; *Westminster Journal and London Political Miscellany*, 31 August – 7 September 1771, [4]; *The Morning Chronicle and London Advertiser*, Monday 3 January 1774, [3]; *Public Advertiser*, 15 April 1779, [3]. For prominent examples, see Francis Ayscough, *A Discourse against Self-Murder* (London: 1755); John Herries, *An Address to the Public, on the Frequent and Enormous Crime of Suicide* (London: 1774); and, Zachary Pearce, *A Sermon on Self-Murder* London: 1774).

27. 'Essay on Suicide', *Westminster Journal and London Political Miscellany*, 4 January 1772; in Robson et al., *History of Suicide in England*, Vol. 6, p. 244.

28. *Gray's Inn Journal*, 24 March 1753; in Robson et al., *History of Suicide in England*, Vol. 6, pp. 192–4.

29. *The Whitehall Evening Post or London Intelligencer*, 29 September – 1 October 1761, [3].

30. *Lloyd's Evening Post*, 30 December 1764 – 2 January, [7].

31. *Public Advertiser* (1779) 15 April, [3].

32. *Middlesex Journal or Universal Evening Post* (1772) 1–3 October, [3]; also MacDonald and Murphy (1990) *Sleepless Souls*, 328; Eric Parisot (2014) 'Suicide Notes and Popular Sensibility in the Eighteenth-Century British Press', *Eighteenth-Century Studies* 47(3): 280.

33. Clare Gittings (1984) suggests the brutality of such traditional rites for suicides may have led to increasing clemency (*Death, Burial and the Individual in Early Modern England* (London and Sydney: Croom Helm), p. 74); cf. Ralph Houlbrooke's (1998) argument that the increase in lunacy verdicts after 1700 may have resulted in the rigorous enforcement of such rites upon the guilty minority (*Death, Religion, and the Family in England, 1480–1750* (Oxford: Clarendon Press), p. 336); see also R. A. Houston (2010) *Punishing the Dead? Suicide, Lordship, and Community in Britain, 1500–1830* (Oxford: Oxford University Press), pp. 189–267.

34. *London Daily Advertiser and Literary Gazette* (1751) 21 June; in Robson et al., *History of Suicide in England*, Vol. 6, pp.186–7.

35. *Gentleman's Magazine* (1751) October, 464–5; also *London Evening Post* (1767) 12–16 May, [4].

36. *Gentleman's Magazine* (1751) November, 504; also *Middlesex Journal or Chronicle of Liberty* (1769) 13–16 May, [3].

37. Houston, *Punishing the Dead?*, p. 270.

38. Miller, *Anatomy of Disgust*, pp. 2, 9; for the moral capacities of disgust, see pp. 1–24, 179–205.

39. Keith Oatley (2004) *Emotions: A Brief History* (Malden, MA: Blackwell), p. 81.

40. A correspondent notes that such methods of deterrence are universally understood; see *Public Advertiser* (1764) 23 June 1764; in Robson et al., *History of Suicide in England*, Vol. 6, p. 224.

41. *The Connoisseur* (1755) 9 January; in Robson et al., *History of Suicide in England*, Vol. 6, pp. 197–201. The authors slightly misquote from *Palamon and Arcite* (2: 576–9); see John Dryden (1956–) *The Works of John Dryden*, gen ed. H. T. Swedenberg, Jr, 20 vols. (Berkeley and Los Angeles, CA: University of California Press), Vol. 7, p. 123.

42. *Gentleman's Magazine* (1755) January, 43; in Robson et al., *History of Suicide in England*, Vol. 6, p. 195.

43. *Town and Country Magazine* (1772) September, 572–73; in Robson et al., *History of Suicide in England*, Vol. 6, p. 262.
44. *Gentleman's Magazine* (1774) November, 537.
45. MacDonald and Murphy (1990) *Sleepless Souls*, p. 326. The authors discovered over 70 eighteenth-century suicide notes in total, including unprinted notes found in coronial records and private papers.
46. Parisot, 'Suicide Notes', 279.
47. Pride 'never fails to produce' an idea of self; see Hume, *Treatise*, p. 287.
48. For more on Mungo Campbell, see Parisot, 'Suicide Notes', 281–4; Houston, *Punishing the Dead?*, 249–51.
49. *Independent Chronicle* (1770) 12–14 March [4].
50. Parisot (2014) 'Suicide Notes', 277–91.
51. *Gentleman's Magazine* (1767) February, 93.
52. G. J. Barker-Benfield (1992) *The Culture of Sensibility: Sex and Society in Eighteenth-Century Britain* (Chicago and London: University of Chicago Press), p. 223.
53. *Public Advertiser* (1774) 5 July, [4].
54. *Morning Post and Daily Advertiser* (1778) 24 September, [1].
55. *Westminster Journal and London Political Miscellany* (1771) 3–10 August, [4].
56. *General Evening Post* (1771) 6–8 August, [3].
57. *Hoey's Dublin Mercury*, 15–17 August 1771, [2].
58. *London Evening Post* (1771) 24–7 August, [2].
59. *Sentimental Magazine, or, General assemblage of science, taste, and entertainment* (1775) September, 390–2; for a similar essay, see *Morning Chronicle* (1778) 21 July, in Robson et al., *History of Suicide in England*, Vol. 6, p. 289.
60. Adam Smith (1976) *The Theory of Moral Sentiments*, eds. D. D. Raphael and A. L. Macfie (Oxford: Clarendon Press), p.140 (III. 3. 9).
61. *Morning Chronicle and London Advertiser* (1779) 9 September, [2].
62. Cf. Smith, *Theory of Moral Sentiments*, 20–1 (I. i. 4. 5).
63. Miller, *Anatomy of Disgust*, p. 191.
64. *Connoisseur* (1755) 9 January, in Robson et al., *History of Suicide in England*, Vol. 6, pp. 197–201.
65. *The World* (1756) 9 September, in Robson et al., *History of Suicide in England*, Vol. 6, pp. 206–9.

11
Passions, Perceptions, and Motives: Fault-Lines in Hutcheson's Account of Moral Sentiment

Glen Pettigrove

1 Introduction

In the 1720s Francis Hutcheson published four treatises, and entered into a series of exchanges in the *London Journal* and the *Dublin Weekly Journal*, in which he developed a systematic account of the origin of ethical ideas and the nature of ethical judgement that was rooted in our affections.[1] Hutcheson's aim in writing was not only to describe the relation of affections to ethical judgement and action; it was also to inspire some of these same affections. In a review of his own book published under the pseudonym Philopatris, he indicated that his intention was to 'raise in Mankind "a *Relish* for a *Beauty* in *Characters*, in *Manners*," as well as in other Things'.[2] And he complained in the preface to Treatises 1 and 2 that modern writers 'have made Philosophy, as well as Religion, by our foolish management of it, so austere and ungainly a Form, that a Gentleman cannot easily bring himself to like it...' (preface to T1 and T2, 9–10). To avoid the shortcomings of his peers, evocative examples are sprinkled liberally throughout the text. This is not merely a stylistic flourish, but is central to his methodology, since he believes that our actions and judgements are a consequence of the sentiments we feel in response to the situations we encounter. Thus, Hutcheson thinks that instructive contributions to the debates carried on in the public sphere (and in the classroom) should be emotionally as well as intellectually engaging.

However, there is a tension within Hutcheson's texts between the judgements he makes when looking at particular cases and the generalised, 'mathematical' account he gives of moral judgement. When judging particular cases, he praises kindness, generosity, friendliness, and mercy. But when he proposes a formula for 'computing the Goodness' of a person's character at the conclusion of his fourth treatise, this formula is at odds with many of his particular judgements. Since a similar issue has been inherited by a number of his intellectual descendants, it is hoped that an investigation of the source of the tension within Hutcheson's framework will be instructive for addressing similar problems in contemporary theories.

Section 2 of this essay identifies the tension in Hutcheson's work between his remarks about individual virtues and his account of 'the most virtuous Temper'. Section 3 traces Hutcheson's attempt to ground moral judgements in what we might call authentic emotions, which he would call 'affections'. The mark of authentic emotions is accuracy: they see the world aright. Section 4 shows how his development of the theory around mathematical calculation and the image of perceptual accuracy lead to the conflict between his account and the emotions of the kind, generous, and loving.

2   Amazing grace

One of the most striking things about Hutcheson's *Inquiry Concerning the Original of Our Ideas of Virtue or Moral Good* is his clear preference for what I shall call gracious virtues.[3] These virtues manifest themselves in beneficial actions that are not determined by the merits of the beneficiary. Seven of the eight most frequently mentioned admirable traits in Treatise 2 are virtues of this type. After benevolence and love – which are mentioned on almost every page – the exemplary traits he names most often are kindness (42),[4] gratitude (37), friendliness (30), generosity (28), beneficence (24), and humanity (22). Counting traits in this way is somewhat inexact, since one could talk about the virtue of generosity, for example, without using the words 'generous' or 'generosity'. Nevertheless, the frequency with which he uses these words is a reasonable proxy for how often he discusses the virtues to which they refer and vividly illustrates their importance for Hutcheson. Gratitude, unlike the other members of the list, is to some degree conditioned on the merits of the person toward whom it is directed: it presupposes that one agent has benefited another. But it also presupposes the admirableness of gracious virtues, since the condition for its possibility is a gracious action. Many of the other admirable traits Hutcheson mentions – liberality, hospitality, patience, cheerfulness, pleasantness of temper, and mercy – are, likewise, manifestly gracious.

The catalogue of gracious virtues includes both some of the most common virtues and some of the least. One of the most common is the love of parents for their children, which is quite clearly gracious, since parental love is not – and could not be – grounded in their children's merits. '[T]he Affection of Parents...cannot be entirely founded on Merit or Acquaintance; not only because it is antecedent to all Acquaintance, which might occasion the Love of Esteem; but because it operates where Acquaintance would produce Hatred, even toward Children apprehended to be vitious' (T2, 148).[5] Less common, but no less admirable, is love for one's enemies.

> Benevolence toward the worst Characters, or the Study of their Good, may be as amiable as any whatsoever; yea often more so than that toward the Good, since it argues such a strong Degree of Benevolence as can surmount the greatest Obstacle, the moral Evil in the Object. Hence the Love of unjust Enemys, is counted among the highest Virtues. (T2, 124)[6]

As these two passages make clear, the gracious virtues are not limited to contexts where the beneficiary simply lacks merit. They extend even to cases of demerit and can be manifested both toward the person whose transgression is out of character as well as 'toward the worst characters'.

To this point I have focused on overtly gracious virtues. But within Hutcheson's framework, one would expect other virtues to be gracious as well, for he contends that all virtues are, at bottom, variants of benevolence or love. 'If we examine all the Actions which are counted amiable any where, and enquire into the Grounds upon which they are approv'd, we shall find, that in the Opinion of the Person who approves them, they always appear as Benevolent, or flowing from Love of others, and a Study of their Happiness.' (T2, 116).

If, as Hutcheson contends, all virtuous actions flow from love of others, and love need not be conditioned on the merits of the beloved, then even virtues whose graciousness is not obvious may prove to be gracious.

One of the reasons Hutcheson offers for writing Treatises 3 and 4 supports such an expectation. He claims that they are needed to counter the influence of other writers, by whom 'many have been discourag'd from all Attempts of cultivating *kind generous Affections* in themselves, by a previous Notion that there are no such Affections in Nature' (preface to T3 and T4, 3–4). And in his 1730 inaugural lecture at the University of Glasgow he pursues a similar theme, arguing that our benevolence and our 'kind and sociable dispositions' are not limited to 'the learned, the elegant, the affable, the liberal, the powerful and honored'. They can, and should, also extend to 'the ignorant, the gloomy, the sour, the boastful, the stingy, and the infamous'.[7]

Read against the backdrop of his enthusiasm for gracious virtues, Hutcheson's remarks about 'the most virtuous Temper' in the final section of Treatise 4 are startling. There he argues that we should love more that which is more lovely. And he concludes that, 'since we cannot apprehend any Goodness in having the *Degree of Love* above the Proportion of its Causes, the most virtuous Temper is that in which the *Love* equals its *Causes*' (T4, 189). Because he includes 'Ties of Blood' among the 'Causes of Love' – along with '*Benefits conferred* upon us and the Observation of *Virtue* in others' (T4, 188) – Hutcheson's formula for calculating goodness of temper need not exclude parents from the class of those who possess 'the most virtuous Temper'. However, it does seem to exclude the person he was lauding in Treatise 2 for loving her enemy, since her love for an unrelated enemy is not proportional to kinship ties, benefits received, or virtues observed. Likewise, it excludes other virtues whose exercise presupposes demerit on the part of the person toward whom they are directed, such as patience and mercy. Furthermore, it leaves out virtues like beneficence, generosity, and hospitality that respond to qualities such as need, rather than kinship, past generosity, or virtue. And it seems to omit virtues like cheerfulness and pleasantness of temper that are best understood in terms of qualities of the agent *from whom* they flow rather than qualities of the agents *to whom* they flow.

One might suspect that what accounts for the discrepancy between the virtues of Treatise 2 and the formula of Treatise 4 is a shift in perspective in the three years between the publication of the *Inquiry* (1725) and the *Essay with Illustrations* (1728). However, the gracious virtues continue to be lauded in his later works, including Treatises 3 and 4. As we saw, he emphasises their importance in the inaugural lecture of 1730, and he devotes a section of the *Metaphysics* – which a former student published without his knowledge in 1742 but which Hutcheson republished in 1744 with his revisions – to the defence of *bonitas vere gratuita*, 'truly gratuitous goodness' (*Metaphysics*, 135). So it does not appear that a shift in Hutcheson's perspective between the earlier and later work will account for the tension between his emphasis on gracious virtues and the formula of Treatise 4. We need to look elsewhere for a suitable explanation.

3 Passions, affections, sentiments, and senses

Before we can diagnose the source of the tension in Hutcheson's theory, we need to get more of the theory on the table. The centrepiece of Hutcheson's moral philosophy is his account of the internal senses. The account begins with the thought that,

> There seems to be some *Sense* or other suited to every sort of Objects which occurs to us, by which we receive either *Pleasure*, or *Pain* from a great part of them, as well as some *Image*, or *Apprehension* of them: Nay, sometimes our only *Idea* is a *Perception of Pleasure, or Pain*. (T3, 15)

If this is our starting point, then we have reason to think our traditional enumeration of senses – sight, sound, smell, taste, and touch – is inadequate. We experience pleasures and pains at moments when the traditional five senses do not appear to be doing any relevant work, such as when we experience the pain of grief at the memory of a deceased friend. Even in moments where one of the traditional senses is operative, it is often not responsible for the pleasure or pain we experience, such as when we feel sympathetic pain upon seeing a child graze her knee. From observations like these Hutcheson concludes, 'If we may call *every Determination of our Minds to receive Ideas independently on our Will, and to have Perceptions of Pleasure and Pain, A SENSE*, we shall find many other *Senses* besides those commonly explained' (T3, 17; similarly T2, 90).

In addition to the five external senses, Hutcheson identifies a number of 'internal senses'.[8] The sense of beauty brings us pleasure when we encounter 'Uniformity amidst Variety' (T1, 67; similarly T3, 17). The *sensus communis*, which he variously calls 'a Publick Sense' and 'sympathy', responds to factors that bear on another person's happiness, bringing us pleasure when they are happy and displeasure when they suffer (T3, 17; *Short Intro*, 33). The 'sense of honour' brings pleasure when others approve our actions and displeasure when they dislike, condemn, or resent something we have done (T3, 18; *Short Intro*, 41–2). The 'moral sense' or the 'sense of the fitting and the good' brings the pleasure of approbation and the displeasure of disapprobation when we observe or reflect upon affections, tempers, opinions, intentions, or actions, and they strike us as virtuous or vicious (T3, 17–18; *Metaphysics*, 119). And the 'sense of humor' brings pleasure when something appears ridiculous (*Metaphysics*, 120; *Short Intro*, 43).

As should already be clear, what twenty-first century readers would call 'emotions' play a significant role in Hutcheson's moral theory. Before I say more about that role, however, it would be helpful to say something about the terms he uses when talking about emotions. Hutcheson uses four terms to refer to the various 'modifications of the mind' that we would designate with the single term 'emotion', namely, 'affection', 'passion', 'sentiment', and 'emotion'. Of these, the term he uses most frequently is 'affection'.[9] 'Affection' may be used in two different ways, Hutcheson suggests. If we were using it precisely, we would reserve it for desires and aversions (T3, 30, and 49). However, he observes, it is customary to apply the term to a much wider range of 'Modifications of the Mind' than this. 'Affection' is also used to refer to states such as joy, gratitude, compassion, sorrow, and despair.

Hutcheson's characterisation of these other 'modifications of the mind' that we also call 'affections' is not entirely consistent. At times, he defines them in contrast to sensations (T3, 30).[10] At other times, he describes them as being a kind of sensation, such as when he claims, 'Joy and Sorrow are only a sort of Sensations' (T3, 49). Although his use of terms may not be entirely consistent, the general conceptual map is reasonably clear. On the one hand, we have sensations, which divide into two classes: (1) *'direct immediate Perception*[s] of Pleasure or Pain from the present Object or Event'; and (2) *'Perceptions* of Pleasure or Pain, not directly raised by the *Presence* or *Operation* of the Event or Object, but by our *Reflection* upon, or *Apprehension* of their present or certainly future existence' (T3, 30). On the other hand, we have desires and aversions, which 'arise in our Mind, from the Frame of our Nature, upon Apprehension of Good or Evil in Objects, Actions, or Events' (T3, 18). Affections in the narrower sense are simply desires or aversions. Affections in the wider sense combine desires and aversions with sensations raised by apprehension of or reflection upon objects or events (T3, 49).

Understanding what Hutcheson means by 'affections' makes it easier to explain his other three 'emotion' terms. 'Sentiment' and 'Passion' are often used synonymously with 'affection'. In these cases, they refer to *'Modifications, or Actions of the Mind consequent upon the Apprehension of certain Objects or Events, in which the Mind generally conceives Good or Evil'* (T3, 15). Nevertheless, 'passions' can also be distinguished from sentiments/affections:

When the word Passion is imagined to denote anything different from the *Affections*, it includes, beside the *Desire* or *Aversion*, beside the *calm Joy* upon apprehended Possession of Good or *Sorrow* from the Loss of it, or from impending Evil, 'a *confused Sensation* either of Pleasure or Pain, occasioned or attended by some violent bodily Motions, which keeps the Mind much employed upon the present Affair, to the exclusion of every thing else, and prolongs or strengthens the Affections sometimes to such a degree, as to prevent all *deliberate Reasoning* about our Conduct'. (T3, 30–31)[11]

Passions are affections-plus. What distinguishes them from other affections is their strength, confusion, and agitation as well as bodily motions that contribute to them. This strong mental and physical agitation is what he refers to as 'emotion' (T4, 188).[12]

We are now in a better position to understand the roles of what we would call emotions in Hutcheson's moral theory. First, they factor in moral perception. If calm affections are in part sensations, and if sensations are part of the way in which we perceive the objects of the senses, then calm affections can be part of the way in which we perceive the objects of the internal senses. Hutcheson illustrates the necessity of affections and sentiments for the perceptions of the internal senses when he argues that 'a Being naturally incapable of Fear' would lack the 'Power of perceiving' certain moral and aesthetic qualities. In the same passage he goes on to liken approbation and delight to the perception of colour and flavour (T1, 70–1). It is an illuminating comparison. Like the secondary qualities – colour, flavour, sound, texture, and smell – moral and aesthetic qualities will be partly constituted by other qualities of the objects in which they inhere and will be partly constituted by our perceptual apparatus. His wording sometimes emphasises one of these sources of constitution, such as when he defines 'Moral Goodness' in terms of a 'Quality apprehended in Actions, which procures Approbation, and Love toward the Actor, from those who receive no Advantage by the Action' (T2, 85). At other times he emphasises the other, such as when he asserts, 'Our *Senses* constitute Objects, Events or Actions *good*' (T3, 39). But the full picture is one in which moral qualities, like secondary qualities, involve both what the world brings to the subject and what the subject brings to the world; and our affections are an important constituent of our perceptions of good, virtue, beauty, honour, and their opposites.[13]

Hutcheson ties the value of a person's sentiments to their perceptual accuracy. This contrasts with later variants of sentimentalism that celebrated the moral agent's emotionality as a good in itself and encouraged many readers of Henry Mackenzie's first novel, *The Man of Feeling*, to continue to admire the benevolent sentiments of the main character, Harley, even when they contribute to the gross misreading of his social circumstances.[14] Whereas Harley's sentiments make him 'unfit for the world',[15] Hutcheson's are meant to fit the world and thus make one better able to navigate it.

The second role for affections is in reflection. Affections can arise as we reflect upon other perceptions of good or evil, virtue or vice. For example, we may experience pride when we reflect upon the fact that the person whose virtue we are perceiving is our friend, or shame when we realise the vice we disapprove in another is one we share (T3, 30). It is here that the growing eighteenth-century print culture comes into the picture by offering readers texts that encourage reflection. Essayists, novelists, playwrights, poets, and preachers could help educate and refine the sentiments of their readers by drawing their attention to qualities or situations they might otherwise have overlooked. And they could encourage people to link ideas that, on first glance, did not appear related, so that when they encounter either idea in the future they will feel the same sentiment (or discourage links they have already made).

A third place affections play a role is in motivating us to pursue certain goods or avoid certain evils. Since desires and aversions are part of affections, our affections can move us to go after the goods we perceive and to flee the evils we observe. Fourth, affections play a role in shaping our temperament. The more frequently we are moved by particular affections, the more disposed we are to be moved by the same affections in the future (T3, 47–8). Finally, certain affections are part of the expression of certain virtues. Experiencing public affections, for example, is an important aspect of being benevolent (T3, 28).

The picture sketched thus far has a number of attractive features. It helps explain where moral ideas and judgements come from: one need not posit innate ideas in order to account for ethics because ethical ideas can be acquired through the operations of the internal senses. It enables Hutcheson to respond to sceptical egoists like Hobbes and Mandeville, insofar as he can show that the objects of many of our valuing emotions have no direct bearing on our individual welfare. When we sympathise with another it is our perception of her welfare (not our own) that explains our response. Hutcheson's framework also enables him to explain how moral judgements can be motivating, which he takes to be an important respect in which his account is preferable to writers like Gilbert Burnet and Samuel Clarke who attempted to ground moral judgements in a faculty of reason. There is much to recommend it, then, in Hutcheson's context as well as our own.

However, Hutcheson's account also has a number of key features that lead to the tension described in part 1. Insofar as we wish to avoid a similar conundrum, identifying the sources of the tension in Hutcheson can be instructive. Where, then, did Hutcheson go astray?

4 Hutcheson's fall from grace

Since his fellow sentimentalists – Anthony Ashley Cooper (the third Earl of Shaftesbury), David Hume, and Adam Smith – did not run into the same difficulty with gracious virtues, one place to look for an explanation of Hutcheson's problem is at the differences between his theory and theirs.[16] Perhaps the most striking difference between the theories is Hutcheson's enthusiasm for mathematics as a tool for doing moral philosophy. Michael Gill has noted that one interesting difference between the moral rationalists – like Cudworth, Clarke, and Balguy – and the moral sentimentalists is the tendency of the former to look to mathematics for the key to understanding morality while the latter sought the key in aesthetics.[17] What Gill fails to mention is that Hutcheson does both. Hutcheson's enthusiasm for mathematics *and* aesthetics is evident, among other places, in the title page of the 1725 London edition of

> An INQUIRY into the ORIGINAL of Our IDEAS of BEAUTY and VIRTUE; In TWO TREATISES. IN WHICH The Principles of the late Earl of SHAFTESBURY are Explain'd and Defended, against the Author of the *Fable of the Bees*: AND THE Ideas of *Moral Good* and *Evil* are establish'd, according to the Sentiments of the Antient *Moralists*. With an Attempt to introduce *Mathematical Calculation* in Subjects of *Morality*.[18]

And his ongoing commitment to each is still on display three years later when he publishes Treatises 3 and 4.

It was quite common in the century prior to the publication of Hutcheson's four treatises for theorists to look to mathematics for their model of analytic rigour, so it is difficult to say with confidence who inspired Hutcheson to do so. Aaron Garrett suggests Hutcheson's 'desire to render morals into mathematically quantifiable ratios likely derives from Richard Cumberland'.[19] Although Hutcheson cites Cumberland on several occasions, and Cumberland does draw an analogy between moral judgement and mathematical judgement,[20] the inspiration is more likely to have come from Malebranche, whose influence on Hutcheson is even more pronounced than Cumberland's. In a section of *The Search after Truth*, entitled 'Geometers proceed properly in the search after truth', Malebranche offers geometry and algebra as exemplars of proper method.[21] In another passage he asserts, 'Analysis or the Algebra of kinds is assuredly the most beautiful, i.e., the most fruitful and the most certain, of all sciences. Without it, the mind has neither penetration nor scope; and with it it is capable of knowing nearly everything that can be known with certitude and clarity'.[22] What makes algebra stand out is that its practitioners use variables to reduce complex problems to a manageable size.

> [B]ecause they see their mind incapable of attending to several figures simultaneously, . . . they avail themselves of ordinary letters, which are perfectly familiar to us, in order to express and simplify their ideas. With the mind neither hampered nor occupied with having to represent a great many figures and an infinite number of lines, it can thus perceive at a single glance what it could not otherwise see, because the mind can penetrate further and embrace more things when its capacity is used economically.[23]

This is exactly what Hutcheson does. For example, in Treatise 2 he says, 'The moral Importance of any Agent, or the Quantity of publick Good produc'd by him, is in a compound Ratio of his Benevolence and Abilitys: or (by substituting the initial Letters for the Words, as $M = $ Moment of Good . . .) $M = B \times A$' (T2, 128). Similarly, in Treatise 4 he writes, 'The *Quantity of Love* toward any Person is in a compound Proportion of the apprehended *Causes of Love* in him, and of the *Goodness of Temper* in the Observer. Or $L = C \times G$' (T4, 189). Further support for the hypothesis that Malebranche contributed to Hutcheson's enthusiasm for using mathematical calculation in moral philosophy can be found in the similarity between Hutcheson's proportionality principle – which appears immediately after the passage just quoted – and parallel passages in Malebranche.[24] Whether Hutcheson's mathematical muse was Malebranche, Cumberland, or one of the many other mathematical enthusiasts of the day, one thing is clear: his attempt to introduce mathematical calculation into morality distinguishes him from other sentimentalists of the period. So it is reasonable to ask whether this is the feature of his system that generated the tension between his commitment to gracious virtues and his defence of a proportionality principle that seems to rule out many of them.

Since Aristotle famously suggests that ethics is a subject matter in which we should not expect the same degree of precision that we expect in the natural sciences,[25] it would seem incumbent on an author who intends both to establish 'ideas of moral good according to the sentiments of the ancient moralists' and to 'introduce mathematical calculation in subjects of morality'[26] to give the reader an explanation of how he can resolve the tension between these two aims. Unfortunately, Hutcheson does not explain why we should take mathematics to provide the model for rigorous thought in ethics. However, even if we accept Hutcheson's mathematical model, if his calculation is to produce reliable results, it will need to include the requisite data. And this is where the problem is introduced. In his enthusiasm for the simplifying techniques of mathematics, Hutcheson oversimplifies the domain he is analysing. In particular, he pays insufficient attention to two variables: needs and character.

The problem is reinforced by his account of the internal senses, which is a second respect in which he differs from some of his fellow sentimentalists. Even though the comparison with secondary qualities permits the perceiver to add something to the equation, the comparison with perception nevertheless invites one to forget what the perceiver adds. It is easy to think of the perceiver functioning in the way a window might: it can be clean or dirty, clear or distorting. Even at its best, however, the window doesn't leave one better able to see what is on the other side of the glass than one could in its absence. The most one will expect is that it will avoid inhibiting one's perception. Similarly, if goodness is the property one is concerned to track and one explains such tracking by appealing to senses, it is easy to think of the perceiver in much the same way.[27] Qualities of a perceiver's character might influence where or how attentively she looks, but they will not alter her sight.

This perspective is further encouraged by the tradition on which Hutcheson is building, according to which what distinguishes affections from passions is whether they are built around clear and distinct ideas, or confused and obscure ones. Within Malebranche's discussion, for example, what the perceiver adds to perception is confusion. Clear, accurate perception involves getting ourselves out of the way so that we can grasp ideas as they are in the mind of God.[28] Hutcheson adopts a different metaphysical framework, but he seems to accept at least this aspect of Malebranche's epistemic framework, distinguishing between the confusion of passions and the clear-sightedness of calm affections.[29] The principal agent-provided influences other than passions that he considers – 'Custom, Education, Habits, and Company' (T3, 47) – are likewise treated as distorters of perception. That is, they are treated as bad habits, confused customs, faulty education, and corrupting company. For example, Hutcheson observes,

> the *Laws* or *Customs* of a Country, the *Humour* of our Company may have made strange *Associations* of *Ideas*, so that some Objects, which of themselves are indifferent to any Sense, by reason of some *additional* grateful *Idea*, may become very desirable; or by like *Addition* of an ungrateful *Idea* may raise the strongest Aversion. (T3, 20)

There is not a parallel discussion of how good habits, customs, education, and company might improve our perceptual capacities, except insofar as the removal of distortion counts as an improvement. The upshot is that the perceptual metaphor effectively silences questions about what the agent might add. It invites one to think that the moral agent's job is to see accurately, report reliably, and respond efficiently to the goods that are available for her pursuit. Such a framework gives priority to states of affairs external to the agent. And it is easy to pay insufficient attention to factors the agent adds to the equation, reducing her to merely a reactive system responding to external stimuli.

Although the perceptual metaphor encourages one to neglect or overlook valuable qualities that a moral agent might add, it is not by itself incompatible with gracious virtues. One might introduce other qualities of character to explain certain admirable aspects of our behaviour. Part of what is so surprising about Hutcheson's fall from grace is that he explicitly draws attention to a number of features that could provide a corrective to the misleading tendencies of the perceptual metaphor. In particular, he discusses propensities, motives, and qualities of temperament. He introduces the first of these by contrasting them with actions performed from sensation or desire:

> We may further observe something in our Nature, determining us very frequently to Action, distinct from *Sensation* and *Desire*; if by Desire we mean a distinct Inclination to something apprehended as Good either publick or private, or as the Means of avoiding Evil: viz. a certain *Propensity of Instinct* to Objects and Actions, without any Conception of them as Good, or as the Means of preventing Evil. These Objects or Actions are generally, tho not always, in effect the *Means* of some Good; but we are determined to them even without this Conception of them. (T3, 51)

He suggests that various propensities commonly accompany our particular affections. For example, we have propensities to fame, to violence when angry, to seek the company of those we love, to be present at an accident scene or to observe those who have suffered some tragedy, and to cry out and run away when we are threatened with danger, to name just a few (T3, 51–2). Some such propensities could be the source of gracious actions and one might expect them to be the raw materials for developing gracious virtues. Our propensity to be drawn to an accident scene, for instance, could readily be combined with compassion for the vulnerable and a disposition to offer assistance. Insofar as the compassion felt and the assistance offered are determined not by the merits of the recipient but by their current suffering and need, these affections and actions would be gracious. To the extent that the compassion is paired with a desire for the happiness or relief of suffering of the person we are assisting, we love them, on Hutcheson's account (T4, 188). And provided the object of our compassion is not a family member, a benefactor, or someone whose virtue we have observed – the causes Hutcheson considers – that love would not be proportional to its causes. So including propensities in conjunction with other features of Hutcheson's account would provide the resources needed to challenge his proportionality principle. Unfortunately, Hutcheson overlooks the resource propensities provide, lumping them in with passions: 'These *Propensities*, along with the Sensations abovementioned, when they occur without rational Desire, we may call *Passions*, and when they happen along with Desires, denominate them *passionate*' (T3, 52). Since passions are, by definition, confused, the consequence of classifying propensities with passions is that they, too, are classified as confused. So whereas Hutcheson's initial characterisation of propensities defined them as operating independently of a perception of good or evil, by including them in the class of passions he transforms them into a confused perception of good or evil.

A second resource that could help a theory maintain space for gracious virtues is an emphasis on motives. While some motives are identified in terms of that *for which* someone acts, others are characterised in terms of that *from which* they act. For example, a person who visits a friend who is ill may do so in order to cheer her up. The phrase 'in order to cheer her up' identifies something about the intention that makes sense of her action. It is that for which she is acting and we often call this her motive for going to see her friend. However, we also use the term 'motive' to identify another feature that helps make sense of her action. She is not only visiting in order to cheer her friend up, she is also going out of friendship. The latter motive is part of what distinguishes this visit from, say, sending flowers to a convalescing person she does not know. Both actions may be done in order to cheer someone up, but only one of them is done out of the motive(s) of friendship.[30] Hutcheson's framework includes a place for motives. In fact, they play a central role within his theory. As noted above, he claims,

> If we examine all the Actions which are counted amiable any where, and enquire into the Grounds upon which they are approv'd, we shall find, that in the Opinion of the Person who approves them, they always appear as Benevolent, or flowing from Love of others, and a Study of their Happiness. (T2, 116)

This passage looks as though it is drawing attention to both the forward- and the backward-looking dimensions of motivation. However, he tends to analyse that from which we act in terms either of intentions or of the affections. Since Hutcheson understands affections to be (or to be the effects of) perceptions or corruptions of perception, that aspect of the theoretical framework which might have been used to make space for grace is closed off, for the reasons discussed above. He analyses intentions in terms of the reasons for which we act, given our desire to obtain and promote the good. And this desire he takes to be governed by the proportionality principle: '[A]nyone who has carefully examined the things which arouse desire, and has directed the powers of his mind to this thing, will find that all his appetites and desires will be stronger or milder in proportion to the goods themselves' (*Metaphysics*, 131). So motives, like propensities, end up being closed off as a resource for explaining gracious virtues.

The third resource for preserving gracious virtues within Hutcheson's framework is his discussion of temperament. Some people are more disposed to generosity, friendship, or general benevolence than others. These different constellations of dispositional, motivational, and volitional tendencies which differentiate some personalities from others he calls 'temperaments'. And in the *Metaphysics* he offers a prime example of graciousness that appears to be explained in terms of temperament (or some analogous divine dispositions). 'All intentions for his [God's] own actions seem to emanate ... from his unwavering benevolence and his natural and unchangeable will to share his felicity with others' (*Metaphysics*, 173). This claim would have been unremarkable in Hutcheson's Presbyterian context. Within Presbyterian circles, God's creation of the world was not explained by the world's goodness (as if the possible goodness of non-existent objects obliged God to bring them into existence). Rather, God's creative activity was understood to be an overflow of God's being. God's good nature expressed itself by bringing other good things into existence and lavishing gifts on them. The explanation of our existence and God's love for us was to be sought in God's goodness, not ours. This was an important aspect of a Reformed theology of grace. Given that another tenet of Reformed faith was that human beings were made in God's image and were called to imitate God in various respects, it would have been fairly straightforward for Hutcheson to have argued that human nature could express itself in a similar way. There could be gracious human ways of being that expressed themselves by making things around them better. And the goodness of gracious actions could be explained not by the qualities of what they brought about or of the person whose happiness they promoted, but rather, like God, by the qualities of the agent from whom the actions flowed.

However, that was not the direction Hutcheson turned. Instead, having recognised that people with different temperaments respond to the same situations in different ways, he attempts to subsume these differences under a more general regularity.

> However these *Affections* [for family members, benefactors, and the virtuous] are very different from the *general Benevolence* toward all, yet it is very probable, that there is a *Regularity* or *Proportion* observed in the Constitution of our Nature; so that, abstracting from some acquired *Habits*, or *Associations of Ideas*, and from the more sudden *Emotions* of some particular Passions, *that* Temper which has the most lively *Gratitude*, or is the most susceptive of *Friendship* with virtuous Characters, would also have the strongest *general Benevolence* toward indifferent Persons: And on the contrary, where there is the weakest *general Benevolence*, there we could expect the least *Gratitude*, and the least *Friendship*, or *Love toward the Virtuous*. (T4, 188)

This claim enables him to isolate the variable of good temperament. We all love proportionally, he claims. It is just that some of us are better attuned to the goods around us than others. By this move he undermines temperament as a possible foundation for gracious virtues and ends up reducing it to a ratio of love to causes.

> The *Goodness of any Temper* is therefore as the *Quantity of Love*, divided by the apprehended *Causes*, or $G = L/C$. And since we cannot apprehend any Goodness in having the *Degree of Love* above the *Proportion*

of its Causes, the most virtuous Temper is that in which the *Love* equals its *Causes*. (T4, 189)

Thus, Hutcheson's enthusiasm for mathematical simplification led him to conclusions that were at odds with the perceptions of his own internal senses.

5   Conclusion

There are a number of places in which, had Hutcheson made a different choice, he might have avoided the tension we have been exploring. Neither his enthusiasm for introducing mathematical calculation into moral subjects, nor his adoption of an account of internal senses, needs to have led to a neglect of character or to an endorsement of a proportionality principle that would exclude the gracious virtues. Other features of his account offered resources that would have enabled him to develop a more consistent theory. However, we noted how an account of moral judgement built around a perceptual model might nudge one in the direction Hutcheson ended up going. If the goodness one sees determines the degree to which one does and should love, then it looks as though there is little room for gracious affections.

Happily, Hutcheson's contributions to the public sphere and to the positive role of gracious affections did not end with the publication of Treatises 3 and 4 in 1728. Over time, his enthusiasm for the introduction of 'mathematical calculation into subjects of morality' appears to have waned. In the third edition of Treatise 4, published in 1742, and in later editions of Treatise 2, Hutcheson deleted formulas like 'G = L/C' and 'toned down or removed' much of the other 'mathematical language'.[31] Although the proportionality principle still appears in the third edition of Treatise 4, that seems to be a relic of the earlier work rather than a sign of Hutcheson's ongoing commitment. In his mature project, *A System of Moral Philosophy*, on which he was working for much of the 1730s and 1740s, very little of his youthful mathematical enthusiasm is still in evidence. His aesthetic predilection had won out over his mathematical one. And, correspondingly, the passages in which he dealt with the evaluation of character[32] were reworked in ways that made space for grace.[33]

Notes

1. Both of Hutcheson's major works from the 1720s were divided into two treatises. When, in footnotes to these works, he directs his reader to something

he has said elsewhere, he refers to them as Treatises 1, 2, 3, and 4 (see the preface to *An Essay on the Nature and Conduct of the Passions and Affections, with Illustrations on the Moral Sense*, p. 11). I shall adopt his convention, and use Treatise 1 (or T1 for short) to refer to 'An Inquiry Concerning Beauty, Order, &c.'; Treatise 2 to 'An Inquiry Concerning the Original of Our Ideas of Virtue or Moral Good'; Treatise 3 to 'An Essay on the Nature and Conduct of the Passions'; and Treatise 4 to 'Illustrations on the Moral Sense'. The page numbers for T1 and T2 refer to *An Inquiry into the Original of Our Ideas of Beauty and Virtue* (2004) ed. Wolfgang Leidhold (Indianapolis, IN: Liberty Fund); those for T3 and T4 refer to *An Essay on the Nature and Conduct of the Passions and Affections, with Illustration on the Moral Sense* (2002) ed. Aaron Garrett (Indianapolis, IN: Liberty Fund).

2. *The London Journal*, 296 (27 March 1725), 1; reprinted in the *Collected Works of Francis Hutcheson* (1990) Vol. 7 (Hildesheim: Georg Olms Verlag), p. 12. The quote within the quote is from page 9 of the preface to Treatises 1 and 2.

3. For further discussion of gracious virtues, see Glen Pettigrove (2012) 'Forgiveness and Grace', in *Forgiveness and Love* (Oxford: Oxford University Press), pp. 124–50.

4. The number indicates how often he uses 'kind', 'kindly', or 'kindness' in T2. Similarly, the number that follows 'humanity' includes both 'humane' and 'humanity', etc.

5. As Wolfgang Leidhold points out, in T1 and T2 'the reader is confronted with an irritating number of terms used to describe love: affection, intention, sentiment, design, disposition, inclination, motive, determination, instinct, even passion' ('Introduction', *Inquiry*, xiv, note 12).

6. Elizabeth Radcliffe claims that, for Hutcheson, 'moral approval and particular benevolence' are 'essential to love' (Elizabeth Radcliffe (2004) 'Love and Benevolence in Hutcheson's and Hume's Theories of the Passions', *British Journal for the History of Philosophy* 12: 631–53, at 635). However, it would be unusual for a Presbyterian minister like Hutcheson to make moral approval an essential constituent of love, given the importance of the command to love our enemies within the moral teaching of the gospels and the Pauline epistles. This passage and others show that he is not breaking ranks with his fellow clergy on this point. Hutcheson's claim is more modest. Love is 'generally attended with some *Approbation*' of its object (T3, 52), but such approbation need not be present in all cases.

7. Francis Hutcheson (2006) *Logic, Metaphysics, and the Natural Sociability of Mankind*, eds. James Moore and Michael Silverthorne (Indianapolis, IN: Liberty Fund), p. 215.

8. Hutcheson's use of the label 'internal sense' shifts over time. Initially (e.g. T1, 67 and T2, 17) he uses it narrowly to refer to what he also calls the 'sense of beauty'. Later, for example, in *Metaphysics*, 117 and *A Short Introduction to Moral Philosophy* (2007 [1747]) ed. Luigi Turco (Indianapolis, IN: Liberty Fund), p. 27, he uses it more broadly to encompass all of the perceptions of pleasure and pain that are not entirely attributable to the five external senses.

9. He uses 'affection' twice as often as 'passion' (which he uses more than 250 times) and nearly nine times as often as 'sentiment' (which he uses 62 times). 'Emotion' is a term he only uses once.

10. Stephen Darwall appears to have such passages in mind when he writes, 'moral sense receives sensation or perception, and Hutcheson explicitly distinguishes between these and desire' (*The British Moralists and the Moral 'Ought': 1640–1740* (1995) (Cambridge: Cambridge University Press), p. 231). Although Darwall's reading reflects what Hutcheson says in some passages, it requires one to overlook a number of other passages in which the distinction between perceptions and desires is blurred in virtue of the fact that affections – broadly construed – have both a perceptual and a conative dimension.

11. Sometimes, Hutcheson uses quotation marks to identify a claim put forward by another author. More often he uses them to set off a definition that he is offering or a claim that he will be considering in the following paragraph(s). In this case, he is doing both. He is putting forward a definition of passions that he will be discussing in subsequent paragraphs. And in defining passions as 'confused' and as 'occasioned' or 'prolonged by bodily Motions' (T3, 50), Hutcheson is attempting to capture the distinguishing features of Malebranche's account of passions in *The Search After Truth* ((1997) trans. and ed. Thomas Lennon and Paul Olscamp (Cambridge: Cambridge University Press), book 5, Chapter 1).

12. Similarly, see Joseph Butler (1860 [1726]) *Fifteen Sermons* (Robert Carter & Brothers), sermon 5, footnote to paragraph 1, p. 65, and sermon 9, paragraph 2, p. 102.

13. Attempting to situate Hutcheson within the conceptual space mapped out by twentieth-century metaethicists, the last 60 years have seen various authors arguing that Hutcheson either is or is not a moral realist. The most influential proponent of a realist interpretation has been David Fate Norton (D. F. Norton (1982) 'Hutcheson's Moral Realism', *David Hume: Common-Sense Moralist, Sceptical Metaphysician* (Princeton, NJ: Princeton University Press)). Recently, Terence Irwin has argued that William Whewell offered a similar, realist reading of Hutcheson in his 1852 *Lectures on the History of Moral Philosophy in England* (T. Irwin (2008) 'Hutcheson: For and Against Moral Realism', *The Development of Ethics: A Historical and Critical Study* (Oxford: Oxford University Press, Vol. 2, p. 400). Anti-realist readings include J. Martin Stafford (1985) 'Hutcheson, Hume and the Ontology of Morals', *Journal of Value Inquiry* 19: 133–51; Elizabeth Radcliffe (1986) 'Hutcheson's Perceptual and Moral Subjectivism', *History of Philosophy Quarterly* 3: 407–21; P. J. E. Kail (2001) 'Hutcheson's Moral Sense: Skepticism, Realism, and Secondary Qualities', *History of Philosophy Quarterly* 18: 57–77; and Irwin, 'Hutcheson: For and Against Moral Realism'. A third position is staked out by Kenneth Winkler, who proposes that Hutcheson's moral theory 'cannot usefully be described in these twentieth century terms' and notes that ' "Realism" was an eighteenth century label for the view that there is a real distinction between vice and virtue. In this sense, largely forgotten in the present century, both Hutcheson and Hume are unhesitating realists' (K. Winkler (1996) 'Hutcheson and Hume on the Color of Virtue', *Hume Studies* 22: 3 and 19). The interpretation offered here should be compatible with variants of each of these ways of interpreting Hutcheson's metaethical position.

14. For a discussion of the contrast between the popular reception of the novel and Mackenzie's own view, which appears to have been much nearer to Hutcheson's, see Henry Mackenzie (2001) 'The Lounger, No. 20', in Brian Vickers (Ed.), *The Man of Feeling* (Oxford; Oxford University Press), pp. 100–3; William Burling (1988) 'A "sickly sort of refinement": The Problem of Sentimentalism in Mackenzie's The Man of Feeling', *Studies in Scottish Literature* 23: 136–49; and Maureen Harkin (1994) 'Mackenzie's *Man of Feeling*: Embalming Sensibility', *English Literary History* 61: 317–40.

15. Mackenzie, *Man of Feeling*, 61.

16. Hume, for example, agrees that our loves are generally explained by factors like those Hutcheson labels 'the causes of love'. However, he does not make the further claims that (a) we only love in proportion to these causes, or (b) we ought to love in proportion to them. For further discussion, see Rico Vitz (2002) 'Hume and the Limits of Benevolence', *Hume Studies* 28: 271–95.

17. Michael Gill (2007) 'Moral Rationalism vs. Moral Sentimentalism: Is Morality More Like Math or Beauty?' *Philosophy Compass* 2: 16–30.

18. Hutcheson (1725) *An Inquiry into the Original of our Ideas of Beauty and Virtue; in Two Treatises* (London: J. Darby in Bartholomew-Close), emphasis in the original.

19. Editor's footnote 55 to Hutcheson, T4, 189.

20. Richard Cumberland (2005) *A Treatise of the Laws of Nature*, trans. John Maxwell (Indianapolis, IN: Liberty Fund), pp. 298–9.

21. Malebranche, *Search after Truth*, book 3, Chapter 3, Section 3, p. 209.

22. Malebranche, *Search after Truth*, book 4, Chapter 11, Section 2, pp. 314–15.

23. Malebranche, *Search after Truth*, book 3, Chapter 3, Section 3, p. 209. See also book 5, Chapter 2, p. 345.

24. See especially Malebranche, *Search after Truth*, book 4, Chapter 1, p. 266. For further discussion of Malebranche's influence on Hutcheson, see Jeffrey Barnouw (1992) 'Passion as "Confused" Perception or Thought in Descartes, Malebranche, and Hutcheson', *Journal of the History of Ideas* 53: 397–424.

25. Aristotle (2000) *Nicomachean Ethics*, ed. Roger Crisp (Cambridge: Cambridge University Press), i.3, 1094b.

26. From the title page of the 1725 edition of T1 and T2 cited above.

27. Whether one takes Hutcheson to be a realist or an anti-realist about moral properties, it is clear that he thinks that external properties are reliably correlated with internal perceptions of good and evil, virtue and vice. A properly functioning internal sense will be one that accurately tracks those external properties.

28. See Malebranche, *Search after Truth*, book 1, Chapter 5, p. 24 and book 3.2, Chapter 6, pp. 230–5.

29. See Barnouw, 416–17.

30. See Michael Stocker (1979) 'Good Intentions in Greek and Modern Moral Virtue', *Australasian Journal of Philosophy* 57: 220–4.

31. Garrett, editor's footnote 55 in Hutcheson, T4, 189.

32. Francis Hutcheson (1755) *A System of Moral Philosophy* (R. and A. Foulis), book 2, Chapter 2, pp. 238–51.

33. This project was made possible by a generous grant from the Royal Society of New Zealand and benefited from the gracious hospitality of the

Centre for the Study of Perceptual Experience at the University of Glasgow and the Centre for the History of Emotions at the University of Adelaide. I am grateful for their support as well as for the helpful feedback on earlier drafts of the paper provided by Merridee Bailey, Katie Barclay, Garrett Cullity, David Lemmings, Jonathan McKeown-Green, Jennifer McMahon, and Robert Phiddian.

12
Anatomist and Painter: Hume's Struggles as a Sentimental Stylist

Michael L. Frazer

1 Introduction

When David Hume wrote to Baron de Montesquieu '*J'ai consacré ma vie à la philosophie et aux belles-lettres*',[1] he was not describing himself as having two separate callings. His was a single vocation – one involving the expression of deep thought through beautiful writing.[2] This vocation did not come naturally or easily to Hume. He struggled continually to reshape his approach to prose, famously renouncing the *Treatise of Human Nature* as a literary failure and radically revising the presentation of his philosophy in the *Essays* and two *Enquiries*. This essay will focus on Hume's struggle between two modes of moral–philosophical composition prevalent in his day: the cold, unemotional style associated with experimental science that Hume metaphorically labels 'anatomy' and the warm, rhetorical style which he labels 'painting'.

Hume's literary development over the course of his repeated presentations of his moral–philosophical ideas has already been the subject of considerable scholarly attention. For many years, the conventional wisdom was that enshrined by L. A. Selby-Bigge in the editor's introduction to his edition of the *Enquiries*. The tale told by Selby-Bigge is one of stylistic progress but intellectual decline. While the *Treatise* is 'ill-proportioned, incoherent [and] ill-expressed', the *Enquiries* display 'elegance, lucidity and proportion'.[3] Yet while the *Treatise* is a philosophical masterpiece despite its literary flaws, in the *Enquiries* Hume has come to write works of a 'lower philosophical standard' meant for an elegant but unsophisticated lay audience.[4]

However, just as Bigge's editions eventually came to give way to new editions of Hume's writings, so too has his position on Hume's philosophical decline given way to new, positive evaluations of the *Essays*

223

and *Enquiries* as remarkable philosophical works in their own right.[5] As so often happens, the counter-orthodoxy has become the orthodoxy, and there is now an air of mustiness to any philosophical dissatisfaction with Hume's later work, perhaps something unscholarly about refusing to accede to Hume's own judgement that of all his writings the second *Enquiry* was 'incomparably the best'.[6] Even if I am speaking only for myself, however, I must admit that at least some admirers of Hume's thought still experience considerable disappointment with both the literary style of the *Treatise* and the philosophical depth of the *Essays* and *Enquiries*, finding it unfortunate that Hume was never able to express his best ideas using his best prose. The goal of this essay is not to defend my lukewarm evaluation of these works, but to explain the tensions in the literary culture of his day which led Hume to write as he did, tensions which may in turn then help explain why so many over the centuries have found Hume's stylistic choices to be so deeply problematic.

The key to understanding Hume's literary development is to see that his struggle regarding painting and anatomy was not a solitary or idiosyncratic one. It was instead symptomatic of the conflicting obligations created by the relationship between authors and their readers in the print culture of Enlightenment Britain. Enlightenment authors were believed to have a responsibility to inform their readers, to provide them with accurate information on important topics. Doing so would suggest the adoption of an anatomical style. Yet these authors were also believed to have a responsibility to engage their readers – not only to hold their interest as a necessary prerequisite for the transfer of knowledge, but also to connect with them emotionally so as to allow for the creation of the sort of sentimental community so highly valued in the eighteenth century. Only if authors succeeded in affectively connecting with the readers could texts hope to change hearts as well as minds, evoking proper moral sentiments and hence become vehicles for both ethical improvement and social reform. As a result, while Hume began with a more or less straightforward commitment to the anatomical approach, he came over time to attempt to combine both painting and anatomy in a single text. Doing so, he became convinced, was necessary in order to engage a wide readership emotionally while maintaining philosophical depth and accuracy. It is not clear, however, whether painting and anatomy can actually be combined in the way that Hume wished to combine them. As a result, the tensions between anatomy and painting continued to plague Hume's philosophical composition. The conflicting demands placed on eighteenth-century authors may never have been resolved adequately in his work.

Adam Potkay attributes the rise of a cold style of philosophical prose to the emergence of natural science, which in the minds of most eighteenth-century Britons had reached its apogee with Newton. The Royal Society and other institutional advocates of science in early modern Britain promoted an 'experimental ideal' according to which 'procedural rigor and a transparent language of argumentation should supplant the deceptions of eloquence in all essays addressed to the understanding'.[7] Perhaps the most notable statement of this position is by John Locke:

> If we would speak of things as they are, we must allow that all the art of rhetoric besides order and clearness, all the artificial and figurative application of words eloquence hath invented, are for nothing else but to insinuate wrong ideas, move the passions, and thereby mislead the judgment, and so indeed are perfect cheats. And therefore, however laudable or allowable oratory may render them in harangues and popular addresses, they are certainly, in all discourses that pretend to inform or instruct, wholly to be avoided, and where truth and knowledge are concerned, cannot but be thought a great fault, either of the language or person that makes use of them.[8]

At the same time as this dry style was emerging in the work of philosophers inspired by Newtonian science, however, emotional rhetoric remained highly popular. Peter Jones describes the preachers and teachers of Enlightenment Britain as showing a strong 'bias towards practical eloquence rather than mere learning'.[9] The warm rhetoric of the pulpit and lectern found itself competing with cold empiricism of the laboratory for the loyalties of the British intelligentsia. Enlightenment philosophers' divided allegiances have led historians to debate whose side they were really on. Jones, Nicholas Phillipson, and others emphasise the didactic side of the moral philosophy of the British Enlightenment, while P. B. Wood has criticised this emphasis to focus on its naturalistic, empiricist side. What the former camp sees as the development of an art of secularised preaching, the latter camp sees as the development of a science of human nature explicitly modelled on the natural sciences.[10] The obvious resolution to this debate is that both sides are correct. While some British Enlightenment philosophers were preacherly moralists, others were quasi-scientific investigators of morality. Still others had conflicted loyalties, trying to negotiate a third way between the two camps. Hume's corpus offers an excellent case study of precisely such an attempt at literary triangulation.

2 The literary failure of the treatise

Given that Hume famously believed that 'reason is and ought only to be the slave of the passions',[11] it might seem that his primary loyalties would naturally lie with the rhetorical style. Yet Hume also introduces his philosophical debut, the *Treatise of Human Nature,* as 'an attempt to introduce the experimental method of reasoning into moral subjects' (T Cover). If Hume is indeed merely observing the operations of human passion in the same manner as Newton observed the orbits of the planets – and if his only goal is to describe these motions accurately – then the dry, scientific style would seem to be necessary. The truth about human sentiments, like any other form of empirical fact, can only be determined properly through a combination of observation and inductive reasoning, not through emotional contagion. Hume thus complains in the *Treatise* that too often in philosophy 'it is not reason, which carries the prize, but eloquence; and no man needs ever despair of gaining proselytes to the most extravagant hypothesis, who has art enough to represent it in any favorable colors' (T Intro.2). Leaving warm eloquence to other works, Hume's self-stated goal in the *Treatise* is only to present 'the accurate anatomy of human nature' (T 1.4.7.23) in general and the 'anatomy of the mind' (T 2.1.12.2) in particular.

Yet although Hume at first advocated an unsentimental examination of human sentiments, his commitment to dispassionate prose was soon challenged. Hume's first attempts at literary triangulation began before the *Treatise* was even completed. The most important evidence to this effect comes from a letter of September 1739 – after the publication of Books I and II of the *Treatise,* but before the publication of Book III, 'Of Morals' – in which Hume responds to Francis Hutcheson's feedback on a draft of this first statement of Hume's ethics. 'What affected me most in your remarks', Hume tells his intellectual mentor, 'is your observing that there wants a certain warmth in the cause of virtue, which, you think all good men would relish and could not displease amidst abstract enquiries'. Hutcheson seems to have used a standard metaphor for impassioned eloquence – one even more popular in the eighteenth century than in the twenty-first – in which passionate prose is associated with heat, and dispassionate prose with coldness.[12] Hume insists that his lack of warmth 'has not happened by chance, but is the effect of a reasoning either good or bad'. His reasoning is as follows:

There are different ways of examining the mind as well as the body. One may consider it either as an anatomist or as a painter: either to discover its most secret springs and principles or to describe the grace and beauty of its actions. I imagine it impossible to conjoin these two views. Where you pull off the skin and display all the minute parts, there appears something trivial even in the noblest attitudes and most vigorous actions. Nor can you ever render the object graceful or engaging but by clothing the parts again with skin and flesh and presenting only their bare outside. An anatomist, however, can give very good advice to a painter or statuary, and in like manner I am persuaded that a metaphysician may be very helpful to a moralist, though I cannot easily conceive these two characters united in the same work. Any warm sentiment of morals, I am afraid, would have the air of declamation amidst abstract reasonings, and would be esteemed contrary to good taste. And though I am much more ambitious of being esteemed a friend to virtue than a writer of taste, yet I must always carry the latter in my eye, otherwise I must despair of ever being serviceable to virtue. I hope these reasons will satisfy you, though at the same time, I intend to make a new trial, if it be possible to make the moralist and metaphysician agree a little better.[13]

Neither Hutcheson's initial criticisms nor his response to Hume survive. A letter from the following year, however, finds Hume informing his mentor that he has 'been very busy in correcting and finishing that discourse concerning morals which you perused'. Hume sent Hutcheson the revised version of the conclusion to Book III as evidence.[14] This revised conclusion may be the 'new trial' of which Hume wrote earlier. Sure enough, in the published version of that conclusion, Hume repeats the analogical reasoning he already used in his correspondence. Here, he writes:

The anatomist ought never to emulate the painter; nor in his accurate dissections and portraitures of the smaller parts of the human body pretend to give his figures any graceful and engaging attitude or expression. There is even something hideous or at least minute in the views of things which he presents; and it is necessary the objects should be set more at a distance, and be more covered up from sight, to make them engaging to the eye and imagination. An anatomist, however, is admirably fitted to give advice to a painter, and it is even impracticable to excel in the latter art, without the assistance of the former. We must have an exact knowledge of the parts, their situation and connection, before we can design with any elegance or correctness. And thus the most abstract speculations concerning human nature, however cold and unentertaining, become subservient to practical morality, and may render this latter science more correct in its precepts, and more persuasive in its exhortations. (T 3.3.6.6)

The same double analogy is presented a third time in the first section of the 1748 *Philosophical Essays Concerning Human Understanding* – retitled *An Enquiry Concerning Human Understanding* in 1758 – albeit now with the greater eloquence characteristic of Hume's later work:

An artist must be better qualified . . . who, besides a delicate taste and a quick apprehension, possesses an accurate knowledge of the internal fabric, the operations of the understanding, the workings of the passions, and the various species of sentiment which discriminate vice and virtue. How painful soever this inward search or enquiry may appear, it becomes, in some measure, requisite to those, who would describe with success the obvious and outward appearances of life and manners. The anatomist presents to the eye the most hideous and disagreeable objects, but his science is useful to the painter in delineating even a Venus or a Helen. While the latter employs all the richest colors of his art, and gives his figures the most graceful and engaging airs, he must still carry his attention to the inward structure of the human body: the position of the muscles, the fabric of the bones, and the use and figure of every part or organ. Accuracy is, in every case, advantageous to beauty, and just reasoning to delicate sentiment. In vain would we exalt the one by depreciating the other. (EHU 1.8)[15]

Indeed, the entire first section of the first *Enquiry*, 'On the Different Species of Philosophy', can be read as an elaboration of the analogical reasoning introduced almost a decade earlier.[16] 'As virtue, of all objects, is allowed to be the most valuable', one species of authors 'paint her in the most amiable colors, borrowing all helps from poetry and eloquence'. Such eloquent writers 'make us feel the difference between vice and virtue; they excite and regulate our sentiments'. Hume here indicates for the first time the precise techniques that painters can adopt to evoke moral sentiments in their readers, most notably their use of vivid examples. Painters of virtue, he explains, 'select the most striking observations and instances from common life; place opposite characters in a proper contrast; and alluring us into the paths of virtue by the views of glory and happiness, direct our steps in these paths by the soundest precepts and most illustrious examples' (EHU 1.1). As is typical of pre-romantic aesthetics, Hume sees the painter's art as essentially mimetic. Painters strive to recreate segments of reality as accurately as possible, and their success can be judged by a representation's ability to evoke the same sentiments which the objects depicted would evoke were they directly available to our observation.[17] 'All polite letters', Hume insists, 'are nothing but pictures of human life in various attitudes and situations; and inspire us with different sentiments, of praise or blame, admiration or ridicule, according to the qualities of the object, which they set before us' (EHU 1.2).

Anatomists of morals, on the other hand, 'regard human nature as a subject of speculation, and with a narrow scrutiny examine it in order to find those principles which regulate our understanding, excite our sentiments, and make us approve or blame any particular object, action or behavior'. Anatomists treat their examples as data for use in inductive reasoning rather than as valuable in themselves, 'proceeding from particular instances to general principles, they still push on their enquiries to principles more general, and rest not satisfied till they arrive at those original principles, by which, in every science, all human curiosity must be bounded'. What is more, anatomists, unlike painters, do not attempt to reach a general audience. Since 'their speculations seem abstract, and even unintelligible to common readers, they aim at the approbation of the learned and the wise; and think themselves sufficiently compensated for the labor of their whole lives, if they can discover some hidden truths, which may contribute to the instruction of posterity' (EHU 1.2).

If anatomists do happen to find some common readers, these readers may not only be confused and left cold; they may even be repulsed by what they read. Just as the body of even the greatest beauty disgusts us if it is cut open on a dissecting table, moral anatomy makes even the greatest virtue seem – borrowing Hume's own words – 'trivial', 'disagreeable', and even 'hideous'. This last choice of terms is particularly revealing. As Michael Gill has pointed out, the Oxford English Dictionary gives as a second definition of 'hideous': 'terrible, distressing or revolting to the moral sense', providing examples of this usage from 1692 and 1863.[18]

Hume's analogical use of anatomy to suggest the off-putting effects of a certain kind of moral philosophy is hardly original.[19] Among the treatises written by the hack persona behind Jonathan Swift's 1704 *A Tale of a Tub* – alongside such imagined masterpieces as *A Panegyrical Essay upon the Number Three* and *A General History of Ears* – there is a fictional publication called *Lectures upon a Dissection of Human Nature*. Swift's narrator explains, 'I have ... dissected the carcass of human nature and read many useful lectures upon the several parts, both containing and contained, till at last it smelt so strong I could preserve it no longer'.[20] Even worse, in the introduction to the *Fable of the Bees*, Bernard Mandeville writes that:

> ... as those that study the anatomy of dead carcasses may see that the chief organs and nicest springs more immediately required to continue the motion of our machine are not hard bones, strong muscles and nerves, nor the smooth white skin that so beautifully covers them, but small trifling films and little pipes ... so they that examine into the nature of man ... may observe that what renders him a sociable animal, consists not in his desire of company, good nature, pity, affability, and other graces of a fair outside, but that his vilest and most hateful qualities are the most necessary accomplishments to fit him for the largest, and, according to the world, the happiest and most flourishing societies.[21]

Hume does not want to disgust the reader of the *Treatise* in this way. To the contrary, he hopes that readers of his accurate anatomy of our moral sentiments will become convinced that 'not only virtue must be approved of, but also the sense of virtue – and not only that sense, but also the principles from whence it is derived – so that nothing is presented on any side, but what is laudable and good'. At the conclusion of the *Treatise*, Hume observes that 'were it proper in such a subject to bribe the readers assent, or employ anything but solid argument, we are here abundantly supplied with topics to engage the affections' (T 3.3.6.3). The implication, however, is that while Hume's moral anatomy could conceivably be framed so as to evoke reader's positive emotions, such affective 'bribery' is not proper in philosophy. It would be easy for someone who has demonstrated the truth of an anti-Mandevillian anatomy of virtue to lure readers into a love of morality, but this would be rhetorical eloquence, not 'solid argument', and hence precluded by the genre rules of the philosophical treatise.

Yet if engaging the affections to support the love of virtue were truly impermissible in a philosophical work, Hume could have easily refrained from doing so at all. The conclusion of the *Treatise* is not the transcript of an extemporaneous lecture, but a repeatedly revised piece of polished prose. When Hume insists that evoking rather than merely describing our moral sentiments is impermissible in such a work, it only serves to strengthen the eloquence of this very evocation. Hume employs a similar device in the second *Enquiry*, when he catches himself in the midst of a rhapsody on the virtue of benevolence. 'But I forget', he writes, 'that it is not my present business to recommend generosity and benevolence, or to paint, in their true colors, all the genuine charms of the social virtues'.[22] M. A. Box's analysis of this passage applies equally well to its analogue in the *Treatise:*

> Initially this seems a plain denial of any hortatory intentions. But on the other hand it is also plainly an admission that he has just been engaged in recommending a virtue and painting its charms. Hume is being arch. He has not really caught himself in getting carried away; he is just imitating, as eighteenth-century prose stylists tended to do, the casual discontinuities, hesitations, afterthoughts and backpedallings of actual conversation. If his commendatory painting of benevolence were really a deviation from his intentions, he could easily have struck it out. The only reason for failing to revise his discussion of benevolence is that it did indeed reflect his intentions.[23]

The fact remains, of course, that Hume confines the explicit engagement of the reader's affections to the conclusion of the *Treatise*, and that the rest of the work fails to evoke significant emotional reactions. At the same time, however, it is the moral anatomy which dominated the work until this point that has 'abundantly supplied' the material which is deployed in the conclusion to evoke warm engagement. If nothing else, this proves that moral anatomy can indeed be useful to the painter of virtue – the painter whom Hume himself becomes, however briefly, in the conclusion to the *Treatise*.

Hume did seem to think that a painterly approach might harm the reception of the *Treatise*. He suggested to Hutcheson that moments of warm rhetoric scattered across a work of cold, abstract reasoning would be seen as contrary to good taste. Yet why is so much abstract reasoning necessary in the first place? It must be because Hume essentially agreed with Locke that it was the only sure path to truth. The thrust of the first section of the first *Enquiry* is therefore not a value-neutral description of the two species of philosophy described, but an apology for careful, abstract anatomy addressed to a readership Hume assumes to be favourably disposed only to painting. And if dry argument is indeed the path to truth generally, this truth is of the utmost importance when it comes to moral subjects 'as may have a direct reference to action and society' (EHU 1.6).

If Hume's analogical reasoning holds correct, however, then the only way to prove that the beauty of virtue is more than skin-deep is to flay it, hence destroying this very beauty. Dissection, even of the most genuinely attractive human body, is an inherently grisly business. As Swift noted, it will inevitably produce a stench. Hume is thus deeply concerned that 'there is no virtue or moral duty, but what may, with facility, be refined away ... in sifting and scrutinising it, by every captious rule of logic, in every light or position, in which it may be placed'. To be sure, Hume holds that those who escape the genuine authority of morality in this way are indulging in a 'false philosophy',[24] but there is reason to worry that even accurate moral anatomy may have similar results.

The question is how to conduct an accurate anatomy of morality without dismembering our moral sentiments in the process. By the time of the first *Enquiry*, Hume has abandoned his insistence that painting and anatomy be kept separate. Now, he will instead attempt to 'unite the boundaries of the different species of philosophy' (EHU 1.17), though it is unclear precisely how this is to be accomplished. The literary technique adopted in the *Treatise* – apologetically appending a painterly conclusion to what is otherwise an essentially anatomical work – did not prove successful. This is not to say that the bulk of the *Treatise* was composed without belletristic goals in mind. Box describes Hume's literary intentions in his first work thusly:

> Hume says here that an anatomist should not attempt to prettify the dissected object, but he does not say that the procedures of anatomy themselves cannot be more or less beautiful. Just as the dexterity and precision with which an anatomist wields his scalpel can be marvelous, the manner in which Hume philosophized could be too. Similarly an anatomist's lectures, and Hume's presentation of his findings, could be entertaining as well as instructive. Accordingly in the *Treatise* Hume did not try to beautify moral sentiments in order to recommend morality to his readers, but he did try to make the anatomizing of sentiment as marvelous for readers as he found it himself.[25]

Hume, however, failed to achieve even this relatively modest literary goal. Rather than feeling wonder at his anatomical report, Hume's earliest readers felt at best indifference and confusion, at worst hostility towards an author they saw as seeking to undermine their moral convictions. Although later generations may have come to disagree, for its first readers Hume's anatomy of morals was indeed hideous and disagreeable.

Later in life, Hume was to conclude that his 'want of success in publishing the *Treatise of Human Nature* had proceeded more from the manner than the matter'.[26] While many have interpreted this to imply that Hume wished simply to improve the presentation of his anatomy with a dash of painterly style, Kate Abramson has convincingly demonstrated that Hume now sought a thoroughgoing synthesis of anatomy and painting – one which required him to rethink his entire compositional approach.[27] Success in this regard, however, was not to come until after Hume attempted another failed experiment.

3 Hume's later attempts at literary triangulation

The initial volume of Hume's *Essays Moral and Political* was published a mere year after the third book of the *Treatise*. Hume's literary model for these essays was Joseph Addison. This decision to ape the Addisonian style was not an unusual one in Enlightenment Scotland. Each edition of Addison's hugely popular weekly *The Spectator* was reprinted in Edinburgh after first appearing in London, and its conversational essays were widely imitated throughout Great Britain.[28] In the advertisement to the first, 1741 volume of his essays, Hume makes his debt to Addison explicit, explaining that his initial plan was to follow Addison's model in terms of both literary style and mode of publication: 'Most of these essays were wrote with a view of being published as weekly papers, and were intended to comprehend the designs both of the Spectators and Craftsmen. But having dropped the undertaking... before I ventured on to any more serious compositions, I was induced to commit these trifles to the judgment of the public'.[29]

Hume seems to have been most influenced by Addison's ambition to bring 'philosophy out of closets and libraries, schools and colleges, to dwell in clubs and assemblies, at tea-tables and in coffee-houses'.[30] If only the great philosophers of antiquity had access to the technology of printing, Addison is convinced that they would have made use of it 'to diffuse good sense through the bulk of a people, to clear up their understandings, animate their minds with virtue, dissipate the sorrows of a heavy heart, or unbend the mind from its more severe employments with innocent amusements'.[31] In his early essay 'Of Essay Writing', which seems to have been intended as a mission statement for his aborted periodical, Hume celebrates the 'league betwixt the learned and conversible worlds, which is so happily begun', and presents himself as an 'ambassador from the dominions of learning to those of conversation'.[32] In the name of all those of 'sound understandings and delicate affections', the learned ambassador proposes an alliance against 'our common enemies, against the enemies of reason and beauty, people of dull heads and cold hearts'.[33] Far from a sacrifice on the part of philosophers in service to the multitude – far from a return from the light of reason to the darkness of Plato's cave – this alliance will actually help the learned better achieve their own goal, that of abstract truth. Hume's reasoning here is characteristically empiricist:

> Learning has been a great loser by being shut up in colleges and cells, and secluded from the world and good company ... Even philosophy went to wrack by this moping recluse method of study, and became as chimerical in her conclusions as she was unintelligible in her style and manner of delivery. And indeed, what could be expected from men who never consulted experience in any of their reasonings, or who never searched for that experience, where alone it is to be found, in common life and conversation?[34]

The main problem with this alliance, however, is that the learned are forced to leave their best weapons at the border of the conversible realm. Addison has never been admired as a great thinker, and the highly informal Addisonian essay is an inappropriate form for the communication of correct reasoning on difficult subjects, especially when compared to the success of the dry, Lockean treatise in this regard. Addison's work is, as Hume acknowledges, 'trifling', and Hume in hindsight describes his own worst essays as giving 'neither pleasure nor instruction', being merely 'bad imitations of the agreeable trifling of Addison'.[35] The most Addisonian and trifling of Hume's early essays – including 'Of Essay Writing' itself – were excluded from later collections of Hume's writings.[36] Box gives a devastating account of the intentional 'superficiality', the 'utter emptiness of new or even rigorous thought', which characterises these withdrawn pieces:

> Elsewhere in the *Essays*, where he is not walking so closely in Mr. Spectator's steps, Hume can be found advancing new theories and insights, but not in the apprentice pieces, where instead he propounds the following trivial theses: that learning is a desirable conversational trait, that philosophical enthusiasm is to be eschewed, that members of the middle class should be content with their station, that impudence is to be distinguished from decent self-confidence, that marriages would be happier if spouses did not seek dominance, that it would be good for women to read books of history, and that avarice is a ridiculous vice.[37]

All of these theses may be true (although I have my doubts about the value of middle-class complacency), but these truths are both trivial and were universally accepted in Hume's time. Yet while it is easy to dismiss the early essays as a naked attempt for popular success on the heels of the failure of the *Treatise*, the same is not true of the still-painterly works that followed.[38] A thorough reading of Hume's *Essays* and *Enquiries* (collected together as *Essays and Treatises on Several Subjects*) would reveal that Hume soon improved markedly in his ability to combine eloquent, emotionally evocative writing with profound and original thought.[39] Hume struggled toward a synthesis of Locke and Addison, developing (in Box's apt phrase) a unique genre of 'essays which are not quite essays',[40] as the change in the title of the first *Enquiry* seems to indicate.[41] As has already been mentioned, Hume insisted at the end of his life that of all his writings *An Enquiry Concerning the Principles of Morals* is 'incomparably the best'.[42] Commentators now generally agree that it was here that Hume came closest to a successful combination of anatomy and painting.[43]

Contrasting Book III of the *Treatise* with the second *Enquiry*, Hume scholars have noted two major changes. First, the most difficult and controversial arguments of the *Treatise* have either been removed or confined to a series of appendices, keeping the stench of anatomy away from the main body of the work. Second, Hume illustrates virtually every point with concrete examples, drawing most of them from actual history. As Hume already noted in the first *Enquiry*, vivid illustrations are the central technique of moral painting, engaging the reader in a way that general principles never could. Our moral sentiments are not affective responses to abstractions, after all, but to the observable behaviour of particular individuals. As Hume put it in his (withdrawn, Addisonian) essay 'On the Study of History', 'When a philosopher contemplates characters and manners in his closet, the general abstract view of the objects leaves the mind so cold and unmoved, that the sentiments of nature have no room to play, and he scarce feels the difference between vice and virtue'. A historian, by contrast, 'places the objects in their true point of view', and hence develops 'a lively sentiment of blame and praise'.[44]

As this passage indicates, it is not poets and preachers, but historians, who are for Hume the best painters of virtue. Hume writes that while poets 'can paint virtue in the most charming colors', their undisciplined imaginations often lead them to 'become advocates for vice'. By contrast, 'historians have been, almost without exception, the true friends of virtue, and have always represented it in its proper colors, however they may have erred in their judgments of particular persons'.[45] It is in the second *Enquiry* that Hume combined the anatomy of his *Treatise* with the accurate and emotionally evocative narrative paintings of his (at the time much more successful) *History of England*.[46]

Such, at least, was Hume's goal. Whether he was fully successful in attaining it is another matter. Certainly, Hume was well aware that he might successfully identify the proper norms of a communicative practice without possessing the talents necessary to master it himself. For example, although Hume felt that the art of oratory was an indispensable means of instilling proper moral sentiments in a political community, he was so abashed about his Scottish accent that he tried to avoid speaking in public.[47] While Hume undoubtedly had a far higher estimation of his literary than his oratorical abilities, Stephen Buckle interprets the apologetic tone of the first section of the first *Enquiry* as an indication of 'Hume's awareness that his success in combining the two kinds of philosophy was likely to be judged (or prejudged) as less than total, at least by his suspected audience'.[48]

4   Conclusion: Hume and Adam Smith

There is admittedly something awkward about the second *Enquiry*'s excess of appendices, and something off-putting about its continuous digressions from philosophy into the deeds of ancient Greeks and Romans. It is not implausible to claim, with Box, that Hume never quite attained what he was trying to achieve in the second *Enquiry*, and that his friend Adam Smith's *Theory of Moral Sentiments* might serve as a better example of success in the genre.[49] Clearly expressing a profound and original moral theory without artificial recourse to appendices, Smith continuously integrates concrete examples into his theory in the form of eloquent narratives – narratives drawn, less often from history and the classics, and more often from homely experiences that his readers could recognise from their own lives.[50] For most of the twentieth century, when Hume's work loomed over all Anglo-American ethics and Smith's moral philosophy was essentially ignored, it might have seemed absurd to suggest that Smith's *Theory* was literarily superior to Hume's second *Enquiry*. Today, however, as Smith's ethics becomes ever-more appreciated, Box's judgement is gaining increasing plausibility.

Smith's *Theory* was certainly praised by Smith's contemporaries for its literary achievements in terms that Hume must have envied. Edmund Burke praises Smith in his correspondence for his 'elegant painting of the manners and passions',[51] and goes on to praise the *Theory* in print as 'one of the most beautiful fabrics of moral theory, that has perhaps ever appeared'. Such a work, Burke continues, must not be subject to the deformations of anatomical dissection. 'A dry abstract of the system would convey no juster idea of it', he says, 'than the skeleton of a departed beauty would of her form when she was alive; at the same time the work is so well methodised, the parts grow so naturally and gracefully out of each other, that it would be doing it equal injustice to show it by broken and detached pieces'.[52] To be sure, we might dismiss this praise of Smith as the sort of hyperbolic flattery often exchanged by eighteenth-century men of letters seeking to win one another's good graces. Even if Burke's praise of Smith is exaggerated, however, the anti-anatomical language used to formulate this praise is suggestive of the eighteenth-century literary ideals which Hume struggled so long to meet, and which he may never have succeeded in meeting to either his or others' satisfaction.

Yet, Hume's failures as a philosophical–literary stylist do nothing to diminish his achievements, not merely as a philosopher in general, but as a philosophical theorist of literary style itself. An eighteenth-century author who was somehow able to fuse the compositional modes of the anatomist and the painter without significant strain might never have been so acutely aware of the conflicting demands of the literary norms of the era. While Hume began his literary career with a pure commitment to a cold, anatomical approach, both he and his contemporaries quickly came to see this as an unacceptable authorial practice. Hume thus began a series of attempts to combine both painting and anatomy in a single text, none of which proved entirely successful. While many commentators have been dissatisfied with either the lack of authentic emotion in Hume's earliest work or with the lack of philosophical depth in his latter publications (or both), these problems must be understood in light of Hume's continual efforts to meet the multiple, conflicting imperatives of Enlightenment print culture. Hume's authorial struggles remain an invaluable resource, not only for historians of the print culture of eighteenth-century Britain, but also for philosophers and writers who still wrestle with analogous problems today.

Notes

1. Letter 65, 10 April 1749, in *The Letters of David Hume* (1932) ed. J. Y. T. Greig (2 vols, Oxford: Oxford University Press), Vol. I, pp. 133–8, 138.
2. I owe this observation to M. A. Box (1990) *The Suasive Art of David Hume* (Princeton, NJ: Princeton University Press), pp. 16–17.

3. L. A. Selby-Bigge, 'Introduction', in D. Hume (1777) *Enquiries Concerning Human Understanding and Concerning the Principles of Morals* (1777 ed. repr. with introduction and analytical notes by L. A. Selby-Bigge), 3rd ed., with text revised and notes by P. H. Nidditch (New York: Oxford University Press, 1893–1975), p. x.

4. Selby-Bigge, 'Introduction' to Hume, *Enquiries*, p. xiv.

5. For a monograph devoted to refuting Bigge's view of the first *Enquiry*, see Stephen Buckle (2001) *Hume's Enlightenment Tract: The Unity and Purpose of 'An Enquiry Concerning Human Understanding'* (New York: Oxford University Press). Other contributions to the voluminous literature devoted to salvaging the reputation of Hume's later philosophical writings will be cited throughout this essay as the occasion arises.

6. D. Hume (1985) 'My Own Life', in *Essays Moral Political and Literary*, ed. Eugene F. Miller, revd. edn (Indianapolis, IN: Liberty Fund), pp. xxxi–xli, xxxvi (henceforth cited as 'EMPL').

7. Adam Potkay (1994) *The Fate of Eloquence in the Age of Hume* (Ithaca, NY: Cornell University Press), p. 4.

8. John Locke (1975 [orig. 1690]) *An Essay Concerning Human Understanding* 3.10.34, ed. Peter H. Nidditch (New York: Oxford University Press), p. 508. As with all quotations from early modern English-language sources in this essay, I have modernised punctuation and spelling.

9. Peter Jones (1983), 'The Scottish Professoriate and the Polite Academy, 1720–1746', in Istvan Hont and Michael Ignatieff (Eds.), *Wealth and Virtue: The Shaping of Political Economy in the Scottish Enlightenment* (New York: Cambridge University Press), pp. 89–118, 90. See also Nicholas Phillipson (1983) 'Adam Smith as Civic Moralist', in Hont and Ignatieff, *Wealth and Virtue*, pp. 179–202.

10. P. B. Wood (1995) 'Hume, Reid and the Science of the Mind', in M. A. Stewart and John P. Wright (Eds.), *Hume and Hume's Connexions* (State College, PA: Penn State University Press), pp. 119–39.

11. David Hume, *A Treatise of Human Nature* (2000 [orig. 1739–40]) eds. David Fate Norton and Mary J. Norton (New York: Oxford University Press), 2.3.3.4. Henceforth cited as 'T'.

12. 'Heat', Potkay observes, 'fairly pervades earlier eighteenth-century discussions of eloquence' (Potkay, *Fate of Eloquence in the Age of Hume*, p. 26).

13. Letter 13, 17 September 1739, in Greig, *The Letters of David Hume*, Vol. I, pp. 32–3.

14. Letter 15, 4 March 1740, in Greig, *The Letters of David Hume*, Vol. I, pp. 36–8.

15. D. Hume (2000) *An Enquiry Concerning Human Understanding*, ed. Tom L. Beauchamp (New York: Oxford University Press). Henceforth cited as 'EHU'.

16. For a close reading of this section of the first *Enquiry*, see Buckle, *Hume's Enlightenment Tract*, pp. 121–8.

17. The Third Earl of Shaftesbury, himself clearly a painter of morality, provides a helpful description of the goals of such painting along these pre-romantic lines. For a thorough analysis of Shaftesbury's *The Moralists: A Philosophical Rhapsody* as a piece of pre-romantic moral painting, see Michael B. Gill (2006), *The British Moralists and the Birth of Secular Ethics* (New York: Cambridge University Press), pp. 100–12.

18. Michael B. Gill (1996) 'A Philosopher in his Closet: Reflexivity and Justification in Hume's Moral Theory', *Canadian Journal of Philosophy* 26(2): 231–55, 236, n. 10.

19. For a thorough review of Hume's predecessors in this regard, see M. A. Stewart (2002) 'Two Species of Philosophy: The Historical Significance of the First *Enquiry*', in Peter Millican (Ed.), *Reading Hume on Human Understanding* (New York: Oxford University Press), pp. 67–96, 71–2.

20. Jonathan Swift (1986) 'A Tale of a Tub', *A Tale of a Tub and Other Works*, ed. Angus Ross and David Woolley, Oxford World Classics (New York: Oxford University Press), pp. 2, 59.

21. Bernard Mandeville (1714–29) *The Fable of the Bees, or Private Vices, Publick Benefits*, ed. with a commentary F. B. Kaye, 2 vols. (Indianapolis, IN: Liberty Fund, 1988), p. 3.

22. D. Hume (1998) *An Enquiry Concerning the Principles of Morals*, ed. Tom L. Beauchamp (New York: Oxford University Press), 2.1.5. Henceforth cited as 'EPM'.

23. Box, *The Suasive Art of David Hume*, p. 16. My application of Box's point to the conclusion of the *Treatise* serves as a refutation of Gill's contrary reading in Gill, *British Moralists*, pp. 310–11.

24. Hume, 'Of the Original Contract,' in EMPL, pp. 465–87, 482.

25. Box, *The Suasive Art of David Hume*, p. 238.

26. Hume, 'My Own Life', in EMPL, pp. Xxxi–xli, xxxv.

27. See Kate Abramson (1997) *Hume's Peculiar Sentiments: The Evolution of Hume's Moral Philosophy* (Ph.D. dissertation, Department of Philosophy, University of Chicago); K. Abramson (2000) 'Sympathy and the Project of Hume's Second Enquiry', *Archiv für Geschichte der Philosophie* 83: 45–80; K. Abramson (2006) 'Happy to Unite, or Not?', *Philosophy Compass* 1(3): 290–302; and K. Abramson (2007) 'Hume's Distinction between Philosophical Anatomy and Painting', *Philosophy Compass* 2(5): 680–98.

28. For the influence of Addison on the Scottish Enlightenment, see Phillipson, 'Adam Smith as Civic Moralist'.

29. As cited in Box, *The Suasive Art of David Hume*, p. 113. Despite Hume's mention of the partisan political weekly *The Craftsman*, it is clear that the non-partisan Hume's literary debts were primarily to the *Spectator*.

30. 'Joseph Addison, *Spectator*, 10 (12 March 1711)', in Erin Mackie (Ed.) (1998) *The Commerce of Everyday Life: Selections from The Tatler and The Spectator* (Boston, MA: Bedford/St Martin's), p. 89. Hume may have also been inspired in this regard by the third Earl of Shaftesbury, who complained that philosophy 'is no longer active in the world, nor can hardly, with any advantage, be brought upon the public stage. We have immured her (poor lady!) in colleges and cells, and have set her servilely to such works as those in the mines'. 'The Moralists' 1.1, as included in *Characteristicks of Men, Manners, Opinions, Times* (2001 [orig. 1732]) ed. Douglas Den Uyl, 3 vols. (Indianapolis, IN: Liberty Fund), Vol. II, pp. 101–247, 105. Hume and Addison, however, were united in rejecting Shaftesbury's ornate, aristocratic style with a simpler mode of composition more amenable to public tastes.

31. 'Addison, *Spectator*, 124 (23 July 1711)', in Mackie, *The Commerce of Everyday Life*, pp. 95–6.

32. 'Of Essay Writing', in EMPL, pp. 533–7, 535.

33. 'Of Essay Writing', in EMPL, p. 536. Hume's extended ambassadorial metaphor is problematically gendered – depicting women as the sovereigns of the kingdom of affection and conversation, while men are sovereigns of the realm of learning – in ways that relate in very complex ways with today's feminist critique of the opposition to emotion in mainstream Anglo-American philosophy. On this topic, see Lívia Guimarãs (2004) 'The Gallant and the Philosopher', *Hume Studies* 30(1): 127–48, as well as the essays collected in Anne Jaap Jacobsen (Ed.) (2000) *Feminist Interpretations of David Hume* (University Park, PA: Pennsylvania State University Press).

34. 'Of Essay Writing', in EMPL, pp. 534–5.

35. Letter 468, To William Strahan, 7 February 1772, in Greig, *The Letters of David Hume*, Vol. II, p. 257.

36. See Box, *The Suasive Art of David Hume.*, Chapter 3; Norah Smith (1972) 'Hume's Rejected Essays', *Forum For Modern Language Studies* 8: 354–71.

37. Box, *The Suasive Art of David Hume*, p. 127.

38. John Immerwahr warns us against the tendency of philosophers today to dismiss all of Hume's work except the *Treatise*, seeing all of the later, more popular work as evidence that Hume had 'sold out, deserting his serious work to write popular trifles for fame and profit'. See John Immerwahr (1991) 'The Anatomist and the Painter: The Continuity of Hume's *Treatise* and *Essays*', *Hume Studies* 17(1): 1–14, 12. Such a dismissive attitude is, however, justified to a significant extent if it is limited only to the withdrawn essays, which even Hume himself admitted were mere 'trifles', and bad ones at that.

39. Perhaps the greatest of Hume's *Essays* in this regard is the sequence of four pieces on happiness named after the schools of Hellenistic philosophy: 'The Epicurean', 'The Stoic', 'The Platonist', and 'The Skeptic'. For my own take on these essays, see M. Frazer (2010) *The Enlightenment of Sympathy: Justice and the Moral Sentiments in the Eighteenth Century and Today* (Oxford: Oxford University Press), pp. 61–3. For a fuller discussion, see Colin Heydt (2007) 'Relations of Literary Form and Philosophical Purpose in Hume's Four Essays on Happiness', *Hume Studies* 33(1): 3–19. Heydt notes that, in these four essays, Hume 'provides us with a rhetorical performance that might have satisfied Hutcheson's expectations for a work on morals' (p. 9).

40. Box, *The Suasive Art of David Hume*, p. 174.

41. M. A. Stewart has observed that there appears to have been a similar change in the title of the second *Enquiry*, albeit one made before its initial publication. See Stewart, in Millican, *Reading Hume on Human Understanding*, p. 81, n. 30. That said, it is important to realise that the English-language genre names for different types of philosophical writing – like the philosophical terminology of the time more generally – was never terribly precise. The words 'essay' and 'treatise' were used loosely, and sometimes even interchangeably, as is evidenced by the fact that the second of Locke's *Two Treatises of Government* is described on its title page as 'An Essay Concerning the True Original, Extent, and End of Civil Government'. See Box, *The Suasive Art of David Hume*, p. 94.

42. 'My Own Life', in EMPL, p. xxxvi.

43. See e.g. Anette Baier (1986) 'Extending the Limits of Moral Theory', *The Journal of Philosophy* 83(10): 538–45, 543; Baier (2011) '*Enquiry Concerning the Principles of Morals*: Incomparably the Best?' in Elizabeth S. Radcliffe (Ed.), *A*

Companion to Hume (Malden, MA: Wiley-Blackwell), pp. 293–320; Abramson, 'Sympathy and the Project of Hume's Second Enquiry', p. 64; and Box, *The Suasive Art of David Hume*, p. 238.

44. 'On the Study of History', in EMPL, pp. 563–8.

45. Hume, 'Of the Study of History', in EMPL, pp. 563–8.

46. For an alternative account of Hume's turn to history, see James Noxon (1973) *Hume's Philosophical Development: A Study of his Methods* (New York: Oxford University Press). Noxon argues that Hume has now come to realise that moral, political, and social theory 'can be based directly upon the historical study of political events without involving any intricate psychological investigation' (p. 25). There is no contradiction between Noxon's explanation and my own; history may both be more emotionally engaging than moral anatomy and capable of standing on its own as a source of moral and political insight, hence rendering Hume's turn to history over-determined. For a recent attempt to read Hume's *History* as a kind of political theory, see Andrew Sabl (2012) *Hume's Politics: Coordination and Crisis in the 'History of England'* (Princeton, NJ: Princeton University Press).

47. See Marc Hanvelt (2012) *The Politics of Eloquence: David Hume's Polite Rhetoric* (Toronto: University of Toronto Press). Hanvelt insists that the fascinating analysis of Hume's position on oratory thus cannot be applied to Hume's own communicative practices, which were largely limited to the written word (see, e.g., p. 34). Yet much, though not all, of Hanvelt's analysis can in fact be applied to Hume's writing if we make allowances for the different applications of the underlying principles of rhetoric to various media of communication.

48. Buckle, *Hume's Enlightenment Tract*, p. 23.

49. See Box, *The Suasive Art of David Hume*, p. 255.

50. On Smith's use of these homely yet literary 'illustrations', see Phillipson, 'Adam Smith as Civic Moralist', p. 182.

51. Letter 38, Edmund Burke to Smith, 10 September 1759, *Correspondence of Adam Smith*, ed. Ernest Campbell Mossner and Ian Simpson Ross (1987), (Indianapolis, IN: Liberty Fund), pp. 46–7, 47.

52. Edmund Burke (1760) 'The Theory of Moral Sentiments, by Adam Smith, Professor of Moral Philosophy, in the University of Glasgow', *The Annual Register, or a View of the History, Politics and Literature of the Year 1759* (London: R. and J. Dodsley), pp. 484–9, 484–5. Burke himself was of course a master of evoking emotion in his readers. Thomas Paine complains that, in the *Reflections on the Revolution in France*, 'the tragic paintings by which Mr. Burke has outraged his own imagination and seeks to work upon that of his readers ... are very well calculated for theatrical representation ... and accommodated to produce ... a weeping effect'. See Thomas Paine (1995 [orig. 1791]) *Rights of Man*, repr. in *Collected Writings* (New York: Library of America), pp. 431–662, 446.

Part IV
Afterword

13
Printed Passion: Sympathy, Satire, and the Translation of Homer (1675–1720)

Conal Condren

1 Introduction: The contingency of eighteenth-century stability

Whatever value there may be in the notion of a long eighteenth century, it needs to be overlaid with a sense of the fragmented continuation of the seventeenth. For any growth of stability associated with party government, and civilised accommodation, gathered around the importance of sentiment, the values of politeness, sociability, sympathy, and being candid with one's fellows, did not come easily. Such values and achievements were periodically over-shadowed by passionate discord and enthusiasm coming from the Civil Wars.[1] The French Revolution and its immediate aftermath in the early nineteenth century could still conjure up fears of indigenous revolutionary violence. The stability of the eighteenth century (bracketing the odd war and riot) has been an achievement of retrospective celebration as much as anything lived through.

Formulations designed to articulate what was new and positive about that long eighteenth century have been various but never entirely convincing: the Williamite regime saw the beginnings of the party system, of confessional toleration, and the rise of the public sphere. The notion of a change in emotional regime may prove to be a fruitful addition to the mix. And it is aspects of this hypothesis that the essays in this volume have been exploring.

In each of these notions, the emphasis on beginnings is both potent and problematic. It helps us determine some overall shape, but allows for a lot of ambiguous or contradictory evidence to be noted but discounted; after all, beginnings are only beginnings. It is a problem of history by origin. Although, for example, during the eighteenth century the terms Whig and Tory had some fluid meaning variably tied to Civil War divisions, *party* was a term of opprobrium; the notion of there being a system and widespread, stable party commitments is a projection from later times. Confessional toleration partially stretched to non-conformity, but stopped short of Catholicism throughout the eighteenth century, in part because of the continuing fears of civil war violence erupting in 1715 and 1745. The Gordon Riots following the Papist Act of 1778 were occasioned by distrust of Catholics remarkably similar to the fears that had got William Cavendish into trouble as one of Charles I's commanders; he preferred loyal Catholics in his army to disloyal Protestants. But again, a degree of accommodation and religious toleration was established, and the eighteenth century can provide a lineage of arguments and attitudes leading in this direction, themselves stemming from marginal voices in the turmoil of the 1640s.

In contrast to these embryonic features of eighteenth-century England, the 'public sphere' has proved a conceptually confused red herring. Initially it was presented as a theoretical model of the preconditions necessary for an idealised participatory democracy, defined by equality of information and voice among post-Kantian rational actors. As such, it was never a suitable subject for an historical search, despite Habermas's own sketchy gestures in the directions of coffee houses and the collapse of censorship.[2] Conceptual models are not found in the evidence; they are applied to it. And as the public sphere was putatively only just beginning with the long eighteenth century, the model did not have to fit anything very well for faith in it to have been maintained. As the essays in this volume have helped illustrate, what has been lauded as an indispensable concept for understanding the early modern world has little saliency or explanatory power.[3] The best application of it can do is draw attention to the diverse vibrancy of a print culture. And it is perhaps just this that the phrase 'public sphere' has come to mean here, so severed from its defining criteria.

The phrase is none the less important for this. The destabilising potential of the printed word had been noted since the sixteenth century: Montaigne's extreme scepticism was in part driven by his awareness that effective communication could be perilously uncertain where authors and readers were independent, often isolated, and of necessity inventive in what they did to a received text. During the seventeenth century there was widespread concern that the wayward printed word expressed passion and prejudice, incited violence, and might be without credibility. The printed word had been one dimension of the Civil Wars; it solidified and spread destructive passion – metaphorically speaking, it might have been a carrier of 'emotional contagion' (see Chapter 1, and Chapter 2, Parrott). Words that might die on the tongue were dyed on the press and could circulate to the four imagined corners of the world. '*Oh Printing*! How hast thou disturbed the Peace of Mankind! That Lead, when founded into Bullets, is not so mortal as when founded into Letters'.[4] With the invasion of 1688/89, itself being blown on the winds of pamphlet propaganda, then fixed in print to become a sort of constitutional and bloodless revolution, there was little sense of assured peace in the early eighteenth century.

2 Sympathy and the modality of sanctioned passion

There is, however, evidence to suggest something like the beginnings of a shift in what has been called an emotional regime (Chapter 1, Chapter 2). It is a helpful phrase, with qualifications: helpful because it brings to the fore what contemporaries believed and explored, that passions were explanatory categories of great importance. They might be authentic in the sense of being sanctioned socially and so praiseworthy if sincerely manifested. They might be authentic in the sense of being intrinsic to human nature, whether of positive or negative value. And even when in one meaning they might be unauthentic, assumed, or pretended, their explanatory importance was hardly discounted. No one had provided a more far-reaching or elegant analysis, partially with internecine war in mind, than Hobbes; and no one was to capitalise more on the contingent stability of the eighteenth century in understanding the passion and largely habit- and sentiment-dependent character of civilisation than David Hume. With emotional regimes in mind, one long eighteenth century might run from Hobbes, via Mandeville to Hume and Smith. And the shift in regime may well hinge on a greater emphasis on socialising passions, among which a notion of sympathy becomes isolated as of paramount importance.[5]

But if there is mileage in the notion of stability in part being a function of emotional regime, qualifications are needed. First, the word emotion in the modern sense appears only occasionally and casually before the nineteenth century (Chapter 1, Chapter 2) and carrying no burden of analytic attention.[6] Only a hundred years earlier, John Evelyn had recommended the French 'Emotion' be imported into English, as the language lacked a proper equivalent.[7] When it is found before the late eighteenth century, it was predominantly as an altogether more general term for movement or upheaval. In its modern meaning, emotion was a small part of many changes to the shape and content of intellectual disciplines during the early nineteenth century, such as psychology, chemistry, and political economy (political science, economics, and English literature would be established only later). Consequently, it would be perilously modernising to read emotion as a simple synonym for passion. This is not least because a case has now to be made that the emotions have explanatory power and cannot be considered as peripheral to understanding the past (i.e. Chapter 1). No one in the seventeenth or eighteenth centuries would have needed to urge such a case for the passions. It was much more a question of what passions and proclivities were of positive value to civilisation, what were negative, and after Mandeville, what negative passions might have positive results.

Second, print culture does not give us direct access to either emotions or passions. Rather, their explanatory importance and any authenticity in them has to be conjectured, historically speaking, largely from the evidence of words, even if such conjecture is partially guided and reshaped with the benefit of psychological theory. What the vocabulary of passion leaves us with is what a number of authors in the volume make clear, expressions appropriate to, even defining a presented persona. Expressions of appropriate passion can be remarkably diverse: those fitting for a heroine in a novel or play (see Chapter 5, Hultquist, and Chapter 9, Dale), a satirist, (Chapter 3, Phiddian), or a philosopher like Hume (Chapter 12, Frazer) were hardly identical. This leads to a third qualification. What for convenience we might call emotional patterning is not uniform to a community, let alone an historical epoch, but modal. As such, print-presented passions were an aspect of an authenticating or persuasive ethos. This leads to a final qualification, that to treat the vocabulary of the passions in isolation is itself to diminish them; they were part and parcel of a moral economy. Glen Pettigrove illustrates this through the analysis of Hutcheson's naturalistic ethics; morality and passion may be distinguished, but their separation is artificial. So also for Smith, as Laura Rosenthal shows, the importance of sympathy as fellow-feeling arising from any passion is that it makes morality, not just exchange, possible (Chapter 7).[8] Indeed, one feature of the later shift from the passional to the emotional was that it aided a more decisive separation between the categories of emotion, reason, and morality than is historically warranted.

A soul, for example, as God's property and existing in obedient relationship to Him never has a morally unproblematic relationship to the passionate desperation of an act of suicide (Chapter 10, Parisot).

It continued to rely upon, as it had for John Donne, a casuistic morality.[9] As Robert Phiddian emphasises (Chapter 3), the satirist's expression of disgusted indignation was a moral one; in a wicked world deserving of censure, anything less was an abrogation of the censor's duty. It is a theme I shall return to below. Again, as Aleksondra Hultquist argues (Chapter 5) Haywood presents a persona in which the cultivation of certain passions is an expression of virtue appropriate to the rational philosopher. The spiritual exercises often associated with the process of becoming a philosopher are extended to those who would not now be counted as such. But they might well lay some claim to that title as the word philosophy was used in the early modern world.[10] This is less because of the propositions they put forward, than because of the passion for virtue that could be taken as preconditional for philosophising. Similarly, in Kathrine Cuccuru's analysis of John Dennis (Chapter 6), the critic's reaction to the sublime is both passionate and ethical. Recognition of the sublime is at once the highest state of virtue and the cause of attraction to it.

In the light of this slippery modality, there are at least three variables that need to be juggled. First, there is the vocabulary of ethical passion that is fairly specific to a given sense of integrity: the indignation and scorn of the satirist can be a vice in another writer; the dispassion of the philosopher, the self-conscious intellectual anatomist discussed by Michael Frazer, is not normally fitting for the parent or the lover. The dissimulation of the actor is necessary in putting virtue before us (Chapter 7, Rosenthal), but that of the politician is a mark of corruption. Anger may be an expression of virtue in a king; it is most likely to be a sin in subjects. Second, other terms, however, have a more general positive colouring across the landscape of moral and social being, such as love, sympathy, or charity. Even so, in such a context of ethico-passional expression, they take on differing meanings in more specific contexts. Justice as a relational virtue is appropriate to all, but what counted as just was usually conditional on who was acting in what capacity. Third, there are shifts over time within a given economy. Hobbes's insistence on the necessity for the philosopher to be singular, to have the courage to stand alone and not rely on the received authority of a body of knowledge, and specifically his boast in *De cive* (1642), to have originated political science or philosophy, rendered him vulnerable to accusations of an arrogant disrespect for tradition, inimical to the philosophical virtues of openness and intellectual modesty. Descartes shared with Hobbes a similar understanding of the qualities necessary for philosophy. Yet within a generation of one encomiast praising Descartes for his over-riding passion to be distinct, the virtues of originality were becoming more broadly acceptable.[11] Edward Young's *Conjectures on Original Composition* (1759), was an encomium for many beside those who might claim to be philosophers. By the end of the eighteenth century originality was established coin in the currency of praise.

A similar story might be told of the sublime. For John Dennis, the future of poetry depended greatly on reaching the sublime, once the notion was denuded of passionate enthusiasm. Understanding and embracing it was intimately tied to the guiding office of the critic, the infant realm of intellectual responsibility that Ben Jonson had tried to establish in the rapidly growing and unruly forest of print.[12] As I shall illustrate in discussing early eighteenth-century translations of Homer, despite its Greek origin, the sublime could be an invaluable, if treacherous descriptor for the poet. Yet, by the end of the eighteenth century, the passion for the sublime could be little more than the enthusiasm of the nature lover for big rocks and crags.

Finally, the question needs to be asked here how far the early eighteenth century did see any significant shift from the passions and values that were expressed in the violent instability of the seventeenth century; or how far they were still encoded in the indirect and veiled speech of civility. Dennis's purging enthusiasm from the sublime is some support for a wider pattern of change. Yet as Emily Cock's argument shows (Chapter 8), the symbolic and semiotic dimensions of displayed passion and virtue may point in another direction. The pox was not just a disease; it remained, as it had been for Sir William Cornwallis, a sign of unruly passion and moral corruption, the social grace of courtly life.[13] There is far more in the world of print than direct propositional communication. The more of that print there is, the more publics can be created or imagined, the more room for diversity of expression there is in trying to reach them.

3 Translation and the taming of Homer

In this light, I want to turn to an important but recalcitrant body of evidence; namely, the translation of work from other times and cultures. Across Europe, the seventeenth and eighteenth centuries put remarkable energies into translating; it was part of an intense and sustained scrutiny of the past and a sense that continuity and adaptation of an inheritance was integral too, and part of the work of maintaining civilisation.[14] Translation was thus an ambivalent exercise in negotiated relevance. But the interpretation of the end results, especially of poetic translation, is particularly difficult because, like the physical signs of some diseases, it is symbolically resonant and multi-dimensional.

Why a poem was selected for translation and, once chosen, why a word or rhyme was employed, why something was omitted, compressed, or enlarged may be subject to a variety of over-lapping and often inconclusive, or partial explanations. But in early modern translation, there was always likely to be more at stake than establishing a verbal equivalence, or gaining access to an alien world – a rationale that became of principal importance only from the late eighteenth century.[15] A translation might be an advertisement for one's capacities, a substitute for direct expression; it might be an exercise in piety or political appropriation. It might proclaim the maturity of a vernacular tongue. Consequently, the very notion of a translation was broader than it is now, and left much room for creative manoeuvre. As Vives had remarked, if we are dealing with more than replacing one set of words with another, with sense, meaning, ideas, then either expansion or compression may be needed.[16] Translation could be critical and inventive, ventriloquistic, and even parodic.[17] So translation into English in the early eighteenth century is likely to be an attempt both to enrich and participate in the culture more broadly. But any conclusions we might draw now need to be cautious. With these caveats in mind, I want to look briefly at the specific problem of Homer and what this might vicariously tell us about passions and the character of argument in the early eighteenth century.

The ancient inheritance of which Homer was a major part came to be pitted, somewhat artificially, against what were considered as the main characteristics of modernity: the battle between the ancients and moderns.[18] This was an established *topos* from earlier times, and was flexible enough to structure argument in many fields; but it is probably fair to say that in the late seventeenth to early eighteenth centuries, it was driven mostly by the attitudes of self-styled ancients to an abstracted modernity. This modernity comprised a syndrome of characteristics: Whig politics, low-church Protestantism, natural and experimental philosophy, mathematics, materialist metaphysics, and philological scholarship. Added to which were professional writing and a relative openness to the spread of education, inescapably significant aspects of a vibrant print culture (see the chapters by Chapter 4, McBain; Chapter 9, Dale; and Chapter 10, Parisot). Finally, modernity exhibited a sceptical attitude to the authority of ancient texts. I have already noted Hobbes's vulnerability on this score. Self-styled ancients were not neatly and uniformly opposed to all of these. They did, however, have a strong *a priori* preference for ancient texts as fonts of wisdom and moral guidance superior to modern learning and philosophy. They were apt to be Tory rather than Whig. Translation of ancient texts, then, was an activity redolent of many issues, a means of affirming or subverting social positions, attitudes, and groupings. It was far more than a matter of making an alien text available to those who did not know the original language. In fact, the principal audience for translations from Latin would have been for those with linguistic familiarity.

It was in this general context that Homer proved problematic, in an age in which Greek was a more familiar language than it had been in the past. He was renowned as the father of poetry, even as a divinely inspired philosopher. He nevertheless made disciples of antiquity queasy. In comparing Homer and Virgil, René Rapin had effectively ejected him from the pantheon so that antiquity might get the uncritical respect it otherwise deserved. Homer was violent and irrational, quite unfitted for a world of Christian morality and civility;[19] as Paul Davis puts it, for the anti-Homerians, the *Iliad* was an atavistic monstrosity.[20] It was mad, bad, and dangerous to read. Swift, in a typically backhanded way, acknowledged the vulnerability of Homer to such moral critique by parodying the extremes of praise that had been lavished on him. Homer is obviously worthless, he says nothing about the Church of England and his treatise on tea is pathetic.[21] The fact that his status had long been debated is an indication that the softer socialising passions and virtues associated with the eighteenth century had antecedents. But what I shall suggest we do see in translating Homer is a taming of destructive passion and an extension of pity (*eleemosune*) as mercy, from pitiable (*aleeinos*), to become a more general socialising sympathy; the instance discussed fits a broader pattern.[22]

Simon Haines has stated that European literature began with *menin*: the accusative singular of wrath or anger, the first word in the *Iliad*. Literature began with a passion, specifically the causes and consequences of the wrath of Achilles.[23] It is hardly a savoury tale, or an exhibition of the virtues of sociability and human understanding. This is more than a matter of having heroes cry and run away and of gods being as petty as the mortals who are supposed to worship them (one of Plato's original complaints). It was a matter of extremity of action and reaction, relentless antisocial, uncivilised competition, of the poet himself wallowing in violence and revenge, through rolling sequences of catalectic hexameters used to present honour (*time*) in battle, that confront the reader with a manic blood-lust. Additionally, there is the seeming complicity in the sheer social irresponsibility of the wrathful Achilles – for all his eloquence, as it were, an emotional child, feeling humiliated, and sulking in his tent because he had taken from him the enslaved Briseis, a woman whom his sense of honour, or lust demanded.

To make Homer fit for the eighteenth century meant modifying the passion. Analogically it was also to reject the violent enthusiasms of the seventeenth century – during which time the bloodshed consequent upon that Achillean wrath had been adapted by Hobbes in a rather different way. His own translations of Homer, his longest works and the fruits of his old age, were printed between 1675 and 1677, and these too needed countering. For Hobbes, both at a philosophical and political level, Homer was made to speak with something close to his own voice, as both Paul Davis and Eric Nelson have forcefully evidenced.[24] The *Iliad* and *Odyssey* became ways of showing that the horrors of destructive passion inherent in humanity made absolute sovereign authority the indispensible condition for civilisation. Thus, making the Homeric violence immediate had a political point; Hobbes's robust simplicity of tone, the direct informality of his verse, and the casual or ironic way in which he treated matters touching spirituality, give decidedly mundane and worldly texts. For Hobbes, poets and the Homeric voice itself are hardly ever seen as inspired by, or in touch with, a higher spiritual order, so Homeric authority and allegorical value are subverted. There is nothing sublime in Hobbes's understanding of the Homeric world.[25] His translations proved popular, and as a result Homer needed not only accommodating, but rescuing. It is, then, not surprising that in the early eighteenth century there was a flurry of attempts to re-translate all or part of the Homeric epics.[26]

Ozell's and Pope's translations drew heavily on Anne Dacier's French prose rendition of Homer as a philosopher poet, who if read allegorically was in no way antithetical to Christian morality and social decency.[27] In general terms, part of the process of adjustment involved distancing the author from the action. Homer was giving a poetic account of earlier times. Such philologically based arguments went in tandem with elevating Longinus' aesthetic concept of the sublime (*huplos*). Homer's indecorum becomes not a sign of his moral primitiveness and passionate irresponsibility (contra Rapin), but a function of his craft, a virtue beyond accepted rules of decorum. As Bezaleel argued in a satiric poem on the translators, all were bound to fail in the presence of sublime genius, so we had best just stand back in awe.[28] Redescription through the concept of the sublime, however, was not self-evident commendation. Pope's praise of the untamed Homer was taken by

Dacier as denigration. Pope, whom she had considered a staunch ally of the ancients, had stabbed Homer in the back with such an assessment. Sublimity hardly went with an allegory of ordered Christian philosophy.[29]

Homer was also made to speak to the eighteenth century through a modification of exhibited passion. The tone is altered to something suggestive of sociability and sympathy; and with Pope's spectacularly successful work, even a compassion for others helps shape the text's narrative trajectory. I shall concentrate on book 1, not just because it is vital for the subsequent plot development, but also because it was sometimes translated in isolation. In the process I shall also make passing comparison with Hobbes's treatment of the epics, to illustrate how he too had adjusted them, and how he too was being repudiated not just as a translator but as a corrupting philosopher.

It is Agamemnon's passionate irrationality against all good advice that starts the whole sorry tale. The Trojan priest Chryses comes to the Greek camp laden with gifts, to beg for the return of his captured daughter, Chryseis. The Greeks are very willing to make the exchange. For them, it is a rare conjunction of what the Romans would call *utilitas* and *honestas*. To accept the offer and return the girl to her father is to show due respect to the god through his priest, and it is also to reap considerable material rewards. Agamemnon, however, ignores all advice, rejects the offer out of hand, abuses and threatens the priest, and gloats over his daughter's plight: she will become a sexual slave in a foreign country until he tires of her.[30] The terrified Chryses flees and prays to Apollo for revenge. The god duly obliges by loosing arrows of a devastating plague on the Greeks. Agamemnon is forced to return the priest's daughter, and in compensation takes Achilles' slave Briseis. The angered Achilles, retires to his tent, refusing to participate in the war, until enraged and distraught by the death of his companion Patrochlus, he re-emerges to seek revenge.

Agamemnon was the supreme war leader of the Greeks, a king (*basileus*), who had behaved in a tyrannical fashion, and he is roundly accused of this. For Hobbes, being a *basileus* had meant Agamemnon was a sovereign, not to be gainsaid by his army and certainly not to be accused of tyranny. Thus Agamemnon contradicts the advice of the 'princes', not all the rest of the Greeks (*alloi*), is given an abbreviated outburst, and implications of tyranny disappear.[31] As for the hapless priest's daughter, Hobbes's Agamemnon states simply that she will '...make *my* Bed, and labour at the Loom'.[32] The sexual lust, so often taken as an expression of the licentiousness that defined tyranny, is also greatly downplayed. As Nelson also stresses, in keeping with Hobbes's long-standing suspicions of eloquence as dangerous and destabilising, the wrathful Achilles ceases to be the master of rhetoric that he is in the original.[33]

Ozell, who has no problem with the democratic implications of a whole army giving advice, and certainly not with seeing Agamemnon as a tyrant, nevertheless also discounts his sexual lust. This partly involves a defensive misreading of the verb form *antoosan*, literally meaning to go with a purpose, but which was usually euphemistic of intercourse, in this case, to go to my bed with a purpose. For Ozell, the girl is simply to be a chambermaid.[34] Dryden's 1700 translation had been explicit and by all standards correct: 'the Captive-maid is mine', she will attend 'my Royal Bed' and 'ascend' to it.[35] Maynwaring would shortly provide evasive locutions for the lust, but he also balances the implacable Apollo's wrath at Agamemnon by attributing to the god a sympathetic 'compassion' for the priest, absent from the Greek.[36] In short, if for Hobbes, the need for social control over human passion makes Agamemnon the answer, for the other translators, his own tyrannical passion is the problem.

Ozell's work carries a translation of Dacier's preface to her version of the *Iliad* and argues that only English, and only blank verse English at that, can get close to the epic grandeur of the original – French being good only for talking about food. And in making specific allusion to Milton – the English Homer, as Ozell calls him –, and citing his view that rhyme is a modern slavery, we see a further dimension of the politics of translation. This is a patriotic Whig appropriation of Homer, one highly critical of Hobbes's tone, omissions, and understanding of the Greek.[37] Thomas Tickell's aborted translation was also sponsored by the Whig Joseph Addison.[38]

Neither satisfied the Tory Catholic Pope any more than had Hobbes's rhyming royalist Homer, poetically beneath Pope's contempt and suspected by him of being deliberately subversive.[39] In a number of ways, Pope's *Iliad* exudes a high church, even Catholic, respect for the cloth. The holiness and the independent power of the priest Chryses are stressed; but more importantly it asserts the necessity of accepting divine mystery beyond the earthly pride and posturing of kings. The poetic voice, especially Homer's, is a mediator of this spiritual realm. This is to bring into relief further dimensions of dispute with the Hobbes translation. Modesty in the face of divine mystery was itself, for Pope and his friends, a form of philosophical virtue, an awareness of human limitation, quite uncharacteristic of the intellectually insatiable modern philosopher. This cap fits Hobbes fairly well and Pope rejected what went with it: a restricted conception of the poet as subordinate to the philosopher; and most emphatically, a total denial of the independence of any priestly class from the sovereign. Hobbes had even slyly satirised Homeric accounts of the afterlife, suitable subjects for Christian allegorical adaptation. Thus ghosts in Hades call themselves 'incorporeal substances', Hobbes's own dismissive oxymoron for what he took to be a particular form of scholastic nonsense.[40] In both his *Iliad* and *Odyssey,* the poetic voice is almost entirely denuded of the Homeric epithets suggesting intellectual authority, inspiration, and the status of mediator of the divine.[41] Pope, however, went so far in the other direction, that John Dennis called his *Iliad* a work of 'arbitrary and popish doctrine' – an obvious echo of Civil War confessional politics.[42]

But Pope also domesticated Homeric passion, even with the tyrannical and wayward Agamemnon. Thus in the abusive dismissal of Chryses, Agamemnon states of the priest's daughter that 'time' not Agamemnon himself 'shall rifle every useful grace'. Although her status as a sex slave is evident enough, he continues, that in old age she will be 'doom'd to deck the bed she once enjoy'd'.[43] The enjoyment is absent from the Greek and Pope thereby turns aggressive passion suggestive of rape into an intimation of mutual engagement.

The story of Pope's Achilles is easily enough construed as one of developing human self-awareness, a growth of moral maturity. But this, I think, would be to read the work through a later perspective focused on an abstracted 'self' or individual as a locus of moral agency, of emotional and ethical development. Paul Davis is convincing in arguing that the shift from Achilles' tented isolation to his participation in the conflict and finally to his recognition of others in a 'humane mutuality', is analogous to Pope's own changing sense of specifically poetic responsibility. It was a journey away from an heroic Miltonic ideal, towards a sympathetic engagement with other worthy poets, hence society.[44] On this reading, Achilles, restored as the master of rhetoric he had ceased to be for Hobbes, would become an allegorical figure for the ethico-passional economy of the poet's office. This Pope regarded in the most elevated, if conventional terms, as giving a form of philosophical guidance.

Appropriately, at the end of Pope's *Iliad* there is a touching sympathy shown by Achilles to King Priam, who comes to him to ask for the remains of his despoiled son Hector. Thus, the poem goes back to its beginning: a father as gift-bearing suppliant pleads for his child before a victor. Crucially, however, the result is different, the remains are returned for proper burial.[45] With Pope's Achilles the anger is largely abated more clearly than in earlier translations. There is a sparkle of it kindling in his eyes;[46] but he exhibits a humane generosity, a sympathetic recognition of the shared human condition and of a community joined beyond war. Priam is told to stop pleading for the body, 'move me no more',/'To yield thy Hector I myself intend'.[47] Achilles acknowledges he has been visited by a vision of his mother in the night, then again tells Priam to cease trying to 'shake the purpose of my soul'.[48] None of this is entirely at odds with the text, but the original is decidedly less assuaging. The human sympathy is glossed largely from Achilles tears for himself and his father; and moreover from his distress at the need to placate the shade of his friend Patrochlus if the abused body is properly buried. Yet he shows pity as Priam asks (*auton t' eleeson*). This Homeric pity, however, is more the condescension towards the pitiable or wretched (*eleeinos*) than, as it is with Dacier and Pope, a generosity of spirit at one with Christian imperatives. The continuing anger of the original is also more evident than in Pope's kindling of it in the eyes. The threats and dire warnings echo Agamemnon's to Chryses in book 1, and they seriously scare the old king.[49] It is clearer in the Greek than in Pope's English that Achilles is returning the body because he has been ordered by Zeus to do so, with the consequence of dishonouring Patrochlus. This situation explains the depth of frustrated anger. Priam should provoke him (*erethixe*) no further, an expression that is both repeated and far stronger than Pope's 'move me' and 'shake the purpose of my soul'.[50] Albeit often only by shifts of emphasis, Pope spins one concluding moral image from the text, as Hobbes had briskly fashioned another more bathetic one, a tidying up of loose ends of a good yarn to get to the funeral. If, then, Pope's Achilles is a figure for the poet, both the conjuring of a general human sympathy and a potential for anger are necessary, and fit Pope's more explicit expressions of poetic and satiric responsibility in the face of modernist corruptions.

4 Satire and the passions of cultural purging

So, was Pope's morally decorous Homer any more authentic than the versions by Hobbes and others he was determined to displace? To be sure, by modern standards it was lacking. But these obscure what was so often at issue in translation. Bezaleel's satiric squib probably provided the safest conclusion; if accuracy is sought, all translations were wanting. Accept that the sublime will never be captured.[51] Substitutional accuracy, however, was not the whole point. Enlistment of an authoritative text to a cause assumed a more obvious importance before narrower understandings of translation and its significance came to hold sway, and translation for those who did not know the original became such a driving force. As I have argued elsewhere, part of what was at stake, was the matter of philosophic responsibility towards society. Hobbes would deny and Pope reassert the independent philosophic authority of the poet; and Homer was a battleground.[52] It is largely modern academic conceptions and the institutionalised separation of literature and philosophy that have obscured the earlier contested fluidity of intellectual demarcation, and of which, in complementary ways, Hultquist and Frazer have fruitfully reminded us. We are returned to the importance of keeping in mind later disciplinary and language changes, such as the crafting of a modern conception of the emotions, when dealing with earlier times preoccupied with the passions.

Nevertheless, Pope's efforts in particular attracted the ire of Richard Bentley and certainly for reasons that went well beyond linguistic fastidiousness. Writing directly to Pope, he took Pope's efforts to be fundamentally versifications of Dacier's prose: 'translated from the French, by a woman too. How the devil could it be Homer? You know no Greek, you can barely construe Latin'.[53] Here is the voice of Pope's arch pedant, the irascibly brilliant philologist and terminally embattled Master of Trinity College Cambridge. Translation was not Bentley's interest, the recovery of the authentic Greek was, together with a little revenge. The poems had survived wanting the archaic letter digamma, and his plan was to produce a corrected original. And had he finished his work (for all but a notebook was lost in a fire), he would have offered a more alien and awkward text for those like Pope and Dacier to assimilate to the modern world.[54] As for revenge, Bentley's outburst comes towards the end of a troubled relationship with Pope and his satiric poetic circle, the Tory wits. He had persistently been a butt of their humour and an object of satiric scorn. So a concluding word is in order on satire and humour in the early eighteenth century, through the glass of these poisoned relationships.

Laughter as an expression of passion was of uncertain standing: extensively theorised in antiquity and from the Renaissance into the eighteenth century, it was recognised to be physiologically healthy, a disturbance, an emotion of the body, such as the spontaneous laughter at an unexpected meeting of old friends. It was, perhaps increasingly taken as a sign of good humour, empathy and fellowship; but it was also, as Addison echoes from centuries of reflection, still seen as an expression of anger and cruelty.[55] Its provocation was recognised as a powerful tool in rhetoric, social control, and the isolation of those who were to be shamed. As Hobbes had asserted in his famous analysis of laughter: it is those grimaces arising from the passion of 'sudden glory' that give pleasure through self-satisfaction or through some perceived deformity in another; laughter is a sign of meanness.[56] So (Hobbes's rider is often overlooked), it is a passion evidencing a moral weakness.

Homer had set a precedent for the laughter of social aggression and control. There is, for example, the entrapment of Aphrodite/Venus and Ares/Mars, caught in a net and humiliated before the other gods and laughed at by Odysseus and his hosts, who revelled in the story. The story demeans the gods and is told by a poet who, for once, Hobbes credits with inspiration. This is unlikely to be coincidental.[57]

To risk a generalisation, it may be that older theories of the aggressive functions of laughter, prominent in satire, survived as a sort of surrogacy for the violence that had so undermined sociability. Certainly the effectiveness of such damaging mirth was probably greater than it is now, simply because, as Craig Muldrew has shown, social credit was both fragile and important. Without reputation or good character, there were serious risks to life and well-being. Managing the ubiquity of debt was dependent upon social credit; at law, reputation could be the difference between an innocent and guilty verdict. And it was social credit that satire attacked; the effective provocation of laughter was a sign of its being diminished.[58] Robert Phiddian (Chapter 3) aptly cites Pope's *Epilogue to the Satires*, men 'Safe from the Bar, the Pulpit, and the Throne,/Yet touch'd and sham'd by *Ridicule* alone'. It was ridicule to which Bentley was subject, safe both from pulpit and bar, protected by the Throne, despite the fellowship of Trinity's best efforts to destroy him.[59]

The moral judgement inherent in the provocation of aggressive humour is a corollary of the social engagement Pope considered to be part of his poetic responsibility. The point of ridicule was to expose and purge society of those who corrupted its standards; it was not simply trade in the currency of safe ethical generalities. Bentley had been the prime target of Swift in *The Battle of the Books*, and was to remain in range in other works up to and including in *The Dunciad*.[60]

The ostensible problem was that Bentley was a modern. For the ancients, like Swift and Pope, accurate philology involving the re-writing and de-mythologising of a cultural inheritance of ancient texts, was profoundly worrying because potentially destructive of civilisation; so scholarship becomes the pedantry pilloried in *The Dunciad*. To this end, they ruthlessly exploited Bentley's own violent passions, making things worse by associating him outrageously with that other icon of hated modernity, Hobbes, who quite openly had dismissed most ancient literature as useless or dangerous. He too, as a leader of the moderns and, arguably, as the spider in the rafters, had been a target in *The Battle of the Books*. Bentley, who quite violently attacked Hobbes's philosophy as mad and wicked, directed his philological energies towards purifying the inheritance of antiquity that it may remain valuable.[61]

The Battle of the Books was in part occasioned by Bentley's decisive proof that a hallowed ancient text was entirely spurious.[62] The attacks on him largely ignored his overwhelming evidence and careful argument. Bentley was to be scoffed into isolation, not because rational standards of proof and inference were beyond his enemies, but because the self-appointed ancients were defending a truth (as they saw it) above such standards, an inheritance of moral standards, attitudes, and emotional/passional responses on which civilisation depended.[63] Satiric exhibition of heightened indignation in the name of higher truth may well have been the expression of genuine feeling, but it was also a legitimating display precisely because satirists like Swift and Pope took satire as being a moral office of critique and purification. The rationale, as Phiddian has illustrated (Chapter 3), licensed passions in the ambit of anger and required they loom large in print. If Pope did associate himself figuratively with Achilles, even the wrath of the hero had some sanction. Predictably, the satirist could in turn be accused with the armoury of antisocial passion: spite, envy, cruelty, pusillanimity, unwarranted wrath. Here we see a final case of the intricate and resourcefully manipulated relationships between proclaimed moral standing and passion. Swift and Pope's exploitation of Bentley's own irascible personality certainly touched on a danger of philological scholarship, what I have elsewhere called the paradox of relevance. It had been recognised since the sixteenth century and has since flowed through to historiography. The effect of trying to understand the past more precisely with more nuanced detail in order to press it into more effective service to the present (Bentley's enterprise), can be to make it alien, unusable, or to expose it as myth, the consequence feared by Swift and Pope.[64]

But the point of satire has also been, as Rosenheim emphasised some years ago, punitive and vengeful.[65] And this, with the fears and violence of the long seventeenth century still with us in the age of Pope and Swift, suggests another vicarious target, for which Bentley stood as symptom: not just modernity, but low-church modernity. For those of the high Anglican Church, this was the thin end of the wedge, or rather the blunt end of the axe that had taken off the head of Charles I. James

VI & I had said much earlier, 'no bishops no king'. And the king killing Presbyterians and independents had a minimal respect for the authority of the cloth. At the other extreme, the Catholics were considered to have too much – no bishops, no pope. And in sniffing 'arbitrary and popish' doctrine in Pope's Homer, the Whig modern Dennis had alighted on the enhanced respect Pope shows for divinely inspired priests and priest-like poets, with interpretative authority, and powers independent of earthly rulers. The abused priest Chryses is able to call down the wrathful vengeance of Apollo on a king who had behaved as a tyrant.

5   Conclusion

What can we suggest from this concerning the emotions in the eighteenth century? On this sort of evidence, the picture cannot be clear-cut. Nevertheless, it does suggest that sensitivity to the violence of the seventeenth century still informs the early eighteenth, and this sensitivity is focused on the problematics of passion in a world in which, increasingly, it is spread through printer's ink: Marvell's 'Lead...founded into Letters'. A Hobbesian solution might not have been acceptable for many, but there remained a continuity of fears about passionate expressions gathered around religion and the functions of priests, political society, and the standing of a cultural inheritance. On all these problematic areas of dispute, Hobbes had set a forceful, if reductive, agenda.

Second, although what was seen as an overly passionate age needed to be put into the past, any textual inheritance also required modification for the present: in continuity there had to be change and translation was apt to disguise it. In Homer's case, the need was acute. Alteration, as Hobbes's translations illustrate, could often be draconian. But the processes of adjustment do not evidence any straightforward charting of the passions, either as expressed, or as played upon. This raises the question of how far the satirists' alleged and loud passion for the 'truth', as a proper moral standard, can be an inauthentic feigning of something else, or an exaggeration deemed necessary by the communicative uncertainties of the printed world? Regardless of how we might answer this, what we do see through satire are attempts to shift the shape and content of social groups, to constitute an audience through print. In the process, old divisions are vicariously perpetuated, and issues encoded that have now fallen from sight – and all by means at odds with later and even contemporary standards of rationality and propositional transparency. In so far as satire helped define the limits of civility and belonging, we are a long way from a public sphere in any Habermasian sense, but we may be closer to a taming of destructive passion. What Hobbes had called 'COMPASSION' and 'in the phrase of this present time a FELLOW-FEELING' was expanded to become the sympathy preconditional for civil society that he had denied it could be.[66] In this continuity, the importance he gave to antisocial passion in explaining the very existence of society, is firmly consigned to the past. It is a trajectory that does something to conjoin the notions of the long seventeenth with the long eighteenth century.

Notes

1. For a bracing overview of the seventeenth century and its shadowing significance for more recent times, see J. Scott (2000) *England's Troubles: Seventeenth-Century English Political Instability in European Context* (Cambridge: Cambridge University Press).
2. J. Habermas (1962) *Strukturwandel der Öffentlicheit* (Darmstadt und Neuweid: Luchterhand Verlag); trans. T. Burger with F. Lawrence (1989) as *The Structural Transformation of the Public Sphere: An Inquiry into a Category of Bourgeois Society* (London: Polity Press). There is now a large historiographical literature *searching* for the origins of this model. For details and for a critique of the category mistake involved, and its deleterious consequences, see C. Condren (2009) 'Public, Private and the Idea of the "Public Sphere" in Early-Modern England', *Intellectual History Review* XIX(1): 15–28.
3. M. McKeon, (2004) 'Parsing Habermas's "Bourgeois Public Sphere", *Criticism* XLVI(II): 273–7.
4. Scott, *England's Troubles*, p. 51, quoting Andrew Marvell (1672) *The Rehearsal Transpros'd* (London).
5. A. Smith (1982 [1759]) *The Theory of Moral Sentiments*, ed. D. D. Raphael and A. L. Macfie (Indianapolis, IN: Liberty Fund), pp. 9–16.
6. See, for example, Smith, *Moral Sentiments*, p. 9, where pity is called an emotion, though the emphasis of the work is upon passion.
7. John Evelyn (2014 [1655–98]) *Letterbooks*, ed. D. D. C. Chambers and D. Galbraith (Toronto: Toronto University Press), Vol. 1, 'To Sir Peter Wiche Knight', 20 June 1665, p. 373.
8. Smith, *Moral Sentiments*, e.g. pp. 10–16.
9. J. Donne (1624, 1700) *Biathanatos* (London).
10. I. Hunter (2001) *Rival Enlightenments: Civil and Metaphysical Philosophy in Early Modern Germany* (Cambridge: Cambridge University Press); for a diversity of explorations of this theme, see C. Condren, S. Gaukroger, and I. Hunter (Eds.) (2006) *The Philosopher in Early Modern Europe* (Cambridge: Cambridge University Press).
11. S. R. (1693) *The Life of M. Descartes* (London), pp. 251–2.
12. A. Williams (2005, 2009) *Poetry and the Creation of a Whig Literary Culture, 1681–1714* (Oxford: Oxford University Press), pp. 183–6; B. Jonson (1875 [1641]) *Timber, or Discoveries made upon Men and Matter*, in *Works*, ed. W. Gifford (London: Bickers and Sotheran), Vol. 9, pp. 129–228.
13. Sir William Cornwallis (1616) *Essays of Certain Paradoxes* (London).

14. P. Burke (2007) 'Cultures of Translation in Early Modern Europe', in P. Burke and R. Po-chia Hsia (Eds.), *Cultural Translation in Early Modern Europe* (Cambridge: Cambridge University Press), pp. 7–38; P. Davies (2008) *Translation and the Poet's Life: The Ethics of Translating in English Culture, 1646–1726* (Oxford: Oxford University Press).

15. Burke, 'Cultures of Translation', pp. 7–15.

16. J. L. Vives (1536) *De ratione dicendi* (Basel) III, pp. 225–6.

17. H. Weinbrot (1966) 'Translation and Parody: Towards a Genealogy of Augustan Imitation', *English Literary History* IV: 434–47.

18. For invaluable accounts, see J. M. Levine (1991) *The Battle of the Books: History and Literature in the Augustan Age* (Ithaca, NY: Cornell University Press); J. M. Levine (1999) *Between the Ancients and the Moderns: Baroque Culture in Restoration England* (New Haven, CT: Yale University Press).

19. R. Rapin (1706) 'A Comparison of Homer and Virgil', in W. Kennet (Ed.), *The Whole Critical Works*, Vol. 1, pp. 116–210; H. D. Weinbrot (1988) *Eighteenth-Century Satire: Essays on Text and Context from Dryden to Peter Pindar* (Cambridge: Cambridge University Press), pp. 101–4.

20. Paul Davis (2008) *Translation and the Poet's Life: The Ethics of Translating in English Culture, 1646–1726* (Oxford: Oxford University Press), p. 255.

21. J. Swift (1963 [1704]) *A Tale of a Tub and the Battle of the Books*, with introduction by L. Melville (London: Dent), pp. 82–3.

22. See M. Strawn (2012) 'Homer, Sentimentalism and Pope's Translation of Homer', *Studies in English Literature* LII(3): 585–608, for a catalogue of changes towards the sympathetic, but discussed rather loosely through the notions of sentiment and emotion. Priam's plea is not discussed.

23. S. Haines (2005) *Poetry and Philosophy From Homer to Rousseau: Romantic Souls, Realist Lives* (Basingstoke: Palgrave), p. 1; Homer (1999) *Iliad*, trans, A. T. Murray, rev. W. F. Wyatt (Cambridge, MA: Harvard University Press), 2 vols, though there have been variations on the opening lines, p. 12.

24. For excellent accounts of the persistent political features of the work, P. Davis (1997) 'Thomas Hobbes's Translations of Homer: Epic and Anticlericalism in late Seventeenth-Century England', *Seventeenth Century* XII(2): 231–55; E. Nelson (2008) 'General Introduction', *Thomas Hobbes: Translations of Homer*, Vol. 1, *The Iliad*, Vol. 2, *The Odyssey*, ed. E. Nelson (Oxford: Clarendon Press) Vol. 1, pp. xii–lxxvi; for a general outline of the political readings of Homer, J. Lynch (1998) 'Political Ideology in the Translations of the *Iliad*, 1660–1715', *Translation and Literature* LXXI: 23–41.

25. Davis, 'Hobbes's Translations' at length; Nelson, 'Introduction', pp. lxix–lxxiv; C. Condren (2014) 'The Philosopher Hobbes as the Poet Homer', *Renaissance Studies* XXVIII(1): 71–89.

26. J. Dryden (1700, 1721) *Iliad*, Book One, in *Fables Ancient and Modern* (London); A. Maynwaring (1967 [1704]) *Iliad* I (fragment) in *The Twickenham Edition of the Poetry of Alexander Pope*, general ed. J. Butt, Vols 7–10, ed. M. Mack (London: Methuen and Yale University Press), Vol. 7, Appendix F, pp. 560–72; J. Ozell, et al. (1712) *The Iliad of Homer with Notes* (London), further editions, 1714, 1734; Thomas Tickell (1715, 1721) *The First Book of Homer's Iliad*, in *The Poetical Works of Thomas Tickell* (London), pp. 86–116; A. Pope (1715–20) *The Iliad of Homer* (London), 6 vols, see also, *Twickenham Edition*, ed. Mack, Vols 7–10.

27. Anne Dacier (1711) *L'Iliade d'Homère, Traduite en Francois avec des Remarques Par Madame Dacier* (Paris); see also F. Moore (2000) 'Homer Revisited: Anne Le Fèvre Dacier's Preface to her Prose. Translation of the *Iliad* in Early Eighteenth-Century France', *Studies in the Literary Imagination* 33(2): 87–107.
28. M. Bezaleel (1721, 1733) *On the English Translations of Homer: A Satire* (London).
29. Moore, 'Homer Revisited', 101; Weinbrot, *Eighteenth Century Satire*, p. 108.
30. Homer, *Iliad*, lines 25–32, pp. 14/15.
31. Hobbes, *Iliad*, ed. Nelson, book 1, line 26, p. 4 and note.
32. Hobbes, *Iliad*, book 1, line 34.
33. Nelson, 'Introduction', pp. lviii–lx.
34. Ozell, *Iliad*, p. 6 and note, defending Chapman's much earlier reading.
35. Dryden, *Fables*, lines 44–9.
36. For discussion and further detail, see Condren, 'The Philosopher Hobbes', 84–5.
37. Ozell, *Iliad* 'Preface', A3–5, A5v.
38. Davis, *Translation and the Poet's Life*, p. 247; see more broadly, Williams, *Poetry and the Creation of a Whig Literary Culture*.
39. Davis, 'Hobbes's Translations', 231–5.
40. Hobbes, *Odyssey*, ed. Nelson, book XI, line 206, and note to p. 107; Davis, 'Hobbes Translations', 234–5; Condren, 'The Philosopher Hobbes', 83–4.
41. Nelson, 'General Introduction', pp. lxxii–lxxiv, and numerous notes to the text; Condren, 'The Philosopher Hobbes', 82–3.
42. Lynch, 'Ideology', 28.
43. Pope, *Iliad*, book 1, lines 41, 44, 34.
44. Davis, *Translation and the Poet's Life*, pp. 265–73, 261.
45. Homer, *Iliad*, book 24, lines 465–550.
46. Pope, *Iliad*, book 24, lines 706, 442 (1720, pagination continuous with earlier volumes).
47. Pope, *Iliad*, book 24, lines 705, 708; see also 'Argument', p. 426.
48. Pope, *Iliad*, book 24, lines 709, 716–19, 442.
49. Homer, *Iliad*, book 24, lines 558–65, quotation from line 503.
50. Homer, *Iliad*, book 24, lines 559–63.
51. Bezaleel, *On the English Translations*.
52. Condren, 'The Philosopher Hobbes', 76–89.
53. R. Bentley, *A Letter to Mr. Pope Occasioned by Sober Advice from Horace*, London 1735; quoted, Levine, *Battle of the Books*, 222, 240–1.
54. R. Bentley, Trinity College MS, B. 17.17; the notes extend only to book 6 of the *Iliad*, erratically cross-referenced to the *Odyssey*.
55. J. Addison (1711, 1906) *The Spectator*, 47, 24 April, 1711, in G. Gregory Smith (Ed.), *The Spectator by Joseph Addison, Richard Steele and Others* (London: Dent), 4 vols, Vol. 1, pp. 174–7.
56. T. Hobbes (2012 [1651]) *Leviathan,* ed. N. Malcolm (Oxford: Clarendon Press) 3 vols, Vol. 1, pp. 88–9; the Latin makes more explicit that deformity may be moral rather than physical.
57. Homer (1995) *Odyssey*, trans. A. T. Murray, rev. G. E. Dimock (Cambridge, MA.: Harvard University Press), book 8, lines 265–370; Hobbes, *Odyssey*, book 8, lines 260–315.

58. C. Muldrew (1988) *The Economy of Obligation: The Culture of Credit and Social Relations in Early Modern England* (New York: St Martin's Press).

59. The Mastership of Trinity is by royal appointment.

60. For example, J. Arbuthnot (? c. 1714, 1768) *Virgilius restauratus*, in J. Swift, *Works* (Edinburgh), 13 vols, Vol. 6, pp. 128–33.

61. R. Bentley (1693) *The Folly and Unreasonableness of Atheism*, p. 40.

62. R. Bentley (1699, 1836) *A Dissertation on the Epistles of Phalaris with an Answer to the Objections of the Honorable Charles Boyle*, in A. Dyce (Ed.), *The Works of Richard Bentley* (London: Francis Macpherson), Vol. 2, pp. 130–81.

63. C. Condren (2012) *Hobbes, The Scriblerians and the History of Philosophy* (London: Pickering and Chatto), pp. 87–91.

64. Condren, *Hobbes, The Scriblerians*, pp. 27–30.

65. E. W. Rosenheim (1963) *Swift and the Satirist's Art* (Chicago: Chicago University Press), pp. 13–17.

66. Hobbes, *Leviathan*, Chapter 6, 90; the phrase is absent from the Latin, p. 91.

Select Bibliography of Secondary Sources

Abramson, K. (2008) 'Sympathy and Hume's Spectator-centered Theory of Virtue' in Elizabeth Radcliffe (ed.) *A Companion to Hume* (Malden: Blackwell), pp. 240–256.

—— (2007) 'Hume's Distinction Between Philosophical Anatomy and Painting' *Philosophy Compass* 2.5: 680–698.

—— (2006) 'Happy to Unite, or Not?' *Philosophy Compass* 1.3: 290–302.

—— (2000) 'Sympathy and the Project of Hume's Second Enquiry' *Archiv für Geschichte der Philosophie* 83: 45–80.

—— (1997) *Hume's Peculiar Sentiments: The Evolution of Hume's Moral Philosophy* (Ph.D. Dissertation, Department of Philosophy, University of Chicago).

Agnew, J.-C. (1986) *Worlds Apart: The Market and the Theater in Anglo-American Thought, 1550–1750* (Cambridge: Cambridge University Press).

Ahmed, S. (2004) *The Cultural Politics of Emotion* (Edinburgh: Edinburgh University Press).

Aldridge, A. O. (1945) 'Shaftesbury and the Test of Truth' *PMLA* 60.1: 129–156.

Alexander, M. (2013) *A History of English Literature* (3rd edn.) Palgrave Foundations Series (Basingstoke; New York: Palgrave Macmillan).

Allen, C. (1998) 'Painting the Passions: The *Passions de l'Âme* as a Basis for Pictorial Expression' in S. Gaukroger (ed.) *The Soft Underbelly of Reason: The Passions in the Seventeenth Century* (London: Routledge), pp. 79–111.

Alliston, A. (2011) 'Female Quixotism: Character and Plausibility, Honesty and Fidelity' *The Eighteenth Century* 52.3–4: 249–269.

Anderson, B. (2009) 'Affective Atmospheres' *Emotion, Space and Society* 2: 77–81.

Anderson, C. and D. Keltner (2004) 'The Emotional Convergence Hypothesis: Implications for Individuals, Relationships, and Cultures' in L. Z. Tiedens and C. W. Leach (eds.) *The Social Life of Emotions* (Cambridge: Cambridge University Press), pp. 144–163.

Anderson, E. H. (2009) *Eighteenth-Century Authorship and the Play of Fiction: Novels and the Theater, Haywood to Austen* (New York: Routledge).

Andrew, D. T. (2013) *Aristocratic Vice: The Attack on Duelling, Suicide, Adultery, and Gambling in Eighteenth-Century England* (New Haven, CT and London: Yale University Press).

Armstrong, N. and L. Tennenhouse (2006) 'A Mind for Passion: Locke and Hutcheson on Desire' in V. Kahn, N. Saccamano and D. Coli (eds.) *Politics and the Passions 1500–1850* (Princeton, NJ: Princeton University Press), pp. 131–150.

Arrizabalaga, J., J. Henderson, and R. French (1997) *The Great Pox: The French Disease in Renaissance Europe* (New Haven, CT: Yale University Press).

Averill, J. R. (1982) *Anger and Aggression: An Essay on Emotion* (New York: Springer-Verlag).

—— (1980) 'A Constructivist View of Emotion' in R. Plutchik and H. Kellerman (eds.) *Emotion: Theory, Research, and Experience: Vol. 1. Theories of Emotion* (New York: Academic Press), pp. 305–339.

Bagnoli, C. (ed.) (2011) *Morality and the Emotions* (Oxford: Oxford University Press).

Baier, A. (1986) 'Extending the Limits of Moral Theory' *The Journal of Philosophy* 83.10: 538–45.

Ballaster, R. (2012) 'Rivals for the Repertory: Theatre and Novel in Georgian London' *Restoration and 18th Century Theatre Research* 27.1: 5–24.

——, G. Egan, and K. Lawton-Trask. *The Georgian Theatre and the Novel: 1714–1830* http://georgiantheatrenovel.wordpress.com, accessed 9 June 2014.

Barclay, K. (2011) *Love, Intimacy and Power: Marriage and Patriarchy in Scotland, 1650–1850* (Manchester and New York: Manchester University Press).

Barish, J. A. (1982) *Anti-Theatrical Prejudice* (Berkeley, CA: University of California Press).

Barker-Benfield, G. J. (1992) *The Culture of Sensibility: Sex and Society in Eighteenth-Century Britain* (Chicago and London: University of Chicago Press).

Barnouw, J. (1992) 'Passion as "Confused" Perception or Thought in Descartes, Malebranche, and Hutcheson' *Journal of the History of Ideas* 53: 397–424.

Barrett, L. F. (2006) 'Emotions as Natural Kinds?' *Perspectives on Psychological Science* 10: 20–46.

Batson, C. D. (1991) *The Altruism Question: Toward a Social-Psychological Answer* (Hillsdale, NJ: Lawrence Erlbaum).

Bell, M. (2000) *Sentimentalism, Ethics, and the Culture of Feeling* (Basingstoke: Palgrave).

Berlant, L. (2008) 'Intuitionists: History and the Affective Event' *American Literary History* 20.4: 845–860.

Berry, C. (2003) 'Sociality and Socialisation' in A. Broadie (ed.) *The Cambridge Companion to the Scottish Enlightenment* (Cambridge: Cambridge University Press), pp. 243–257.

Berry, H. M. (2003) *Gender, Society and Print Culture in Late-Stuart England: The Cultural World of the Athenian Mercury* (Burlington, VT: Ashgate).

Boiger, M. and B. Mesquita (2012) 'The Construction of Emotion in Interactions, Relationships, and Cultures' *Emotion Review* 4.3: 221–229.

Box, M. A. (1990) *The Suasive Art of David Hume* (Princeton, NJ: Princeton University Press).

Bray, J. (2009) *The Female Reader in the English Novel: From Burney to Austen* (New York: Routledge).

Brennan, T. (2004) *The Transmission of Affect* (Ithaca, NY: Cornell University Press).

Brewer, D. A. (2012) 'Print, Performance, Personhood, Polly Honeycombe' *Studies in Eighteenth Century Culture* 41: 185–194.

Brissenden, R. F. (1974) *Virtue in Distress: Studies in the Novel of Sentiment from Richardson to Sade* (London: Macmillan).

Broadie, A. (2009) 'Hutcheson on Connoisseurship and the Role of Reflection' *British Journal for the History of Philosophy* 17: 351–364.

—— (2006) 'Sympathy and the Impartial Spectator' in K. Haakonssen (ed.) *The Cambridge Companion to Adam Smith* (Cambridge: Cambridge University Press), pp. 158–188.

Buckle, S. (2001) *Hume's Enlightenment Tract: The Unity and Purpose of 'An Enquiry Concerning Human Understanding'* (New York: Oxford University Press).

Burke, P. (2007) 'Cultures of Translation in Early Modern Europe' in P. Burke and R. Po-chia Hsia (eds.) *Cultural Translation in Early Modern Europe* (Cambridge: Cambridge University Press), pp. 7–38.

Burling, W. (1988) 'A "sickly sort of refinement": The Problem of Sentimentalism in Mackenzie's The Man of Feeling' *Studies in Scottish Literature* 23: 136–149.

Burnyeat, M. F. (1980) 'Aristotle on Learning to be Good' in A. Rorty (ed.) *Essays on Aristotle's Ethics* (Berkeley, CA: University of California Press), pp. 69–92.

Caradonna, J. L. (2010) 'Grub Street and Suicide: A View from the Literary Press in Late Eighteenth-Century France' *Journal for Eighteenth-Century Studies* 33.1: 23–36.

Carlile, S. (ed.) (2010) *Masters of the Marketplace: Women Novelists of the 1750s* (Lanham, MD: Lehigh University Press).

Carroll, J. (2004) *Literary Darwinism: Evolution, Human Nature, and Literature* (New York: Routledge).

Chandler, J. (2013) *An Archaeology of Sympathy: The Sentimental Mode in Literature and Cinema* (Chicago: University of Chicago Press).

—— (2010) 'The Politics of Sentiment: Notes Toward a New Account' *Studies in Romanticism* 49.4: 553–575.

—— (2008) 'The Languages of Sentiment' *Textual Practice* 22.1: 21–39.

Chentsova-Dutton, Y. E., N. Senft, and A. G. Ryder (2014) 'Listening to Negative Emotions: How Culture Constrains What We Hear' in W. G. Parrott (ed.) *The Positive Side of Negative Emotions* (New York: Guilford Press), pp. 146–178.

Clery, E. (1995) *The Rise of Supernatural Fiction, 1762–1800.* Cambridge Studies in Romanticism (Cambridge: Cambridge University Press).

Cohon, R. (2008) *Hume's Morality: Feeling and Fabrication* (New York: Oxford University Press).

Cole, L. (1995) '*The London Merchant* and the Institution of Apprenticeship' *Criticism: A Quarterly for Literature and the Arts* 37.1: 57–84.

Condren C. (2014) 'The Philosopher Hobbes as the Poet Homer' *Renaissance Studies* 28.1: 71–89.

—— (2012) *Hobbes, The Scriblerians and the History of Philosophy* (London: Pickering and Chatto).

—— (2009) 'Public, Private and the Idea of the "Public Sphere" in Early-Modern England' *Intellectual History Review* 19.1: 15–28.

——, S. Gaukroger, and I. Hunter (eds.) (2006) *The Philosopher in Early Modern Europe* (Cambridge: Cambridge University Press).

Crawford, K. (2007) *European Sexualities, 1400–1800* (Cambridge: Cambridge University Press).

Csengei, I. (2012) *Sympathy, Sensibility and the Literature of Feeling in the Eighteenth Century* (Basingstoke: Palgrave Macmillan).

Daniel, C. (1987) 'The Fall of George Barnwell' *Restoration and Eighteenth-Century Theatre Research* 2.2: 26–37.

Darwall, S. (1995) *The British Moralists and the Moral 'Ought': 1640–1740* (Cambridge: Cambridge University Press).

Davis, M. H. (2004) 'Empathy: Negotiating the Border Between Self and Other' in L. Z. Tiedens and C. W. Leach (eds.) *The Social Life of Emotions* (Cambridge: Cambridge University Press), pp. 19–42.

Davis P. (2008) *Translation and the Poet's Life: The Ethics of Translating in English Culture, 1646–1726* (Oxford: Oxford University Press).

—— (1997) 'Thomas Hobbes's Translations of Homer: Epic and Anticlericalism in late Seventeenth-Century England' *Seventeenth Century* 12.2: 231–255.

Delehanty, A. T. (2007) 'Mapping the Aesthetic Mind: John Dennis and Nicolas Boileau' *Journal of the History of Ideas* 68.2: 233–253.

De Rivera, J. and D. Páez (2007) 'Emotional Climate, Human Security, and Cultures of Peace' *Journal of Social Issues* 63.2: 233–253.

De Sousa, R. (2014) 'Emotion' in *The Stanford Encyclopedia of Philosophy*, E. N. Zalta (ed.) Spring 2014 http://plato.stanford.edu/archives/spr2014/entries/emotion/

Dickie, S. (2011) *Cruelty and Laughter: Forgotten Comic Literature and the Unsentimental Eighteenth Century* (Chicago: University of Chicago Press).

Dixon, T. (2012) ' "Emotion": The History of a Keyword in Crisis' *Emotion Review* 4: 338–344.

—— (2003) *From Passions to Emotions: the Creation of a Secular Psychological Category* (Cambridge: Cambridge University Press).

Doherty, F. (1992) *A Study in Eighteenth-Century Advertising Methods: The Anodyne Necklace* (Lewiston: Edwin Mellon).

Dror, O. E. (1999) 'The Scientific Image of Emotion: Experience and Technologies of Inscription' *Configurations* 7: 355–401.

Edmond, M. 'Davenant, Sir William (1606–1668)' in H. C. G. Matthew and B. Harrison (eds.) *Oxford Dictionary of National Biography* (Oxford: Oxford University Press). Online edition, L. Goldman (ed.) http://www.oxforddnb.com/view/article/7197, accessed 12 February 2011.

—— (1987) *Rare Sir William Davenant* (Manchester: Manchester University Press).

Eisenberg, I. (1982) 'History of Medicine: A History of Rhinoplasty' *South African Medical Journal* 62: 286–292.

Ekman, P. (1973) *Darwin and Facial Expression: A Century of Research in Review* (New York: Academic Press).

—— (1972) *Emotion in the Human Face: Guidelines for Research and an Integration of Findings* (New York: Pergamon Press).

Elias, N. (2000) *The Civilising Process: Sociogenetic and Psychogenetic Investigations* translated by E. Jephcott, revised and edited by E. Dunning, J. Goudsblom and S. Mennell (Oxford: Blackwell).

Ellis, M. (1996) *The Politics of Sensibility: Race, Gender, and Commerce in the Sentimental Novel* (Cambridge: Cambridge University Press).

Ellison, J. (1999) *Cato's Tears and the Making of Anglo-American Emotion* (Chicago: University of Chicago Press).

Elster, J. (1999) *Alchemies of the Mind: Rationality and the Emotions* (Cambridge: Cambridge University Press).

Elton, M. (2008) 'Moral Sense and Natural Reason' *The Review of Metaphysics* 62: 79–110.

Emsley, J. (2005) *The Elements of Murder: A History of Poison* (Oxford: Oxford University Press).

Eustace, N. (2008) *Passion is the Gale: Emotion, Power and the Coming of the American Revolution* (Williamsburg, VA: Omohundro).

Fairclough, M. (2013) *The Romantic Crowd: Sympathy, Controversy and Print Culture* (Cambridge: Cambridge University Press).

Fara, P. (1996) *Sympathetic Attractions: Magnetic Practices, Beliefs and Symbolism in Eighteenth-Century England* (Princeton, NJ: Princeton University Press).

Fiering, N. S. (1976) 'Irresistible Compassion: An Aspect of Eighteenth-Century Sympathy and Humanitarianism' *Journal of the History of Ideas* 37.2: 195–218.

Fischer, A. H. and A. S. R. Manstead (2008) 'Social Functions of Emotion' in M. Lewis, J. M. Haviland-Jones and L. F. Barrett (eds.) *Handbook of Emotions*, 3rd edn. (New York and London: Guilford Press), pp. 456–468.

Forget, E. L. (2005) 'Evocations of Sympathy: Sympathetic Imagery in Eighteenth-Century Social Theory and Physiology' *History of Political Economy* 35: 282–308.

Frazer, M. L. (2010) *The Enlightenment of Sympathy: Justice and the Moral Sentiments in the Eighteenth Century and Today* (New York: Oxford University Press).

Freeman, J. I. (2012) 'Jack Harris and "Honest Ranger": The Publication and Prosecution of Harris's List of Covent-Garden Ladies, 1760–95' *The Library: The Transactions of the Bibliographical Society* 13.4: 423–456.

Freeman, L. (2002) *Character's Theater: Genre and Identity on the Eighteenth-century English Stage* (Philadelphia, PA: University of Pennsylvania Press).

—— (1999) 'Tragic Flaws: Genre and Ideology in Lillo's *London Merchant*' *South Atlantic Quarterly* 98.3: 539–561.

Frevert, U. (2011) *Emotions in History: Lost and Found* (Budapest and New York: Central European University Press).

Frevert, U. et al. (2014), *Learning How to Feel: Children's Literature and Emotional Socialization, 1870–1970* (Oxford: Oxford University Press).

Fridlund, A. J. (1994) *Human Facial Expression: An Evolutionary View* (San Diego, CA: Academic Press).

Frijda, N. H. (2005) 'Emotion Experience' *Cognition and Emotion* 19.4: 473–497.

——(1986) *The Emotions* (Cambridge: Cambridge University Press).

—— and W. G. Parrott (2011) 'Basic Emotions or Ur-emotions?' *Emotion Review* 3: 406–415.

Gallagher, C. (1999) *Nobody's Story: Gender, Property, and the Rise of the Novel* (Durham, NC: Duke University Press).

Gardiner, H. M., R. C. Metcalf, and J. G. Beebe-Center (1937) *Feeling and Emotion: A History of Theories* (New York: American Book Company).

Garrett, A. (2003) 'Anthropology: the "Original" of Human Nature' in A. Broadie (ed.) *The Cambridge Companion to the Scottish Enlightenment* (Cambridge: Cambridge University Press), pp. 79–93.

Gaukroger, S. (1998) 'Introduction' in S. Gaukroger (ed.) *The Soft Underbelly of Reason: The Passions in the Seventeenth Century* (London and New York: Routledge), pp. 1–13.

Gerrard, C. (2005) 'Pope, Peri Bathous, and the Whig Sublime' in D. Wormersley (ed.) *'Cultures of Whiggism': New Essays on English Literature and Culture in the Long Eighteenth Century* (Newark, DE: University of Delaware Press), pp. 200–215.

Gill, M. B. (2007) 'Moral Rationalism vs. Moral Sentimentalism: Is Morality More Like Math or Beauty?' *Philosophy Compass* 2: 16–30.

—— (2006) *The British Moralists and the Birth of Secular Ethics* (New York: Cambridge University Press).

—— (1996) 'Fantastick Associations and Addictive General Rules: A Fundamental Difference between Hutcheson and Hume' *Hume Studies* 22: 23–48.

—— (1996) 'A Philosopher in his Closet: Reflexivity and Justification in Hume's Moral Theory' *Canadian Journal of Philosophy* 26.2: 231–255.

—— (1995) 'Nature and Association in the Moral Theory of Francis Hutcheson' *History of Philosophy Quarterly* 12: 281–301.

Gilman, S. L. (1998) *Creating Beauty to Cure the Soul: Race and Psychology in the Shaping of Aesthetic Surgery* (Durham, NC: Duke University Press).

Gittings, C. (1984) *Death, Burial and the Individual in Early Modern England* (London and Sydney: Croom Helm).

Gnudi, M. T. and J. P. Webster (1950) *The Life and Times of Gaspare Tagliacozzi Surgeon of Bologna 1545–1599, With a Documented Study of the Scientific and Cultural Life of Bologna in the Sixteenth Century* (New York: Herbert Reichner).

Gordon, S. P. (2006) *The Practice of Quixotism: Postmodern Theory and Eighteenth-Century Women's Writing* (New York: Palgrave Macmillan).

Goring, P. (2005) *The Rhetoric of Sensibility in Eighteenth-Century Culture* (Cambridge: Cambridge University Press).

Gottlieb, E. (2007) *Feeling British: Sympathy and National Identity in Scottish and English Writing, 1707–1832* (Lewisburg, PA: Bucknell University Press).

Griffin, D. H. (2010) *Swift and Pope: Satirists in Dialogue* (Cambridge: Cambridge University Press).

Gross, D. M. (2008) *The Secret History of Emotion: From Aristotle's Rhetoric to Modern Brain Science* (Chicago: University of Chicago Press).

Guimarās, L. (2004) 'The Gallant and the Philosopher' *Hume Studies* 30.1: 127–148.

Habermas, J. (1991) *The Structural Transformation of the Bourgeois Sphere: An Enquiry into a Category of Bourgeois Society*, trans. T. Burger and F. Lawrence (Cambridge, MA: MIT Press).

Haines, S. (2005) *Poetry and Philosophy From Homer to Rousseau: Romantic Souls, Realist Lives* (Basingstoke: Palgrave).

Hamilton, D. (2012) *A History of Organ Transplantation: Ancient Legends to Modern Practice* (Pittsburgh, PA: University of Pittsburgh Press).

Hanvelt, M. (2012) *The Politics of Eloquence: David Hume's Polite Rhetoric* (Toronto: University of Toronto Press).

Harkin, M. (1994) 'Mackenzie's *Man of Feeling*: Embalming Sensibility' *English Literary History* 61: 317–340.

Harré, R. (1986) *The Social Construction of Emotions* (Oxford: Basil Blackwell).

Harris, J. G. (2004) *Sick Economies: Drama, Mercantilism, and Disease in Shakespeare's England* (Philadelphia, PA: University of Pennsylvania Press).

Hatfield, E., J. T. Cacioppo, and R. L. Rapson (1994) *Emotional Contagion* (Cambridge: Cambridge University Press).

Healy, M. (2001) *Fictions of Disease in Early Modern England: Bodies, Plagues and Politics* (New York: Palgrave).

Heath, M. (2012) 'Longinus and the Ancient Sublime' in T. M. Costelloe (ed.) *The Sublime: From Antiquity to the Present* (Cambridge: Cambridge University Press), pp. 11–23.

Hedrick, E. (2008) 'Romancing the Salve: Sir Kenelm Digby and the Powder of Sympathy' *The British Journal for the History of Science* 41.2: 161–185.

Heydt, C. (2009) 'Hutcheson's *Short Introduction* and the Purposes of Moral Philosophy' *History of Philosophy Quarterly* 26: 293–309.

—— (2007) 'Relations of Literary Form and Philosophical Purpose in Hume's Four Essays on Happiness' *Hume Studies* 33.1: 3–19.

Hilgard, E. R. (1980) 'The Trilogy of Mind: Cognition, Affection, and Conation' *Journal of the History of the Behavioral Sciences* 16: 107–117.

Hirschman, A. O. (1977) *The Passions and the Interests: Political Arguments for Capitalism Before its Triumph* (Princeton, NJ: Princeton University Press).

Hitchcock, T. (1997) *English Sexualities, 1700–1800* (New York and Basingstoke: St Martin's Press and Macmillan).

Hont, I. and M. Ignatieff (eds.) (1983) *Wealth and Virtue: The Shaping of Political Economy in the Scottish Enlightenment* (New York: Cambridge University Press).

Houlbrooke, R. (1998) *Death, Religion, and the Family in England, 1480–1750* (Oxford: Clarendon Press).

Houston, R. A. (2010) *Punishing the Dead? Suicide, Lordship, and Community in Britain, 1500–1830* (Oxford: Oxford University Press).

Hunter, I. (2001) *Rival Enlightenments: Civil and Metaphysical Philosophy in Early Modern Germany* (Cambridge: Cambridge University Press).

Immerwahr, J. (1991) 'The Anatomist and the Painter: The Continuity of Hume's *Treatise* and *Essays*' *Hume Studies* 17.1: 1–14.

Ingram, A., S. Sim, C. Lawlor, R. Terry, J. Baker, and L. Wetherall-Dickson (2011) *Melancholy Experience in Literature of the Long Eighteenth Century: Before Depression, 1660–1800* (Basingstoke: Palgrave Macmillan).

Izard, C. E. (1977) *Human Emotions* (New York: Plenum).

Jacobsen, A. J. (ed.) (2000) *Feminist Interpretations of David Hume* (University Park, PA: The Pennsylvania State University Press).

James, S. (1998) 'Explaining the Passions: Passions, Desires, and the Explanation of Action' in S. Gaukroger (ed.) *The Soft Underbelly of Reason: The Passions in the Seventeenth Century* (London and New York: Routledge), pp. 17–33.

—— (1997) *Passion and Action: The Emotions in Seventeenth-century Philosophy* (Oxford: Clarendon Press).

Johnson, C. (1995) *Equivocal Beings: Politics, Gender, and Sentimentality in the 1790s: Wollstonecraft, Radcliffe, Burney, Austen* (Chicago: University of Chicago Press).

Justman, S. (1996) 'Regarding Others' *New Literary History* 27.1: 83–93.

—— (1993) *The Autonomous Male of Adam Smith* (Norman, OK: University of Oklahoma Press).

Kahn, V., N. Saccamano, and D. Coli (eds.) (2006) *Politics and the Passions 1500–1850* (Princeton, NJ: Princeton University Press).

Kail, P. J. E. (2001) 'Hutcheson's Moral Sense: Scepticism, Realism, and Secondary Qualities' *History of Philosophy Quarterly* 18: 57–77.

Karian, S. E. (2010) *Jonathan Swift in Print and Manuscript* (Cambridge: Cambridge University Press).

Kelly, D. R. (2011) *Yuck!: The Nature and Moral Significance of Disgust* (Cambridge, MA: MIT Press).

Kelly, J. R. and S. G. Barsade (2001) 'Mood and Emotion in Small Groups and Work Teams' *Organizational Behavior and Human Decision Processes* 86.1: 99–130.

King, K. R. (2008) 'Eliza Haywood, Savage Love, and Biographical Uncertainty' *Review of English Studies* 59.242: 722–739.

—— (2005) 'New Contexts for Early Novels by Women: The Case of Eliza Haywood, Aaron Hill, and the Hillarians, 1719–1725' in P. R. Backscheider and C. Ingrassia (eds.) *A Companion to the Eighteenth-Century English Novel and Culture* (Malden, MA: Blackwell), pp. 261–275.

Klein, L. E. (1994) *Shaftesbury and the Culture of Politeness: Moral Discourse and Cultural Politics in Early Eighteenth-Century England* (Cambridge: Cambridge University Press).

Kristjánsson, K. (2002) *Justifying Emotions: Pride and Jealousy* (London and New York: Routledge).

Lamb, J. (2009) *The Evolution of Sympathy in the Long Eighteenth Century* (London: Pickering and Chatto).

Larlham, D. (2012) 'The Felt Truth of Mimetic Experience: Motions of the Soul and the Kinetics of Passion in the Eighteenth-Century Theatre' *The Eighteenth Century* 53.4: 432–454.

Lemmings, D. and A. Brooks (eds.) (2014) *Emotions and Social Change: Historical and Sociological Perspectives* (New York: Routledge).

Levine, J. M. (1999) *Between the Ancients and the Moderns: Baroque Culture in Restoration England* (New Haven, CT: Yale University Press).

—— (1991) *The Battle of the Books: History and Literature in the Augustan Age* (Ithaca, NY: Cornell University Press).

Loveman, K. (2008) *Reading Fictions, 1660–1740: Deception in English Literary and Political Culture* (Aldershot: Ashgate).

Lupton, C. (2012) *Knowing Books: The Consciousness of Mediation in Eighteenth-Century Britain* (Philadelphia, PA: University of Pennsylvania Press).

Lutz, C. and L. Abu-Lughod (1990) *Language and the Politics of Emotion* (Cambridge: Cambridge University Press).

Lynch, D. (2000) 'Personal Effects and Sentimental Fictions' *Eighteenth-Century Fiction* 12.2–3: 345–368.

—— (1998) *The Economy of Character: Novels, Market Culture, and the Business of Inner Meaning* (Chicago and London: Chicago University Press).

Lynch, J. (1998) 'Political Ideology in the Translations of the *Iliad*, 1660–1715' *Translation and Literature* 71: 23–41.

MacDonald, M. and T. R. Murphy (1990) *Sleepless Souls: Suicide in Early Modern England* (Oxford: Clarendon Press).

Macfarlane, A. (1986) *Marriage and Love in England: Modes of Reproduction, 1300–1840* (Oxford and New York: Blackwell).

Mandell, L. (1999) *Misogynous Economies: the Business of Literature in Eighteenth-Century Britain* (Lexington, KY: University of Kentucky Press).

Manstead, A. S. R. and A. H. Fischer (2001) 'Social Appraisal: The Social World as Object of and Influence on Appraisal Processes' in K. R. Scherer, A. Schorr and T. Johnstone (eds.) *Appraisal Processes in Emotion: Theory, Methods, Research* (Oxford: Oxford University Press), pp. 221–232.

Markus, H. R. and S. Kitayama (1994) 'The Cultural Construction of Self and Emotion: Implications for Social Behavior' in S. Kitayama and H. R. Markus (eds.) *Emotion and Culture: Empirical Studies of Mutual Influence* (Washington, DC: American Psychological Association), pp. 89–130.

Marsden, J. (1996) *Fatal Desire: Women, Sexuality, and the English Stage, 1660–1720* (Ithaca, NY: Cornell University Press).

Marshall, D. (1988) *The Surprizing Effects of Sympathy: Marivaux, Diderot, Rousseau and Mary Shelley* (Chicago: University of Chicago Press).

—— (1986) *The Figure of the Theatre: Shaftesbury, Defoe, Adam Smith and George Eliot* (New York: Columbia University Press).

—— (1984) 'Adam Smith and the Theatricality of Moral Sentiments' *Critical Inquiry* 10.4: 592–613.

McKenzie, A. T. (1990) *Certain Lively Episodes: The Articulation of Passion in Eighteenth-Century Prose* (Athens, GA: University of Georgia Press).

McKeon, M. (2005) *The Secret History of Domesticity: Public, Private, and the Division of Knowledge* (Baltimore, MD: The Johns Hopkins University Press).

—— (2004) 'Parsing Habermas's "Bourgeois Public Sphere" *Criticism* 46.2: 273–277.

Mendelson, B. (2013) *In Your Face: The Hidden History of Plastic Surgery and Why Looks Matter* (Melbourne: Hardie Grant).

Miller, W. I. (1997) *The Anatomy of Disgust* (Cambridge, MA and London: Harvard University Press).

Millican, P. (ed.) (2002) *Reading Hume on Human Understanding* (New York: Oxford University Press).

Milner, M. (2012) *Fever Reading: Affect and Reading Badly in the Early American Public Sphere* (Durham, NH: University of New Hampshire Press).

Monk, S. H. (1960) *The Sublime: A Study of Critical Theories in XVII-Century England* (Ann Arbor, MI: University of Michigan Press).

Montagu, J. (1994) *The Expression of the Passions: The Origin and Influence of Charles Le Brun's* Conférence sur l'expression générale et particulière (New Haven, CT: Yale University Press).

Moore, J. (2000) 'Homer Revisited: Anne Le Fevre Dacier's Preface to her Prose Translation of the *Iliad* in Early Eighteenth-Century France' *Studies in the Literary Imagination* 33.2: 87–107.

Morillo, J. (2000) 'John Dennis: Enthusiastic Passions, Cultural Memory, and Literary Theory' *Eighteenth-Century Studies* 34.1: 21–41.

Morris, D. B. (1972) *The Religious Sublime: Christian Poetry and Critical Tradition in 18th-Century England* (Lexington, KY: The University Press of Kentucky).

Morrissey, L. (1998) 'Sexuality and Consumer Culture in Eighteenth Century England: "Mutual Love from Pole to Pole" in *The London Merchant*' *Restoration and 18th Century Theatre Research* 13.1: 25–39.

Muldrew, C. (1998) *The Economy of Obligation: The Culture of Credit and Social Relations in Early Modern England* (New York: St Martin's Press).

Mullan, J. (1990) *Sentiment and Sociability: the Language of Feeling in the Eighteenth Century* (Oxford: Clarendon Press).

Nachumi, N. (2008) *Acting Like a Lady: British Women Novelists and the Eighteenth-Century Theater* (New York: AMS Press).

Nevitt, M. (2009) 'The Insults of Defeat: Royalist Responses to Sir William Davenant's *Gondibert* (1651)' *The Seventeenth Century* 24.2: 287–304.

Ngai, S. (2005) *Ugly Feelings* (Cambridge, MA: Harvard University Press).

Nicholson, M. (1970) 'Introduction' in W. Payne (ed.) *The Best of Defoe's Review* (Freeport, NY: Books for Libraries Press), pp. vii–xxi.

Norton, D. F. (1982) *David Hume: Common-Sense Moralist, Sceptical Metaphysician* (Princeton, NJ: Princeton University Press).

Novak, M. E. (2001) *Daniel Defoe: Master of Fictions* (Oxford: Oxford University Press).

Noxon, J. (1973) *Hume's Philosophical Development: A Study of his Methods* (New York: Oxford University Press).

Oatley, K. (2004) *Emotions: A Brief History* (Malden, MA: Blackwell).

Pagden, A. (2013) *The Enlightenment: and Why It Still Matters* (New York: Random House).

Pain, S. (2006) 'A Nose by Any Other Name' *New Scientist* 191.2566: 50–51.

Panksepp, J. (1982) 'Toward a General Psychobiological Theory of Emotions' *The Behavioral and Brain Sciences* 5: 407–467.

Parisot, E. (2014) 'Suicide Notes and Popular Sensibility in the Eighteenth-Century British Press' *Eighteenth-Century Studies* 47.3: 277–292.

Parks, S. (1976) *John Dunton and the English Book Trade* (New York: Garland).

Parkinson, B., A. H. Fischer, and A. S. R. Manstead (2005) *Emotion in Social Relations* (New York: Psychology Press).

Parrott, W. G. (2014) 'Feeling, Function, and the Place of Negative Emotions in a Happy Life' in W. G. Parrott (ed.) *The Positive Side of Negative Emotions* (New York: Guilford Press), pp. 273–296.

—— (2012) 'Ur-emotions: The Common Feature of Animal Emotions and Socially Constructed Emotions' *Emotion Review* 4.3: 247–248.

—— (2010) 'Ur-emotions and Your Emotions: Reconceptualizing Basic Emotion' *Emotion Review* 2: 14–21.

—— (2007) 'Components and the Definition of Emotion' *Social Science Information* 46: 419–423.

—— (2000) 'The Psychologist of Avon: Emotion in Elizabethan Psychology and the Plays of Shakespeare' in B. Landau, J. Sabini, J. Jonides, and E. Newport (eds.) *Perception, Cognition, and Language: Essays in Honor of Henry and Lila Gleitman* (Cambridge, MA: The MIT Press), pp. 231–243.

—— and S. F. Smith (1991) 'Embarrassment: Actual vs. Typical Cases, Classical vs. Prototypical Representations' *Cognition and Emotion* 5: 467–488.

Paster, G. K., K. Rowe, and M. Floyd-Wilson (eds.) (2004) *Reading the Early Modern Passions: Essays in the Cultural History of Emotion* (Philadelphia, PA: University of Pennsylvania Press).

Pearson, J. (1999) *Women's Reading in Britain 1750–1835: A Dangerous Recreation* (Cambridge: Cambridge University Press).

—— (1996) ' "Books, my greatest joy": Constructing the Female Reader in *The Lady's Magazine*' *Women's Writing* 3.1: 3–15.

Peters, J. S. (2000) *Theatre of the Book 1480–1880: Print, Text, and Performance in Europe* (Oxford: Oxford University Press).

Pettigrove, G. and N. Parsons (2012) 'Shame: A Case Study of Collective Emotion' *Social Theory and Practice* 38: 504–530.

Pinch, A. (1996) *Strange Fits of Passion: Epistemologies of Emotion, Hume to Austen* (Stanford, CA: Stanford University Press).

Pinker, S. (2011) *The Better Angels of Our Nature: A History of Violence and Humanity* (London: Allen Lane).

Plamper, J. (2015) *The History of Emotions: An Introduction* (Oxford: Oxford University Press).

Polly, G. (2005) 'A Leviathan of Letters' in D. J. Newman (ed.) *The Spectator: Emerging Discourses* (Newark, DE: University of Delaware Press), pp. 105–128.

Porter, R. (1996) ' "Laying Aside Any Private Advantage": John Marten and VD' in Linda E. Merians (ed.) *The Secret Malady: Venereal Disease in Eighteenth-Century*

Britain and France (Lexington, KY: University Press of Kentucky), pp. 51–67.

Potkay, A. (1994) *The Fate of Eloquence in the Age of Hume* (Ithaca, NY: Cornell University Press).

Probyn, E. (2005) *Blush: Faces of Shame* (Minneapolis, MN: University of Minnesota Press).

Radcliffe, E. (2011) *A Companion to Hume* (Malden, MA: Wiley-Blackwell).

—— (2004) 'Love and Benevolence in Hutcheson's and Hume's Theories of the Passions' *British Journal for the History of Philosophy* 12: 631–653.

——(1986) 'Hutcheson's Perceptual and Moral Subjectivism' *History of Philosophy Quarterly* 3: 407–421.

Radcliffe, S. (2008) *On Sympathy* (Oxford: Oxford University Press).

Reddy, W. M. (2009) 'Historical Research on the Self and Emotions' *Emotion Review* 1.4: 302–315.

—— (2008) 'The Anti-Empire of General de Boigne: Sentimentalism, Love, and Cultural Difference in the Eighteenth Century' *Historical Reflections* 34.1: 4–25.

—— (2001) *The Navigation of Feeling: A Framework for the History of Emotions* (Cambridge: Cambridge University Press).

—— (2001) 'The Logic of Action: Indeterminacy, Emotion, and Historical Narrative' *History and Theory* 40.4: 10–33.

—— (2000) 'Sentimentalism and its Erasure: the Role of Emotions in the Era of the French Revolution' *Journal of Modern History* 72.1: 109–152.

——(1999) 'Emotional Liberty: Politics and History in the Anthropology of Emotions' *Cultural Anthropology* 14.2: 256–288.

—— (1997) 'Against Constructionism: The Historical Ethnography of Emotions' *Current Anthropology* 38.3: 327–351.

Reisenzein, R. (1983) 'The Schachter Theory of Emotion: Two Decades Later' *Psychological Bulletin* 94: 239–264.

Richetti, J. J. (2005) *The Life of Daniel Defoe* (Oxford: Blackwell).

—— (1984) 'Richardson's Dramatic Art in *Clarissa*' in S. S. Kenny (ed.) *British Theatre and the Other Arts, 1660–1800* (Washington, DC: Folger Books), pp. 288–308.

Roach, J. (1985) *The Player's Passion: Studies in the Science of Acting* (Newark, DE: University of Delaware Press).

Robson, M., D. Lee, K. McGuire, J. Merrick, and P. Seaver (eds.) (2013) *The History of Suicide in England, 1650–1850*, 8 vols. (London: Pickering and Chatto).

Rorty, A. O. (1990) ' "Pride Produces the Idea of Self": Hume on Moral Agency' *Australasian Journal of Philosophy* 68: 255–269.

—— (1982) 'From Passions to Emotions and Sentiments' *Philosophy* 57: 159–172.

Rosenheim, E. W. (1963) *Swift and the Satirist's Art* (Chicago: Chicago University Press).

Rosenthal, L. J. (2006) *Infamous Commerce: Prostitution in Eighteenth-Century British Literature and Culture* (Ithaca, NY and London: Cornell University Press).

Rosenwein, B. H. (2014) 'Modernity: a Problematic Category in the History of Emotions' *History and Theory* 53.1: 69–78.

—— (2010) 'Problems and Methods in the History of Emotions' *Passions in Context: Journal of the History and Philosophy of the Emotions* 1: 1–33.

—— (2010) 'Thinking Historically about Medieval Emotions' *History Compass* 8.8: 828–842.

—— (2006) *Emotional Communities in the Early Middle Ages* (Ithaca, NY: Cornell University Press).

—— (2002) 'Worrying About Emotions in History' *The American Historical Review* 107.3: 821–845.

——(ed.) (1998) *Anger's Past: the Social Uses of an Emotion in the Middle Ages* (Ithaca, NY and London: Cornell University Press).

Russell, G. and C. Tuite (eds.) (2002) *Romantic Sociability: Social Networks and Literary Culture in Britain, 1770–1840* (Cambridge: Cambridge University Press).

Sabl, A. (2012) *Hume's Politics: Coordination and Crisis in the 'History of England'* (Princeton, NJ: Princeton University Press).

Samet, E. D. (2003) 'Spectacular History and the Politics of Theater: Sympathetic Arts in the Shadow of the Bastille' *PMLA* 118.5: 1305–1319.

Santoni-Rugiu, P. and P. J. Sykes (2007) *A History of Plastic Surgery* (Berlin: Springer).

Schachter, S. and J. E. Singer (1962) 'Cognitive, Social, and Physiological Determinants of Emotional State' *Psychological Review* 69: 379–399.

Scheer, M. (2012), 'Are Emotions a Kind of Practice (and is that what Makes Them have a History)? A Bourdieuian Approach to Understanding Emotion' *History and Theory* 51: 193–220.

Scherer, K. R. (1984) 'On the Nature and Function of Emotion: A Component Process Approach' in K. R. Scherer and P. Ekman (eds.) *Approaches to Emotion* (Hillsdale, NJ: Erlbaum), pp. 293–317.

Schmitter, A. (2012) 'Family Trees: Sympathy, Comparison, and the Proliferation of the Passions in Hume and his Predecessors' in M. Pickave and L. Shapiro (eds.) *Emotion and Cognitive Life in Medieval and Early Modern Philosophy* (Oxford: Oxford University Press).

Scott, J. (2000) *England's Troubles: Seventeenth-Century English Political Instability in European Context* (Cambridge: Cambridge University Press).

Scott, W. (1968) 'George Colman's *Polly Honeycombe* and Circulating Library Fiction in 1760' *Notes and Queries* 15.12: 465–467.

Sedgwick, E. K., A. Frank and I. E. Alexander (eds.) (1995) *Shame and Its Sisters: A Silvan Tomkins Reader* (Durham, NC: Duke University Press).

Shields, S. A. (2000) 'Thinking about Gender, Thinking about Theory: Gender and Emotional Experience' in A. H. Fischer (ed.) *Gender and Emotion: Social Psychological Perspectives* (Cambridge: Cambridge University Press), pp. 3–23.

Skinner, G. (1999) *Sensibility and Economics in the Novel, 1740–1800: The Price of a Tear* (New York: St Martin's Press).

Smith, E. R., C. R. Seger, and D. M. Mackie (2007) 'Can Emotions be Truly Group Level? Evidence Regarding Four Conceptual Criteria' *Journal of Personality and Social Psychology* 93.3: 431–446.

Staines, J. (2004) 'Compassion in the Public Sphere of Milton and King Charles' in G. K. Paster, K. Rowe, and M. Floyd-Wilson (eds.) *Reading the Early Modern Passions: Essays in the Cultural History of Emotion* (Philadelphia, PA: University of Pennsylvania Press), pp. 89–110.

Stewart, M.A. and J. P. Wright (eds.) (1995) *Hume and Hume's Connexions* (State College, PA: Penn State University Press).

Stone, L. (1992) *Uncertain Unions: Marriage in England, 1660–1753* (Oxford and New York: Oxford University Press).

—— (1977) *The Family, Sex and Marriage in England 1500–1800* (London: Weidenfeld and Nicolson).

Strier, R. (2004) 'Against the Rule of Reason: Praise of Passion from Petrarch to Luther to Shakespeare to Herbert' in G. K. Paster, K. Rowe, and M. Floyd-Wilson (eds.) *Reading the Early Modern Passions: Essays in the Cultural History of Emotion* (Philadelphia, PA: University of Pennsylvania Press), pp. 23–42.

Sutton, C. (2006) 'Syphilis' in A. L. Nelson and J. Woodward (eds.) *Sexually Transmitted Diseases: A Practical Guide for Primary Care* (Totowa: Humana), pp. 205–227.

Symons, J. (2001) 'A Most Hideous Object: John Davies (1796–1872) and Plastic Surgery' *Medical History* 45: 395–402.

Teirney-Heinz, R. (2012) *Novel Minds: Philosophers and Romance Readers* (Basingstoke: Palgrave MacMillan).

Telfer, E. (1995) 'Hutcheson's Reflections upon Laughter' *The Journal of Aesthetics and Art Criticism* 53: 359–369.

Tiedens, L. Z. and C.W. Leach (2004) *The Social Life of Emotions* (Cambridge: Cambridge University Press).

Tileagă, C. and J. Byford (eds.) (2014) *Psychology and History: Interdisciplinary Explorations* (Cambridge: Cambridge University Press).

Tillotson, G. (1958) *Pope and Human Nature* (Oxford: Clarendon Press).

Totterdell, P. (2000) 'Catching Moods and Hitting Runs: Mood Linkage and Subjective Performance in Professional Sport Teams' *Journal of Applied Psychology* 85.6: 848–859.

Tsai, J. L., B. Knutson, and H. H. Fung (2006) 'Cultural Variation in Affect Valuation' *Journal of Personality and Social Psychology* 90: 288–307.

Turco, L. (2003) 'Moral Sense and the Foundations of Morals' in A. Broadie (ed.) *The Cambridge Companion to the Scottish Enlightenment* (Cambridge: Cambridge University Press), pp. 136–156.

Van Sant, A. J. (1993) *Eighteenth-century Sensibility and the Novel: the Senses in Social Context* (Cambridge: Cambridge University Press).

Vitz, R. (2002) 'Hume and the Limits of Benevolence' *Hume Studies* 28: 271–295.

Von Sneidern, M-L. (2005) *Savage Indignation: Colonial Discourse from Milton to Swift* (Newark, DE: University of Delaware Press).

Waddell, M. A. (2003) 'The Perversion of Nature: Johannes Baptista Van Helmont, the Society of Jesus, and the Magnetic Cure of Wounds' *Canadian Journal of History* 38: 179–197.

Wahrman, D. (2006) *The Making of the Modern Self: Identity and Culture in Eighteenth-century England* (New Haven, CT: Yale University Press).

Warner, W. B. (2000) 'Staging Readers Reading' *Eighteenth-Century Fiction* 12.2–3: 391–416.

Weinbrot, H. D. (1988) *Eighteenth-Century Satire: Essays on Text and Context from Dryden to Peter Pindar* (Cambridge: Cambridge University Press).

—— (1966) 'Translation and Parody: Towards a Genealogy of Augustan Imitation' *English Literary History* 4: 434–447.

Williams, A. (2005, 2009) *Poetry and the Creation of a Whig Literary Culture, 1681–1714* (Oxford: Oxford University Press).

Williams, G. (1994) *A Dictionary of Sexual Language and Imagery in Shakespearean and Stuart Literature*, 3 volumes (Atlantic Highlands, NJ: Athlone).

Wilputte, E. (2011) 'Eliza Haywood's *Poems on Several Occasions*: Aaron Hill, Writing and the Sublime' in L. V. Troost (ed.) *Eighteenth-Century Women: Studies in their Lives Work and Culture*, vol. 6 (New York: AMS), pp. 79–102.

Winkler, K. (1996) 'Hutcheson and Hume on the Color of Virtue' *Hume Studies* 22: 3–22.

Wispé, L. (1986) 'The Distinction Between Sympathy and Empathy: To Call Forth a Concept, a Word is Needed' *Journal of Personality and Social Psychology* 50.2: 314–321.

Wright, L. M. and D. J. Newman (eds.) (2006) *Fair Philosopher: Eliza Haywood and the Female Spectator* (Lewisburg, PA: Bucknell University Press).

Wrigley, E. A. and R. S. Schofield (1983) 'English Population History from Family Reconstitution: Summary Results 1600–1799' *Population Studies* 37.2: 157–184.

Zeis, E. (1977) *The Zeis Index and History of Plastic Surgery 900BC to 1863AD* [1863–1864], translated by T. J. S Patterson (Baltimore, MD: Williams and Wilkins).

Zillman, D. and J. R. Cantor (1977) 'Affective Responses to the Emotions of a Protagonist' *Journal of Experimental Social Psychology* 13: 155–165.

Index

Note: Locators followed by 'n' refer to notes section.

Printed and bound in the United States of America